Value-Based Metrics: Foundations and Practice

Edited by

Frank J. Fabozzi, Ph.D., CFA
and
James L. Grant, Ph.D.

Published by Frank J. Fabozzi Associates

FJF
To my wife Donna and my children,
Francesco, Patricia, and Karly

JLG
To my mother and father

© 2000 By Frank J. Fabozzi Associates
New Hope, Pennsylvania

ISBN: 1-883249-76-7

Printed in the United States of America

Table of Contents

Preface   iv

About the Editors   vii

Contributing Authors   viii

1. Value-Based Metrics: Motivation and Practice   1
   Frank J. Fabozzi and James L. Grant

2. Value-Based Metrics in Financial Theory   7
   Frank J. Fabozzi and James L. Grant

3. Closing the GAAP between Earnings and EVA   51
   Al Ehrbar

4. Value-Based Measures of Performance   67
   Pamela Peterson

5. Does Value-Based Management Discourage Investment in Intangibles?   99
   Stephen F. O'Byrne

6. Integrating EVA® into the Portfolio Management Process   133
   Jason L. Wolin and Steven Klopukh

7. Economic Margin: The Link Between EVA and CFROI   157
   Daniel J. Obrycki and Rafael Resendes

8. Value-Based Management and Economic Value Added: A Global Perspective   179
   S. David Young

9. EVA and the OECD Principles of Corporate Governance   195
   Robert Straw, Simon Peck, and Hans-Ueli Keller

10. The Implementation of Value-Based Metrics and the Next Steps in Corporate Valuation   229
    Raja Gupta and Craig MacDonald

11. Allocating Risk Capital in Banking   253
    Ralph C. Kimball

12. Internal Use of Value-Based Metrics   269
    Bernard L. Lorge

Index   279

Preface

Value-Based Metrics: Foundations and Practice is designed to meet two primary objectives: (1) to provide a solid foundation on the theory of economic profit measurement and wealth creation, and (2) to bring together key players and metrics in today's value-based movement. In this latter context, this book sheds light on how value-based (economic profit) measurement can be used to enhance shareholder value in banks, corporations, investment management firms, and even (quasi) governmental organizations.

We coauthored the first two chapters. In Chapter 1 we provide a motivation for value-based metrics and a review of economic profit measures used in practice. In Chapter 2 we provide a theoretical and empirical foundation on value-based metrics that, in turn, sets the stage for practical discussion and application of prominent value-based metrics — like CFROI, EM, EVA, and SVA — in chapters that follow. Specifically, in Chapter 2 we emphasize the role of value-based metrics in financial theory, how to use economic profit measures in enterprise valuation, VBM measurement and capital structure issues, and some empirical evidence for wealth creators and wealth destroyers.

Chapter 3 by Al Ehrbar focuses on how to close the "GAAP" between accounting and economic profit measures. In this chapter, he offers both practical and strategic insight on several accounting adjustments that are linked to economic profit and wealth creation. These EVA-based adjustments include research and development, strategic investments, accounting for acquisitions, expense recognition, depreciation, restructuring charges, among other value-based accounting adjustments. Chapter 4 by Pamela Peterson follows with an insightful discussion of value-based measurement tools including EVA and CFROI, along with a case study application of metrics using financial statement data for McDonald's Corporation.

Stephen O'Byrne in Chapter 5 expands upon the earlier VBM foundations and measurement chapters. In this regard, he provides quantitative insight on the valuation role of "economic profit improvement" and how this key concept impacts a firm's future growth value. This is important knowledge in the wealth creation process since much of a firm's enterprise value is derived from economic profit generated by its anticipated future assets not currently in place. He then provides rigorous numerical examples on how to handle economic depreciation, acquisition goodwill, spontaneous sources of financings, environmental liabilities, and the like in a robust shareholder value added context.

In Chapter 6, Jason Wolin and Steven Klopukh build on a growing trend of economic profit applications in investment management. Just like corporations have employed economic profit concepts to maximize shareholder value, they argue that money management firms should employ a disciplined economic profit approach to create "investor value added." Along this line, they believe that an economic profit framework provides a foundation on three key elements that determine overall portfolio success — namely, an organizational focus on generating risk-adjusted returns, a measurement system that eliminates unnecessary risk exposure, and a favorable stock selection technique.

Daniel Obrycki and Rafael Resendes in Chapter 7 promote an interesting new metric called Economic Margin (EM). After examining the benefits and limitations of CFROI and EVA, they show how EM — or spread between a firm's operating cash flow return and its cost of invested capital — is a natural link between these sophisticated approaches to value-based measurement. More importantly, they offer key insight on the nature of competition by relating the "decay rate" in a firm's economic profit margins to EM level, EM variability, EM trend, and firm size defined by invested capital.

Chapters 8 and 9 are devoted to the expanding role of value-based metrics in world economic and financial markets. In Chapter 8, David Young sets the global stage by arguing that financial capital has attained a degree of mobility that is "unprecedented" in human history. Today's capital flows transcend the boundaries of North America, Europe, Asia, and Latin America and move rapidly whenever investors believe that their funds can be more productively employed elsewhere. Hence, global-minded companies must be cognizant of their capital costs — otherwise their cost of capital will be unproductively higher than that of competitors.

Moreover, in Chapter 9, Robert Straw, Simon Peck, and Hans-Ueli Keller provide an interesting discussion on the role of value-based measurement in the OECD's international set of principles on "good" corporate governance. EVA and value-based metrics are offered up as the best present solution to joining the complex disciplines of corporate governance and financial performance measurement. They also argue in favor of a balanced metric for establishing international standards of corporate governance — one that jointly maintains the benefits of value-based principles and preserves the business of "thinking globally, while acting locally."

In Chapter 10, Raja Gupta and Craig MacDonald provide three illustrative case studies based on consulting experiences with companies using CFROI, EVA, and blended CFROI/EVA approaches to value-based management. In each case study, they shed practical insight on the process of metric selection, initial corporate expectations, VBM implementation, compensation tie-ins, results and next steps, and value-based advice for others. After recommending a set of "best practices" on value-based implementation, they provide a foundation on an enterprise risk model that focuses on economic profit from both physical and intangible capital assets — especially, the value of intellectual capital in a knowledge-based economy.

Chapter 11 by Ralph Kimball extends the value-based focus to banks and financial services companies. While recognizing that the opportunity cost of equity capital is essential to understanding a bank's true profitability, he argues that the allocation of equity capital in banks and financial services companies is a complex decision. Because of cross dependencies in business unit and/or product line revenues and expenses, Kimball argues that inefficient allocations of bank equity capital can result in the absence of a systematic measurement system that accounts for interrelatedness in business unit activities. To resolve this value-based dilemma, he develops an "internal beta" approach to measuring and allocating equity capital at risk in banks and financial services companies.

In Chapter 12, Bernard Lorge provides an interesting corporate perspective on VBM issues that must be addressed for successful implementation of an internal value-based measurement program — a program whereby all internal players, including senior managers, product line managers, and employees are moving in the same direction of creating shareholder value added. In this context, he argues that a successful VBM implementation involves a careful examination of four internal program considerations, including metric calculation, reporting, compensation, and just as importantly, value-based training.

We wish to thank all of the authors for their insightful contributions on value-based measurement. We know of no other book that brings together the value-based thinking of major players in academia, corporations, consulting firms, and investment management firms. As evidenced in Chapter 2, we have benefited from helpful discussions with James Abate of Credit Suisse Asset Management on economic profit issues and applications in equity portfolio management. Also, we thank Al Ehrbar of Stern Stewart & Co. for providing EVA and MVA data from the Stern Stewart Performance 1000 Universe.

Frank J. Fabozzi
James L. Grant

About the Editors

Frank J. Fabozzi is editor of the *Journal of Portfolio Management* and an Adjunct Professor of Finance at Yale University's School of Management. He is a Chartered Financial Analyst and Certified Public Accountant. Dr. Fabozzi is on the board of directors of the Guardian Life family of funds and the BlackRock complex of funds. He earned a doctorate in economics from the City University of New York in 1972 and in 1994 received an honorary doctorate of Humane Letters from Nova Southeastern University. Dr. Fabozzi is a Fellow of the International Center for Finance at Yale University.

James L. Grant is President of JLG Research, a company specializing in economic profit research and customized seminars in investment management. Dr. Grant holds a Ph.D. in Business from the University of Chicago's Graduate School of Business, and has been a featured speaker at industry conferences on value-based metrics. Dr. Grant is also a research consultant to Credit Suisse Asset Management. He has published several articles in investment journals, including the *Journal of Portfolio Management* and the *Journal of Investing*. Dr. Grant is the author of *Foundations of Economic Value Added* (published in 1997 by Frank J. Fabozzi Associates), which has been translated into Japanese, and the coauthor with Frank Fabozzi of *Equity Portfolio Management* (published in 1999 by Frank J. Fabozzi Associates).

Contributing Authors

Al Ehrbar	Stern Stewart & Co.
Frank J. Fabozzi	Yale University
James L. Grant	JLG Research
Raja Gupta	World Research Advisory
Hans-Ueli Keller	University of St. Gallen, Switzerland
Ralph C. Kimball	Babson College and Federal Reserve Bank of Boston
Steven Klopukh	CDC Investment Management
Bernard L. Lorge	Polaroid Corporation
Craig MacDonald	World Research Advisory
Daniel J. Obrycki	The Applied Finance Group, Ltd.
Stephen F. O'Byrne	Shareholder Value Advisors Inc.
Simon Peck	City University Business School, London
Pamela Peterson	Florida State University
Rafael Resendes	The Applied Finance Group, Ltd.
Robert Straw	University of St. Gallen, Switzerland
Jason L. Wolin	CDC Investment Management
S. David Young	INSEAD

Chapter 1

Value-Based Metrics: Motivation and Practice

Frank J. Fabozzi, Ph.D., CFA
Adjunct Professor of Finance
School of Management
Yale University

James L. Grant, Ph.D.
President
JLG Research

INTRODUCTION

During the past two decades the U.S. stock market provided investors with a total return of 2,495%. This cumulative return performance represents an annualized growth of 17.68% that bests a long term estimate on U.S. equities by some 577 basis points.[1] Several macroeconomic and geo-political reasons are offered to account for the unprecedented stock market growth. These include (1) deregulation of commercial and product markets during the 1980s, (2) deregulation of financial services and telecommunication industries during the 1990s, and (3) the economic benefits derived from democratization and movement toward free market economies around the world.

In the often-cited views of market strategists' Abby Joseph Cohen and Steven Einhorn of Goldman Sachs, today's managers and investors are reaping the benefits of a "brave new" global economy.[2] Moreover, coincident with these structural themes, James Abate of Credit Suisse Asset Management points to U.S. stock market benefits over the past two decades attributed to (1) lower inflation volatility, (2) lower

---

[1] The 20-year stock market performance cited in the text reflects the cumulative return experience of the S&P 500 over the 1979 to 1998 period. At 11.91%, the longer-term return estimate for U.S. large cap stocks was estimated over the 1960 to 1998 years (a period of 39 years). Annual total returns on the S&P 500 were obtained from Standard and Poor's Corporation.

[2] For an interesting stock market interpretation of the "brave new" global economy — using macro economic profit analysis — see Steven G. Einhorn, Gabrielle Napolitano, and Abby Joseph Cohen, "EVA® and Valuation of the S&P," *U.S. Research* (Goldman Sachs, January 8, 1998). EVA® is a registered trademark of Stern Stewart & Co.

GDP volatility — due to variable versus fixed infrastructure — and, (3) reduced uncertainty in Federal Reserve monetary and interest rate policy.[3]

Along with pervasive macro themes, it is important to note that abnormal stock market growth over the past 20 years is also due to powerful microeconomic happenings at the corporate level — as manifest in the adoption by U.S. and international corporations (either directly or indirectly) of value-based metrics that are designed to give shareholders their due. These so-called economic profit measures — with value defined acronyms, EVA and MVA (Stern Stewart) [4,5] CFROI (HOLT/BCG),[6] and SVA and TSR (LEK/Alcar Consulting Group)[7] — represent a practitioner-driven rebirth in the microeconomic theory of the firm. Indeed, the theoretical roots of this value driven revival date back in the 20th century to the wealth-creating ideas of Miller and Modigliani in 1958, to the pioneering investment theory of Irving Fisher during the 1930s.[8] In turn, the oft-cited classical tenets of economic profit theory date back to the late 19th century writings of Alfred Marshall, and even — in the context of political economy — to Adam Smith's notions about the wealth building power of the "invisible hand" in the 1776 publication of *The Wealth of Nations.*[9]

If the past two decades of U.S. stock market growth truly represent a "golden era" of investing, then this unusual (yet exciting) period of wealth accumulation can also be viewed as a blossoming time for value-based management

---

[3] James Abate's comments on macro (and micro) factors that have generated abundant growth in the U.S. stock market over the past few decades were presented at the September 1999 Information Management Network's Inaugural Conference on Value-Based Metrics (cited more formally below).

[4] For an insightful discussion of the Stern Stewart economic profit model, along with many applications in a corporate finance setting, see G. Bennett Stewart III, *The Quest for Value* (New York: Harper Collins, 1991) and Al Ehrbar, *EVA: The Real Key to Creating Wealth* (New York: John Wiley and Sons, 1998).

[5] That a significant interest exists among today's academics and practitioners on EVA and economic profit is evidenced in the following non-exhaustive list of published works: Pamela P. Peterson and David R. Peterson, *Company Performance and Measures of Performance* (Charlottesville VA: Association for Investment Management and Research, 1996); James L. Grant, "Foundations of EVA for Investment Managers," *Journal of Portfolio Management* (Fall, 1996), and *Foundations of Economic Value Added* (New Hope, PA: Frank J. Fabozzi Associates, 1997); Jeffrey Bacidore, John Boquist, and Todd Milbourn, "The Search for the Best Financial Performance Measure," *Financial Analysts Journal* (May/June 1997), Gary C. Biddle, Robert M. Bowen, and James W. Wallace, "Does EVA® Beat Earnings: Evidence on Associations with Stock Returns and Firm Values," *Journal of Accounting and Economics* (December 1997); Aswath Damodaran, "Value Creation and Enhancement: Back to the Future," *Contemporary Finance Digest* (Winter 1998); and Stephen F. O'Byrne, "Does Value-Based Management Discourage Investment in Intangibles?" in Chapter 5 — among other EVA focused chapters in this book.

[6] CFROI is the financial and investment advisory product of HOLT Value Associates, LP, and is promoted by the Boston Consulting Group (BCG). For rigorous development and application of the CFROI approach to corporate valuation and performance measurement, see Bartley J. Madden, *CFROI Valuation: A Total Systems Approach to Valuing the Firm* (Woburn, MA: Butterworth-Heinemann, 1999).

[7] SVA and TSR — for Shareholder Value Added and Total Stock Returns, respectively — are financial measurement tools of the LEK/Alcar Consulting Group (the shareholder value consulting arm of L.E.K. Consulting of London) that are grounded in the corporate valuation and performance measurement analysis of Alfred Rappaport. See Alfred Rappaport, *Creating Shareholder Value: A Guide for Managers and Investors* (Free Press, 1997, revised from the original 1986 edition), and "New Thinking on How to Link Executive Pay with Performance," *Harvard Business Review* (March/April 1999).

systems (and the associated value-based metrics) that channel economic and financial resources — via wealth maximizing internal or external acquisition/ divestiture decisions by corporate managers — to their highest valued use. In light of these *jointly* profound macro and microeconomic developments that have occurred over the past two decades, this chapter and the next one provide a value-based foundation on the strategic role of economic profit measures — such as EVA (Economic Value Added) and CFROI (Cash Flow Return on Investment) — for futuristic looking corporate managers and investors.

In this chapter we will look at today's value-based metric players. In Chapter 2 we cover value-based metrics in the context of: (1) role of value-based metrics in financial theory, (2) value-based measurement issues, (3) traditional versus economic profit approach to corporate valuation, (4) capital structure and cost of capital issues, and (5) empirical evidence on the relationship between value-based metrics and shareholder wealth. In these contexts, Chapter 2 provides a foundation on the role of value-based (economic profit)[10] measures in enhancing stockholder wealth as well as providing a value focused foundation on the chapters that follow — with economic profit applications in banking, corporate finance, and investment management.

TODAY'S VALUE-BASED METRICS PLAYERS

While the theory and application of value-based metrics (VBM) is not new,[11] today's economic profit players include a wide and growing range of constituents

[8] A theoretical foundation on value based metrics — expressed in the context of NPV analysis and the irrelevance of capital structure mix in a perfect capital market — is spelled out by Modigliani and Miller in their 1958 and 1961 papers. See Franco Modigliani and Merton H. Miller, "The Cost of Capital, Corporation Finance, and the Theory of Investment," *American Economic Review* (June 1958), and "Dividend Policy, Growth and the Valuation of Shares," *Journal of Business* (October 1961).

For Irving Fisher's pioneering work on the NPV theory of the firm, see Irving Fisher, The Theory of Investment (New York: Augustus M. Kelley Publishers, 1965, Reprinted from the original 1930 edition).

[9] A classical foundation on the concept of economic profit can be found in Alfred Marshall, *Principles of Economics* (New York: Macmillan & Co.: Volume 1, 1890), p. 142.

[10] In this chapter and the next, we use the terms "value-based metrics" and "economic profit" interchangeably. Also, the overriding goal of this chapter and the next is to examine and promote the role of value-based measurement in enhancing stockholder wealth. We do not recommend the shareholder value benefits of any one economic profit metric over another — such as EVA over CFROI.

[11] It is common knowledge among academics and practitioners that value-based measurement theory — along with its corporate valuation implications — is not new. This point was recently emphasized at the 1999 Information Management Network's Conference on Value-Based Metrics (covered in the text that follows), and in an interesting article by Aswath Damodaran ["Value Creation and Enhancement: Back to the Future," *Contemporary Finance Digest* (Winter 1998)].

What is not so well known is that the application of economic profit concepts — in a much simpler form than today's sophisticated value-based metrics — was applied by major corporations several decades ago. For examples, Stephen O'Byrne points out in Chapter 5 of this book that in 1922 General Motors adopted an incentive compensation plan that provided for a bonus pool of 10% of profit in excess of a 7% return on capital. More recently, in 1984, Walt Disney gave Michael Eisner a bonus incentive equal to 2% of net income in excess of a 9% return on stockholders' equity.

— from academia, consulting firms, banks, corporations, money management firms, and even (quasi) governmental bodies.[12] Current interest in value-based metrics can be distinguished from the past in terms of the sophistication of VBM employed as well as the heightened awareness among corporate managers and investors alike in the primacy of shareholder value-added principles in increasingly competitive capital markets — where the flow of investment moneys transcend international borders when seeking the best risk-adjusted returns.

Recent interest in the theory and application of value-based metrics is evidenced in the context of three prominent finance and investment conferences. These include (1) Credit Suisse First Boston's landmark 1996 "Economic Value Added Conference" — that is now an annual client event sponsored by this investment banking firm — (2) Goldman Sachs' client conference of May 1997 — titled "EVA and Return on Capital: Roads to Shareholder Wealth" — when Steven Einhorn directed the "roll-out" of the firm's EVA-based company research platform, and (3) the Information Management Network's September 1999 "Inaugural Conference on Value-Based Metrics." Attendees at the September 1999 IMN conference included a broad range of VBM participants who play a key role in shaping today's value-based management systems, metrics, and economic profit research.

Although it is commonly acknowledged by VBM players that varying economic profit measures must in theory give the same valuation results — for both the enterprise value of the firm and its outstanding shares — the value-based metrics promoted by today's management consulting firms can be differentiated in several ways according to (1) the number of accounting adjustments made to obtain a "true" cash-based measure of a firm's operating profit and economic capital, (2) whether the value metric provides an answer that is stated in dollars or percentage terms, and (3) whether the value-based analysis is conducted using nominal or inflation-adjusted inputs of operating profit and capital. In each case, however, the major VBM consultants — like Stern Stewart, HOLT Value Associates, and LEK/Alcar Consulting Group — recognize the shareholder value imperative of linking operating profit with economic capital, and the opportunity cost of invested capital.[13]

With respect to some of the key adjustments made by VBM consultants to estimate economic profit, Stern Stewart's *dollar*-based EVA measure is based on a limited (and often customized) number of significant accounting adjustments — such as research and development, treatment of acquisition goodwill, and spe-

---

[12] It is interesting to note that value-based principles are now emphasized in the Office of Economic and Community Development's (OECD) global corporate governance initiatives. The growing role of economic profit concepts in the international arena is explained by David Young of INSEAD and Robert Straw, Simon Peck, and Hans-Ueli Keller. See Chapters 8 and 9 of this book.

[13] For examples, Stern Stewart estimates the cost of capital as a weighed average cost of debt and equity financing — where the cost of equity capital is estimated using the traditional CAPM. HOLT Value Associates estimates a corporate "hurdle rate" as an average historical return on capital stated in real terms. We cover cost of capital theory and estimation issues in Chapter 2.

cial capital investment "banks" having a memory for deferred opportunity costs.[14] Also, HOLT Value Associates' CFROI is much like a *percentage*-based internal rate of return (IRR) measure that gets compared to a corporate-wide "hurdle rate." As explained in more detail later, CFROI is calculated in real terms after (1) "grossing up" of the firm's past capital investments, and (2) inflation-adjusting downward the future nominal cash flow and terminal value estimates.

In terms of financial advisory, Stern Stewart generally serves the corporate world with its MVA and EVA metrics, while HOLT Value Associates primarily serves institutional investors worldwide with its CFROI measure. Also, the LEK/Alcar Consulting Group (the shareholder value advisory arm of L.E.K. Consulting)[15] focuses on enhancing shareholder value added (SVA) in the context of improving total stockholder returns (TSR) — hence the acronyms, SVA and TSR. Arthur Andersen — working in conjunction with the Applied Finance Group of Chicago — emphasizes a value-focused measurement system that attempts to blend EVA and CFROI concepts in the context of a firm's "Economic Margin."[16] Also, we would be remiss for not mentioning the financial advisory efforts of Marakon Associates — with a shareholder value focus dating back to the late 1970s.

While economic profit measures were applied early on in the corporate world — as evidenced by Coca-Cola's embracing during the 1980s of the economic profit measure of corporate success — then energized during the 1990s by several prominent Wall Street players — such as CS First Boston, Goldman Sachs and Salomon Smith Barney — they now play a growing role in the evolving world of banking and financial services. For example, Al Ehrbar[17] notes that in 1994 Centura Banks became the first U.S. bank to employ Stern Stewart's EVA measure of corporate success. Banc One "rolled out" EVA incentives and a financial management system in 1997, while economic profit concepts have been promoted at banks around the world including Citibank, ANZ bank in Australia, and ABSA bank in South Africa. Moreover, on the asset management and research side, Credit Suisse Asset Management, CDC Investment Management, and Goldman Sachs U.S. Research employ economic profit models in their intrinsic valuation analysis of companies, industries, and even the macro economy.[18]

---

[14] We discuss some of the important accounting adjustments made by VBM players in the next chapter. More detailed discussions on value-based accounting issues are provided in Chapter 3 by Al Ehrbar and Chapter 4 by Pamela Peterson.

[15] At the time of this writing, L.E.K. was integrating all of its consulting advisory groups — including business strategy, mergers and acquisitions, and shareholder value advisory (LEK/Alcar Consulting Group) — into L.E.K Consulting.

[16] The "economic margin" approach to value-based measurement used by Arthur Andersen and the Applied Finance Group is covered in Chapter 7.

[17] See Ehrbar, *EVA: The Real Key to Creating Wealth.*

[18] For pioneering research by Wall Street firms that look at companies, industries, and/or the macro-economy in an economic profit context, see (1) Al Jackson, Michael J. Mauboussin, and Charles R. Wolf, "EVA Primer," *Equity-Research Americas* (CS First Boston: February 20, 1996), (2) Steven G. Einhorn, Gabrielle Napolitano, and Abby Joseph Cohen, "EVA: A Primer," *U.S. Research* (Goldman Sachs, September 10, 1997), and (3) James A. Abate, "Select Economic Value Portfolios," *U.S. Equity Product Overview* (Credit Suisse Asset Management, January 1998).

REFLECTION

In this chapter, we introduce some of the evolutionary developments and players that shape today's world of value-based metrics. By doing so, we have opened the lid on a box that is filled with robust financial theories and practitioner models that recognize the importance of wealth creation for companies, industries, and even nations of the world. Before proceeding to expand the value-based metrics focus, we emphasize that one of the most important aspects of today's evolving world of value-based metrics is the synergy that is now being realized between classical economic tenets of the firm and value-driven practitioner models used in practice — with applications by sophisticated VBM players in banking, corporate finance, and investment management. These value-based theories and models recognize the importance of measuring "profit" — albeit economic profit — in the context of (1) linking operating profit with economic capital, and (2) recognizing that "profit" is not economic or true profit without a proper accounting for the opportunity cost of invested capital.

As we move forward to Chapter 2, it is important to emphasize a central tenet of value-based metrics theory. That is, invested capital — more aptly, equity capital as a primary source of funding for that capital — is not "free capital" for any company, for any industry, or for that matter, any country. With a proper understanding of how wealth is created at the microeconomic level in the context of positive and sustainable growth in economic profit — more specifically, favorable EVA generation from invested assets both now and in the future — one has the beginnings of a financial understanding of why some companies and industries can create wealth, while other companies and industries will destroy it. Economic profit generation also has spillover effects at the macroeconomic level and can explain why a capitalistic and open market economic system will, on the average create wealth, while economic systems such as socialism and communism will waste wealth — with an unfortunate, yet concomitant decline or collapse in the general standard of living.

As we see it, the "good news" about value-based metrics is that corporate managers, investors, and governmental policy makers alike can employ the principles of economic profit and wealth creation to bring about positive change within their general sphere of influence. However, the "bad news" is that some corporate managers or government policy makers may still choose to ignore the wealth-creating role of economic profit creation by making inept managerial or governmental policy decisions that result in what history reveals as a prolonged and painful period of wealth destruction. Even within the world's most developed free market economy, "Corporate America" is still littered with too many companies that have negative economic profit — for some unfortunate examples, see the 10 largest U.S. "wealth destroyers" that we discuss in Chapter 2. Moreover, without a recent history or memory of the importance of economic profit and wealth creation by Russia's government policy officials, it is little wonder why their stock and currency markets collapsed in the Russian financial debacle of August 1998.

Chapter 2

Value-Based Metrics in Financial Theory

Frank J. Fabozzi, Ph.D., CFA
Adjunct Professor of Finance
School of Management
Yale University

James L. Grant, Ph.D.
President
JLG Research

INTRODUCTION

One of the most exciting aspects of value-based metrics (economic profit measures) is that they directly measure the value that the firm's managers add to the physical (and human) capital in their employ. Anyone who has had a basic course in finance knows that managers should invest in wealth creating projects that have a positive net present value (NPV). But what does it mean for corporate managers to invest in positive NPV projects when most of the available financial data have little if any resemblance to the kind of cash flow information that is required in capital budgeting decisions?[1]

This is precisely where value-based metrics as a practitioner's guide to measuring shareholder value go to the head of the corporate finance class — or better yet to the head of the corporate board! Consider EVA, the value-based metric that was successfully developed by Joel Stern and G. Bennett Stewart in 1982. In their economic profit framework (which, as we noted before, rests on microeconomic tenets of the firm), the link between EVA and shareholder value added is transparent. In principle, the NPV of any firm can be expressed in terms of the present value stream of economic profit generated by both the firm's current and anticipated future assets not currently in place.[2]

In this chapter, we'll look at the role of value-based metrics in the theory of finance. We'll begin with the link between NPV and its *annualized* EVA equivalent in the context of the "two-period" Fisherian Wealth Model.[3] We'll then show that other

---

[1] For a basic illustration on how to calculate a company's EVA and NPV from a Value Line report — along with some difficulties due to information shortfall — see James L. Grant, *Foundations of Economic Value Added* (New Hope, PA: Frank J. Fabozzi Associates, 1997).

prominent value-based measures such as Cash Flow Return on Investment (CFROI) evolve out of the same market value rule that leads corporate managers to act in the wealth creating interest of the firm's owners —namely, those investors that hold the firm's existing securities. We'll also explore the theory of value-based metrics in terms of the firm's capital structure decision as well as the *real* meaning of the firm's enterprise value-to-book capital ratio. We conclude the chapter with an empirical examination of the NPV-EVA relationship for wealth creators and wealth destroyers.

TWO-PERIOD NPV MODEL

Consider a two-period world where an investment today of say $100 (or 100% of the initial capital investment) leads to an unlevered expected after-tax cash flow of $130 (or 130% of the capital invested) in the future period. For convenience, we'll denote this one-time expected cash flow as "NOPAT."[4] Further suppose that the firm's *weighted average cost of capital* (*wacc*) is 10%. Based on these figures, the *gross present value* (GPV) of the firm's investment decision is:

---

[2] The division of a firm's value into a pricing contribution from the firm's existing and future investment (or growth) opportunities is explained in Eugene F. Fama and Merton H. Miller, *The Theory of Finance* (Holt, Rinehart, and Winston, Inc., 1972). For economic profit (EVA) interpretations of the classic "Investment Opportunities Approach to Valuation (IOAV)," see (1) Grant, *Foundations of Economic Value Added*, (2) Aswath Damodaran, "Value Creation and Enhancement: Back to the Future," *Contemporary Finance Digest* (Winter 1998), and (3) Chapter 5 of this book by Stephen F. O'Bryne — "Does Value-Based Management Discourage Investment in Intangibles?" Economic profit for a time is also consistent with the "franchise factor" model of Kogelman and Leibowitz — see Stanley Kogelman and Martin L. Leibowitz, "The Franchise Factor Valuation Approach: Capturing the Firm's Investment Opportunities," *Corporate Financial Decision Making and Equity Analysis* (Charlottesville VA: Association for Investment Management and Research, 1995).

[3] The basic link between NPV and EVA in a "two-period" wealth model is explained in Grant, *Foundations of Economic Value Added*. Without getting into the detail in this chapter, the "two-period" economic profit model is robust in a multi-period setting.

[4] In practice, NOPAT refers to a firm's net operating profit after tax. Because we are using a two-period model to show the basic link between NPV and economic profit (EVA), the "NOPAT" figure (at $130) shown in the text includes the initial capital investment (at $100) and the dollar return on that capital (at $30). In equation form, this can be expressed as $I \times (1 + ROC)$, where ROC is the after-tax return on the firm's invested capital. This two-period interpretation of NOPAT is of course different from the conventional view of NOPAT as after-tax operating profit or the dollar return on the existing capital in place, $I \times ROC$, for an ongoing concern.

However, since the "capital charge" in the two-period model must include both the "interest" on borrowed funds (measured by $I \times wacc$) plus the return of the borrowed "loan principal," — $I \times (1 + wacc)$, as opposed to just $I \times wacc$ for an ongoing concern — the reader will shortly see that the resulting EVA expression in the two-period NPV model is consistent with the conventional view of economic profit — and indeed, is the theoretical justification for the popular interpretation of EVA.

In this context, we show that EVA is the "spread" between the after-tax return on invested capital (ROC) and the cost of capital (*wacc*), multiplied by the initial capital investment — namely, EVA= $I \times$ [ROC – *wacc*], which, in turn, has a net present value of EVA/(1 + *wacc*). In a multi-period framework the economic profit generated by the firm's existing assets (as opposed to expected future assets) would be valued at EVA/*wacc*, while the present value of the perpetual capital charge on any existing assets is, $I \times wacc/wacc = I$.

$$GPV = \text{Present value of unlevered after-tax cash flow}$$
$$= NOPAT/(1 + wacc)$$
$$= \$130/(1 + 0.1) = \$118.18$$

In turn, the net present value (NPV), or *market value added* (MVA) in Stern Stewart terminology, from the firm's corporate investment strategy, I, is given by:

$$NPV = GPV - \text{Capital Investment}$$
$$= NOPAT/(1 + wacc) - I$$
$$= \$118.18 - \$100 = \$18.18$$

Due to the wealth-creating capital investment, the firm's managers have added $18.18 (or 18.18%) to the initial capital employed by the firm. The corporate or "enterprise" value of the firm is therefore:

$$\text{Enterprise Value} = \text{Market Value of Debt} + \text{Market Value of Equity}$$
$$= \text{Capital} + \text{Net Present Value}$$
$$= \$100 + \$18.18 = \$118.18$$
$$\text{(or 118.18\% of the initial capital)}$$

Exhibit 1 provides a visual representation of the two-period Fisherian Wealth Model. Assume that the firm's ability to transform current resources into future resources can be represented by a Production Possibilities Curve (PPC). Also, assume that the firm has no internal start up funds such that the total invested capital, $I = \$100$, is raised entirely from external capital market sources. The length "$I = \$100$" in Exhibit 1 represents the amount borrowed to finance the capital investment, I. Also assume that the initial corporate investment generates an unlevered cash flow, NOPAT of $130, in the future period — which in a multiperiod context can be viewed as the after-tax cash flow generated next period plus the present value of all future after-tax cash flows thereafter.

Exhibit 1: Wealth Creation with Positive NPV

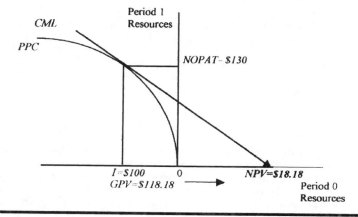

At NOPAT equal to $130, the after-tax cash flow from the firm's productive investment decision is represented by the vertical distance in Exhibit 1 from length "I" up to the PPC. At $118.18, the present value of the anticipated NOPAT is the firm's gross present value. The horizontal length GPV in the exhibit represents this distance. Moreover, the firm's net present value, at $18.18, is measured along the horizontal axis by the difference between its gross present value, GPV = $118.18, and the total invested capital of $100. Equivalently, the exhibit shows that the firm's NPV of $18.18 is obtained by "passing" a Capital Market Line (CML) down through the point of tangency with the PPC and then reading off the NPV dollar value on the horizontal axis — labelled "Period 0 Resources."

ECONOMIC PROFIT LOOK AT THE NPV MODEL

Up to this point nothing has been said about the role of value-based metrics as a financial tool in measuring the NPV of the firm's corporate investment decision. This means that, in principle, we can speak in terms of wealth creation without formally introducing an annualized measure of economic profit. Having said that, it is important to emphasize that one of the major goals of the value-based metrics revolution is to promote an operating measure of profit — albeit economic profit as opposed to accounting profit — that at the very least is consistent with the measurement and creation of shareholder value.

Based on the figures supplied in our two-period NPV illustration, the firm's expected future EVA is $20. This economic profit figure results from subtracting the expected financing payment of $110 — including the return of "loan principal" (at $100) to external suppliers of capital — from the expected future cash flow, denoted previously as "NOPAT."[5]

$$\begin{aligned} EVA &= NOPAT - \$ \text{ Capital Charge} \\ &= \$130 - \$100 \times (1 + 0.1) = \$20 \end{aligned}$$

With positive EVA, at $20, the firm's NOPAT is more than sufficient to cover its anticipated expenses including a "rental charge" (again, we include the return of borrowed loan principal in the two period application), $I \times (1 + wacc) = \$110$, for the economic capital employed in the business.

---

[5] For an ongoing concern, a firm's economic profit, EVA, is the difference between its unlevered net operating profit, NOPAT, and a charge for the capital employed in the business — as measured by the weighted average cost of capital, *wacc*, times the amount of capital invested:

$$\begin{aligned} EVA &= NOPAT - \$ \text{ Capital Charge} \\ &= [S - CGS - SGA - D] \times (1 - t) - I \times wacc \\ &= EBIT \times (1 - t) - I \times wacc \end{aligned}$$

where NOPAT is expressed in simple terms in the context of the firm's pretax operating profit, EBIT, less unlevered operating taxes. EBIT is a function of the firm's sales less expenses including cost of goods sold, CGS, selling, general and administrative expenses, SGA, and *economic* depreciation, *D*. Based on this EVA formulation, the invested capital term, *I*, is net of accumulated economic depreciation. In practice, there are many accounting adjustments that must be made to estimate a company's economic profit.

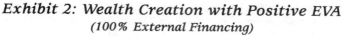

Exhibit 2: Wealth Creation with Positive EVA
(100% External Financing)

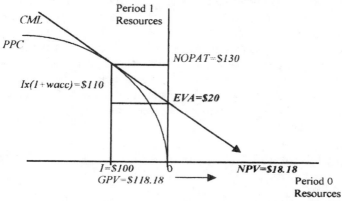

Exhibit 2 shows how the firm derives its net present value from anticipated economic profit. Recall that EVA is simply the difference between the firm's estimated NOPAT and the dollar capital charge, $I \times (1 + wacc)$. At $20, this economic profit amount is labeled "EVA" in Exhibit 2. Upon discounting the firm's economic profit back to the current period by the weighted average cost of capital, at 10%, we again obtain the firm's net present value, at $18.18. Alternatively, we again see that the firm's NPV of $18.18 can be located where the CML intersects the axis labelled "Period 0 Resources." Hence, the two-period wealth model shows that the firm's net present value is in fact equal to the present value of its anticipated future EVA.

Relatedness of Economic Profit Measures

In an attempt to show the basic relationship between today's popular value-based metrics, such as EVA and CFROI, we can express (in the two-period model) the firm's unlevered net operating profit after tax, NOPAT, as:

$$NOPAT = I \times (1 + CFROI)$$

In this expression, CFROI is the firm's "cash flow return on investment" and "I" is its initial capital investment. With this development, we can express the firm's NPV directly in terms of related value-based metrics including CFROI and EVA according to:[6]

$$
\begin{aligned}
NPV &= NOPAT/(1 + wacc) - I \\
&= I \times (1 + CFROI)/(1 + wacc) - I \times (1 + wacc)/(1 + wacc) \\
&= I \times [CFROI - wacc]/(1 + wacc) \\
&= EVA/(1 + wacc)
\end{aligned}
$$

---

[6] In this NPV illustration, we assume a perfect world where all VBM players make the same correct accounting adjustments when estimating economic profit.

In principle, we see that the firm's NPV derives its sign from the difference between the cash flow return on investment, CFROI, and its weighted average cost of capital, *wacc*. The spread between CFROI (or after-tax return on capital, ROC) and *wacc* is often referred to in the value-based metrics literature as the firm's *residual return on capital* (RROC). This key return difference is also referred to as the *surplus return on capital*, the firm's *excess return on invested capital*, the *EVA spread*, and the *economic margin*. Furthermore, the above development shows that the net present value of the firm is equal to the present value of its anticipated economic profit stream — as measured by its economic value added, EVA = NOPAT − $Capital Charge.

Upon substituting the numerical values into the "two-period" NPV formulation, we obtain:

$$
\begin{aligned}
\text{NPV} &= \text{MVA} \\
&= \$130/(1 + 0.1) - 100 \\
&= \$100(1 + 0.3)/(1 + 0.1) - \$100 \\
&= \$100(0.3 - 0.1)/(1.1) \\
&= \$20/(1.1) = \$18.18
\end{aligned}
$$

In this combined illustration, the firm's anticipated CFROI is 30%, the assessed residual return on capital (RROC) is 20% (measured by the EVA spread), and the firm's assessed economic profit is equal to $20. The conceptual relationship between NPV, EVA, and CFROI and other prominent value-based metrics follows from this result.

In sum, the two-period wealth model is robust. It shows that the firm makes a positive NPV addition to invested capital if and only if the assessed Cash Flow Return on Investment, CFROI, is greater than the weighted average cost of capital, *wacc*. Another way of saying the same thing is that the firm's NPV is positive because its discounted economic profit, EVA/(1+*wacc*), is positive. In principle, value-based metrics such as EVA and CFROI are strategic measures of corporate operating profit because they directly measure whether the firm makes a positive NPV (or MVA) addition to the firm's economic capital.

INTERNAL VERSUS EXTERNAL FINANCING

The "just right" way of financing a company's growth opportunities is a controversial issue in the study of corporate finance. With perfect capital markets, the method of financing a firm's growth opportunities has no meaningful impact on the net present value created by the firm's productive-investment decision. In this Miller and Modigliani context,[7] the market value of the firm and its outstanding shares are invariant to its capital structure decision. The value-based metrics interpretation of the Modigliani-Miller position on capital structure is shown in Exhibit 3.[8]

---

[7] See Franco Modigliani and Merton H. Miller, "The Cost of Capital, Corporation Finance, and the Theory of Investment," *American Economic Review* (June 1958), and "Dividend Policy, Growth and the Valuation of Shares," *Journal of Business* (October 1961).

Exhibit 3: Wealth Creation with Positive EVA
(100% Internal Financing)

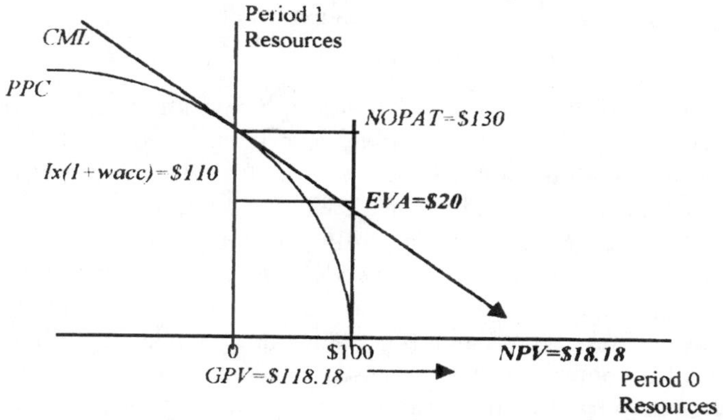

Suppose in contrast to the external financing assumption (Exhibit 1 or 2), that the firm's current owners provide the firm's initial capital, $I = \$100$. Exhibit 3 shows that the Production Possibility Curve shifts to the right by this amount and now begins at "100" rather than at "zero." According to Miller and Modigliani arguments, nothing of any real value has changed. With internal financing, the PPC merely shifts to the right (by $100) without any impact on shareholder wealth — measured by the firm's NPV. As Exhibit 3 shows, the net present value added to the firm's invested capital is still equal to $18.18. As before, there are several ways of interpreting this NPV result. We'll look at the market value added (NPV) to the owner's initial investment from an economic profit (EVA) perspective.

Looking up in Exhibit 3 from the invested capital of $100 — along the positive side of the horizontal axis — we again see the anticipated NOPAT of $130. Upon subtracting the capital charge, at $110, from NOPAT we obtain the estimated EVA of $20. This results because the future capital charge of $110 (including the $10 opportunity cost and return of the owners' initial capital investment of $100) still applies even though the firm is financed entirely with internal equity financing. In this context, the capital charge must still be "paid" regardless of whether the initial invested capital is supplied by external investors — our first NPV example (shown graphically in Exhibit 1 or 2) — or to the firm's existing owners — as in our second financing illustration (see Exhibit 3). Moreover, upon discounting the EVA of $20 back to the present yields the same NPV figure, at $18.18, that we obtained before with 100% external financing. This is the essence of the original Modigliani-Miller position on capital structure from an economic profit lens.

---

[8] Fama and Miller employ a "two-period" NPV model to show the irrelevance of internal *versus* external financing decisions in a perfect capital market — see Fama and Miller, *The Theory of Finance*. We illustrate the irrelevance of corporate debt policy in an NPV-EVA context.

We can also reconcile the Miller-Modigliani application in the context of the value-based formulation that we explained before:

$$NPV = EVA/(1 + wacc)$$
$$= I \times [CFROI - wacc]/(1 + wacc)$$

Specifically, since NOPAT is the net operating profit after tax generated by the *unlevered* firm, and "*I*" is the initial capital investment, the impact of internal versus external financing on enterprise value boils down to the impact of corporate financing on the firm's weighted average cost of capital, *wacc*.

As shown by Modigliani and Miller in their 1958 paper,[9] the weighted average cost of capital, *wacc*, is *independent* of the particular method (debt versus equity) of financing. Therefore, if *wacc* is unaffected by corporate leverage, then the firm's assessed future EVA and its present value equivalent, NPV, must also be independent of the internal versus external financing decision. Moreover, in the MM world of corporate finance, the source of the firm's positive NPV — and therefore its annualized EVA equivalent — are derived from wealth enhancing investment decisions in real assets — both now and in the future — that have a CFROI that on the average exceeds the *wacc*.

Impact of Corporate Taxes on WACC

The capital structure irrelevance argument of Miller and Modigliani depends on the assumption of a perfect capital market. In the real world, market imperfections exist such that the capital structure mix of internal versus external financing may impact the enterprise value of the firm and the price of its outstanding shares. Perhaps the most significant imperfection — and the one most often cited in the theory and practice of corporate finance — is the issue of tax deductibility of debt interest expense that in turn leads to a debt tax subsidy. In a world with taxes and deductibility of corporate interest expense, the firm's weighted average cost of capital can be expressed as:

$$\text{Levered } wacc = \text{Unlevered } wacc \, [1 - t_e \times (D/C)]$$

where, t_e, is the firm's "effective" debt tax subsidy rate, and (D/C) is its "target" debt to capital ratio.

As long as the firm's debt tax subsidy rate is positive, then the levered firm's cost of capital is lower than the cost of capital for an equivalent business risk unlevered firm. When this happens, both the anticipated future EVA and (therefore) the currently measured NPV of the levered firm is higher than that available to unlevered shareholders. However, Miller argues[10] that even in a world with corporate taxes and progressive income taxation, the firm's effective

---

[9] See Modigliani and Miller, "The Cost of Capital, Corporation Finance, and the Theory of Investment."
[10] See Merton H. Miller, "Debt and Taxes," *Journal of Finance* (May 1977).

debt tax subsidy rate, t_e, in the levered cost of capital formulation is close to zero. If correct, then the levered firm's cost of capital is again equal to the unlevered firm's cost of capital such that the firm's assessed future EVA and its current NPV are independent of the particular method of corporate financing — including the "just right" mix of debt versus equity financing.

Like most corporate finance practitioners, we do not question the existence of a debt tax subsidy on enterprise value. However, we also recognize that the benefit of a debt induced tax subsidy to the levered firm's shareholders may be overestimated by corporate managers — especially, as Miller points out, when one considers the offsetting tax effects of leveraged capital structures. Moreover, its seems that shareholders are better served when managers focus their investment decisions on real economic profit enhancement as opposed to corporate financing strategies that merely repackage the mix of debt and equity securities on the firm's corporate balance sheet. In this context, we emphasize the EVA importance of wealth creation via positive NPV decisions as opposed to capital structure changes that merely give investors the illusion of economic profit creation.[11]

REAL MEANING OF THE VALUE/CAPITAL RATIO

Wall Street analysts often speak in terms of the "price/earnings" and "price/book value" ratios. Along this line, one of the key benefits of the value-based metrics approach to measuring corporate success is that we can see why a firm has a price/book ratio, for example, above or below unity. We can show this by dividing the enterprise value of the firm, V, by total capital employed, I, according to:

$$V/I = I/I + NPV/I$$
$$= 1 + NPV/I$$

From this, we see that a firm's value-to-capital ratio, V/I, exceeds one if and only if — in a well functioning capital market — the firm has positive NPV. In contrast, the V/I ratio falls below unity when the firm invests in wealth destroying or negative expected NPV projects — such that the NPV/I ratio turns negative.[12] Substituting our (two-period) present value-based EVA and CFROI relationships into the "value/capital" ratio produces:

---

[11] We are aware of — but do not cover in this chapter — the positive NPV (and therefore EVA) role that levered capital structures may have in disciplining corporate managers (agents) to act in the best interests of shareholders (owners) in a world with agency costs. For a practitioner-oriented discussion of the transactions cost role of corporate debt policy in creating ownership value, see Michael C. Jensen, "Eclipse of the Modern Corporation," *Harvard Business Review* (September/October 1989). See also the value-focused corporate leverage comments by David Young in Chapter 8 and Robert Straw, Simon Peck, and Hans-Ueli Keller in Chapter 9 of this book.

[12] At a later point, we examine the empirical relationship between the NPV-to-Capital ratio and the EVA-to-Capital ratio for wealth creators and wealth destroyers. This updates some earlier empirical work on economic profit by Grant in *Foundations of Economic Value Added*.

$$V/I = 1 + [EVA/(1 + wacc)]/I$$
$$= 1 + [I \times [CFROI - wacc]/(1+wacc)]/I$$
$$= 1 + [CFROI - wacc]/(1+wacc)$$

Wealth creating firms have a value/capital ratio that exceeds unity because they have positive NPV. The positive NPV is due to the discounted positive-assessed EVA. In turn, economic profit is positive because the firm's CFROI, exceeds the *wacc*. These developments point to the theoretical role of value-based metrics as strategic measures of economic profit that are directly linked to shareholder value.

Substituting the assumed values from our two-period NPV example into the value/capital ratio yields:

$$V/I = 1 + [\$20/(1.1)]/\$100$$
$$= 1 + [0.3 - 0.1]/(1.1) = 1.1818$$

Hence, with value-based metrics, there is little uncertainty as to (1) why a wealth creating firm has a value/capital ratio that exceeds one, and (2) why a wealth waster has a value-to-capital ratio that lies below unity. Value-based metrics can — from an economic profit perspective — give corporate managers and investors alike the necessary financial tools to see the direct relationship between corporate investment decisions — made both now and in the future — and their expected impact on shareholder value.[13]

VBM MEASUREMENT ISSUES

The two-period wealth model is helpful in showing how value-based metrics like EVA and CFROI are grounded in financial theory. However, the simple NPV model *belies* the complexity of the economic profit calculation in practice. In this context, Stern Stewart, Goldman Sachs U.S. Research, and David Young of INSEAD point out that there are some 160 accounting adjustments that can be made to a firm's financial statements to convert them to a value-based format emphasizing cash operating profit and asset replacement cost considerations. Many of the potential adjustments can have a material impact on the analyst's estimate of a company's after-tax return on capital through their joint impact on the firm's unlevered net operating profit (NOPAT) and the dollar estimate of economic book capital.

Also, there are significant empirical anomalies and academic issues involved when estimating the firm's weighted average cost of debt and equity capital.[14] Consequently, we'll provide an overview of the two key elements of economic profit, including (1) the major accounting adjustments that are necessary to

---

[13] That value-based metrics can be used in a meaningful corporate valuation way, however, is based on the assumption that the capital market is reasonably efficient. If the capital market were price inefficient, then this would create active investment opportunities for informed investors that seek to trade the equity *and* debt securities of mispriced firms.

calculate a firm's NOPAT in practice, and (2) cost of capital estimation challenges that an analyst must address when estimating economic profit in practice. While we focus primarily on EVA in the illustration of value-based adjustments, the same accounting and cost of capital issues arise in the estimation of other prominent value-based metrics such as CFROI and SVA.

NOPAT ESTIMATION

Due to practical considerations, the major economic profit players — including Stern Stewart, HOLT Value Associates, LEK/Alcar Consulting Group, CS First Boston, and Goldman Sachs — have generally narrowed the list of possible accounting adjustments to measure a firm's NOPAT. In this context, Exhibit 4 shows Stern Stewart's "bottom up" and "top down" income statement approaches to calculating a firm's unlevered NOPAT while Exhibit 5 shows how economic book capital can be estimated in practice with some key balance sheet adjustments based on the equivalent "asset approach" and "financing sources of assets approach" to measuring the firm's economic capital.[15]

The Stern Stewart Approach

In Stern Stewart's "bottom up" approach to estimating unlevered NOPAT, the financial analyst begins with a firm's operating profit after depreciation and amortization. Accounting items that get added back to this figure include the increase in LIFO reserve, goodwill amortization, and the change in *net* capitalized research and development. Two other accounting figures that are shown in Exhibit 4 include the *implied* interest expense on operating leases as well as the (net) increase in bad-debt reserve.

The rise in LIFO reserve is added back to the firm's accounting-based operating profit to give the analyst a better gauge of the cash operating profit derived from the actual inventory units used to manufacture the firm's product. In a period of rising prices (inflation), LIFO inventory cost understates corporate profit due to the higher cost of goods sold figure resulting from inventory costing (last in, first out) of newly produced products at near-to-current market prices. Coincidentally, current assets on the firm's balance sheet are understated due to an *incorrect* assumption about the replacement cost of inventory — namely, those units still in inventory having an assumed purchase cost based on the initial inventory units.

---

[14] From an academic perspective, we argued that the Modigliani-Miller theory of capital structure provides some meaningful insight on how to interpret the value-based role (or lack thereof) of corporate debt policy on the firm's cost of capital and its economic profit. Also, in addition to the empirical anomalies that we cover shortly, it is important to note that published financial statements do not provide the external capital market information that is needed to estimate the firm's cost of equity capital — financial statement omissions that include the risk-free rate of interest and the investor's required premium for bearing business and financial risk.

[15] For a more comprehensive discussion of EVA-based accounting adjustments, see Stewart, *The Quest for Value*.

Exhibit 4: Calculation of NOPAT from Financial Statement Data

---

A. *Bottom-up approach*

Begin:

   Operating profit after depreciation and amortization

Add:

   Implied interest expense on operating leases

   Increase in LIFO reserve

   Goodwill amortization

   Increase in bad-debt reserve

   Increase in net capitalized research and development

Equals:

   Adjusted operating profit before taxes

Subtract:

   Cash operating taxes

Equals:

   NOPAT

B. *Top-down approach*

Begin:

   Sales

Add:

   Increase in LIFO reserve

   Implied interest expense on operating leases

   Other income

Subtract:

   Cost of goods sold

   Selling, general, and administrative expenses

   Depreciation

Equals:

   Adjusted operating profit before taxes

Subtract:

   Cash operating taxes

Equals:

   NOPAT

Note: Exhibit based on information in G. Bennett Stewart III, *The Quest for Value* (New York: Harper Collins, 1991).

Also, the change in goodwill amortization on the income statement is added back to the operating profit because the companion accumulated goodwill figure on the firm's balance sheet — arising from patents, copyrights, internal software, and even corporate acquisitions (price paid for target firm in excess of underlying value of target's *physical* assets) — is viewed as a form of economic capital or asset investment. Since research and development are also viewed as capital investment, the value-based convention is to "capitalize" it on the balance sheet while writing it off over a reasonable period of time on the income statement — rather than "expense" all R&D expenditures in the year incurred.[16] With these adjustments, the analyst arrives at NOPAT by subtracting "cash taxes" from the firm's estimated pre-tax cash operating profit. In practice, this means that the accrual-based "income tax expense" item on the income statement needs to be increased by the interest tax subsidy on debt (as well as debt equivalents like leases), while the accounting tax item should be decreased by the tax on the firm's *non*-recurring income sources.

Exhibit 5: Calculation of Capital Using Accounting Financial Statements

A. Asset *approach*
Begin:
      Net (short term) operating assets
Add:
      LIFO reserve
      Net plant and equipment
      Other assets
      Goodwill
      Accumulated goodwill amortization
      Present value of operating leases
      Bad-debt reserve
      Capitalized research and development
      Cumulative write-offs of special items
Equals:
      Capital

B. Source of financing approach
Begin:
      Book value of common equity
Add equity equivalents:
      Preferred stock
      Minority interest
      Deferred income tax reserve
      LIFO reserve
      Accumulated goodwill amortization
Add debt and debt equivalents:
      Interest-bearing short-term debt
      Long-term debt
      Capitalized lease obligations
      Present value of noncapitalized leases
Equals:
      Capital

Note: Exhibit based on information in G. Bennett Stewart III, *The Quest for Value* (New York: Harper Collins, 1991).

---

[16] Al Ehrbar notes in Chapter 3 that Stern Stewart typically uses a 5-year average write-down of R&D investment. Like R&D, the value-based convention is to capitalize marketing and corporate training expenditures.

Exhibit 4 shows Stern Stewart's "top down" approach to estimating the firm's unlevered NOPAT. As shown here, the analyst begins with sales (revenue), then subtracts the usual operating expenses such as cost of goods sold and selling, general, and administrative expenses. The increase in LIFO reserve is added to the revenue figure, while accounting depreciation[17] (in the Stern Stewart and Goldman Sachs approaches) is subtracted on the path to NOPAT. Since the benefits of corporate debt financing (if any) are already reflected in the dollar cost of capital, the cash tax figure should be based on the marginal tax rate paid by the unlevered firm. A rigorous application of Stern Stewart's approach to adjusting the firm's accounting operating profit to a cash operating profit figure for the EVA calculation is shown in an Association for Investment Management and Research (AIMR) publication by Pamela Peterson and David Peterson.[18]

Impact on Invested Capital

As Stern Stewart points out, the amount of capital employed within a firm can be estimated by making adjustments to the left hand or right hand side of the firm's balance sheet. As revealed in Exhibit 5, it is possible to estimate the firm's operating capital using the "asset approach" or the equivalent "sources of financing approach." The asset approach begins with the "net (short-term) operating assets." This figure represents current operating assets[19] less *non*-interest bearing current liabilities (accounts/taxes payables, and accrued expenses for examples). To this amount, Stern Stewart adds familiar items like the accumulated LIFO reserve, net plant and equipment, and goodwill-related items. The capitalized value of research and development and cumulative write-offs from special items like restructurings are also figured into their asset-based view of capital.

In the equivalent "sources of financing" approach, the firm's economic capital estimate is obtained by adding "equity equivalents" to the firm's book value of common equity, along with debt and "debt equivalents." Exhibit 5 shows that in the Stern Stewart model, equity equivalents consist of preferred stock, minority interest, deferred income tax reserve, LIFO reserve, and accumulated goodwill amortization.

---

[17] Goldman Sachs and Stern Stewart do not make any explicit cash adjustments to accounting depreciation on the income statement and (therefore) accumulated depreciation on the balance sheet. This approach to handling economic depreciation seems at odds with the long established view that managers can manipulate earnings by the judicious use of accounting depreciation policies. For a rigorous explanation on how to incorporate economic depreciation into the EVA calculation, see Chapter 5 of this book by Stephen O'Byrne.

[18] Using the 1993 Annual Report for Hershey Foods Corporation, Peterson and Peterson provide a step-by-step instruction on how to calculate the firm's cash operating profit, dollar cost of capital, and economic value added (EVA). This practical guide can be found in Pamela P. Peterson and David R. Peterson, *Company Performance and Measures of Value Added* (Charlottesville, VA: The Research Foundation of the Institute of Chartered Financial Analysts, 1996). The reader is also referred to the value-based application of McDonald's Corporation by Pamela Peterson in Chapter 4 of this book.

[19] In the value-based metrics realm, short-term operating assets typically include (1) a normal level of operating "cash," (2) accounts receivable, and (3) inventory. Excess cash is often excluded from operating capital because it can be viewed as a form of "negative debt."

Likewise, debt and debt equivalents consist of interest bearing short-term liabilities, long-term debt, as well as capitalized lease obligations. With the income statement (Exhibit 4) and balance sheet (Exhibit 5) converted to a cash operating basis, an analyst is able to jointly estimate the firm's unlevered net operating profit after tax and the economic book capital employed within the firm. With these figures, the firm's after-tax return on capital is calculated by dividing NOPAT by employed capital.

Overview of Goldman Sachs' Approach

Like Stern Stewart and others, Goldman Sachs has narrowed the field from 160 possible accounting adjustments down to a select number of accounting adjustments that can have a meaningful impact on the firm's cash operating profit and its economic book capital.[20] Some of the key "equity equivalents" used by Goldman's U.S. Equity Research Group to measure the firm's economic book capital include accumulated amortization of intangibles, deferred taxes, LIFO reserves, capitalized leases, and cumulative non-recurring charges. Based on the "sources of financing approach," they (too) begin with stockholders' equity on the firm's balance sheet and then "add back" equity equivalents. On the income side, the accompanying increase in equity equivalents is added back to accounting net income.

Like Stern Stewart, Golman Sachs recognizes that the taxes used in measuring a company's post-tax capital returns should be a reflection of the cash taxes actually paid by the *unlevered* firm — as the interest tax subsidy (if any) is already reflected in the cost of capital calculation for the levered firm. On the tax issue, Goldman Sachs uses the *statutory* corporate tax rate rather than the firm's effective tax rate.

COST OF CAPITAL ESTIMATION

Aside from any further accounting difficulties that may arise when estimating NOPAT in practice, there remains many "cost of capital" issues that can impact the estimation of economic profit.[21] These cost of capital challenges have both theoretical and empirical foundations. From a theoretical perspective, Merton Miller argues that corporate debt policy has little if any impact on enterprise value — and therefore its annualized economic profit equivalent — even in a world with corporate taxes, deductibility of debt interest expense, and progressive income taxation at the personal level.[22] Extending the original 1958 capital structure the-

---

[20] See Steven G. Einhorn, Gabrielle Napolitano, and Abby Joseph Cohen, "EVA: A Primer," *U.S. Research* (Goldman Sachs, September 10, 1997).

[21] It is interesting to note that the question of how to estimate a firm's cost of capital — as opposed to the plethora of NOPAT accounting adjustments — was the most important economic profit issue that surfaced at the September 1999 IMN Conference on Value-Based Metrics.

[22] We explained Merton Miller's 1977 "Debt and Tax" argument earlier.

ory of Modigliani and Miller, he argues (in 1977) that levered firms should be priced in the capital market "as if" they were in fact equivalent business risk unlevered firms. As mentioned before, this implies that the cost of capital for a levered firm is the same as the cost of (equity) capital for an unlevered firm with the same amount of business uncertainty.

Yet, in spite of Miller's widely acclaimed view on corporate debt policy, today's value-based players — including Stern Stewart, CS First Boston, and Goldman Sachs — assume in their economic profit calculations that corporate debt is a "cheaper" source of financing when compared to equity financing. This seemingly tax advantaged source of financing gives corporate managers an economic profit incentive — via a lower cost of capital for levered firms due to a debt-interest tax subsidy — to finance long-term growth with debt rather than equity. However, without revisiting capital structure theory, suffice it to say that the enterprise valuation role of corporate debt policy is likely to be much smaller than that typically assumed by proponents of value-based metrics.[23]

CAPM ANOMALIES

Another problematic cost of capital issue arises for corporate managers and investors when estimating the required return on the firm's common stock. In principle, using the standard CAPM to estimate the firm's cost of equity capital seems reasonable enough because this *single factor* model is an integral component of established financial theory. However, in recent years CAPM has been challenged by many empirical studies that question the validity of the one-factor expected return-risk predictions of the model.[24]

Specifically, in this asset pricing framework, *beta* is considered to be the systematic (or market) risk factor that drives the expected rate of return on the firm's outstanding common stock which is an estimate of the cost of equity capital. In this model, stocks of companies with high betas should offer relatively high expected returns, while stocks of firms with low betas should offer comparably lower anticipated returns. Over time, these positive expected return-risk anticipations should be revealed in *real-time* capital markets. However, recent empirical research does not seem to verify the systematic risk and return predictions of the single-factor CAPM.

---

[23] Having said that, the financial analyst should be aware that the unlevered firm's cost of capital *is* impacted by economywide changes in interest rates and the market-assessed business risk premium. This means that a firm's required return on invested capital (and therefore its economic profit) can change independently of managerial decision making at the micro level.

We'll also look at the valuation role of company specific risk and cost of capital change — based on a required return on invested capital model developed by Credit Suisse Asset Management — later in this chapter.

[24] See, for example, Eugene F. Fama and Kenneth French, "The Cross Section of Expected Stock Returns," *Journal of Finance* (June 1992).

Exhibit 6: Security Selection Analysis: Decomposition of Expected Return on (Equity) Capital

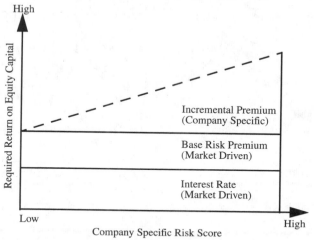

Source: James A. Abate, "Select Economic Value Portfolios," *U.S. Equity Product Overview* (Credit Suisse Asset Management, January 1998).

CAPM Alternatives

Fortunately, there are alternative approaches to using CAPM when estimating a firm's cost of equity capital. In this context, James Abate at Credit Suisse Asset Management (CSAM) has developed a proprietary model that estimates a firm's required return on capital (largely, the expected return on equity capital) based on a model that incorporates (1) the market risk premium, (2) well-known fundamental factors including size and leverage considerations, and (3) the growth and stability in the firm's economic profit over time.[25] Holding the first two equity risk considerations the same, firms that have demonstrated stability in their real economic profit growth will be assigned a *lower* cost of capital score than firms that otherwise demonstrate substantial specific volatility in their economic profit.

Exhibit 6 shows how the required return on invested capital (cost of capital) is estimated in the CSAM model. As with CAPM, the firm's cost of equity is based on a market driven "base risk premium." To the estimate of the systematic market premium, CSAM adds a "company specific" premium to arrive at the firm's overall cost of capital — based on established fundamental factors (size, etc.) and their proprietary scoring measure on the volatility of a company's economic profit. The lower the EVA-based volatility score, the lower the required return on invested capital (largely cost of equity capital). Other things the same, the higher the company-specific risk score, the higher the assessed cost of (equity) capital.

---

[25] See James A. Abate, "Select Economic Value Portfolios," *U.S. Equity Product Overview* (Credit Suisse Asset Management, January 1998).

Exhibit 7: Cost of Capital in Value-Based Metrics
Shifts in Company-Specific Risk Impact Stock Price Performance

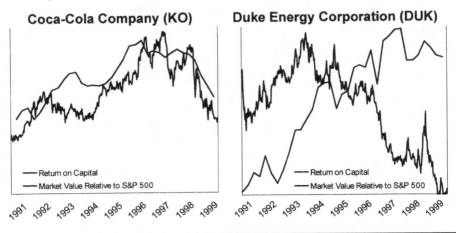

Exhibit 7 shows the time series relationship between the return on capital and stock price for two large companies that — according to Credit Suisse Asset Management — have different economic profit risk characteristics: Coca-Cola (KO) with stable and predicable capital returns, and Duke Energy Corporation (DUK) having invested capital returns that seem less certain. Accordingly, CSAM analysts — and presumably other knowledgeable investors — assign a relatively lower company-specific risk score to Coca-Cola compared with the economic profit risk score that they assign to Duke Energy Corporation. With a lower cost of capital, Coke's shareholders have benefited over time — both in absolute terms and relative to the investors holding stock of Duke Energy Power — due to a lower specific risk component of the firm's economic profit volatility. Other things the same, the reduced company-specific risk for Coca-Cola leads to a more stable relationship between its stock price and the underlying return on invested capital.

A closer look at Exhibit 7 shows that Coca-Cola and Duke Energy stock prices were rising during the early to mid 1990s. During that time span, the invested capital returns for both companies were positive and rising. When Coke's return on capital began to falter in the post 1997 period, the beverage company's stock price followed a somewhat smooth decline, coincident with the firm's slowing growth in economic profit. In relative terms, the exhibit also shows that the adverse wealth impact of Coca-Cola's declining stock price[26] during 1998 and 1999 was noticeably different from the negative wealth effect that was experienced by Duke Energy shareholders in the post 1995 years.

---

[26] The fact that Coca-Cola's stock price declined somewhat after 1997 should not overshadow the role of this beverage firm as a powerful U.S. wealth creator. As we will see in the empirical section, Coke ranks among the "top 10" U.S. wealth creators.

The sharp decline in Duke Energy's stock price after 1995 was precipitated by a volatile change in the firm's capital returns. According to CSAM, the heightened company-specific risk lead to a rising cost of capital for Duke Energy Corporation and, consequently, a falling share price. Indeed, Exhibit 7 suggests that when Duke's invested return on capital began to slow after 1995, the firm's stock price began a long and precipitous decline. This had serious wealth consequences for Duke Energy investors. The CSAM illustration is one example of the role of company-specific risk assessment and its possible impact on cost of capital as an important source of stock price change for firms having dissimilar economic profit risk.[27]

Moreover, there are well-known factor-based equity models that can be used in lieu of the single-factor CAPM to estimate a firm's cost of equity capital. In this context, the analyst might consider the benefits of using a multi-factor approach to estimating the firm's expected return on common stock, and (therefore) the required return on invested capital. Fundamental factor models (like BARRA) have been used to build forecasts of equity returns based on beta, size, book-to-price ratio, dividend yield, and earnings momentum — among other "common factors" that influence security return. Also, macro-factor models — such as Burmeister, Ibbotson, Roll, and Ross — have been used in practice to estimate the expected return on common stocks in the context of interest rate and economywide changes in corporate profits, among other macro-factors.

CASH FLOW RETURN ON INVESTMENT (CFROI)

Although EVA is perhaps the most popular value-based metric, it is not the only one used in practice by corporate managers and investors. As we explained before, another prominent measure that is also consistent with the principles of wealth maximization is cash flow return on investment (CFROI). This metric is generally promoted by two consulting advisory firms — Holt Value Associates, LP (dealing primarily with investment management firms) and Boston Consulting Group (on the corporate side). Although differences exist, Holt's CFROI measure is similar in concept to the well-known internal rate of return (IRR) method used in capital budgeting analysis.

In principle, CFROI can be viewed as the after-tax internal rate of return on the firm's existing assets. CFROI is that rate which sets the present value of the after-tax cash flows generated by the firm's existing assets equal to their investment cost. As a result, the firm's net present value is positive if CFROI exceeds

---

[27] IDC Portfolio Management, Inc. (among others) also looks beyond the single-factor CAPM to assess the cost of equity capital. This research advisory firm also models the firm-specific risk component of economic profit volatility. See "S&P 500 Stock Valuations," product report (IDC Portfolio Management, Inc.: September 10, 1999). Also, HOLT Value Associates avoids CAPM-related beta issues altogether by assessing a firm's "hurdle rate" (or cost of capital) in the context of a historical model of real returns on invested capital — as opposed to a market driven model of capital market equilibrium.

the "hurdle rate" or cost of capital, while the firm's NPV is negative when the Holt estimated CFROI metric falls short of the required return on the firm's existing capital.

Since Holt's CFROI metric is based on both current *and* distant cash flows while Stern Stewart & Co.'s EVA measure appears — on the surface — to be a snapshot of the firm's current economic profit, it is tempting to argue that the former firm's measure is more closely aligned with promoting shareholder value added over the long term. Such a comparative interpretation is incorrect however when one realizes that economic profit (EVA) is the *annualized* equivalent of the firm's net present value. Also, if for some reason the firm's managers compare CFROI to a hurdle rate that is inconsistent with the required return on the firm's invested capital, *wacc*, then a wealth-destroying *agency* problem exists between the firm's managers and owners.

CFROI: Real World Considerations

Pamela Peterson and David Peterson point out that the proprietary CFROI measure is very informative yet more complex than a typical IRR calculation.[28] The estimation difficulty arises because the inputs to the model are stated in *real* as opposed to nominal dollars.

Using the 1993 Annual Report for Hershey Foods Corporation, they provide an insightful discussion on how to calculate CFROI (as well as EVA) along with the important issues that arise when interpreting the results. After intensive examination of Hershey's financial statements, Peterson and Peterson discover the gross cash flow and gross investment items that are pertinent to the CFROI calculation. Their *nominal* findings from information gleaned from the Hershey Corporation financial reports at year-end 1993 are shown below:

Gross Cash Investment	=	$2,925.863 million
Gross Cash Flow (payment)	=	$427.156 million
Nondepreciating Asset (future value)	=	$522.968 million
Asset Life	=	18 years
CFROI (nominal)	=	13.31%
CFROI (real)	=	10.25%

Based on the information provided in Hershey's 1993 Annual Report, they find that the internal rate of return on the firm's *existing* assets is 13.31%. Although many calculations were involved to arrive at this point, the estimated IRR percentage is *not* the firm's actual CFROI. As noted by Peterson and Peterson, there are two practical differences between the standard IRR and CFROI calculations. First, the inputs to the CFROI model are stated in current monetary equivalents: past investments are "grossed up" to the current period by a historical inflation factor while gross cash flows are inflation-adjusted back to the present time period.

---

[28] See Peterson and Peterson, *Company Performance and Measures of Value Added.*

In light of the current dollar adjustments supplied by Holt Value Associates (to Peterson and Peterson), the CFROI measure for Hershey Foods Corporation drops from 13.31% to 10.25%. This percentage estimation difference is important. If the firm's "hurdle rate" were somewhere between the two figures, the unsuspecting (or less informed) analyst with a CFROI estimate of 13.31% might incorrectly gauge the firm as a "wealth creator" with positive NPV. Second, in the Holt/BCG approach, the firm's CFROI is actually stated in *real* terms as opposed to nominal terms. Hence, the real CFROI measure is impacted by the inflation assumption used by the analyst in the future cash flow and gross investment estimation processes (aside from the many nominal accounting adjustments that were already mentioned in calculating a firm's economic profit).

Peterson and Peterson also point out that CFROI measurement concerns arise because the estimated *real* return on the firm's existing assets is *not* compared to an inflation-adjusted hurdle measure using the standard *wacc* formulation. If correct, then the Holt/BCG approach to shareholder value added may give rise to an agency conflict between managers and owners, unless of course their estimated "hurdle rate" — perhaps in light of the many empirical challenges to CAPM — is somehow a more descriptive measure of the equilibrium expected rate of return on the firm's economic book capital. However, given the proprietary nature of their related cost of capital benchmark, one may wonder how the capital market would generally know this in setting the equilibrium real rate in the first instance.

ENTERPRISE VALUATION APPROACHES

In recent years there has been an increased focus by corporate managers and investors alike on discounted cash flow procedures that begin by looking at the firm's aggregate corporate value and then its stock price. While several approaches to enterprise valuation are employed by today's value-based players — such as Stern Stewart, HOLT Value Associates, LEK/Alcar Consulting Group, CS First Boston, and Goldman Sachs — the DCF models are in large part grounded in two of the more often cited approaches including (1) the traditional free cash flow model and (2) the economic profit approach to enterprise valuation. We'll cover corporate valuation models in the next section[29] with the recognition that both traditional and modern approaches to enterprise value must in principle give the same intrinsic worth of the firm and its outstanding shares.[30]

---

[29] The DCF models covered in this chapter are drawn from Frank J. Fabozzi and James L. Grant, *Equity Portfolio Management* (New Hope, PA: Frank J. Fabozzi Associates, 1999). Additional insights on these enterprise valuation models are covered in Chapter 5 by Stephen F. O'Byrne.

[30] That corporate valuation models must in theory provide the same intrinsic worth of the firm and its outstanding shares is an outgrowth of the "equal rate of return principle" explained by Eugene Fama and Merton Miller in Chapter 2 of *The Theory of Finance*.

FREE CASH FLOW MODEL

In the most general form of the free cash flow model, the firm's enterprise value, V, is expressed as the present value of its anticipated free cash flow according to:

$$V = \sum \frac{FCF_t}{(1 + r)^t} \tag{1}$$

where FCF_t is the estimated free cash flow at time period t, and r is the firm's expected return or weighted-average cost of capital.[31] Unless otherwise noted, t runs from 1 to infinity.

In turn, the firm's anticipated free cash flow can be expressed in one of two ways. One approach looks at the firm's free cash flow in terms of its *gross* operating profit after tax, GOPAT, less *gross* capital investment (including working capital additions) during time period t:[32]

$$\begin{aligned} FCF_t &= GOPAT_t - Gross\ Investment_t \\ &= [EBIT_t(1-t_u) + D] - [Net\ Inv._t + D] \\ &= [NOPAT_t + D] - [Net\ Inv._t + D] \end{aligned} \tag{2}$$

The first term in the second cash flow expression of equation (2) shows that *GOPAT* is equal to the (unlevered) firm's tax-adjusted *EBIT* plus depreciation, while gross investment is the sum of its net investment plus depreciation. Investment expenditures are included in free cash flow model because the firm cannot expect to grow its future earnings — beyond that generated on its maintained existing assets — without making future investments in real operating capital (including tangible and intangible assets, as well as human capital).

Equivalently, upon subtracting depreciation, D (presumed equal to an appropriate charge for economic obsolescence), from both right hand side terms of the gross cash flow formulation, we express the firm's free cash flow in terms of its familiar *net* operating profit after tax, *NOPAT*, and *net* capital investment (namely, gross investment — including working capital additions — minus a yearly depreciation charge) according to equation (3):

$$\begin{aligned} FCF_t &= EBIT_t(1 - t_u) - Net\ Investment_t \\ &= NOPAT_t - Net\ Inv._t \end{aligned} \tag{3}$$

---

[31] For convenience, we use the letter "r" to denote a firm's weighted average cost of capital in the detailed valuation expressions that follow. We'll return to the more descriptive "*wacc*" at a later point.

[32] In the free cash flow expression that follows, it should also be noted that GOPAT can be expressed as:

$$GOPAT = EBITD(1-t_u) + t_u D$$

where *EBITD* is the firm's operating profit before interest, taxes, and depreciation, and $t_u D$ is the yearly tax subsidy received by the *unlevered* firm from the deductibility of depreciation in computing corporate taxes — at the unlevered corporate tax rate, t_u.

As Fama and Miller point out, the gross operating profit, GOPAT, and net operating profit, NOPAT, approaches to free cash flow estimation differ only in form rather than substance.[33]

Two-Stage Free Cash Flow Model

To operationalize the free cash flow (FCF) model, we'll express the firm's enterprise value in terms of (1) the intrinsic value of its ability to generate free cash flow during a finite growth period, T, plus (2) the present value of mature or competitive growth in the firm's remaining cash flow for years $T+1$ to infinity. This two-phase interpretation of the FCF model can be expressed as:[34]

$$V = \frac{\sum\limits_{t}^{T} FCF_t}{(1+r)^t} + \frac{1}{(1+r)^T} \frac{NOPAT_T}{r} \tag{4}$$

where, the first term on the right hand side of equation (4) is the assessed value of the firm's estimated free cash flow during its finite growth years when "discounted" back to the current period at the firm's weighted average cost of capital, r.

As shown, the firm's "residual value" at T is based on the simplifying assumption that capital investment (beyond maintenance of existing assets) ends at that time. That is, during the post-horizon years, gross annual investment is equal to depreciation while net capital investment equals zero. The $NOPAT/r$ term is therefore the "residual value" of the firm at time period T. Discounting this residual value figure back to the current time period gives the present value contribution of the firm's anticipated free cash flows from years $T+1$ to infinity.

Free Cash Flow Estimation: Horizon Years

When using the free cash flow model, the financial analyst needs to know how to calculate the firm's cash flow over the estimated horizon years (and thereafter). To assist in this development, we'll employ a sales forecasting model with simple assumptions about the firm's (1) anticipated revenue growth, g, (2) pre-tax *net* (of depreciation) operating margin, p, (3) unlevered tax rate, t_u, (4) *net* capital investment (gross investment less depreciation) as a function f of increased sales, and (5) working capital additions as a function w of increased revenue.[35] We'll also show how the firms' free cash flow can be expressed in two equivalent ways: the NOPAT and GOPAT approaches.

Based on the sales forecasting parameters, the firm's estimated free cash flow, $FCF(t)$, during the horizon years (period 1 to T) can be expressed in NOPAT form as equation (5):

---

[33] See Chapter 2 in Fama and Miller, *The Theory of Finance* — with the understanding that our cash flow labels are different.

[34] We could, of course, describe the firm's enterprise value in the context of a two- or three-phase geometric FCF model. However, in the application that follows, we estimate the year-to-year free cash flow during the horizon years (T), with a simple "no-growth" assumption about free cash flow generation thereafter.

Exhibit 8: Estimating Free Cash Flow: NOPAT Approach
(in $ millions)

Period	1	2	3	4	5	6	7	8	9	10
Sales	115.00	132.25	152.09	174.90	201.14	231.31	266.00	305.90	351.79	404.56
Op. Exp.	92.00	105.80	121.67	139.92	160.91	185.04	212.80	244.72	281.43	323.64
EBIT	23.00	26.45	30.42	34.98	40.23	46.26	53.20	61.18	70.36	80.91
Taxes	8.05	9.26	10.65	12.24	14.08	16.19	18.62	21.41	24.63	28.32
NOPAT	14.95	17.19	19.77	22.74	26.15	30.07	34.58	39.77	45.73	52.59
NCapInv.	3.00	3.45	3.97	4.56	5.25	6.03	6.94	7.98	9.18	10.55
Work Cap	1.50	1.73	1.98	2.28	2.62	3.02	3.47	3.99	4.59	5.28
Net Inv.	4.50	5.18	5.95	6.84	7.87	9.05	10.41	11.97	13.77	15.83
FCF	10.45	12.02	13.82	15.89	18.28	21.02	24.17	27.80	31.97	36.76

$$FCF_t = S_{t-1}(1 + g)p(1 - t_u) - (w + f)(S_t - S_{t-1})$$
$$= EBIT_t(1 - t_u) - (w + f)(S_t - S_{t-1})$$
$$= NOPAT_t - Net\ Investment_t \tag{5}$$

where the first term on the right hand side of the sales forecasting equation is the firm's (accounting) net operating profit after tax (NOPAT) and the second term reflects the horizon year's *net* capital investment and working capital additions as a proportion of increased (or decreased) dollar revenue.[36]

Based on this sales forecasting technique, Exhibit 8 shows 10 years of free cash flow figures based on (1) a revenue base of say $100 million (or 100% of the initial sales base), (2) annualized revenue growth of 15%, (3) pre-tax net operating margin of 20%, (4) net capital investment at 20% of increased sales, and (5) working capital additions at 10% of anticipated sales change. A corporate tax rate of 35% (for equivalent unlevered firm) is also used in the cash flow illustration. Also, the free cash flow representation in Exhibit 8 is important because it causes the financial analyst to realize that future investment — beyond that required to maintain existing assets — is required to generate a future stream of revenue and earnings. In this context, the *net* capital investment figures — defined by $f(S_t - S_{t-1})$ — for years 1 through 10 represent gross capital investment less a "depreciation" charge associated with maintaining the productive capacity of the firm's existing assets.

---

[35] For consistency with the traditional approach to free cash flow estimation, we employ the sales forecasting technique described by Alfred Rappaport in "Strategic Analysis for More Profitable Acquisitions," *Harvard Business Review* (July/August 1979). As we noted in Chapter 1, Alfred Rappaport is one of the financial pioneers in the LEK/Alcar Consulting Group. For additional insights beyond this book on free cash flow and enterprise valuation models, see Thomas Copeland, Timothy Koller, and Jack Murrin, *Valuation: Measuring and Managing the Value of Companies, Second Edition* (New York: John Wiley & Sons, 1994).
[36] Consistent with the free cash flow approach employed by Rappaport, f is net of depreciation cost to maintain existing assets. See Rappaport, "Strategic Analysis for More Profitable Acquisitions."

Exhibit 9: Estimating Free Cash Flow: GOPAT Approach
(in $ millions)

Period	1	2	3	4	5	6	7	8	9	10
Sales	115.00	132.25	152.09	174.90	201.14	231.31	266.00	305.90	351.79	404.56
Op. Exp.	92.00	105.80	121.67	139.92	160.91	185.04	212.80	244.72	281.43	323.64
EBIT	23.00	26.45	30.42	34.98	40.23	46.26	53.20	61.18	70.36	80.91
Taxes	8.05	9.26	10.65	12.24	14.08	16.19	18.62	21.41	24.63	28.32
NOPAT	14.95	17.19	19.77	22.74	26.15	30.07	34.58	39.77	45.73	52.59
Deprec.	0.90	1.04	1.19	1.37	1.57	1.81	2.08	2.39	2.75	3.17
GOPAT	15.85	18.23	20.96	24.11	27.72	31.88	36.66	42.16	48.49	55.76
G.CapInv.	3.90	4.49	5.16	5.93	6.82	7.84	9.02	10.37	11.93	13.72
Work Cap	1.50	1.73	1.98	2.28	2.62	3.02	3.47	3.99	4.59	5.28
Gross Inv	5.40	6.21	7.14	8.21	9.44	10.86	12.49	14.36	16.52	19.00
FCF	10.45	12.02	13.82	15.89	18.28	21.02	24.17	27.80	31.97	36.76
NCapInv.	3.00	3.45	3.97	4.56	5.25	6.03	6.94	7.98	9.18	10.55

Exhibit 9 shows that the firm's free cash flow can also be expressed in the context of its GOPAT less gross capital additions (including working capital). To estimate the firm's free cash flow this way, recall that GOPAT can be expressed as:

$$GOPAT_t = EBIT_t(1 - t_u) + D$$
$$= NOPAT_t + D \tag{6}$$

Upon *adding* back depreciation in equation (6) to the firm's estimated NOPAT, we can express the firm's yearly free cash flow figures in terms of its GOPAT and *gross* capital investment at t. This GOPAT way of estimating the firm's free cash flow during the horizon years is shown in Exhibit 9. Since the firm's annual depreciation charge (D) is added back to NOPAT, it must also be added back to the firm's *net* capital investment for each year.

Free Cash Flow Estimation: Residual Period
In the two-stage free cash flow model — as well as other multi-stage versions — some assumption needs to be made about cash flow generation after the finite horizon period (T). One simplifying assumption employed by financial analysts assumes that the firm's existing assets in place at T generate a NOPAT perpetuity thereafter. In this context, the firm's *gross* capital investment in the post horizon years is assumed to equal depreciation, while working capital additions are assumed to equal zero. That is, gross capital additions in years $T+1$ to infinity are just enough to maintain (measured by economic depreciation) the productive capacity of the firm's existing assets in place at termination of the finite horizon period. This, of course, implies that the firm's net capital investment in the post horizon years is zero.

Exhibit 10: Free Cash Flow Valuation
(in $ millions, except per share values)

Year	NOPAT	Net Invest	FCF	Pres.Val. 10%	Cum. PV 0.00
1	14.95	4.5	10.45	9.50	9.50
2	17.19	5.18	12.01	9.93	19.43
3	19.77	5.95	13.82	10.38	29.81
4	22.74	6.84	15.9	10.86	40.67
5	26.15	7.87	18.28	11.35	52.02
6	30.07	9.05	21.02	11.87	63.88
7	34.58	10.41	24.17	12.40	76.29
8	39.77	11.97	27.8	12.97	89.26
9	45.73	13.77	31.96	13.55	102.81
10	52.59	15.83	36.76	14.17	116.98
11 Plus	52.59				

Residual Value	525.9	202.76
Corporate Value		319.74
LT Debt		12.00
Equity		307.74
Share OS		5.00
Price		61.55

With a zero growth assumption, we can represent the firm's free cash flow for the post horizon or residual years (years $T+1$ to infinity) as equation (7):

$$FCF_t = NOPAT_T - Net\ Investment_t$$
$$= NOPAT_T - (D - D)$$
$$= NOPAT_T \tag{7}$$

Present Value of Free Cash Flows

Exhibit 10 shows how to "roll up" the firm's free cash flow estimates — for years 1 to infinity — into the estimated value of the firm and its outstanding shares. In this context, the top portion of Exhibit 10 shows the "intrinsic value," at $116.98 million, of the estimated yearly free cash flow sequence during the horizon period — namely, years 1 through 10. As shown, this figure results from first calculating the present value of each free cash flow estimate at an assumed cost of capital of 10%, and then cumulating or summing-up the yearly present value results. In turn, the lower portion of Exhibit 10 shows how to calculate the firm's "residual value" — which is equal to the present value of the firm's expected corporate value at year 10.

With zero growth at termination of the horizon period, the firm's enterprise value at T (for 10 years) can be expressed as equation (8):

$$V_T = \frac{NOPAT_T}{r} = \frac{\$52.59}{0.1} = \$525.90 \tag{8}$$

Exhibit 11: Cost of Capital Sensitivity Analysis
Free Cash Flow Model

Rate %	Basis Pt. Change	Horiz. Val.*	Resid. Val.*	Corp. Val.*	% Change Corp. Val.
8	−200	130.46	304.49	434.95	36.03
8.5	−150	126.89	273.65	400.54	25.27
9	−100	123.46	246.83	370.29	15.81
9.5	−50	120.16	223.38	343.54	7.44
10	0	116.98	202.76	319.74	0
10.5	50	113.92	184.54	298.46	−6.66
11	100	110.97	168.38	279.35	−12.63
11.5	150	108.13	153.98	262.11	−18.03
12	200	105.39	141.11	246.50	−22.91

* In $ millions.

Discounting $525.90 million back 10 years at 10% yields the firm's residual value in the current period, at $202.76 million. Upon adding the two present value figures ($116.98 + $202.76), we obtain the firm's overall enterprise value, V, at $319.74 million.

If we assume that long-term debt is, say, $12 million, and the firm has 5 million common shares outstanding, then the intrinsic worth of its stock is currently $61.55. This per share figure is calculated by dividing the firm's estimated equity capitalization, E, by its outstanding shares according to equation (9):

$$\text{Stock Price} = \frac{\text{Corporate Value} - \text{LT Debt}}{n} = \frac{E}{n}$$

$$= \frac{(\$319.74 - \$12)}{5} = \$61.55 \tag{9}$$

The two-stage free cash model could of course be expanded to more than two stages. The only difference is that more than one abnormal free cash flow growth rate would be used in the enterprise valuation process, up to the termination of the overall finite growth years, T. Either zero or long-term constant growth in free cash flow is generally assumed thereafter (years $T+1$ to infinity).

Cost of Capital Change: FCF Model

When the firm's free cash flow estimates were discounted at 10% — a standard rate used in many present value illustrations — we found that the firm's enterprise value was $319.74 million. Exhibits 11 and 12 (table and graph, respectively) show what happens to the firm's market value when the cost of capital rises and falls in increments of 50 basis points from a base rate of 10%. The corporate pricing relationships shown in these exhibits are consistent with the principles of financial theory in a number of interesting respects.

Exhibit 12: Corporate Valuation and the Cost of Capital: Free Cash Flow Model

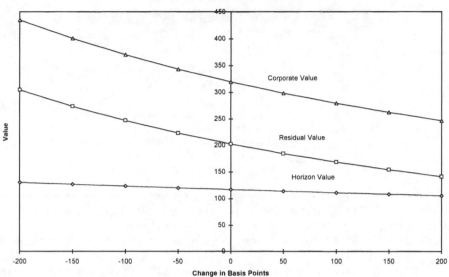

First, Exhibit 11 shows that an *inverse* relationship exists between enterprise value and the weighted average cost of capital. As the discount rate rises in the marketplace — due perhaps to a rise in either the risk-free rate of interest or the business risk premium required by investors in the unlevered firm — the market value of the firm goes down. Conversely, when the firm's cost of capital goes down — due this time to either a fall in the risk-free rate or a decline in the required business risk premium — corporate value goes up.[37]

Second, it's also interesting to see that the relationship between enterprise value and the cost of capital is *convex*. For example, when the cost of capital rises by 100 basis points — from 10% to 11% — the market value of firm falls by 12.63%. In contrast, when the corporate discount rate falls by 100 basis points — from 10% to 9% — the market value of firm rises by 15.81%. Likewise, an asymmetric pricing response arises when the cost of capital rises or falls by 200 basis points. These corporate valuation findings are consistent with well-known pricing relationships in the fixed income market. In effect, the "convexity" in the corporate value-cost of capital relationship reveals that firm values are more sensitive to cost of capital (or interest rate) declines than to equivalent basis point increases in the weighted average cost of capital.

---

[37] From a real world perspective, James Abate of Credit Suisse Asset Management contends that abnormal U.S. stock market growth during the 1990s is due in part to a significant decline in the business risk component of the U.S. cost of capital. His insightful cost of capital views were presented at the September 1999 IMN Conference on Value-Based Metrics.

Additionally, Exhibit 12 shows that the residual value function is more sensitive to cost of capital changes than the horizon value function. This is also consistent with known present value relationships in the sense that long *duration* assets (and, therefore, cash flows) are more sensitive to interest rate changes than short duration assets. In our illustration, the residual value function is a present value reflection of distant cash flows generated in the post horizon years, $T+1$ to infinity. Consequently, the firm's residual value is like a long duration asset that is highly sensitive to cost of capital changes. In contrast, the firm's horizon value can be viewed as a relatively short duration asset, and thereby less sensitive to cost of capital change. For instance, when the firm's cost of capital declines by 100 basis points, the firm's residual value rises by 21.74% ($246.83/$202.76), while its horizon value increases by a much smaller percentage, at 5.54% ($123.46/$116.98).

ECONOMIC PROFIT MODEL

The *economic profit approach* to enterprise valuation also looks at the firm's aggregate value, *V.* In this value-based framework, the firm's corporate value (debt plus equity capitalization) is expressed as the sum of its economic book capital (*TC*) *plus* the net present value (*NPV*) generated by the firm's existing and anticipated future assets. That is,

$$V = Debt\ Value + Equity\ Value = TC + NPV \tag{10}$$

In contrast with the free cash flow approach, the economic profit model provides a *direct* assessment of whether the firm's managers are investing in wealth-creating (namely, positive NPV) or wealth-destroying (negative NPV) investment projects.[38]

NPV and Economic Profit

In principle, the firm's net present value is equal to the present value of anticipated economic profit, or economic value added, that is generated by both its existing and expected future assets. In this context, we can express the firm's NPV in terms of its discounted stream of anticipated economic value added according to:[39]

$$NPV = \sum \frac{EVA_t}{(1 + r)^t} \tag{11}$$

---

[38] This does *not* mean that the economic profit model gives a valuation answer that is different from the free cash flow model – or even a dividend discount model. Indeed, these equity valuation procedures are all derived from the "equal rate of return principle" explained by Fama and Miller. See Chapter 2 in *The Theory of Finance.*

[39] For a theoretical and empirical foundation on the economic profit approach to equity valuation, see Grant, *Foundations of Economic Value Added.*

where EVA_t in equation (11) is the firm's expected economic value added at period t, and r is the firm's weighted average cost of capital (typically assumed constant for all future years). As with the free cash flow approach, we can operationalize the economic profit model by looking at two distinct stages of growth; in this instance, EVA growth during the anticipated horizon years, T, followed by mature economic profit growth (if any) for years $T+1$ to infinity.

With two stages of economic profit growth, the firm's aggregate net present value can be expressed as equation (12):[40]

$$NPV = \sum_{}^{T} \frac{EVA_t}{(1+r)^t} + \frac{1}{(1+r)^T} \frac{EVA_{T+1}}{r - g_{LT}} \tag{12}$$

where EVA and r were defined before, and g_{LT}, is the firm's long-term economic profit growth rate. This value is assumed to be equal to zero (presumably due to competitive forces) in the two-stage economic profit illustration that follows.

Estimating Economic Profit

At this point, it is helpful to recall that the firm's economic value added for any given year is equal to its *unlevered* net operating profit after tax less the dollar capital charge on the firm's economic capital at the start of period t (equivalently, the end of period $t-1$). For consistency with estimation procedures used by Stern Stewart and Goldman Sachs, we express the firm's economic profit in terms of its accounting-based NOPAT and total capital.[41] In their economic profit models, NOPAT is net of the firm's accounting depreciation, while TC is a reflection of the firm's *net* physical capital (gross plant and equipment *less* accumulated depreciation) and short-term operating capital (namely, operating current assets less *non*-interest bearing short-term liabilities). We show this as equation (13):

$$EVA_t = NOPAT_t - rTC_{t-1}$$
$$= EBIT_t(1 - t_u) - rTC_{t-1} \tag{13}$$

Given the net operating profit after tax and net investment information shown in Exhibit 8, we now show that the economic profit and free cash flow approaches yield the same enterprise value of the firm and, thereby, are equivalent estimates of its stock price. The difference between the two approaches to equity

---

[40] Applications of the two-stage EVA growth model can also be found in: (1) Al Jackson, Michael J. Mauboussin, and Charles R. Wolf, "EVA Primer," *Equity-Research Americas* (CS First Boston: February 20, 1996), (2) Einhorn, Napolitano, and Cohen, "EVA: A Primer," and (3) Grant, *Foundations of Economic Value Added.*

[41] The "NOPAT" approach to estimating the firm's economic profit is described in (1) G. Bennett Stewart III, *The Quest for Value* (Harper Collins, New York: 1991), and (2) Einhorn, Napolitano, and Cohen, "EVA: A Primer."

valuation is largely one of interpretation — where (1) the free cash flow model looks at the firm's after-tax profitability *net* of required yearly investment to sustain a growing earnings stream, and (2) the economic profit model (in its most meaningful form) provides a *direct* present value assessment of whether the firm is a wealth creator or wealth waster. The firm's wealth creator status is in turn determined by the sign of its net present value generated by existing and anticipated future assets not currently in place.

Exhibit 13 provides the yearly EVA estimates for illustration of the economic profit approach to enterprise valuation. As shown, the economic profit estimate for any given year is obtained by subtracting the total dollar capital charge from the firm's net operating profit estimate for that year. With an initial capital base of $40 million, and a cost of capital of 10%, the firm's capital charge for year 1 is $4 million. Subtracting this figure from the corresponding NOPAT estimate, $14.95 million, we obtain the firm's anticipated economic profit for year 1, at $10.95 million. The economic profit estimates shown in Exhibit 13 for the rest of the horizon period — namely, years 2 through 10 — are obtained in a similar manner.

With zero-expected growth in the firm's economic profit *beyond* the horizon period, the firm's estimated economic profit for years 11 to infinity is forecasted at $39.45 million. This EVA perpetuity is calculated by subtracting the firm's dollar cost of capital (cost of capital *times* economic book capital in place at the end of year 10), at $13.14 million, from its estimated net operating profit after tax perpetuity (NOPAT in this case), at $52.59 million. We now show how the economic profit estimates in Exhibit 13 can be used to assess the firm's NPV and its enterprise value.

Exhibit 13: Estimation of Economic Profit
(in $ millions)
Cost of Capital = 10%

Year	Yearly Net Inv.	Total Net Capital	NOPAT	Capital Charge	Economic Profit
0		40			
1	4.5	44.5	14.95	4.00	10.95
2	5.18	49.68	17.19	4.45	12.74
3	5.95	55.63	19.77	4.97	14.80
4	6.84	62.47	22.74	5.56	17.18
5	7.87	70.34	26.15	6.25	19.90
6	9.05	79.39	30.07	7.03	23.04
7	10.41	89.8	34.58	7.94	26.64
8	11.97	101.77	39.77	8.98	30.79
9	13.77	115.54	45.73	10.18	35.55
10	15.83	131.37	52.59	11.55	41.04
11 Plus			52.59	13.14	39.45

Exhibit 14: Valuation of Economic Profit
(in $ millions, except per share values)

Year	EVA	Pres.Val.	Cum. PV 0
1	10.95	9.95	9.95
2	12.74	10.53	20.48
3	14.80	11.12	31.60
4	17.18	11.73	43.34
5	19.90	12.36	55.69
6	23.04	13.00	68.70
7	26.64	13.67	82.37
8	30.79	14.36	96.73
9	35.55	15.08	111.81
10	41.04	15.82	127.63
	Residual Value	394.53	152.11
	NPV		279.74
	Capital		40.00
	Corp.Val		319.74
	LT Debt		12.00
	Equity		307.74
	Share OS		5.00
	Price		61.55

Present Value of Economic Profit

Exhibit 14 illustrates the pricing results of our application of the two-stage economic profit approach to corporate valuation. The top portion of the exhibit shows how to calculate the *net* present value of the firm's estimated economic profit during the horizon years, 1 though 10, when discounted at 10%. As shown, the cumulative present value of that anticipated EVA stream is $127.63 million. In turn, the residual value at T (equivalently, the net present value at T) of the firm's estimated EVA stream in the post-horizon years is $394.53 million. This residual value estimate is calculated by discounting the EVA perpetuity (assuming *zero*-growth due to long term competitive forces) by the firm's weighted average cost of capital according to equation (14):[42]

$$\text{NPV}_T = \frac{\text{EVA}_{T+1}}{r} = \frac{\$39.453}{0.1} = \$394.53 \tag{14}$$

---

[42] With an unlimited economic profit "franchise," it should be apparent that the firm's EVA capitalization rate (in the valuation expression that follows) becomes $1/(r-g_{LT})$: where g_{LT} is the firm's long-term EVA growth rate covering the post-horizon years. Also, we have noticed that the appropriate "fade" period in a company's long-term economic profit is a controversial issue among proponents of value-based metrics.

Discounting the residual value figure (at T) back to the current period yields the intrinsic value of the firm's anticipated EVA stream in the post-horizon years, at \$152.11 million (rounded). Upon summing the NPV of the firm's EVA stream during *both* horizon and post-horizon periods — \$127.63 million and \$152.11 million respectively — we obtain the firm's estimated *total* net present value in the current period of \$279.74 million. This expected NPV figure represents the aggregate value added to the firm's initial capital of \$40 million due to positive economic profit that is generated by the firm's existing assets and anticipated future assets *not* currently in place. In the valuation illustration shown in Exhibit 14, the firm is a "wealth creator" because the positive stream of economic profit is the underlying source of its positive net present value.

At \$319.74 million, the firm's estimated enterprise value is equal to the sum of its initial economic book capital, \$40 million, plus the overall value added by the firm's managers as given by equation (10):[43]

$$V = TC + NPV = \$40 + \$279.74 = \$319.74$$

Upon subtracting the firm's (assumed) long-term debt, \$12 million, from its intrinsic corporate value, we obtain the firm's equity capitalization of \$307.74 million. Dividing this latter figure by the assumed number of common shares outstanding yields the intrinsic worth of the firm's stock, at \$61.55. That is,

$$\text{Stock Price} = \frac{\text{Equity Capitalization}}{n} = \frac{\$307.75}{5} = \$61.55$$

As expected, the underlying value of the firm and its outstanding shares are the same as the figures obtained previously using the free cash flow approach to enterprise valuation.

Cost of Capital Change: Economic Profit Model

When discounting the firm's anticipated economic profit by 10% (our *previous* economic profit illustration), the firm's enterprise value was estimated to be \$319.74 million. Exhibits 15 and 16 (table and graph, respectively) show the pricing impact of cost of capital variation on both the firm's net present value and corporate value in the economic profit model. This time, the corporate value-cost of capital relationship manifests itself in the inverse relationship between the firm's net present value and its underlying weighted average cost of capital. This happens because corporate value in the economic profit approach is equal to the sum of the firm's initial invested capital (a "sunk cost") and the aggregate NPV generated by the firm's existing and anticipated future assets.

---

[43] Of course, this valuation statement must be qualified by the fact that corporate value is also influenced by sector and macroeconomic forces (such as interest rate changes) that are independent of managerial decision making.

Exhibit 15: Cost of Capital Sensitivity Analysis
Economic Profit Model

Rate %	Basis Pt. Change	NPV*	Tot. Cap.*	Corp. Val.*	% Change Corp. Val.
8	−200	394.95	40.00	434.95	36.03
8.5	−150	360.54	40.00	400.54	25.27
9	−100	330.29	40.00	370.29	15.81
9.5	−50	303.54	40.00	343.54	7.44
10	0	279.74	40.00	319.74	0.00
10.5	50	258.46	40.00	298.46	−6.66
11	100	239.35	40.00	279.35	−12.63
11.5	150	222.11	40.00	262.11	−18.03
12	200	206.50	40.00	246.50	−22.91

* In $ millions.

Exhibit 16: Corporate Valuation and the Cost of Capital: Economic Profit Model

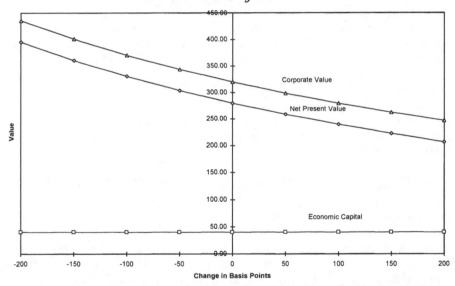

Although the *absolute* price changes in NPV and corporate value are the same in response to fluctuations in the cost of capital, the percentage responses — or duration estimates — are of dissimilar magnitude. For example, Exhibit 15 shows that if the cost of capital declines by 100 basis points — from 10% to 9% — then corporate value rises from $319.74 million to $370.29 million. This represents an absolute change in value of $50.55 million and a percentage change of 15.81%. In response to the 100 basis point decrease in the cost of capital, the firm's underlying NPV rises from $279.74 million to $330.29 million. This too represents a price change of $50.55 million, yet a percentage change of 18.07%. The difference in price elasticity is explained by the fact that the firm's NPV makes up 87.5% of its enterprise valuation while the initial capital accounts for the remaining capitalization weight ($40/$319.74 × 100 = 12.5%).

Also, since the firm's net present value is derived from the present value of its anticipated economic profit stream (again, from existing and expected future assets), the sensitivity of the firm's market value is fundamentally related to the sensitivity of its economic profit stream to underlying changes in the corporate-wide hurdle rate. Moreover, the source of the cost of capital variations shown in Exhibits 15 and 16 may be due to unforeseen changes in the risk-free rate of interest (which in many instances are linked to unanticipated changes in the inflation rate) and investors' (debt and equity holders in total) perception of the required premium for bearing the firm's underlying business risk.[44]

INVESTMENT OPPORTUNITIES APPROACH TO VALUATION

With some simple rearrangements to the basic economic profit model, we can look at what part of a firm's enterprise value is attributed to economic profit generation by existing assets and the EVA contribution to corporate value from future assets not currently in place. Based on the "Investment Opportunities Approach to Valuation (IOAV)" described by Fama and Miller, the firm's enterprise value can be separated into two components: (1) the present value contribution of the unlevered after tax cash flows generated by the firm's existing assets, NOPAT in our notation, plus (2) the present value contribution of the firm's anticipated future growth opportunities.[45]

$$V = \text{NOPAT}/wacc + G_f$$

Since NOPAT is equal to the capital charge earned on the firm's existing assets, plus the economic profit (EVA) generated by the assets already in place, we can unfold the firm's market value into its total capital, TC, plus the NPV contribution of all future economic profit generated by both existing assets and expected future assets according to:

---

[44] The firm's cost of capital, and therefore enterprise value, may also change due to variation in its "target" debt-to-capital ratio. However, once set in place, it seems unlikely that the firm would make significant changes to what it perceives as an "optimal" debt-to-equity, or debt-to-capital ratio. Also, the enterprise valuation impact of leveraged-induced changes in the firm's cost of capital — even in a world of corporate taxes and deductibility of debt-interest expense — is muted according to Merton Miller in "Debt and Taxes."

[45] The Investment Opportunities Approach to Valuation is explained in detail by Fama and Miller in *The Theory of Finance*. As noted before, several economic profit interpretations of the classic IOAV approach to corporate valuation have been developed. Also, we now return to "*wacc*" to denote a firm's weighted average cost of capital.

$$V = [wacc \times TC + EVA]/wacc + G_f$$
$$= TC + [EVA/wacc + G_f]$$
$$= TC + NPV$$

Hence, as before, the firm's market value is equal to its total capital plus its NPV. The firm's aggregate net present value is in turn equal to the present value of all future economic profit generated by existing assets, $EVA/wacc$, and the NPV contribution attributed to economic profit "improvement" from anticipated future assets not currently in place, namely G_f. In the empirical section of this chapter, we'll look at the decomposition of enterprise value for wealth creators in the context of the IOAV-EVA growth model described above.

RECENT EMPIRICAL EVIDENCE

Let's now look at some empirical evidence for companies that have created wealth and firms that, unfortunately, have destroyed it.[46] We'll begin the empirical journey by looking at the performance of powerful wealth creating firms using the Stern Stewart Performance 1000 Universe. This informative annual survey lists MVA, total capital, NOPAT, EVA, return on capital, *wacc*, and related value-based data for large U.S. firms as of the previous year end. In our case, we'll use the 1998 Performance Universe which covers economic profit information for U.S. firms through year-end 1997.

Wealth Creators

One of the primary tenets of the value-based metrics movement is that wealth is created when value is added to invested capital. To see this in practice, Exhibit 17 reports the enterprise value versus capital employed for the "top 10" U.S. wealth creators in the 1998 Performance Universe covering U.S. firms at year-end 1997. At that time, General Electric had a market value — consisting of debt plus equity value — of $255.08 billion with $59.25 billion of capital employed. GE's net present value for 1997 was thus an astounding $195.83 billion. Likewise, Coca-Cola had a corporate value of $169.2 billion with only $10.96 billion of invested capital — resulting in a 1997 NPV of $158.24 billion.

---

[46] We do not in this section assess the *relative* information content of EVA (or CFROI) over traditional measures such as ROA and ROE. We are aware that recent empirical research suggests that the relative information content of value-based metrics over traditional metrics is weak, at best. But we are also aware that — unlike value-based metrics — accounting measures of corporate profit do not fully account for the opportunity cost of capital as required in the NPV theory of the firm.

For some interesting empirical evidence on the relative information content of value-based metrics over traditional accounting profit measures, see (1) Gary C. Biddle, Robert M. Bowen, and James W. Wallace, "Does EVA® Beat Earnings: Evidence on Associations with Stock Returns and Firm Values," *Journal of Accounting and Economics* (December 1997), and (2) Chapter 4 of this book by Pamela Peterson.

Exhibit 17: Top Ten U.S. Wealth Creators in 1997: Enterprise Value versus Capital Employed

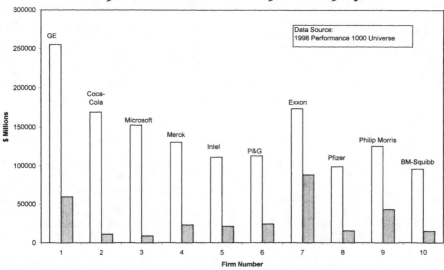

In the technology sector, Microsoft and Intel added $143.74 billion and $90.01 billion, respectively, to their relatively small capital bases of $8.68 billion and $21.44 billion. In the health care sector, powerful wealth creators such as Merck, Pfizer, and Bristol-Myers Squibb had net present values at year-end 1997 ranging from $107.42 billion for Merck down to $81.31 billion for Bristol-Myers-Squibb. Although Exhibit 17 reveals that large U.S. wealth creators added tremendous value to a comparatively small amount of invested capital, a noticeable exception to this efficient utilization of invested capital rule is Exxon — with a 1997 enterprise value of $173.68 billion and a relatively large amount of capital employed, at $88.12 billion.

For the 10 U.S.wealth creators shown in Exhibit 17, the combined NPV was $1,117 billion. The average dollar amount of value added to the capital employed of these firms was $111.71 billion. Moreover, the NPV of the 10 firms ranged from $195.83 billion for General Electric to $81.31 billion for Bristol-Myers Squibb.

Decomposition of the Enterprise Value/Earnings Ratio for Wealth Creators

We noted in the Investment Opportunities Approach to Valuation that enterprise value consists of two components: the NOPAT contribution to market value generated by the firm's existing assets plus the EVA contribution to corporate value generated by expected future assets not currently in place — that is, future growth opportunities. In the IOAV model, we noted that the firm's enterprise value can be expressed as:

$$V = NOPAT/wacc + G_f$$

Exhibit 18: 1997 Growth and Operating Asset Components of the Enterprise Value/Earnings Ratio

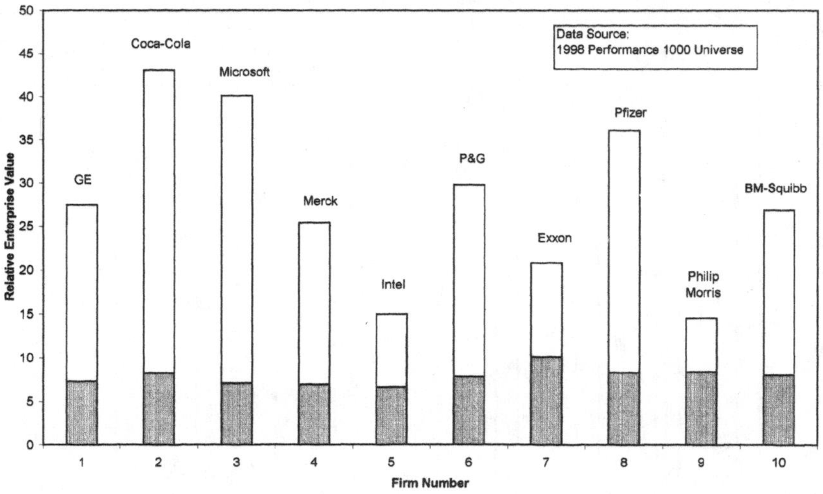

Upon dividing the firm's value by its unlevered net operating profit after tax, we obtain the enterprise value-to-earnings ratio according to:

$$V/E = 1/wacc + G_f/E$$

where "earnings" in the V/E ratio is measured by NOPAT. With this development, we see that the firm's "price-to-earnings" ratio is equal to the "P/E" ratio for a firm having no expected growth, $1/wacc$, plus the EVA contribution to relative corporate value generated by expected future assets, G_f/E.

From a real world perspective, Exhibit 18 shows the decomposition of enterprise value-to-earnings ratio for the 10 largest U.S. wealth creators in the Performance 1000 Universe at year-end 1997. Not surprisingly, the exhibit reveals that the contribution to the value/earnings ratio from positive growth opportunities — namely, G_f/E — makes up most of the observed relative value ratio for wealth creating firms. For examples, the 1997 value-to-earnings ratios for General Electric, Coca-Cola, Microsoft, and Merck were 27.45, 43.09, 40.11, and 25.37, respectively.

In turn, the growth multiples (of NOPAT) for these U.S. wealth creators were 20.19, 34.85, 33.07, and 18.48, respectively. Expressed in percentage terms, the NPV (and discounted future EVA) contribution of expected future assets to the value/earnings ratio for GE and Merck was about 73%, while the growth relative contribution for Coca-Cola and Microsoft was up to 81-82%. Conversely, the anticipated NOPAT perpetuity from existing assets made up only 18-19% of the observed value-to-earnings ratio for powerful wealth creators like Microsoft and Coca-Cola.

Exhibit 19: MVA-to-Capital versus EVA-to-Capital Ratio:
50 Largest Wealth Creators in 1998 Performance 1000 Universe

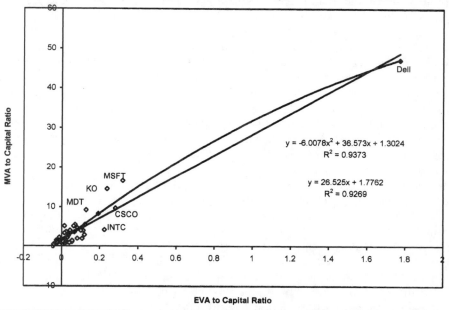

EVA to Capital Ratio

At 48% and 58%, the highest contribution among the "top 10" wealth creators (based on Exhibit 18) from existing assets to relative enterprise value is observed on Exxon and Philip Morris. At value-to-earnings multiples of 10.09 and 8.38, earnings from existing assets — measured by NOPAT — comprise a relatively high proportion of their observed value/earnings ratios of 20.81 and 14.54, respectively. On the average though, the contribution of existing assets to the enterprise value-to-earnings ratio, V/E, for the 10 U.S. wealth creators at year-end 1997 was about 32%. This implies that the EVA contribution from future assets, at 68%, mostly drives the value-to-earnings ratio for wealth creating firms.

Top 50 U.S. Wealth Creators

Expanding the value-based analysis to include 50 large U.S. wealth creators at year-end 1997 is interesting in several respects. First, it is evident in Exhibit 19 that a strong positive relationship exists between the MVA-to-Capital ratio and the EVA-to-Capital ratio for large U.S. wealth creators.[47] In this context, 40 out of the top 50 wealth creators at year-end 1997 had positive MVA-to-Capital ratios in the presence of their jointly positive EVA-to-Capital ratios. With respect to

[47] The 1997 empirical findings for wealth creators (and wealth destroyers) reported in this section are consistent with the earlier statistical results reported by Grant in (1) "Foundations of EVA for Investment Managers," *Journal of Portfolio Management* (Fall 1996), and (2) *Foundations of Economic Value Added.*

those firms having positive MVA in the presence of currently negative EVA, the capital market — from an efficient market perspective — must have been highly optimistic about the wealth creating potential of these companies to generate positive economic value added for the future.

Exhibit 19 also indicates that "information technology" — firms like Microsoft Corporation, Cisco Systems, Intel Corporation, and Dell Corporation — dominate the U.S. wealth creator list. Although each of these technology firms have strongly positive net present value, Dell leads the technology pack when net present value (MVA) and economic profit (EVA) are scaled by economic book capital. Indeed, during 1997 Dell Corporation generated a sizable MVA, at $25.8 billion, on a relatively tiny amount of book capital, at $0.55 billion. Moreover, several other familiar companies comprised the U.S. wealth creator landscape for 1997 including Coca-Cola in the beverage industry, General Electric in the electrical and appliance sector, and Medronics in the health care industry. Not surprisingly, Cisco Systems and Microsoft had residual return on capital figures (return on capital less cost of capital) of 36.67% and 38.74% that were especially attractive.

The statistical association between the MVA-to-Capital ratio (dependent variable) and the EVA-to-Capital ratio (independent variable) for the 50 largest U.S. wealth creators at year-end 1997 seems strong. Based on linear (and non-linear) regression results, it appears that variation in the EVA-to-Capital ratio explains about 93% of the cross sectional variation in the MVA-to-Capital ratios for wealth producing firms. If correct, this means that when the EVA-to-Capital ratio is high, the NPV-to-Capital ratio is also high. When the EVA/Capital ratio is relatively low, the MVA/Capital ratio for wealth creators is also low — as the theoretical relationship between NPV and EVA would suggest. In turn, the source of the positive EVA for wealth creating companies must in some sense be due to their ability to generate a cash flow return on investment, CFROI, that exceeds the cost of capital — both now and in the future.

Wealth Destroyers

We'll now look at some empirical evidence for companies that have wasted wealth. In this context, Exhibit 20 shows the enterprise value and capital employed for the bottom 10 firms listed in the Stern Stewart Performance 1000 Universe at year-end 1997. Ironically, General Motors — a renowned "pillar of capitalism" — goes to the head of the wealth destroyer heap with a large amount of invested capital, at $75.35 billion, compared to its enterprise value of $61.48 billion. At –$13.87 billion, GM continued an 18-year pattern of wealth destruction since its NPV turned negative, at –$11.36 billion by Stern Stewart estimates, in 1980. Indeed, the large auto-maker's average net present value for the years 1980 to 1997 was astonishingly negative, at –$15.28 billion.

Another disturbing U.S. wealth destroyer is RJR Nabisco. Born out of one of the largest hostile corporate takers in U.S. history, this firm's 1997 invested capital was $35.41 billion in the presence of its enterprise value of $25.88 billion.

Equally troubling is that RJR Nabisco's 1997 NPV of −$9.53 billion continued a 7-year string of adverse net present value figures since the early 1990s. Also, the food products and tobacco maker's average net present value over the 1990 to 1997 period was −$9.22 billion.

Exhibit 20 reveals that wealth destruction seems to plague other capital intensive companies as well — where capital includes buildings, machinery, and inventory. For examples, Loews Corporation's 1997 enterprise value was only 54.73% of its total capital employed, at $22.29 billion, while Kmart's corporate value fell short of its invested capital of $14.73 billion by 15.34%. Exhibit 20 also shows that wealth destruction is not unique to just capital intensive firms — including the above mentioned wealth wasters and Inland Steel and US Steel — but also to companies that fall prey to changing economic conditions and techno-logical change — such as USF&G in the insurance industry and Digital Equip-ment in the technology sector.

On balance, the bottom 10 companies listed in the Performance Universe at year-end 1997 destroyed some $50 billion in shareholder value. The negative NPV figures ranged from −$1.67 billion for Inland Steel down to −$13.87 billion for General Motors. Unfortunately, the average return on capital, at 4.76%, for the 10 largest U.S. wealth destroyers fell short of the average cost of capital of 9.63%.

Exhibit 20: Ten Largest U.S. Wealth Destroyers in 1997: Enterprise Value versus Capital Employed

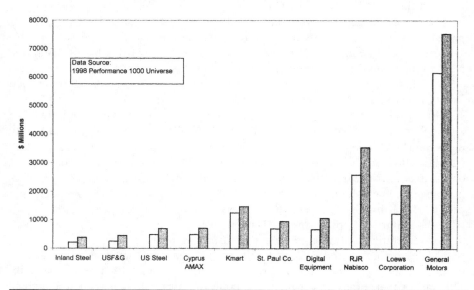

Exhibit 21: MVA-to-Capital versus EVA-to-Capital Ratio: 50 Largest Wealth Destroyers in 1998 Performance 1000 Universe

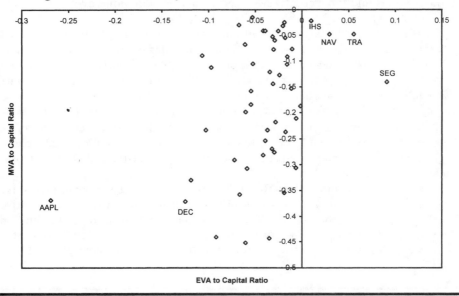

EVA to Capital Ratio

Bottom 50 U.S. Firms

Exhibit 21 reports the capital adjusted MVA-EVA results for the bottom 50 firms listed in the 1998 Performance Universe — where 1000 companies were ranked by Stern Stewart according to their 1997 market value added (or assessed net present value). In contrast with the empirical findings for 50 large U.S. wealth creators (recall Exhibit 19), we see a preponderance of firms having negative NPV in the presence of their currently negative EVA.

Indeed, Exhibit 21 shows that 46 out of the 50 U.S. wealth destroyers had jointly negative MVA-to-Capital and EVA-to-Capital ratios at year-end 1997. For specific wealth destroyers at that time, the exhibit shows that companies like Apple Computer (AAPL) and Digital Equipment Corporation (DEC) had highly negative MVA/Capital ratios, each at −0.37, in the presence of their adverse EVA/Capital ratios, at −0.27 and −0.13, respectively. These findings may indicate that on the average the currently announced EVA for troubled firms has adverse information signaling content about the ability of these firms to create future economic profit. Along this line, it seems that several interesting inferences can be drawn from the empirical findings for wealth destroyers.

Specifically, the large scatter of firms in Exhibit 21 having jointly negative MVA-to-Capital and EVA-to-Capital ratios suggests that a pervasive degree of adverse managerial "noise" is present among companies that destroy wealth. This means that it may be especially difficult for corporate managers to convince shareholders — due in general to the "abundance" of managerial noise that seems to plague wealth wasting firms — that their company is in fact the one that is making conscious efforts to turn the negative economic profit situation around.[48] With a large spread of firms having negative NPV-to-capital ratios for similarly negative EVA-to-Capital ratios, it may be difficult for managers to convince investors that their firm is indeed the turnaround company that will emerge from the *abyss* of wealth destruction.

It is also interesting to see in Exhibit 21 that some firms have negative MVA-to-Capital ratios in the presence of their currently positive EVA-to-Capital ratios — although the list of such companies is quite short. For examples, Seagate Technologies (SEG), Terra Industries (TRA), Navistar International (NAV), and Integrated Health Services (IHS) had positive EVA-to-Capital ratios for 1997 in the presence of their negative NPV-to-Capital ratios. Depending on the degree of capital market efficiency there are at least two explanations for these positive EVA and negative NPV occurrences. Specifically, if the capital market is price efficient, then Seagate et al. have negative NPV because investors are highly pessimistic about the ability of these firms to create economic value added for the future — even though their current EVA (to Capital ratio) looks attractive.

Another possibility is that stocks of companies with such anomalous NPV-EVA combinations are "undervalued" in the capital market. This could happen if the stock price was driven down much too far and too fast in light of the firm's currently successful effort at creating economic profit. Such a delayed reaction in stock price may be a boon to active investors who are able to discern these happenings in their "bottom-up" company analysis using value-based metrics. Discovering those companies among the universe of wealth wasters having positive EVA momentum is, of course, the essence of discovering real value — as opposed to illusory value — among the universe of so-called "value stocks" having low price-to-earnings and price-to-book value ratios.[49]

SUMMARY

We set out in this chapter to provide a foundation on the theory and application of value-based metrics. We examined the role of value-based measures in the context of (1) the theory of finance, (2) measurement differences between accounting profit and economic profit, (3) traditional and value-based approaches to enterprise valuation, (4) cost of capital estimation and its variation impact on eco-

---

[48] This information signaling difficulty for troubled companies is recognized by Grant in *Foundations of Economic Value Added*. As one might expect, there may be firm specific cost of capital implications — beyond the single factor CAPM — for negative EVA firms that have abnormal credit (or default) risk on their outstanding debt and equity securities.

[49] An economic profit framework on "value" and "growth" investing is provided by Grant in *Foundations of Economic Value Added* — and Abate in "Select Economic Value Portfolios."

nomic profit, and (5) how value-based metrics can be used to assess the financial characteristics of wealth creating and wealth destroying firms.

We found that many challenges exist when trying to estimate a company's economic profit. One only needs to witness the plethora of accounting adjustments that are necessary to calculate EVA, CFROI, or SVA. However, the basic fact remains that accounting profit is not economic profit — regardless of how one tries to rationalize the conceptual and empirical relationship between these approaches to measuring corporate success. For this reason, we believe that the goal of measuring economic profit is worth the extra time and effort, as value-based metrics are directly related to the net present value of the firm's present and anticipated future growth opportunities.

In our view, companies that seek to implement an economic profit approach are moving in the direction of shareholder value improvement, because today's value driven metrics are designed to provide a formal link between the firm's cash-adjusted operating profit and its economic capital. Indeed, the essence of today's value-based movement is that it recognizes that invested capital — from debt and equity sources — has an opportunity cost much like that envisioned by financial economists of the 20th century (Modigliani and Miller, for examples) and the capital cost notions of classical economists like Alfred Marshall from days gone by.

Moreover, with the emergence of sophisticated economic profit measures over the past two decades, we have seen a revolution of sorts in the theory and practice of corporate finance and investment management — a value-based revival that we (and apparently other chapter contributors to this book) believe will endure the test of time.

Chapter 3

Closing the GAAP between Earnings and EVA*

Al Ehrbar
Senior Vice President
Stern Stewart & Co.

INTRODUCTION

The accounting profession has labored mightily for the past quarter century to make income statements and balance sheets more accurately reflect the performance and financial condition of corporations. The Financial Accounting Standards Board, the profession's self-regulatory body, has issued more than 100 new rules, many of them numbingly complex, since it replaced the old Accounting Principles Board in 1973. But instead of improving the product, all this toil and trouble by the auditing overseers has moved generally accepted accounting principles farther and farther away from economic reality. As Baruch Lev, a prominent accounting professor at New York University, sums up the matter in one of his many studies of accounting distortions:

> The association between accounting data and market values is not only weak, but appears to have been deteriorating over time. Overall, the fragile association between accounting data and capital market values suggests that the usefulness of financial reports ... is rather limited.[1]

The widening gap, as it were, between accounting and reality grows out of an extreme conservative bias in the auditing profession. When accountants are faced with a choice of several ways to treat an item, they almost invariably choose the option that will put the smallest number on the income statement or balance sheet. They immediately charge off all spending on intangibles such as research and development and employee training even though companies make those

---

[1] See Baruch Lev, "R&D and Capital Markets," *Journal of Applied Corporate Finance*, Vol. 11, No. 4 (Winter 1999).

---

* This economic profit material is adapted from Chapter 11 of Al Ehrbar's book, *EVA: The Real Key to Creating Wealth* (Copyright © 1998 by Al Ehrbar and Stern Stewart & Co. Adapted by permission of John Wiley & Sons, Inc.).

investments only because they expect a positive return in the future. Companies that extend credit to customers have to take a charge against earnings for bad debt losses the instant they make new loans. Some borrowers will default, of course, but most will not. In measuring performance, which is what earnings purport to do, immediately booking losses equal to the percentage of loans that are likely to go bad makes no more sense than immediately booking profits on the rest.

Accountants have plenty of reasons to be conservative, of course. Historically, they have prepared their statements primarily for use by lenders, whose concerns are very different from those of owners and managers. Lenders care much less about profitability and performance than they do about whether they can get their hands on enough stuff to recover their loans if a borrower goes bust. As a result, accounting statements provide a portrait of a company from an undertaker's point of view. Balance sheets, after all the writing down of assets and reserving for possible future expenses, do not provide a measure of the cash that investors have put at risk in a going concern, or what we call capital. Instead, they come much closer to showing the minimum amount that a liquidator could expect to get for the assets in a fire sale.

The securities laws are another important contributor to this abject conservatism. When accountants get sued for securities fraud, it is for overstating earnings or assets, not understating them, so their self-interest is solidly on the side of debiting earnings. In addition, the Securities and Exchange Commission, which is the final arbiter of accounting rules for publicly held corporations, has mandated some of the more foolish provisions in GAAP. It was the SEC, for example, that insisted on the requirement that companies amortize goodwill. The Commission makes these rules out of an abiding fear that shady managers will hornswoggle investors by inflating earnings and assets. The rich history of stock swindles may justify such fears, but the SEC's protective zeal sometimes takes it to absurd extremes. One case in point: back in the 1970s the SEC became concerned that naïve investors were being misled by the emphasis that real estate investment trusts put on cash flow, so it ordered all companies to stop reporting cash flow per share. All were still required to report cash flow and the number of shares outstanding, of course. The threat to the fairness of the markets apparently came from allowing companies to perform the long division for their shareholders.

Finally, the distortions caused by accounting conservatism have been exacerbated by changes in the nature of business over the past few decades. As Baruch Lev points out, a big culprit in the weakening association between financial statements and reality is the "frequent contamination of [earnings] by transitory and arbitrary items, such as asset writeoffs, restructuring charges, goodwill amortization and the full expensing of research and development."[2] Arbitrary refers, of course, to accounting treatments, not business actions. All these areas are ones in which accountants are far too eager to reduce earnings and balance sheets, which means that GAAP is particularly ill suited to the business environment that is likely to prevail in the coming decades.

---

[2] See Lev, "R&D and Capital Markets."

POWER OF EVA

Quantum erring on the side of caution may or may not serve creditors well (a strong case can be made that it often does not), but GAAP plainly fails to meet the needs of managers and shareholders. These optimistic folk rightly view the corporation not as a candidate for interment, but as an enterprise that will continue in operation into the indefinite future and hopefully will provide a handsome return. What they need is a performance measure that provides signals and feedback that confirm or refute the wisdom of capital allocation decisions and serves as a reliable guide to the economic value of a company. Managers in particular need a performance metric that shows, month-to-month and quarter-to-quarter, whether their actions are adding to the value of the business. To achieve that, they do not need liquidation values or even the fair market value of assets. Rather, they need a balance sheet that provides a measure of the cumulative cash outlays expected to contribute to future profits, which constitutes the proper capital base on which to measure rates of return and EVA. They also need a corresponding measure of operating profits that reflects what really is happening in the business.

That's precisely what EVA provides. Companies cannot replace GAAP earnings with EVA in their public reporting, of course. But no regulations prevent them from using a different earnings calculation for internal decisions, or from reporting that number to investors alongside the one mandated by the SEC. The first departure from GAAP accounting is to recognize the full cost of capital. Accountants treat equity as if it were free. EVA also fixes the problems with GAAP by converting accounting earnings to economic earnings and accounting book value to economic book value, or capital. The result is a NOPAT figure (net operating profits after taxes) that gives a much truer picture of the economics of the business, and a capital figure that is a far better measure of the funds contributed by shareholders and lenders.

The first step in calculating EVA for any one company is to decide on which adjustments to make to the GAAP accounts. As you will see, the correct answer usually is far fewer than you might expect, though one could make EVA numbingly complex by insisting on a plethora of unnecessary accounting adjustments. Stern Stewart, for example, has identified more than 160 potential adjustments to GAAP and to internal accounting treatments, all of which can improve the measure of operating profits and capital. Any change in the accounting adjustments will yield a different EVA number, of course. If you think of all the potential EVAs as running along a spectrum, the one at the extreme left in Exhibit 1 is what might be called "basic" EVA. This is the EVA you would get using unadjusted GAAP operating profits and the GAAP balance sheet. Moving to the right, you come to what we call "disclosed" EVA. This EVA, which Stern Stewart uses in its published MVA/EVA rankings, is computed by making about a dozen standard adjustments to publicly available accounting data. At the extreme right in Exhibit 1 is "true" EVA. This is the most theoretically correct and accurate measure of economic profit, calculated with all relevant adjustments to accounting data and using the precise cost of capital for each business unit in a corporation.

Exhibit 1: The EVA Spectrum

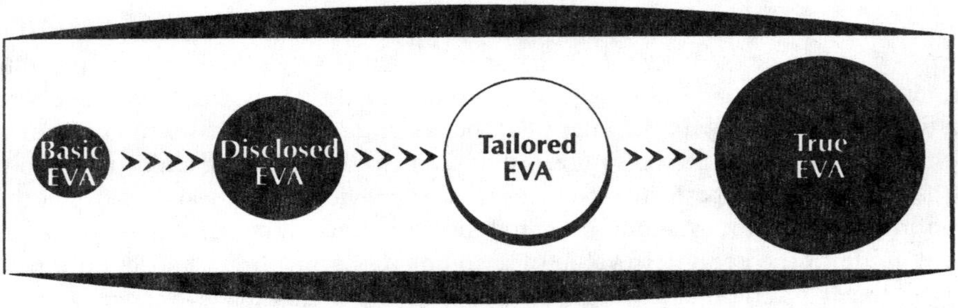

Which EVA should a company use? None of the above. Basic EVA is an improvement on regular accounting earnings because it recognizes that equity capital has a cost, but all the other problems with GAAP remain. At the other extreme, the calculation of true EVA requires more wisdom than mere mortals possess. Disclosed EVA is much, much better than basic EVA. Specifically, disclosed EVA explains about 50% of changes in MVA.[3] But disclosed EVA is not as good as it should be for internal management use. That's partly because publicly reported figures do not include enough detail to fine-tune some of the accounting adjustments. It also reflects the fact that some practical shortcuts are inescapable in doing timely EVA computations for large rankings of companies.

In fact, no off-the-shelf definition of EVA will do. What each company needs is a custom-tailored definition, peculiar to its organizational structure, business mix, strategy and accounting policies — one that optimally balances the tradeoff between simplicity (easy to calculate and understand) and precision (the accuracy with which it captures true economic profit). These custom-tailored EVAs typically explain 60% to as much as 85% of changes in MVA. In Stern Stewart's experience, most companies require no more than 15 accounting adjustments to calculate an optimal EVA, and many can get by with fewer still. Once the formula is set, it should be virtually immutable, serving as a sort of constitutional definition of performance. Top management and the board should be just as circumspect about fiddling with their chosen EVA as Congress is about amending the U.S. Constitution.

The myriad formulas for EVA may make it sound rather muddy and easily manipulated, and one may argue that this is a serious shortcoming of economic profit measures. However, flexibility and customizability are important strengths of EVA, not weaknesses. The purpose, after all, isn't to arrive at some theoretically pristine measure of profits. Rather, it is to change the behavior of managers and workers in ways that will maximize shareholder wealth, and the effectiveness of any measure at shaping behavior will diminish as it becomes more complex

---

[3] Based on research by Stern Stewart and independent published sources.

and difficult to understand. Since particular accounting adjustments may be crucial in some industries and unimportant in others, tailoring allows each company to limit its adjustments to those that are truly necessary. Some competing measures of corporate performance, specific names not mentioned here, start out exceedingly complicated and can never be made simple enough for even the smartest non-financial managers to comprehend. EVA, in contrast, starts out simple and gets only as complicated as it has to be to provide the right information for managers and workers to make wealth-maximizing decisions. But again, once the definition has been decided, it should not be modified lightly.

ACCOUNTING ADJUSTMENTS

The list of potential accounting changes is too lengthy to detail here. The various types of adjustments include the treatment of such things as: the timing of expense and revenue recognition; passive investments in marketable securities; securitized assets and other off-balance-sheet financing; restructuring charges; inflation; foreign currency translation; inventory valuation; bookkeeping reserves; bad debt recognition; intangible assets; taxes; pensions; post-retirement expenses; marketing expenditures; goodwill and other acquisition issues, and strategic investments. Some adjustments are necessary to avoid mixing operating and financing decisions. Some provide a long-term perspective. Some avoid mixing stocks and flows. Some convert GAAP accrual items to a cash-flow basis, while others convert GAAP cash-flow items to additions to capital. Still others, including overhead allocations and transfer pricing issues, change internal accounting treatments to resolve organizational interface problems that distort decisions. The following examples include some of the major adjustments necessary to put NOPAT and capital on an economic basis, and further illuminate ways that GAAP distorts reality.

Research and Development

The treatment of R&D provides an excellent example of the difference between accounting and economics. As noted earlier, shareholders and managers rightly regard outlays on R&D as investments in future products and processes. GAAP, however, requires companies (software developers are the signal exception) to immediately expense (deduct from earnings) all outlays for research and development. GAAP is saying, in effect, that the more than $100 billion a year that U.S. corporations invest in research and development is worthless. This punitive treatment of R&D has particularly perverse consequences for research-intensive high-tech companies. Expensing R&D wrongly reduces their book values by writing one of their greatest assets down to zero. A principal reason that high-tech stocks typically sell at much higher multiples of book value than other companies is that their book values are so egregiously understated.

The EVA treatment is to capitalize R&D investments (add current outlays to the balance sheet as an asset) and amortize them (charge a portion against earnings each year) over an appropriate period. Research by Baruch Lev[4] and others indicates that the correct amortization period ranges from as little as three or four years for scientific instruments to eight years or more for pharmaceuticals. The average useful life of R&D for all industries is five years, which is the amortization period that Stern Stewart uses in the Performance 1000. All companies with significant R&D spending should capitalize it. Why? Because the adjustment can occasionally have a material impact on decisions. A CEO playing by the rules according to GAAP might order a cutback in R&D spending in a lean year in order to bolster earnings, even though that means the company is sacrificing shareholder wealth by forgoing an investment that promises to return more than the cost of capital. (If the R&D isn't likely to return more than the cost of capital, the company shouldn't have been doing it in the first place.) Alternatively, the CEO might be reluctant to increase spending to capture a first-strike advantage in a promising technology area.

Research indicates that the GAAP treatment of R&D has pernicious effects even in normal years. Robert Gibbons of Cornell University and Kevin J. Murphy of Harvard studied R&D spending patterns in the final years before CEOs retire. R&D doesn't decline, but the rate of increase in R&D does.[5] Gibbons and Murphy believe that CEOs whose pensions are based on earnings performance in their final years on the job become stingy with R&D dollars to pad their own pensions. The findings also indicate that the CEOs in question understand what they are doing to shareholders. The falloff in R&D is significantly smaller when CEOs hold substantial amounts of stock or options, the value of which would be reduced by curtailing R&D.

Under EVA, and with bonuses and pensions based on EVA instead of earnings, the CEO would not face such destructive temptations; cutting R&D outlays would have no immediate impact on EVA. But, and this is also important, the amortization of R&D in future years makes managers feel accountable for getting results. In too many companies, R&D is simply institutionalized at a certain spending precisely because it is treated as an expense. When R&D is treated as an investment, the system automatically creates more leeway to increase spending on an attractive project, while the charge for the cost of capital and accountability under the EVA bonus system insure that researchers appraise prospective projects objectively.

Strategic Investments

Capital discipline is the essence of EVA, but there are times when companies do not want managers to worry about covering their full cost of capital — at least not immediately. These are the instances when the payoff from an investment is not

[4] See Lev, "R&D and Capital Markets."
[5] See Robert Gibbons and Kevin Murphy, "Does Executive Compensation Affect Investment," *Journal of Applied Corporate Finance*, vol. 5, No. 4 (Summer 1992).

expected to come until some point in the future. A manager at a forest products company, for example, sees great potential in a new, more efficient pulp mill that would take three years to construct and bring up to full capacity. But he may be reluctant to propose it because he knows that his EVA will be reduced by capital charges imposed on the new investment before the mill begins to produce profits.

The same disincentive to investment can dissuade companies from making wealth-creating acquisitions. Monsanto, which implemented EVA in 1996, has completed a number of acquisitions over the past couple years as it spun off its chemical business and refocused itself as a "life sciences" company with extensive operations in food, agriculture and pharmaceuticals. Chief Executive Robert B. Shapiro would have rejected many of those acquisitions if the test had been whether they would immediately contribute to higher EVA. But Monsanto has not been acquiring just to round out the offerings in its catalogs. Instead, it has been buying bio-tech companies whose research will help Monsanto develop more breakthrough products. The EVA payoff will come down the road as the products move from development to market. Similarly, most upscale restaurants operate at a loss — or too small an operating profit to cover the interest on the initial investment in fixtures and kitchen equipment — until they build a loyal customer base, something that rarely happens overnight.

The approach that many non-EVA companies take in situations like these is to define the investments as strategic and basically ignore the immediate impact on profitability. This has great appeal for everyone (except the shareholders) because it is essentially discipline-free. When the time comes for the profits to finally materialize, hardly anyone ever looks back to see if they are as large as promised or large enough to justify the initial investment. Which is why so many people have come to regard strategic as a code word for a project or acquisition that will never pay off. EVA provides a better way — one that encourages managers to propose investments with distant payoffs, but only when they believe (and don't just hope) that the investment will return more than the cost of capital.

The solution is to use a special accounting treatment for strategic investments that is akin to the construction-in-progress accounting used by electric utilities. Instead of applying a capital charge to strategic investments from the day they are made, EVA companies "hold back" the investment in a special "suspension" account. The capital charge on the balance in the suspension account is left out of the EVA calculation until the time that the investment is expected to produce operating profits. In the interim, the capital charges that would have been applied to the suspension account are simply added to it, so that the balance in the account reflects the full opportunity cost — including accrued interest, as it were — of the investment. Then, when the investment is scheduled to begin producing NOPAT, the capital in the suspension account is metered back into the EVA calculation.

This is strategic investment with a memory. The strategic investment treatment stretches out managers' horizons and encourages them to consider opportunities with distant payoffs. A manager proposing an investment understands that he will not be penalized in the short term for taking a long-term view, but also knows that he ultimately will be held accountable for the capital invested. However, as with the EVA formula itself, it is essential that companies establish the rules for strategic treatment in advance and then stick to them.

Accounting for Acquisitions

When one company acquires another and uses the purchase method of accounting to record the transaction, anything it pays in excess of the "fair value" of the acquired company's assets goes on its balance sheet as an asset called goodwill. Arithmetically, goodwill is simply purchase price minus "fair value." Economically, it could represent any number of things. Goodwill may include the value of patents, technological know-how, or R&D projects that are still in process. And some part of goodwill may be exactly what the name implies: the good will that the acquired company and its brands have established with customers and suppliers.

Whatever its true source, goodwill is an intangible, and accountants get very uncomfortable around things they can't touch. So GAAP requires companies to write off goodwill over a period of 40 years or less. This treatment of goodwill plays havoc with the information content in accounting numbers. The annual amortization charge arbitrarily reduces reported earnings, which also reduces conventional profitability measures such as return on equity (ROE) and return on assets (ROA). Ultimately, however, the accumulated amortization charges reduce equity and assets so far that the treatment of goodwill inflates ROE and ROA.

That's just the beginning of the mischief. Since 1970 GAAP has required acquirers to allocate an appropriate share of the purchase price to "identifiable" intangible assets, including R&D. In recent years acquirers have been doing just that by estimating, sometimes with the help of outside appraisers, the market value of in-process R&D. They aren't doing this just to be in compliance with the 1970 accounting rule. Their real motivation is to single out the R&D portion of goodwill so they can write if off immediately. When IBM bought Lotus for $3.2 billion in 1995, for example, it allocated $1.84 billion, or 57% of the purchase price, to in-process R&D. IBM then wrote off the entire amount under the GAAP rule requiring companies to expense R&D. Why jump through these hoops? Because immediately writing off the in-process R&D gets a big chunk of goodwill off the books now, which reduces ongoing goodwill amortization charges and boosts reported earnings. The writeoff also puts more zing in ROE and ROA by immediately shrinking shareholders equity and assets.

Baruch Lev calls this the "flash-then-flush" maneuver.[6] The acquirer flashes the estimated market value of acquired R&D to shareholders and then flushes it off the balance sheet. Interestingly, Lev's examination of nearly 400 instances in which acquirers used flash-then-flush shows that the estimated market values of the in-process R&D correlated highly with the stock-market valuations of the acquiring companies. Lev's research also provides an empirical

---

[6] See Lev, "R&D and Capital Markets."

validation of the EVA treatment of R&D. He also found that the valuations that acquirers put on in-process R&D were close to the book values that the R&D would have had using the EVA approach of capitalizing and amortizing outlays.

The proper economic treatment of goodwill is to write it off over its estimated economic life. For practical reasons, Stern Stewart recommends leaving goodwill on the balance sheet and never writing it off. First, this focuses managers on cash flows rather than mere bookkeeping entries. Second, most goodwill represents assets with indefinite lives, such as brands, reputation and market position. Finally, managers shouldn't be concerned about how a prospective acquisition will affect reported earnings, but they should be constantly aware that shareholders will expect them to produce a return on the acquisition price that equals or exceeds the cost of capital in perpetuity. Thus, the EVA adjustment is to add the current period's goodwill amortization back to NOPAT and to add the goodwill amortized in past years back to capital.

Pooling-of-interest acquisitions present an entirely different set of problems. In these cases, the balance sheets of the two companies are simply added together and goodwill isn't accounted for at all. The absence of goodwill means there are no ongoing amortization charges to penalize reported earnings. This makes poolings very attractive to managers of acquiring companies; so attractive, as mentioned before, that they are willing to pay higher acquisition premiums than companies using purchase accounting. However, the pooling treatment distorts EVA because it understates capital and the capital charge. Thus, the proper EVA treatment is to convert pooling acquisitions to purchase accounting so that managers will focus on the true capital costs of an acquisition instead of the impact on accounting earnings.

Expense Recognition

Some companies should make changes in things as basic as when they recognize revenues and expenses. Many companies willingly incur marketing costs to establish new brands, enter new markets or gain market share. America On Line, for example, must have sent 20 or 30 disks to access its service to every PC owner in the U.S. Similarly, cellular telephone companies typically spend $250 to $300 to acquire a new customer, both by selling cellular phones far below cost and by paying finder's fees to telephone retailers. All these outlays are investments to acquire new assets called customers.

Yet GAAP accounting says they must be treated as current period expenses and deducted from earnings immediately. Thus, the more successful a cellular company is at landing new subscribers, the less profitable it appears. But is it less profitable? What the cellular company has done is acquire a subscriber who is going to run up monthly charges. If cellular companies capitalized customer acquisition costs and amortized them over the appropriate period, which is the proper economic treatment, their earnings and book values would be much higher. More important, a growing company would not have any reason to cut back on profitable marketing outlays just to make a quarterly earnings number look better.

Depreciation

For most companies, the straight-line depreciation of plant and equipment used in GAAP accounting works acceptably well. While straight-line depreciation doesn't attempt to match the actual economic depreciation of physical assets, the deviations from reality ordinarily are so inconsequential that they do not distort decisions. That's not true, however, for companies with significant amounts of long-lived equipment. In those cases, using straight-line depreciation in calculating EVA can create a powerful bias against investments in new equipment. That's because the EVA capital charge declines in step with the depreciated carrying value of the asset, so that old assets look much cheaper than new ones. This can make managers reluctant to replace "cheap" old equipment with "expensive" new gear.

Companies with long-lived equipment can eliminate this distortion by replacing straight-line depreciation with "sinking-fund" depreciation.[7] Under a sinking fund schedule, the annual depreciation charge follows the same pattern as the principal payment in a mortgage, starting out small in the early years and rising rapidly in the last years. The sum of the depreciation charge and the EVA capital charge remain constant from year to year, just like a mortgage payment. The switch to sinking fund depreciation, which effectively makes owning an asset look just like leasing, eliminates any bias against new equipment. It also happens to be much closer to economic reality. Most long-lived equipment depreciates very little in the first few years, and then tumbles in value in the later years when obsolescence and physical deterioration gang up on it.

Restructuring Charges

Nothing in GAAP provides worse signals to managers than the treatment of restructuring charges. To see this, think about what a restructuring charge represents. In the GAAP view, the charge is a belated recognition of the loss on an investment that went bad. This has some intellectual merit, but it doesn't capture the dynamics of a restructuring from a managerial perspective. Viewed from the executive suite, a restructuring should be thought of as a redeployment of capital that is intended to improve profitability going forward by reducing the ongoing losses from past mistakes. The GAAP treatment focuses entirely on the past mistakes aspect, and turns a restructuring into a painful mea culpa that most managers would do anything to avoid. The EVA treatment focuses on the likely improvement in shareholder wealth, turning restructurings into opportunities that managers should be eager to seize.

Consider this example of a highly simplified company with a $500 factory that produces zero operating profits. That's breakeven under GAAP, but much worse under EVA. If the company's cost of capital is 10%, the capital charge for the factory is $50 and, with zero operating profits, EVA is minus $50. The com-

---

[7] For a detailed illustration of the EVA impact of straight line depreciation versus "sinking fund" depreciation, see Chapter 5 of this book by Stephen F. O'Byrne.

pany could sell the factory and distribute the proceeds to shareholders, but would get only $200 for it. Under GAAP, the company reports a $300 restructuring charge for the loss on the sale of the factory, which is treated as a $300 reduction in earnings. The balance sheet decline by $500 as the asset is fully written off and the $200 dividend paid to shareholders. Few managers who focus on earnings would close the plant. Why take a $300 hit to earnings, a $500 reduction in assets, and a shrinkage in operations if you can continue breaking even under GAAP?

Look at the same situation under EVA. The company takes the $500 factory off its books. But instead of flowing a $300 restructuring charge through the income statement, it adds a $300 restructuring investment to the balance sheet. Capital declines not by $500, but by the $200 actually paid to shareholders from the sale of the factory. This, after all, is the amount of capital management actually returned to shareholders. Now look at what happens to EVA: operating profits remain at zero (since the factory no longer is operating), but the capital charge drops to $30 (10% of the $300 restructuring investment), and EVA rises from minus $50 to minus $30. A manager whose bonus was based on changes in EVA would sell the factory in a New York minute.

Taxes

The mismeasurement of taxes arises because companies calculate their pretax profits one way for shareholders and a second way for the Internal Revenue Service. The profit — and tax liability — they report to the IRS usually is much lower. Depreciation is the biggest difference between the two sets of books, but not the only one. Companies use accelerated depreciation of fixed assets in computing taxable profits for the IRS and a slower depreciation schedule (usually straight-line) in the profits they report to shareholders. The provision for income taxes used in GAAP earnings statements, commonly referred to as book taxes, isn't the same as the cash taxes companies actually pay. It is the taxes they would owe if they used GAAP earnings on their tax return. The difference — the taxes they don't really pay — goes into a liability account called deferred taxes.

The trouble with this accounting treatment is that most companies never will pay their deferred taxes. Even if a company's fixed assets grow slowly, the depreciation charges on its tax return will keep the deferred tax account rising indefinitely. From an economic standpoint, the only taxes a company should deduct from current earnings are the ones it pays now, not taxes that it might — or might not—have to pay at some distant date. So for the purposes of calculating NOPAT and EVA at the corporate level, companies should deduct only the cash taxes they pay in the period being measured. Correspondingly, the deferred taxes that were deducted from earnings in the past should be moved from the liability portion of the balance sheet and added back to shareholder funds for the purposes of calculating capital and the cost of capital.

Most non-EVA companies use pre-tax operating profits to evaluate business units, and some EVA companies do so as well. However, most companies should use after-tax NOPAT and EVA at the business-unit level. Since taxes are an inescapable cost of doing business, operating managers should take them into account if they can affect cash tax liabilities through their decisions. When they are charged for taxes actually paid, managers will have the incentive to collaborate with the tax department at the planning stages of new ventures to determine the most tax-efficient organization instead of calling in the tax experts after the fact to minimize the damage already done by failing to consider taxes until all other decisions had been made.

Balance Sheet Adjustments

All the adjustments mentioned thus far can have a significant impact on the measurement of capital, or economic book value. Capitalizing R&D and adding back amortized goodwill and tax reserves all add to capital, for example. Several other adjustments that affect the balance sheet directly bear mention. One adjustment that many EVA companies make is to subtract passive investments (such as the large cash reserves that some companies hold in marketable securities) because they do not represent capital used to produce operating profits. What's more, passive investments should be valued in the market at the cost of capital inherent in the investments themselves rather than at the company's cost of capital. Needless to say, the income on those investments should be subtracted from NOPAT. Another balance-sheet adjustment is to subtract the free financing all companies enjoy, which comes in the form of accrued expenses and non-interest-bearing accounts payable.[8] These adjustments limit the capital charge to the net assets employed in operations. Finally, companies should move all off-balance-sheet items, such as uncapitalized leases and securitized receivables, back onto the balance sheet. This is essential to avoid mixing operating and financing decisions. An uncapitalized lease item, for example, will appear cheaper than it really is if managers look only at the implicit lending rate in the lease.

In tailoring EVA to a specific company, Stern Stewart applies a series of tests to determine which accounting adjustments are optimal. The first and most important is whether an adjustment is material. By material, we aren't referring to the accountant's test of whether a number is large relative to a company's earnings or assets. In our world, material means that the numbers involved are significant down at the levels of decision-makers even if they cancel out at the corporate level. Material also means that the change in accounting could alter decisions in ways that affect shareholder wealth. If a change cannot affect decisions, it usually isn't worth making.

The other tests of potential adjustments are whether:

- The necessary data are available
- The change is understandable to operating managers

---

[8] For an interesting example of the EVA treatment of such "spontaneous" sources of financing, see Chapter 5.

- The change can be explained to employees, directors and stockholders
- The change is definitive
- The change aligns calculated EVA more closely with the market value of the firm
- The change involves items that are manageable by those affected

By definitive, we mean that the adjustment can be cast in concrete and left unchanged for a minimum of three years. By aligned, we mean that the adjustment moves the NOPAT calculation closer to economic earnings, and that anyone can make the adjustment automatically without any subjective judgements. By manageable, we are referring to whether an operating manager can influence expenses or capital outlays in ways that benefit shareholders. One example is the allocation of corporate overhead, which often is charged to business units on the basis of sales. In those cases, the only way a business unit can affect its allocated overhead expense is by getting sales down, something that presumably is not a good thing for shareholders. The manageability test would dictate that the company either not allocate corporate overhead at all or allocate it according to an activity-based-costing formula that a business unit could manage by using fewer corporate services.

COST OF CAPITAL

The other element in crafting a company's EVA formula is to define the cost of capital.[9] The cost used in all EVA calculations is the weighted average cost of debt and equity capital. This is the percentage of capital provided by lenders multiplied by the company's cost of debt, plus the percentage supplied by shareholders multiplied by the cost of equity capital. That rate, when multiplied by total capital, is the profit that must be earned in order to make interest payments on the debt and leave enough additional profit to provide shareholders with a minimum acceptable return on their investment.

Perhaps the easiest way to understand the cost of capital for any company is to divide it into three basic components. The first is the risk-free rate of interest, which usually is measured by the government bond rate. The risk-free interest rate reflects the fact that capital is scarce and that any use of it has a minimum time value, even when the person providing the capital is absolutely certain of getting it all back. The second component of the cost of capital is a premium over the risk-free rate to compensate for business risk. Business risk varies with the level of uncertainty in a company's industry. Food processing, for example, is much less risky than making auto parts or operating theme parks, and the cost of capital for each reflects its relative risk. The third component is a reduction in the cost of capital to reflect the savings most companies get from being able to deduct interest

---

[9] Cost of capital estimation and its variation impact on EVA and corporate value are explained in Chapter 2 of this book.

payments from their taxable profits, commonly referred to as the tax subsidy on debt. For the vast majority of companies, the sum of the three components comes to a figure that is 1 to 7 percentage points higher than the government bond rate.

What about the separate costs of debt and equity? For the most part, they don't really matter. Apart from the effect of the tax subsidy on debt, the overall cost of capital in a business is purely a function of the underlying business risk and, within reasonable leverage limits, is not affected by the mix of debt and equity. To be sure, the cost of debt is considerably cheaper than equity, for the simple reason that debt holders get paid first. Superficially, it would appear that substituting cheaper debt for more expensive equity is a way to bring down the average cost of capital. However, higher debt gives rise to greater financial risk. Shareholders demand to get paid for that type of risk as well. The required return on equity rises as more fixed interest payments are subtracted from uncertain operating profits and make the bottom-line profits available to shareholders riskier or more volatile over a business cycle. One of the contributions that Miller and Modigliani made some 40 years ago was to show that, apart from the tax subsidy on debt, the cost of greater financial risk exactly offsets the savings from substituting debt for equity.[10]

In practice, of course, companies do calculate separate costs for debt and equity capital. Debt is simple. It is the company's after-tax cost of borrowing at current interest rates. Current interest rates, rather than the rates on existing debt, are the appropriate ones to use because that is the cost the company would pay on new debt or would save if it repurchased debt. The cost of equity is considerably more complicated. Financial economists and consultants have devised a variety of ways to estimate the cost of equity down to as many decimal places as anyone would like. We each have our preferred method, none of which is worth going into here. Suffice it to say that the differences in estimates produced by the various methodologies usually are less important than the answers to questions about things such as whether to use different costs of capital in different countries, and whether a company should use one cost of capital for every business unit. In answer to the second, Stern Stewart usually recommends using just one cost of capital for the sake of simplicity and ease of administration, and to forestall pointless arguments over the "right" cost. Some cases are exceptions, however, especially when the costs of capital in business units are radically different. Telecom New Zealand uses one cost of capital for its conventional, wired service, and a second, higher one for its wireless phone business.

The specific estimating technique also is much less important for getting the benefits of EVA than the fact that managers explicitly recognize that capital has some cost, and their bonuses depend upon covering that cost. As with so many other things in business, the calculation of the cost of capital is subject to the 80/

---

[10] See Franco Modigliani and Merton H. Miller, "The Cost of Capital, Corporation Finance, and the Theory of Investment," *American Economic Review* (June 1958), and "Dividend Policy, Growth and the Valuation of Shares," *Journal of Business* (October 1961).

20 rule, which says that about 80% of the benefits of determining the right cost come from the first 20% of the effort. Whether the true weighted average cost of capital is 11.5% or 13.2% is of far less importance than having everyone understand that capital is expensive and behave accordingly. Some companies prefer to keep the cost-of-capital issue as simple as possible, figuring that refinement would merely confuse some people without improving decisions. Coca-Cola, for example, uses 12% as its single cost of capital worldwide, expressed in dollars. Why 12%? Because it is 1% a month.

Chapter 4

Value-Based Measures of Performance

Pamela Peterson, Ph.D., CFA
Professor of Finance
College of Business
Florida State University

INTRODUCTION

Evaluating a company's performance using traditional measures derived directly from financial statements, such as return on asset or return on equity, is often criticized as inadequate measurement of a company's or a division's performance. Though accounting principles are updated regularly to provide for the best representation of a companies' operating performance and financial position, there are concerns about whether financial statement information is really useful in financial analysis and valuation because we apply a set of general accounting principles to companies in a variety of businesses and that financial information can be managed through a judicious use of accounting principles.

So why not just look at stock prices as a measure of performance? If we dispose of financial statement information and focus solely on stock prices we have simply substituted one set of concerns for another. Evaluating a company's performance is much more challenging than looking at stock prices. If stock prices rise in a given period, does that mean the company is doing well? Not necessarily — the stock price may not be as high as it should be given economic and market conditions. If a company's stock price declines during a given period, does that mean that the company is doing poorly? Not necessarily — the stock's price may be higher than expected given current economic and market conditions.

Arising from the need for better methods of evaluating performance, several consulting companies have advocated performance evaluation methods that are applied to evaluate a firm's performance as a whole and to evaluate specific managers' performances. These methods are, in some cases, supplanting traditional methods of measuring performance, such as the return-on-assets. As a class, these measures are often referred to as value-based metrics or economic value added measures, though there is a cacophony of acronyms to accompany these measures, including EVA®, MVA, CFROI, and SVA.[1]

A company's management creates value when decisions are made that provide benefits that exceed the costs. These benefits may be received in the near or distant future, and the costs include both the direct cost of the investment, as well as the less obvious cost, the cost of capital. The *cost of capital* is the explicit and implicit cost associated with using investors' funds. It is the attention to the cost of capital that sets the value-based metrics apart from traditional measures of performance.

The value-based metrics are based on the idea that a company should only invest in projects that enhance the value of the firm. So where do these value-enhancing projects come from? In a competitive market for investment opportunities where many companies compete for available investment opportunities, there should be no value-enhancing projects. In other words, the cost of a project should be bid upward through competition so there is no net benefit from investing in the project. This explanation is rather gloomy and ignores the true source of value-enhancing projects: a firm's comparative or competitive advantage. It is only through some advantage vis-a-vis one's competitors that allows companies to invest in projects that enhance value.[2] In cases where there are no impediments to investment (that is, there is a competitive market for investments), it is only through having some type of advantage that a company can invest in something and get more back in return. Stepping back from looking at individual projects to looking at an entire firm, we can apply the same basic principles. If the firm's investments provide future benefits greater than its costs, the investments enhance the value of the firm. If the firm's investments provide future benefits that are less than the investments costs, this is detrimental to the value of the firm.[3]

From the perspective of analysts, the focus of performance evaluation is on the company as a whole, not on individual investment decisions within the firm. The key to evaluating a firm's performance is therefore whether the firm's investment decisions, as a whole, are producing value for the shareholders. But there is no obvious technique to accomplish this because: (1) we do not have the ability to perfectly forecast future cash flows from these investments, (2) we do

---

[1] As noted in Chapter 1, EVA and MVA are economic value added and market value added, respectively, promoted by Stern Stewart & Co., CFROI is cash flow return on investment, promoted by Holt/Boston Consulting Group, SVA is shareholder value added, promoted by the LEK/Alcar Consulting Group. EVA is a registered trademark of Stern Stewart & Co.

[2] A comparative advantage is the advantage one company has over others in terms of the cost of producing or distributing goods or services. A competitive advantage is the advantage one company has over another because of the structure of the markets (input and output markets) in which they both operate.

[3] The idea of producing current value from future investment opportunities is reflected in the concept of franchise value, which is discussed by Stanley Kogelman and Martin L. Liebowitz in their decomposition of the price-earnings (P/E) ratio into a franchise P/E and a base P/E. In their analysis, future investment opportunities in excess of market returns are reflected in above-market P/E ratios. See Stanley Kogelman and Martin L. Liebowitz, "The Franchise Factor Valuation Approach: Capturing the Firm's Investment Opportunities," *Corporate Financial Decision Making and Equity Analysis*, ICFA Continuing Education (Charlottesville, Va.: Association for Investment Management and Research, 1995), pp. 5-10.

not have accurate measures of the risks of each investment, and (3) we do not know the precise cost of capital. Therefore, we are left with using proxies (however imperfect) to assess a firm's performance.

The most prominent of recently developed techniques to evaluate a firm's performance is the value-added measures of economic value added (EVA®) and market value added (MVA).[4,5] These measures have links to our fundamental valuation techniques. Value-added measures are based on the same valuation principles as the net present value capital budgeting technique. A net present value for a specific investment project is the estimate of change in the value of the firm's equity if the company invests in the project. The value-added measures also produce an estimate of the change in the value of the firm, but relate to a company or a division as a whole, rather than a specific project. Further, whereas net present value is forward looking, assisting management in making decisions dealing with the use of capital in the future, measuring a period's performance using value-added measures focuses on the decisions that have been made during a period and the cost of capital that supported those investment decisions to help us gauge how well the company has performed.

There are a number of value-added measures that an analyst can calculate. The most commonly used measures are economic value added and market value added. Economic value added is simply another name for a company's *economic profit*. Key elements of estimating economic profit are:

- the calculation of the firm's operating profit from financial statement data, making adjustments to accounting profit to better reflect a firm's results for a period;
- the calculation of the company's cost of capital; and
- the comparison of operating profit with the cost of capital.

The difference between the operating profit and the cost of capital is the estimate of the firm's economic profit, or economic value-added.

A related measure, *market value-added*, focuses on the market value of capital, as compared to the cost of capital. The key elements of market value-added are:

---

[4] A description of the value-added methods can be found in G. Bennett Stewart III, *The Quest for Value* (Harper Collins Publishers, Inc., 1991); Pamela P. Peterson and David R. Peterson, *Company Performance and Measures of Performance*, Research Foundation of the Institute of Chartered Financial Analysts (Charlottesville, VA.: Association for Investment Management and Research, 1996); James L. Grant, *Foundations of Economic Value Added* (New Hope, PA: Frank J. Fabozzi Associates, 1997); Al Ehrbar, *The Real Key to Creating Wealth* (New York: John Wiley & Sons, 1998); and, Aswath Damodaran, "Value Creation and Enhancement: Back to the Future," *Contemporary Finance Digest* (1999), pp. 1-46.

[5] Another prominent valuation approach is the discounted cash flow approach, advocated by McKinsey and Co. This approach involves forecasting future periods' free cash flows, forecasting a company's continuing value at the end of the forecast period, and discounting the future free cash flows and the continuing value at the company's weighted average cost of capital. Because this approach involves valuation based on forecasts, it is not a suitable device for evaluating performance, though it is useful in setting performance targets. See Thomas Copeland, Timothy Koller, and Jack Murrin, *Valuation: Measuring and Managing the Value of Companies, second edition* (New York: John Wiley & Sons, 1994).

- the calculation of the market value of capital;
- the calculation of the capital invested; and
- the comparison of the market value of capital with the capital invested.

The difference between the market value of capital and the amount of capital invested is the market value-added. The primary distinction between economic value-added and market value-added is that the latter incorporates market data in the calculation.

The purpose behind the use of the value-based metrics is to improve upon the traditional performance measures, such as the return on assets. What makes a good performance measure? Ideally, a measure of a firm's performance should have several characteristics:

1. The measure should not be sensitive to the choice of accounting methods.
2. The measure should evaluate the firm's current decisions considering expected future results.
3. The measure should consider the risk associated with the decisions made by the firm.
4. The measure should neither penalize nor reward the company for factors outside of its control, such as market movements and unanticipated changes in the economy.

The different performance measures discussed in the following sections are judged by these characteristics.

TRADITIONAL PERFORMANCE MEASURES

The most widely cited performance measures are return on investment ratios, including the return on assets and the return on equity. Generally, higher return ratios are associated with better performance. Return ratios are typically used in two ways. First, return ratios are often compared over time for a given firm, where it is the trend, rather than the actual return for a particular period, that indicates performance. Second, return ratios are often compared across companies or compared to a benchmark, such as an industry average return or the return for the industry leaders.

An advantage of using return ratios in evaluating companies' performances is the ease of calculation. All information necessary for the calculation is readily available, either from financial statements or from market data. And, since the return is expressed as a percentage of the investment, its interpretation is straightforward.

An attractive feature of return ratios is the ability to decompose the return ratio to examine the source of changes in returns. For example, the Du Pont system can be used to analyze return ratios by breaking the return ratios into their activity and profit components. This allows us to further evaluate the source of the return changes from year-to-year and to evaluate differences across companies.

Return on investment measures are not good measures of performance for a number of reasons. First, the return on investment ratios are formed using financial statement data in the numerator and/or the denominator and therefore these ratios are sensitive to the choice of accounting methods. And this sensitivity to accounting methods makes it difficult to compare return ratios across companies and across time, requiring an adjustment of the accounting data to place return ratios on the same accounting basis.[6]

Second, return on investment ratios are backward-looking, not forward-looking. Though the immediate effects of current investments influence the return ratios, the expected future benefits from current period decisions are generally not incorporated in the return ratios.

A third reason for the deficiency of return-on-investment ratios is that they fail to consider risk. These ratios simply use historical financial statement data that in no way reflect the uncertainty the firm faces.

Finally, the return-on-investment ratios do not adjust for controllable versus non-controllable factors. Ideally, we would want to isolate the performance of the company from factors that are outside the control of management. Yet, the return on investment ratios simply reflect the bottom line and do not consider any other factors.

MEASURES OF VALUE-ADDED

It is difficult to measure whether a company's management has increased or decreased a company's value during a period since a company's value may be affected by many factors. Currently advocated performance measurement techniques, such as Stern Stewart's EVA® and MVA, are based on valuation principles. However, there is an important distinction between valuation and performance measurement: valuation relies on forecasts, whereas performance measurement must rely on actual results. The value-added measures described in this section are presented as they are commonly used in performance measurement.

Economic Profit

Many U.S. corporations, including Briggs and Stratton, Coca-Cola, and Harnischfeger, have embraced a method of evaluating and rewarding management performance that is based on the idea of compensating management for economic profit, rather than for its accounting profit. What is economic profit? Basically, it

---

[6] A related measurement issue is that these ratios use financial data that is an accumulation of monetary values from different time periods. For example, the gross plant account includes the cost of assets purchased at different points in time. If there is significant inflation in some of the historical periods, this results in an "apples and oranges" addition problem for most accounts that affect total assets and equity, distorting the calculated returns on investment.

is the difference between revenues and costs, where the costs include not only expenses, but also the cost of capital. And though the application of economic profit is relatively new in the measurement of performance, the concept of economic profit is not new — it was noted for example by Alfred Marshall in the nineteenth century.[7] What this recent emphasis on economic profit has done is focus attention away from accounting profit and towards the cost of capital.

The estimation of economic profit is analogous to the net present value method of evaluating investments. The net present value method, as applied in the context of evaluating performance of companies and management, was brought to prominence by G. Bennett Stewart III, in his book entitled *A Quest for Value*, which was published in 1991, and through the consulting work by Stern Stewart. Though attractive in principle, there are many pitfalls associated with its application of these valuation principles to actual companies. These pitfalls include (1) the use of accounting data to determine economic profit, and (2) the estimation of the cost of capital.[8]

The profit that is considered economic value added is not accounting profit, but rather economic profit. There are two important distinctions between accounting profit and economic profit. The first distinction deals with the cost of capital. Accounting profit is the difference between revenues and costs, based on the representation of these items according to accounting principles. Economic profit is also the difference between revenues and costs, but, unlike the determination of accounting profit, the cost of capital is included in the costs. The second distinction between accounting and economic profit deals with the principles of recognition of revenues and costs. Accounting profits, for the most part, are represented using the accrual method, whereas economic profits reflect cash-basis accounting. However, since the only data reported in financial statements is in terms of accrual accounting, analysts calculating economic profit must first start with accounting profit and then make adjustments to place the data on a cash basis.

Further adjustments must be made to accounting profits to compensate for distortions that may arise from the choice of particular accounting methods. For example, goodwill is typically amortized over forty years in the U.S., yet goodwill does not represent a cost; goodwill amortization must be added back to reported net income in calculating economic profit. Unlike accounting profit, economic profit (at least in theory) cannot be manipulated by management through the choice of accounting methods.

The cost of capital is the rate of return that is required by the suppliers of capital to the company. For a business that finances its operations or investments using both debt and equity, the cost of capital includes not only the explicit interest on the debt, but also the implicit minimum return that owners require. This minimum return to owners, also referred to as the required rate of return, is necessary so that the owners keep their investment capital in the company.

---

[7] Alfred Marshall, *Principles of Economics Volume 1* (New York: MacMillan & Co., 1890), p. 142.

[8] The cost of capital is an opportunity cost of funds, typically measured as the weighted average of the marginal costs of debt and equity capital.

Calculating Economic Profit

Economic profit is the difference between operating profits and the cost of capital, where the cost of capital is expressed in dollar terms. The application to an entire company involves, in theory, calculating the net present value of all investment projects, both those involving existing assets (that is, past investment decisions) and those projected. In application, however, the measure focuses on profit from existing assets.

Economic profit can be written as:[9]

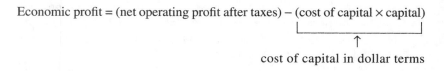

Economic profit = (net operating profit after taxes) − (cost of capital × capital)

cost of capital in dollar terms

or, equivalently, using the spread between the rate of return and the percentage cost of capital,

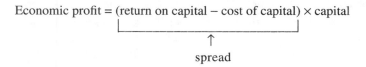

Economic profit = (return on capital − cost of capital) × capital

spread

where the return on capital is the ratio of net operating profit after taxes to capital.

Application of this formula produces an estimate of the economic profit for a single period. In evaluating a company's performance for a given period, economic profit reflects whether value is added (a positive economic profit) or reduced (a negative economic profit).

Net Operating Profit After Taxes

NOPAT, as the name implies, is operating income. But what is different from the operating income reported in financial statements is that this amount has been "cleansed" of the results of financing decisions (e.g., the financing component of operating leases) and accounting distortions. Why remove the results of financing decisions? Because the calculation of economic profit is the difference between the profit generated from the assets and the cost of capital, where the cost of capital reflects the costs of financing; failure to remove the effects of financing decisions would result in a double-counting of these elements.

Operating income *after* depreciation is used rather than the traditional cash flow measures, calculated *before* depreciation because depreciation is considered an economic expense:[10] depreciation is a measure of how much of an

---

[9] Stewart, *The Quest for Value*, p. 136.

[10] For a rigorous discussion on how to measure depreciation in an economic profit context, see Chapter 5 by Stephen F. O'Byrne.

asset is used up in the period, which gives us an idea of how much must be expended to maintain operations at the existing level.

One distortion of accounting income results from the deferral of taxes; to compensate for this, taxes are placed on a cash basis. Taxes are adjusted further to remove the effect that financing decisions may have on taxes for the period. The result of these two manipulations is cash operating taxes.

In addition to cash operating taxes, there are several adjustments intended to alter accounting profit to better reflect economic profit. However, because these adjustments involve adjusting accounting profit to arrive at economic profit, these adjustments must be tailored to the company's specific accounting practices and situation. In fact, there may be over one-hundred adjustments to accounting profit. Hence, it is not possible to develop a "cookie cutter" calculation to apply to all companies.

As shown in Chapter 2, NOPAT is calculated using one of two approaches: bottom-up or top-down. Whether you start with operating profit after depreciation (the "bottom-up" approach),

$$
\begin{aligned}
\text{NOPAT} = \ &\text{Operating profit after depreciation and amortization} \\
&+ \text{Implied interest expense on operating leases} \\
& \text{Increase in LIFO reserve} \\
+\ & \text{Goodwill amortization} \\
& \text{Increase in bad debt reserve} \\
&\text{Increase in net capitalized research and development} \\
&- \text{Cash operating taxes}
\end{aligned}
$$

or begin with sales (the "top-down" approach),

$$
\begin{aligned}
&\phantom{\text{NOPAT} = \ } \text{Increase in LIFO reserve} \\
\text{NOPAT} = \ &\text{Sales} + \text{Implied interest expense on operating leases} \\
&\phantom{\text{Sales} + } \text{Other income} \\
\\
&\phantom{\text{Sales} + } \text{Cost of goods sold} \\
&- \text{Selling, general, and administrative expenses} \\
& \text{Depreciation} \\
&- \text{Cash operating taxes}
\end{aligned}
$$

we arrive at net operating profit after taxes (NOPAT).

Let's calculate 1997 NOPAT for McDonald's Corporation to see how these adjustments are made to actual company data. Using the basic income statement data as presented as an example in Exhibit 1, balance sheet data in Exhibit 2, financial statement note information (not shown in table), and using the bottom-up approach, we begin with operating profit after depreciation and amortization (i.e., operating income) of $2,808.3 million.

Exhibit 1: McDonald's Balance Sheet

in millions	1997	1996
ASSETS		
Cash & cash equivalents	$341.4	$329.9
Accounts and notes receivable	483.5	495.4
Inventories	70.5	69.6
Prepaid expenses and other current assets	246.9	207.6
Total current assets	$1,142.3	$1,102.5
Notes receivable due after one year	$67.0	$85.3
Investments in and advances to affiliates	634.8	694.0
Intangible assets – net	827.5	747.0
Miscellaneous	608.5	405.1
Total other assets	$2,137.9	$1,931.4
Gross plant, property & equipment	$20,088.2	$19,133.9
Accumulated depreciation and amortization	(5125.8)	(4,781.8)
Net plant, property & equipment	$14,961.4	$14,352.1
Total assets	$18,241.5	$17,386.0
LIABILITIES		
Notes payable	$1,293.8	$597.8
Accounts payable	650.6	638.0
Taxes payable	52.5	22.5
Other taxes	148.5	136.7
Accrued interest	107.1	121.7
Other accrued liabilities	396.4	523.1
Long-term debt due in one year	335.6	95.5
Total current liabilities	$2,984.5	$2,135.3
Long-term debt	$4,834.1	4,830.1
Other liabilities	427.5	726.5
Deferred taxes	1,063.5	975.9
Common equity put options	80.3	0.0
SHAREHOLDERS' EQUITY		
Preferred stock	0.0	358.0
Common stock	8.3	8.3
Additional paid-in capital	699.2	574.2
Guarantee of ESOP Notes	(171.2)	(193.2)
Retained earnings	12,569.0	11,173.0
Accumulated other comprehensive income	(470.5)	(175.1)
Common stock in treasury	(3,783.1)	(3,027.0)
Total shareholders' equity	$8,851.6	$8,718.2
TOTAL LIABILITIES & EQUITY	$18,241.5	$17,386.0

Source: McDonalds' Corporation, 1997 Annual Report

Exhibit 2: McDonald's Income Statement

in millions	1997	1996
REVENUES		
Sales by Company operated restaurants	$8,136.5	$7,570.7
Revenues from franchised and affiliated restaurants	3,272.3	3,115.8
Total revenues	$11,408.8	$10.686.5
OPERATING COSTS AND EXPENSES		
Company operated restaurants	$6,649.6	$6,163.2
Franchised restaurants - occupancy expenses	613.9	570.1
Selling and general administrative expense	1,450.5	1,366.4
Other operating (income) expense - net	(113.5)	(45.8)
Total operating costs and expenses	8,600.5	8,053.9
Operating income	$2,808.3	$2,632.6
Interest expense	364.4	342.5
Non-operating income and expense	36.6	39.1
Income before provision for income taxes	$2,407.3	$2,251.0
Provision for income taxes	764.8	678.4
Net income	$1,642.5	$1,572.6

Source: McDonald's Corporation, 1997 Annual Report

Much of the information necessary to make the adjustments is available directly from the financial statements or the notes to financial statements. The only adjustment of those listed above that is applicable or practical to do in the case of McDonald's is for implied interest on operating leases, which is calculated using information on future rental commitments, as detailed in *McDonald's Corporation 1997 Annual Report*, "Leasing arrangements" note.[11] McDonald's implied interest expense on operating leases must be calculated using note information. The interest expense is estimated as the interest cost on the change in the average value of leases during the year. This requires estimating the present value of leases at the beginning and end of the year.

The present value of operating leases is determined by discounting minimum rental commitments on operating leases for the next five years. These minimum rental commitments are disclosed in a footnote to the financial statements. In the case of McDonald's, the expected future commitments beyond 1997 are as follows:

Year relative to 1997	Operating lease rental commitment
First year	$538.8
Second year	533.9
Third year	509.9
Fourth year	487.7
Fifth year	464.9
Beyond the fifth year	4,190.4

---

[11] Information on change in the goodwill amortization and bad debt reserve is not available in McDonald's financial statement, likely because these items are immaterial. Therefore, these adjustments are not made. This points to a potential problem in calculating economic profit: the information needed may not be available in published financial reports.

Using a discount rate of 7% (the approximate yield on McDonald's debt in 1997), the present value of the first five years of commitments is $2,090 million. Because financial statements provide only information on the next five years, the value of the commitments beyond the fifth year are often ignored in the determination of capital. In the case of McDonald's, this may amount to a large difference in estimated debt capital, and hence economic profit.[12] Repeating the same analysis for 1996, the present value of the operating leases is $1,950 million. The average lease value for 1997 is therefore ($2,090 + 1,950)/2 = $2,020 million. Using an interest rate of 7%, the interest on the leases is estimated to be $141.4 million. This implied interest is backed out of operating profit because it represents a financing cost that is deducted to arrive at reported operating profit.

Starting with the operating profit after depreciation and amortization from the 1997 income statement, adjusted operating profit before taxes for McDonald's is calculated as:

	Amount, in millions	
Operating profit after depreciation and amortization	$2,808.3	⇒ DEBIT
Add: Implied interest on operating leases	141.4	
Adjusted operating profit before taxes	$2,949.7	

Cash operating taxes are estimated by starting with the income tax expense and adjusting this expense for: (1) changes in deferred taxes, (2) the tax benefit from the interest deduction (for both explicit and implicit interest) to remove the tax effect of financing with debt, and (3) taxes from other non-operating income or expense and special items.[13] The change in deferred taxes is removed from the income tax expense because an increase in deferred taxes indicates that a portion of the income tax expense that is deferred is not a cash outlay for the period, and a decrease in deferred taxes indicates that the income taxes expense understates the true cash expense.

The tax benefit from interest is added back to taxes so that the cash taxes reflect the taxes from operations; this gross-up of taxes isolates the taxes from any direct effects of financing decisions. This tax benefit is the reduction of taxes from the deductibility of interest expense:

$$\text{Tax benefit from interest} = \text{interest expense} \times \text{marginal tax rate}$$

The taxes from other non-operating income and special items (e.g., sales of investment interest) are also removed so that the cash taxes reflect solely those taxes related to operations.

---

[12] If McDonald's rental commitments beyond the fifth year are, say $400 million per year, the difference in estimated debt capital (using a 7% discount rate) is over $4,000 million: discount the $400 per year as a perpetuity to the end of the fifth year ($400/0.07 = $5,714), and then discount this amount back five years (present value = $4,074 million).

[13] The adjustment for the taxes on other non-operating income is suggested by Copeland, Koller, and Murrin in *Valuation: Measuring and Managing the Value of Companies*, though the amount is typically small.

Let's look at an example using the McDonald's 1997 financial data. First, we calculate cash taxes, using a marginal tax rate of 35%:

	Amount in millions	Source of information
Income tax expense	$764.8	Income statement
Subtract: Increase in deferred taxes	(87.6)	Difference between deferred taxes on balance sheets for 1997 and 1996: [$1,063.5 − 975.9 = $87.6]
Add: Tax benefit from interest expense	127.5	Interest expense from income statement, times the marginal tax rate [$364.4 × 0.35 = $127.5]
Add: Tax benefit from interest on leases	49.5	Implied interest from footnote information, times marginal tax rate [$141.4 × 0.35 = $49.5]
Add: Taxes on non-operating expense	12.8	Non-operating income from income statement, times marginal tax rate [$36.6 × 0.35 = $12.8]
Cash operating taxes	$867.0	

Subtracting cash operating taxes from the adjusted operating profit produces net operating profit after taxes (NOPAT):

	Amount, in millions
Adjusted operating profit before taxes	$2,949.7
Less: Cash operating taxes	(867.0)
Net operating profit after taxes	$2,082.7

This approach to calculating NOPAT is a "bottom-up" approach since it starts with operating profit after depreciation and amortization and builds to NOPAT. Another approach is a "top-down" approach, where we start with sales and adjust to arrive at NOPAT. In the case of McDonald's for 1997,

	Amount in millions	Source of information
Revenues	$11,408.8	Income statement
Less: Costs and expenses	(7,263.5)	Income statement (costs and expenses of company operated restaurants and franchised restaurants)
Less: Selling, general & administrative expenses	(1,450.5)	Income statement
Add: Other operating income	113.5	Income statement
Add: Implied interest on operating leases	141.4	Calculated from "Leasing arrangements" note
Adjusted operating profit before taxes	$2949.7	
Less: Cash operating taxes	(867.0)	(see previous calculation)
NOPAT	$2,082.7	

Whether we use the top-down approach or the bottom-up approach, we can arrive at the NOPAT of $2,082.7 million.

Capital

Capital is defined in this context as the sum of net working capital, net property and equipment, goodwill, and other assets. Another way of looking at capital is that it is the sum of the long-term sources of financing, both debt and equity.

Several adjustments to reported accounts are made to correct for possible distortions arising from accounting methods. For example, inventory is adjusted for any LIFO reserve, the present value of operating leases are included, and accumulated goodwill amortization is added to capital. One approach to estimating capital is the asset approach:[14] begin with net operating assets and then making adjustments to reflect total invested capital. For example,

$$\text{Capital} = \text{Net operating assets} + \begin{array}{l} \text{LIFO reserve} \\ \text{Net plant and equipment} \\ \text{Other assets} \\ \text{Goodwill} \\ \text{Accumulated goodwill amortization} \\ \text{Present value of operating leases} \\ \text{Bad debt reserve} \\ \text{Capitalized research and development} \\ \text{Cumulative write-offs of special items} \end{array}$$

For example, it can be argued that goodwill generated from paying more for acquiring a company than its assets' book value is an investment; therefore, both goodwill and prior periods' amortization of goodwill are added to reflect the company's asset investment. Another approach, the source of financing approach, begins with the book value of common equity and adds debt, equity equivalents and debt equivalents:

$$\text{Capital} = \text{Book value of common equity}$$

$$+ \begin{array}{l} \text{Preferred stock} \\ \text{Minority interest} \\ \text{Deferred income tax reserve} \\ \text{LIFO reserve} \\ \text{Accumulated goodwill amortization} \end{array}$$

$$+ \begin{array}{l} \text{Interest-bearing short-term debt} \\ \text{Long-term debt} \\ \text{Capitalized lease obligations} \\ \text{Present value of operating leases} \end{array}$$

Perusal of the footnotes for the financial statements is necessary to arrive at these adjustments and the calculation of capital should, ideally, be tailored to reflect each company's financial accounting. You will also notice that the adjustments made to arrive at NOPAT have companion adjustments to arrive at capital. And, as with the NOPAT calculations, we can arrive at capital by starting at either of two points: total assets (the asset approach) or book value of equity (sources of financing approach).

---

[14] Recall the Stern Stewart approach to measuring capital that was noted in Chapter 3.

Continuing our example using McDonald's, capital calculated using the asset approach is:[15],[16]

	Amount (in millions)	Source of information
Begin with net operating assets	$(105.7)	Current assets, less accounts payable, taxes payable, and accrued expenses, all from the balance sheet
Add: Net plant, property, and equipment	14,961.4	Balance sheet
Add: Other assets	1,310.3	Balance sheet
Add: Intangibles	827.5	Balance sheet (assumption: all intangibles represent goodwill)
Add: Present value of operating leases	2,090.0	Implied from data in note
Capital	$19,083.5	

Alternatively, starting with the book value of equity,

	Amount (in millions)	Source of information
Begin with Book value of equity	$8,851.6	Balance sheet
Add: Common equity in put options	80.3	Balance sheet
Add: Deferred income taxes	1,063.5	Balance sheet
Total equity and equity equivalents	$9,995.4	
Add: Book value of long-term debt	$5,169.7	Current and long-term portions of debt from balance sheet
Add: Accrued interest	107.1	Balance sheet
Add: Interest-bearing short-term debt	1,293.8	Notes payable from balance sheet
Add: Present value of operating leases	2,090.0	Calculated from note data
Add: Other liabilities	427.5	Balance sheet
Total debt and debt equivalents	$9088.1	
Capital	$19,083.5	

Some consultants make a further distinction between invested capital (as described above) and operating capital.[17] *Operating capital* is invested capital less goodwill and excess cash and marketable securities; in other words, operating

---

[15] Information on bad-debt reserve, capitalized research and development, and cumulative write-offs was not available in the financial statements. The extent to which these omissions affect the resultant economic value-added measure is unknown, but these items are also omitted in published examples of economic value added due to unavailability of the data [see, for example, the explanations accompanying the Wal-Mart example in Stewart, *The Quest for Value*, p. 99.

[16] Operating current assets include cash, marketable securities, receivables, inventories, and other current assets; for McDonald's in 1997, these amount to $1,142.3. Net operating assets are operating current assets less accounts payable [$650.6], taxes payable [$201.0], and accrued expenses [$396.4], $1,142.3 − 1,248.0 = $(105.7).

[17] See, for example, Copeland, Koller and Murrin, *Valuation: Measuring and Managing the Value of Companies.*

capital the amount of the investment employed in operations. Goodwill is removed as capital because it tends to be distorted by premiums paid in acquiring other companies. Excess cash and marketable securities are those in excess of the typical need for cash and marketable securities. Copeland, Koller and Murrin estimate that the need for cash and marketable securities is between 0.5% and 2% of sales, varying by industry.[18] In 1997, cash and marketable securities were \$341.4 million for McDonald's, or approximately 3% of revenues. Therefore, no adjustment for excess cash and marketable securities is made. Goodwill for McDonald's in 1997 is \$827.5 million and accumulated goodwill amortization is not determinable from published financial statements. Removing goodwill from invested capital produces operating capital of \$18,256million.

Return on Capital

The *return on capital*, also known as the *return on invested capital* or *ROIC*, is operating income after taxes, divided by capital. This measure is a return on investment measure, using NOPAT instead of accounting profit:

$$\text{Return on capital} = \frac{\text{Net operating profit after taxes}}{\text{Capital}}$$

The return on capital for McDonald's is the ratio of the NOPAT to invested capital, or:

$$\text{McDonald's return on capital} = \frac{\$2,082.7 \text{ million}}{\$19,083.5 \text{ million}} = 10.914\%$$

The return on *operating* capital for McDonald's is,

$$\text{McDonald's return on operating capital} = \frac{\$2,082.7 \text{ million}}{\$18,256 \text{ million}} = 11.408\%$$

Which return measure is best to use in evaluating McDonald's? It depends on whether you are focusing on (1) McDonald's ability to profitably and efficiently use investors' funds (including funds used to acquire other companies at a premium), which requires use of the former measure, or (2) McDonald's ability to profitably and efficiently use its operating assets (allowing better comparability across companies in the same industry), which requires the use of the latter measure.

Cost of Capital

The cost of capital is the cost of raising additional funds from debt and equity sources. For each source, there is a cost. Once the cost of each source of capital is determined, the cost of capital for the company is calculated as a weighted average of each cost, where the weight represents the proportionate use of each source.

[18] Copeland, Koller and Murrin, *Valuation: Measuring and Managing the Value of Companies*, pp. 160-161. The economic profit treatment of "excess cash" is also discussed in Chapter 6 by Jason L. Wolin and Steven Klopukh.

The cost of debt is the after-tax cost of debt, r_d^*, adjusted for the benefit from the tax-deductibility of interest:

$$r_d^* = r_d \times (1 - \text{marginal corporate tax rate})$$

where the before tax rate, r_d, is the prevailing yield on long-term bonds of companies with similar credit risk. For example, in 1997, bonds of similar risk to McDonald's yielded approximately 7%. Using the marginal tax rate of 35%, the after-tax cost of debt for McDonald's is:

$$r_d^* = 0.07 \times (1 - 0.35) = 4.55\%$$

The cost of equity capital is the sum of the risk-free rate of interest and the risk premium,

$$r_e = r_f + \beta(r_m - r_f)$$

where r_f is the risk-free rate of interest, r_m is the expected return on the market, and β is the capital asset pricing model beta.

This calculation is not as straightforward as it looks. One issue is the appropriate proxy for the risk-free rate. The risk-free rate of interest should, theoretically, be the return on a zero-beta portfolio that has a duration similar to the holding period of the investor. Because this estimation task is extremely difficult, an alternative is to proxy the risk-free rate using rates on securities with no default risk; that is, U. S. government debt. However, if a government obligation with a short duration is used, such as a Treasury Bill, there is a mismatch of the duration between the Treasury Bill and the risk-free portfolio. A more suitable proxy would be a 10-year government bond, because this most likely matches the duration of the market portfolio.[19]

Another issue is the premium for market risk, $(r_m - r_f)$. For example, G. Bennett Stewart (1991) advocates a 6% market risk premium, based on the historical spread between the return on the market and the return on long-term government bonds, whereas Copeland, Koller and Murrin (1994) advocate the use of the difference between the geometric mean return on the market and that of the long-term government bonds, both calculated over a long time frame. The estimates using 1926-1993 data produce a market risk premium of 5%.[20]

The market risk premium is tailored to the company's specific risk premium by multiplying the market risk premium by the firm's common stock beta,

---

[19] See Chapter 8 in Copeland, Koller, and Murrin, *Valuation: Measuring and Managing the Value of Companies* for a discussion of the comparability of durations. Stewart in *The Quest for Value* specifies that this rate should be the rate on a long-term government bond. Copeland, Koller and Murrin are more specific, advocating the rate on a 10-year U.S. Treasury bond. Using the latter approach, the risk-free rate for 1993 is 5.87%.

[20] See Copeland, Koller, and Murrin, *Valuation: Measuring and Managing the Value of Companies*, pp. 260-261.

β. The beta is a measure of the sensitivity of the returns on the firm's stock to changes in the returns on the market and are readily available from financial services such as BARRA, Standard and Poor's Compustat, or the Value Line *Investment Survey*. We will use an estimate for McDonald's beta of 0.90.[21] Using the 10-year Treasury bond rate, a market risk premium of 5% and a beta of 0.9, McDonald's cost of equity is:

$$r_e = 0.06 + 0.9(0.05) = 10.5\%$$

Using a market risk premium of 6% produces a higher cost of capital, 11.4%.

In sum, the cost of capital of McDonald's is comprised of the cost of debt of 4.55% and the cost of equity of 10.5% (or 11.4%, using an alternative risk premium). The costs of debt and equity are weighted using the proportions each represents in the capital structure to arrive at a cost of capital for the firm.

The first step in the calculation of the weighted average cost of capital is to determine the values of debt and equity that we can use as weights. The book value weights can be determined from the debt and equity book values that we determined in the calculation of capital. The estimation of the market value of the capital components requires estimating the market value of both debt and equity. McDonald's capital structure at the end of 1997 consists of:[22]

Capital	Book value in millions	Book value proportions	Market value in millions	Market value proportions
Debt capital	$9,088.1	47.6%	$9,088.1	18.6%
Equity capital	9,995.4	52.4%	39,646.8	81.4%
Total	$19,083.5	100.0%	$48,734.9	100.0%

McDonald's capital structure at the end of 1996 (and the beginning of 1997) consists of:

Capital	Book value in millions	Book value proportions	Market value in millions	Market value proportions
Debt capital	$8,321.6	46.2%	$8,321.6	18.0%
Equity capital	9,694.1	53.8%	38,032.9	82.0%
Total	$18,015.7	100.0%	$46,354.5	100.0%

Additions and subtractions to debt and equity capital are made throughout the year. Because of this and the lack of specific data on changes in capital, we can approximate the capital proportions by averaging the beginning and ending capital proportions for the year. Using book values, this gives us approximately 47% debt and 53% equity. The weighted average cost of capital using the book weights and a 10.5% cost of equity, is:

---

[21] The beta of 0.9 is taken from *Value Line Investment Survey*.

[22] In addition to estimating the company's most recent market value capital components, it is useful to look at the capital structure of other companies in the industry and to consider the trends in the company's capital structure over time, since the capital structure of a company at a point in time may not reflect the company's target capital structure.

Cost of capital = $[0.47(0.0455)] + [0.53(0.105)] = 0.077$ or 7.7%

Using market value weights, the cost of capital is greater since approximately 82% of its capital is equity:

Cost of capital = $[0.18(0.0455)] + [0.82(0.105)] = 0.094$ or 9.4%

Using the higher cost of equity estimate of 11.4%, the costs of capital are 8.2% and 10.2%, respectively.

Which do we use, 7.7%, 9.4%, 8.2%, or 10.2%? In most applications, we choose the method that better reflects the marginal cost of funds. If the company raises an additional dollar of capital, in what proportion does it raise these funds? We usually think of this in terms of the market value proportions, using the 9.4% or the 10.2% cost of capital. But in this particular application, we are applying this cost of capital against the estimated invested capital, which is most often stated in terms of book values. Mixing a market-value determined cost of capital with book values of invested capital results in distortions; the extent of the distortion depends on the relation between the market value of capital and the book value of capital.[23]

Pitfalls in Estimating Economic Profit

Economic profit is the profit generated during the period in excess of what is required by investors for the level of risk associated with the firm's investments. Economic profit is analogous to the net present value of capital budgeting, and represents the value-added by the firm's management during the period. Even advocates of economic profit do not prescribe a particular formula for calculating economic profit Economic profit has ambiguous elements, most notably the adjustments to operating income and the cost of capital.[24] Conceivably, two analysts could calculate economic profit, yet draw different conclusions regarding companies' relative performance.

The calculation of operating income (i.e., NOPAT) requires that each company be treated as an individual case. The adjustments to arrive at operating profits after taxes are different for each company and there may be over 150 adjustments. This makes it difficult to apply from the perspective of the financial analyst who must rely on financial statements and other publicly available information to determine economic profit. Though a formula could be developed to deal with the most common adjustments, there are always exceptions to the general rules.[25]

---

[23] For a given company, the cost of debt is less than the cost of equity. Therefore, if book values are used to determine the weights — as is most often the case in applications of these metrics — the cost of capital for companies with high financial leverage is biased low, making the cost of capital an easier hurdle to overcome.

[24] This is not the fault of economic profit, per se, but rather the starting point of the calculations: reported financial statements prepared according to generally accepted accounting principles.

[25] This is the dilemma that plagues accounting principles — developing one set of principles to apply to many companies is challenging and can result in distortions of what you set out to measure.

Consider the issue of operating leases mentioned earlier. In the case of McDonald's, the inclusion or exclusion of operating leases beyond the fifth year makes a difference of over $4 billion in the estimated capital and, hence, affects the estimate of economic profit. Unfortunately, trying to undo the distortions due to a complex set of accounting principles can result in a complex set of adjustments. Accompanying this complexity is the possibility of manipulation because the selection of the adjustments can and does affect the economic profit outcome (which may then affect management compensation based on that profit outcome).

Another source of differences is the estimation of the cost of capital. Consider the sensitivity of economic profit to the estimate of the cost of capital. Continuing the example of McDonald's, suppose we assume that its cost of capital is 8%. Using the two, equivalent economic profit calculations, we see that McDonald's management generated an economic profit in 1997:

$$\begin{aligned}
\text{McDonald's economic profit} &= \text{(net operating profit after taxes)} \\
&\quad - \text{(cost of capital} \times \text{capital)} \\
&= \$2,082.7 \text{ million} - (0.08 \times \$19,083.5 \text{ million}) \\
&= \$2,082.7 \text{ million} - \$1,526.7 \text{ million} \\
&= \$556 \text{ million}
\end{aligned}$$

or,

$$\begin{aligned}
\text{McDonald's economic profit} &= \text{(rate of return} - \text{cost of capital)} \times \text{capital} \\
&= (0.10914 - 0.08) \times \$19,083.5 \text{ million} \\
&= \$556 \text{ million}
\end{aligned}$$

McDonald's earned an economic profit of $556 million in 1997. In other words, McDonald's management added value during 1997.

Looking at a range of cost of capital, plus and minus 100 basis points, gives an idea of the sensitivity of the estimate of the economic profit to the cost of capital:[26]

McDonald's economic profit if the cost of capital is 10%
= $2,082.7 − 1,908.4 = $174.3 million

McDonald's economic profit if the cost of capital is 6%
= $2,082.7 − 1,145.0 = $937.7 million

Consequently, drawing a conclusion regarding the degree of profitability depends, in part, on the estimated cost of capital.

Extending outside of the McDonald's example, consider an example using Stern Stewart's own numbers. If we estimate the cost of capital for Hewlett-Packard is 15% (per Stern Stewart), the economic value added for 1997 is $152 million.[27] On the other hand, if we estimate the cost of capital as, say, 16%, there

---

[26] A detailed assessment of the impact of cost of capital variation on economic profit and corporate value is shown in Chapter 2 by Frank J. Fabozzi and James L. Grant.

[27] The figures are derived from the data provided by Shawn Tully, "America's Greatest Wealth Creators," *Fortune* (November 9, 1998), p. 196.

is an economic loss of $113 million for the year. The slight change in the cost of capital estimate changes the estimated value-added by $265 million — and Hewlett-Packard goes from a value-adding to a value-destroying company. A slight difference in the estimate of the cost of capital can change our view of the company's performance from value-destroying to value-enhancing.

We know from the many years of experience in using the cost of capital in other applications, such as rate regulation, that the estimation of the cost of capital is imprecise and difficult.[28] Consider some of the many ambiguities regarding the measurement of the cost of capital. One issue is determining the best model for the estimate of the cost of equity. Should the analyst use the capital asset pricing model or the dividend valuation model?[29] Suppose the analyst uses the capital asset pricing model, which requires specifying a market risk premium (that is, the additional required return for bearing market risk). Should the market risk premium be 5%? 6%?[30] In some cases the choice matters, making the difference between a value-adding company and a value-destroying company. Another issue is the choice of weights to apply to the difference costs of capital. Though market weights are theoretically appealing, many apply weights based on book values. Whether these issues affect the assessment of performance and relative performance is, of course, an empirical issue.

Is it realistic that large difference can exist in the estimate of the economic profit? Consider Coca-Cola, who reports economic profit in its financial statements and which is an often-cited example of a company that uses economic value added. Displayed in Exhibit 3 are the economic profit amounts for 1992 through 1997 as reported by the company and as reported in the *Stern Stewart 1000*. The difference between the two measures of economic profit is actually widening over time. Consider another example: Monsanto reported an economic profit of $231 million for fiscal year 1997, whereas Stern Stewart reported an economic loss for Monsanto of $239 million for the same year.[31,32]

Market Value-Added

A measure closely related to economic profit is market valued added. Market value added is the difference between the firm's market value and its capital. Essentially, market value added is a measure of what the company's management has been able to do with a given level of resources (i.e., the invested capital):

---

[28] See, for example, Eugene F. Fama and Kenneth R. French, "Industry Costs of Equity," *Journal of Financial Economics* (February 1997), pp. 153-193.

[29] Most applications of economic profit use a CAPM-based cost of equity. The CAPM has been challenged as inadequately capturing the risk and return relationship. See, for example, Eugene F. Fama and Kenneth R. French, "The Cross Section of Expected Stock Returns," *Journal of Finance* (June 1992).

[30] Particular to the applications prescribed by Stewart in *The Quest for Value*, a risk premium of 6% is used, which contrasts with the lower risk premium of 5% used by Copeland, Koller, and Murrin in *Valuation: Measuring and Managing the Value of Companies*.

[31] This is calculated by taking the difference in the cumulative economic profit for 1997 of $273 million and the cumulative economic profit for 1996 of $42 million, using data reported by Monsanto, http://www.monsanto.com.

[32] Tully, "America's Greatest Wealth Creators," p. 198.

Exhibit 3: Comparison of Reported Economic Profit for Coca-Cola, 1992-1997

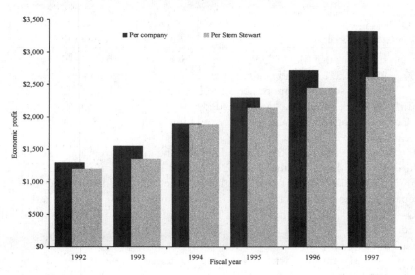

Sources of information:
"Per company" data are taken from published annual reports of Coca-Cola. "Per Stern Stewart" data are taken from the Stern Stewart 1000, various years, as reported in *Forbes*.

Market value-added = (Market value of the firm) – Capital

Like economic profit, market value-added is in terms of dollars and the goal of the company is to increase added value. Being top of the list of companies ranked on the basis of market value added does not mean that the company has outperformed other companies. It merely means that the company has the greatest difference between its book and market values of capital — accumulated over time. Rather, performance is evaluated by looking at the *change* in market value-added over a period. The change in the market value added is a measure of how effectively the firm's management employs capital to enhance the value of capital to *all* suppliers of capital, not just common shareholders.[33] The change in market value added is the change in the market value of capital (debt and equity), less the change in the book value of capital. Looking once again at McDonald's, we see the following for 1997 and 1996:

---

[33] A related issue is whether the company's management should be striving to maximize the value of the company or to maximize the value of shareholders' equity. The market value added measure focuses on the former, whereas more common measures, such as stock returns, focus on the latter. In general, maximizing the value of the company results in the maximization of shareholders' equity.

McDonald's Capital	1997 (in millions)	1996 (in millions)	Change from 1996 to 1997 (in millions)
Market value of equity, plus market value of debt	$48,734.9	$46.354.5	$2,380.4
Less: Invested capital	19,083.5	18,015.7	1,067.8
Market value-added	$29,651.4	$28,338.8	$1,312.6

This analysis tells us that McDonald's management has increased the market value added in 1997, adding $1,312.6 million more in market value in excess of invested capital.

We can see the importance of focusing on the change in market value added if we break the market value added into the layers as it is earned through time. Consider Coca-Cola, which has ranked high in the Stern Stewart Performance 1000 each year over the past few years. Breaking Coca Cola's market value added into the previous year's market value added and the current year's market value, as shown in Exhibit 4, we see that Coca Cola added little market value in 1993, even though it was ranked as the second highest market value added in that years. This discrepancy is due to the fact that ranking companies on the basis of market value added — which is the accumulation of market value added for the company since its incorporation — does not reflect the current period's performance. For example, Comcast added $3,349 million to its market value during 1993 using invested capital of only $3,918 million, whereas Coca-Cola added $1,996 million during 1993 using invested capital of $6,871 million. However, Coca-Cola ranks higher in the Performance 1000 (rank of 2 versus Comcast's rank of 54) because its *accumulated* market value added is much higher. This example points out the need to focus on the changes in market value added over a period and the amount of invested capital.

Exhibit 4: Coca-Cola's Market Value Added Breakdown, 1988-1997

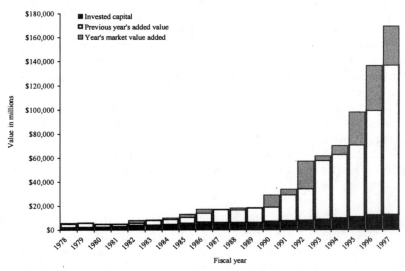

Source: Calculations from data provided in Coca-Cola's 10-K and annual reports

It is often the case in application that the book value of debt and the book value of preferred stock are used in estimating both the market value of capital and the book value of capital.[34] Therefore, the change in market value added from one year to the next amounts to the change in the market value of common equity, plus the change in the *book value* of debt and preferred stock. Because of this measurement of market value added, the change in market value added is determined, in large part, by the change in the market value of the common stock's price. Therefore, the change in market value is affected by the change in the value of the market in general.

Reconciling Economic Value-Added with Market Value-Added

As we have seen, there are two different value-added measures: economic value added (economic profit) and market value added. Economic value added is based on the adjusted operating earnings (after taxes), invested capital, and the firm's weighted average cost of capital. Market value added is based on a comparison of invested capital with the market value of capital. These two measures are both designed to help evaluate the performance of a firm.

There is a logical link, however, between market value-added and economic profit. The market value-added should be equal to the present value of future periods' economic profit, discounted at the cost of capital. If we assume that the company will generate future-period economic profit equivalent to this period's economic profit, in perpetuity, the relation between market value and economic profit is a simple one:

$$\text{Market value-added} = \frac{\text{Economic profit}}{\text{Cost of capital}}$$

Yet, the perpetuity assumption is not valid for most companies because of a very basic notion: economic profits are generated only when a company has some comparative or competitive advantage.[35] Most companies cannot maintain these advantages for long periods of time; for example, government regulations may change, patents are not perpetual, and demographics change, all of which can erode a firm's advantage and, hence, its economic profit. Therefore, the assumption of a perpetual stream of the current period's economic profit is not reasonable in most cases.

Another reason why this relation does not hold in application is that the methods of determining economic profit and market value added are quite different. Economic profit is a single-period measure, estimated using accounting data and an estimate of the cost of capital. Market value added employs market values, which are more forward-looking estimates of performance.

Still another reason why this relation does not hold true is that the estimates of economic profit are just that — estimates. Economic profit is estimated by starting with accounting data and making adjustments to better reflect eco-

---

[34] See, for example, Stewart, *The Quest for Value*, pp. 153-154.

[35] For pricing insight on variable growth economic profit models, see Chapters 2 and 5 of this book.

nomic reality. However careful an analyst is in adjusting the accounting data, the estimated economic profit cannot precisely reflect true economic profit.

Economic profit and market value-added may result in conflicting evaluations of performance. For example, in *The 1998 Stern Stewart Performance 1000*, Exxon is ranked 7th among 1,000 companies by Stern Stewart in terms of its market value-added (of $85.6 billion), implying that Exxon is one of the best companies in terms of providing value to its shareholders. But Exxon has a negative economic profit (of $412 million), which implies the firm's management is losing value. This apparent contradiction between economic profit and market value-added may be due to the fact that economic profit, while theoretically forward-looking, is based on historical, single-period accounting data, whereas market value added is based on forward-looking stock prices.[36,37]

But Do Value Added Measures Add Value?

Whether the value-added measures aid the financial analyst in assessing the operating performance and financial condition of a company is really an empirical issue. What we know from an analysis of the economic profit (a.k.a. economic value added) is that it has a solid foundation in economic and financial theory. Using economic profit instead of accounting earnings is attractive because it avoids the problems associated with accounting earnings — at least in theory.

Are companies that generate more economic profit than others better companies? Not necessarily. First, economic profit is a single period measure, estimated using the current period's financial information. Just like a return on investment ratio based on accounting numbers, focusing on economic profit is short-sighted. It may be the case, for example, that the company is sacrificing future profitability to generate current period economic profit. Second, economic profit is calculated using the company's cost of capital as the "hurdle." But if the company has taken on activities that are riskier than the company's typical activities, the calculation of the cost of capital and economic profit may not reflect this increased risk-taking, resulting in an over-statement of current profitability. Third, the estimates of NOPAT and the cost of capital are just that — estimates. Even slight variations in the assumptions and estimates can result in dramatic changes in measured profitability. Fourth, economic profit is generally stated in dollar terms, but this is misleading when comparing companies of different sizes. According to the *1997 Stern Stewart Performance 1000* rankings, Gillette generated $447 million of economic value added, whereas GTE generated $448.[38] So which one performed better? Comparing economic value added, GTE appears to be approximately the same as Gillette, but once you look at the amount of invested capital (that is, what they invested to generate

---

[36] As previously shown, slight differences in the estimated cost of capital can result in quite different conclusions regarding economic profit and, hence, performance.

[37] As you can see, this equation is nonsensical in the case in which there is an economic loss and a positive market value-added.

[38] Richard Teitelbaum, "America's Greatest Wealth Creators," *Fortune* (November 10, 1997), pp. 265-276.

that economic profit), you get a different picture: Gillette's invested capital is $9,042 million, whereas GTE invested over 4 times the capital, or $41,071.

So if there are so many problems associated with measuring economic profit, what good is it? Well, in theory economic profit is a measure of a company's performance over a period of time. If we can overcome the measurement issues, we have a measure that is superior to accounting income. And if measured in a consistent manner across companies or across time it can be used to compare performance.

Further, in theory economic profit is related to market value added: market value added is the present value of future periods' economic profit. If investors' valuation of future economic profit is market value added and if current and recent periods' economic profit are predictors of future economic profit, then we can use economic profit in assessing the value of a share of stock. This suggests that trends in economic profit suggest future value changes. For example, continued improvements in economic profit suggests that value is being added and we should see an increase in market value added. Coca-Cola is a case in point, where economic profit has increased each year during the past ten years and market value added has increased. In a similar vein, if economic profit is declining, we should see a decline in market value added; a case in point is AT&T, which has had negative economic profit for each of the years 1992-1997 and its market value added increased through 1996 to over $40 billion (rank = 7) and then plunged in 1996 to less than $8 billion (rank = 79). But then, how do we explain the increase in 1997 to more than $35 billion (rank = 29)?[39]

Economic profit failed to predict the destruction in value during 1998 as the markets turned down and market value added declined along with stock prices. During the first nine months of 1998, Coca-Cola lost 11.6% of its common stock's value; this decline in value follows years of value added performance in terms of both economic profit, market value added, and changes in market value added. And that is one of the problems with value added measures as a measure of performance: these measures do not control for uncontrollable factors (e.g., the Asian economic crisis and its effects).

So if use of single-year economic profit figures is flawed, what about multiple years or momentum? Using a strategy based on economic profit momentum or multiple-year economic profit is difficult because it is not clear — either from theory or from the empirical evidence — how many years comprise a momentum: 3? 4? Examples can be found that support and dispute any length of time chosen for momentum.

Suppose that we focus on market value added. Is this a better measure of the performance of a company than, say, stock returns? Going back to the definition of market value added, we see that a company increases its market value when the change in the market value of its capital (that is, the market value of its debt and equity) exceeds the change in its invested capital (that is, book value of its debt and equity). Because most of the measures of market value added use the

---

[39] See Laura Walbert, "American's Best Wealth Creators," *Fortune* (December 27, 1993), pp. 64-76 and Shawn Tully, "America's Best Wealth Creators," *Fortune* (November 28, 1994), pp. 143-162.

market value of equity and assume that the market value of debt is equal to the book value of debt, the change in the market value added is really attributed to the change in the stock's price. Therefore it should be no surprise that the change in the market value added is highly correlated with a company's stock's return and, hence, provides similar measurement of performance.

The Evidence

The key to understanding a performance metric is to see how well it performs in rigorous testing. Are the companies that add value (per the value-added metric) also the companies that benefit shareholders the most? The answer is empirical. Whereas there is a great deal of anecdotal evidence that touts the success of metrics, much of this is provided by consulting firms. There has been very limited independent testing of these metrics.

It is possible to cite successful companies that use economic value added metrics, including Coca-Cola, Sprint, Briggs and Stratton, and Eli Lilly. But it is also possible to cite companies that use or have used these measures without as much success, including Harnischfeger Industries, Quaker Oats, and Whirlpool, and to cite companies that have stopped using value added metrics, including AT&T and Georgia Pacific. Further, it is difficult to separate the factors that are really driving a company's success. For example, Coca-Cola uses economic profit and unit sales for performance measurement. What is to say that their added value is driven by applying economic value added principles?

In a study of both adopters and non-adopters of economic value added measures, Wallace found no difference in subsequent stock performance between adopters versus non-adopters.[40] He also observed that adopters tended to repurchase shares more frequently and decrease new investment. An explanation for these practices is that users of value-added measures have learned to play games: for example, repurchasing shares reduces capital, hence increasing market value added.

In a study funded by the AIMR Research Foundation, David Peterson and I show that value-added metrics do not outperform traditional measures.[41] We looked at companies over the period 1988 through 1992, examining over 250 companies in each year and comparing value-added metrics with both traditional accounting measures and shareholder returns.

Value-added measures are theoretically more closely related to a company's value than the simpler, traditional measures such as return on assets. Empirically, however, both traditional and value-added measures of performance are highly correlated with stock returns, with value-added measures having slight edge over the traditional measures. The commonly-used value added measures, economic profit and market value added, are only slightly more correlated with stock returns than the traditional measures and thus may not be better gauges of performance than traditional measures.

---

[40] James C. Wallace, "Adopting Residual Income-Based Compensation Plans. Do You Get What You Pay For?" *Journal of Accounting and Economics* (December 1997), pp. 275-300.

[41] Peterson and Peterson, *Company Performance and Measures of Performance.*

Exhibit 5: Coca-Cola's Net Income, Free Cash Flow, Economic Profit, and Cash Flow from Operations, 1988-1997

Source: Coca-Cola Company 1997 and 1994 10-K reports.

Further, we altered the value-added measures to reduce the effects of a potential size bias that results because economic profit and market value added are in dollars terms. These enhancements improve the value-added measures somewhat and make them slightly more attractive for performance evaluation than the traditional measures. But because we stacked the deck against the traditional measures in the empirical analysis by using the most naive form of the traditional measures, it is disappointing that the more recently developed measures do not dominate the traditional measures. These findings are supported by other, recent research by academics.[42]

How can it be that these measures that are theoretically more palatable are not necessarily better performance measures? Consider the case of Coca-Cola's economic profit versus other measures of the company's performance over a period: net income, cash flow from operations, and free cash flow. As you can see in Exhibit 5, these measures follow the same general upward trend. The most variable of the measures is free cash flow. This variability is understandable because free cash flow is the firm's cash flow after capital expenditures, which may vary widely from period to period. Because these measures of performance give the same general trend, the use of these in return measures (e.g., return on assets, return on invested capital, return on equity) should result in similar conclusions regarding performance.

[42] See, for example, Jeffrey M. Bacidore, John A. Boquist, Todd T. Milbourn, and Anjan V. Thakor, "The Search for the Best Financial Performance Measure," *Financial Analysts Journal* (May/June 1997), pp. 11-20 and Shimin Chen and James L. Dodd, "Usefulness of Accounting Earnings, Residual Income, and EVA®: A Value-Relevance Perspective," working paper, Drake University, 1997.

Exhibit 6: Correlation Among Performance Measures, 1996

	Return on the common stock	Economic profit	Market value added	Return on assets: basic earning power	Return on assets	Market value of common stock
Return on the common stock	1.000	0.259*	0.221*	0.315*	0.353*	0.122
Economic profit		1.000	0.566*	0.397*	0.460*	0.359*
Market value added			1.000	0.364*	0.459*	0.900*
Return on assets: basic earning power				1.000	0.872*	0.234*
Return on assets					1.000	0.347*
Market value of common stock						1.000

* indicates that the correlation coefficient is different from zero at a 5% level of significance.
Source: Pamela P. Peterson, "Value-Added Measures of Performance," working paper, 1998.

Though the performance measures are similar for Coca-Cola, is this true across many companies? Biddle, Bowen, and Wallace examined whether economic profit provides any information in addition to that provided by accounting profit.[43] They found that earnings before extraordinary items and residual income each explained more of stock returns than did economic profit.

To see the close relation among these measures, consider the correlation matrix for different measures of performance shown in Exhibit 6.[44] The sample of companies is from the 200 largest companies listed in the 1997 Stern Stewart Performance 1000 (which is based on data from 1996) and the value-based measures are produced by Stern Stewart.[45] As you can see in this exhibit, there is a strong correlation between each measure and the return on the common stock, as well as a strong correlation among the value-added and traditional measures. As shown in Peterson and Peterson using a much larger sample and several years, the measures that correlate most strongly with stock returns are the traditional measures in some years and the value-added measures in other years.

Correlations of measures with stock returns may be misleading, however, because as you see in this last exhibit all accounting-based measures are correlated with stock returns. The key is how these measures relate to *future* risk-adjusted performance. David Peterson and I examined raw returns, risk and market adjusted returns, and size-adjusted returns and examined the relation between value-added measures and subsequent returns — all with similar results: neither economic profit nor market value added led to superior future risk-adjusted stock

---

[43] Gary C. Biddle, Robert M. Bowen, and James S. Wallace, "Does EVA® Beat Earnings? Evidence on Associations with Stock Returns and Firm Values," *Journal of Accounting and Economics* (December 1997), pp. 301-336.

[44] The correlation matrix is comprised of pair-wise correlation coefficients, which are a statistical measure of the degree to which the two variables in the pair are related; correlation coefficients range from −1 (perfect negative correlation) to +1 (perfect positive correlation). The degree of correlation is tested using a t-distributed test statistic. Only the upper-diagonal of the matrix is shown in this exhibit.

[45] The correlation coefficients are calculated using 173 companies; 27 companies are dropped because of insufficient data to determine either the year's annual stock return or the traditional measures.

performance. This result is illustrated in Exhibit 7, comparing the return on high and low economic profit portfolios.

Do Value-Added Measures Add Value?

What is the value of value-added measures in financial analysis? In so much as these measures are constructed with care and used properly they may help the analyst get a better picture of a company's performance. Are these value-added measures good performance measures? Let's consider the criteria for a good performance measure.

1. The measure should not be sensitive to the choice of accounting methods. The most attractive feature of economic profit and market value added are that they force the analyst to look beyond the accounting numbers and consider the effects of accounting methods. Therefore, the value-based measures achieve this criteria.

2. The measure should evaluate the firm's current decisions in light of the expected future results. In other words, the measure should be forward-looking. Economic profit, as applied in practice, is a historical measure and therefore is not forward-looking. A company making decisions with the objective of maximizing economic profit may be short-sighted and risks sacrificing future profitability for current-period profitability. Market value added, on the other hand, compares market values with historical values. Because the market is forward-looking in pricing securities, the market value of a company's capital is forward-looking.

Exhibit 7: Returns for High and Low Economic Profit Portfolios

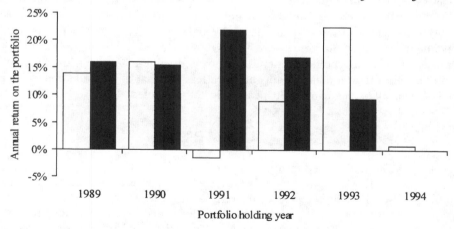

Source: Data drawn from Pamela P. Peterson and David R. Peterson, *Company Performance and Measures of Performance*, Research Foundation of the Institute of Chartered Financial Analysts (Charlottesville, VA.: Association for Investment Management and Research, 1996).

3. The measure should consider the risk associated with the decisions made by the firm. In theory, both economic profit and market value added incorporate risk: economic profit through the use of a cost of capital that reflects risk and market value added through the discounting performed by the market that is assumed to incorporate risk. In practice, however, the cost of capital used in the calculation of economic profit is often the imbedded, or historical cost of capital.

4. The measure should neither penalize nor reward the company for factors outside of their control, such as market movements and unanticipated changes in the economy. If a company's stock increases during a period, has the company added value? Maybe. In a bull market environment, how can the amount of value added, as reflected in market value added, be attributed to decisions the company makes and to factors outside of the company's control? The experience in using economic profit and market value added in the management of a company and as an analysis tool has been primarily in a bull market in which most companies added value. Will the enthusiasm be just as great when or if there is a bear market? The problem is that neither economic profit nor market value added control for factors outside the company's control and this may result in misleading indications of the company's financial health.

Economic profit and market value added measures have helped focus attention away from accounting numbers and directing this attention to value added. However, the value added measures, like any other performance measure, must be used with care. The financial analyst must understand what these measures can and cannot do.

It is far too early in the research of these metrics to discard the familiar, traditional metrics such as return on equity and return on assets. Much more independent testing of the value-added metrics is needed. It seems prudent at the present time to use both traditional metrics and value-added metrics, accompanied by information that explains how the less familiar value-added metrics are calculated. Reliance on a single measure is not warranted.

SUMMARY

- The value-added measures of economic profit and market value added are really nothing new — it is their application in performance measurement within firms and in financial analysis that is new.
- Economic profit (a.k.a. economic value added) is the operating profit of a company less its cost of capital. The calculation of operating profit for this purpose requires adjustments to remove distortions resulting from the prior application of accounting principles. There can be more than one hundred adjustments and these adjustments must be tailored for the individual company.

- Traditional performance measures, such as the return on assets, are not forward-looking, do not capture risk, and do not control for factors outside of the control of the company. Additionally, unless care is taken in the construction of these measures, these measures may be affected by the choice of accounting methods.
- The calculation of economic profit requires financial statement data, notes to financial statements, and, in most cases, information beyond published financial information. This makes the calculation of economic profit challenging to the financial analyst.
- Calculating economic profit also requires determining the amount of company's invested capital. Adjustments to arrive at operating income for the economic profit calculation have companion adjustments to arrive at invested capital.
- The cost of capital is generally determined by using a weighted average of the costs of capital. However, there are many assumptions and complexities in the calculation of the cost of capital and any estimate is subject to possible measurement error because a company's cost of capital cannot be observed.
- Market value added is the difference between the market value of a company's capital and the amount of invested capital (i.e., book values of capital). Performance measurement requires determining the change in market value added because the total market value added is measured over the company's entire history.
- There is limited independent evidence on the value of using value-added measures. However, the evidence that exists suggests that the value-added measures offer little over the traditional measures such as the return on assets.
- If used with the understanding of what the value added measures can and cannot do, the financial analyst may benefit from including these measures along with the traditional measures.

Chapter 5

Does Value-Based Management Discourage Investment in Intangibles?

Stephen F. O'Byrne
Managing Director
Shareholder Value Advisors Inc.

INTRODUCTION

The goal of value-based management is to create an operating measure of period performance that is consistent with shareholder value. An operating measure is an accounting (or non-financial) measure that does not depend on market value and can be measured at the business unit level. An operating measure is completely consistent with shareholder value if maximizing the operating measure over a measurement period also maximizes the dollar excess return computed on a market value basis. One of the most popular value-based operating measures is Stern Stewart's EVA®, which is an economic profit measure, i.e., a profit measure that includes a charge for the opportunity cost of equity capital. The market value of a company, i.e., the present value of its future free cash flow, can be expressed in terms of economic profit (i.e., market value is equal to the sum of book capital and the present value of future economic profit), but this does not imply that maximizing measurement period economic profit also maximizes the dollar excess return.

The first major objective of this chapter is to evaluate the consistency between incentive plan measures of economic profit, which typically reward the change in economic profit over a 3- to 5-year measurement period, and shareholder value, with particular emphasis on investments in intangibles. Intangible investments, such as R&D or acquisition goodwill, are particularly difficult challenges for value-based management because the expected free cash flows from intangible investments are often far in the future. The second major objective, once we show that there is severe conflict between economic profit incentive plans and intangible investments, is to examine the response of operating companies to the conflict: Have they reduced intangible investments? Have they abandoned economic profit as an incentive compensation measure? Have they developed a way to modify economic profit or their incentive plans to mitigate the conflict?

99

The first major finding of our case studies is that companies that have embraced value-based management have, in their initial implementations, greatly underestimated the accounting effort and complexity needed to reconcile economic profit with shareholder value. This is not surprising since value-based management is generally promoted as an attack on accounting with the promise that shareholder value is simply a matter of "getting to cash." "Shareholder value accounting," that is, accounting that makes economic profit consistent with shareholder value, requires economic depreciation, which violates GAAP depreciation standards, and, for acquisitions and R&D, negative economic depreciation, which violates historical cost accounting as well as GAAP depreciation standards. Linking incentive compensation to economic profit also requires significant effort in setting economic profit targets. Managers and directors will challenge the use of economic profit for incentive compensation if performance targets are not perceived to be fair or result in substantial inconsistencies with realized shareholder returns.

A second major finding is that some companies, including AT&T and Monsanto, have abandoned economic profit as a performance measure because they were unable, or unwilling, to resolve the accounting and target setting problems that arise in using economic profit. A third major finding is that other value-based companies, such as Furon and SPX, have found ad-hoc techniques, such as "metering in" acquisitions costs to capital and adjusting compensation targets on a pro-forma basis, to mitigate the conflict between economic profit and shareholder value and to maintain their commitment to value-based management. It is my judgment that the companies that have maintained their commitment to value-based management have been (1) willing to invest much more time and effort in addressing accounting and target setting problems, and (2) willing to do so because they have made contractual commitments to multi-year incentive compensation targets for operating performance (and hence, management's compensation is dependent on the resolution of the accounting and target setting problems).

The following sections of this chapter cover:

- Discounted cash flow (DCF) valuation, the definition of free cash flow (FCF), and the weakness of FCF as a measure of period performance,
- The concept of economic profit (EP) and the opportunity it provides to create a better measure of period performance,
- The economic profit analysis of market value: future growth value and expected EP improvement,
- The Stern Stewart EVA bonus plan design,
- The objectives of shareholder value accounting and their conflict with the objectives of GAAP accounting,
- The conflict between shareholder value and economic profit using straight line depreciation,
- The severe conflict between shareholder value and economic profit created by acquisitions (when economic profit is computed on the basis of historical cost accounting),

- The need for negative economic depreciation to eliminate the conflict created by acquisitions,
- The responses of EVA companies to the conflict created by acquisitions:
  - "Metering" the acquisition cost into capital,
  - Making "dilutive adjustments" to NOPAT to temporarily offset the negative impact of the acquisition on EVA,
  - Recalculating prior year EVA on a pro-forma basis and recalibrating incentive targets for EVA improvement,
  - Excluding acquisition liabilities from capital, and
  - Abandoning EVA as a performance measure

A note on EVA and EP terminology. In this chapter, we use "EVA" when referring to Stern Stewart & Co. client implementations or to policies or programs developed or advocated by Stern Stewart, e.g., the Stern Stewart EVA bonus plan design. We use economic profit, or "EP", when talking about issues or problems that are not specific to EVA, but exist for any economic profit measure. For example, the details of the Stern Stewart EVA bonus plan are discussed in terms of EP because the bonus plan concepts apply to any economic profit measure.

DCF VALUATION AND FREE CASH FLOW

The DCF value of equity is the present value of future dividends discounted at the cost of equity and the DCF value of debt is the present value of future interest and principal payments discounted at the cost of debt. The enterprise value, i.e., the market value of equity plus the market value of debt, is equal to the present value of future free cash flow discounted at the weighted average cost of capital, as long as the cost of capital is the market weighted average of the cost of equity and the after-tax cost of debt. Free cash flow is defined as the net after-tax distribution to investors:

After-tax interest expense + dividends + stock repurchases
+ debt repayments − new stock issues − new debt

FCF can be expressed in operating terms as NOPAT − Δcapital where NOPAT (*Net Operating Profit After Tax*) and capital are defined as:

$$
\begin{aligned}
\text{NOPAT} \ &= \ \text{Operating Profit} \times (1 - \text{tax rate}) \\
&= \ \text{After-tax profit with 100\% equity financing} \\
&= \ \text{Net income} + (1 - \text{tax rate}) \times \text{interest expense} \\
\text{Capital} \ &= \ \text{Equity} + \text{debt}
\end{aligned}
$$

The great virtue of FCF is that it allows market value to be expressed in terms of operating performance and eliminates the need for an explicit forecast of financing costs. As shown by Fabozzi and Grant in Chapter 1, the firm's market value (or enterprise value) can be expressed as the present value of anticipated future free cash flows according to:

$$\text{Market value} = \sum_{i=1}^{\infty} \frac{FCF_i}{(1+c)^i}$$

where c is the cost of capital.

To estimate the enterprise value, we need only forecast the income statement and balance sheet and make the assumption that constant leverage is maintained on a market value basis. We don't need to model the separate cash flows paid to equity and debt holders and our estimate of the enterprise value is correct (assuming our cash flow forecast is correct!) as long as our forecasts adhere to "clean surplus" accounting. FCF, unlike earnings, can be used for valuation analysis because it recognizes that the value of future earnings depends on the level of investment required to produce the earnings.

However, the great weakness of FCF is that it provides a poor measure of annual operating performance. FCF can be negative because investment is high in a profitable business or because NOPAT is low in an unprofitable business. In 1992, when Wal-Mart was at the top of the Stern Stewart Performance 1000 ranking, Wal-Mart had free cash flow of −13% of capital with an EVA return of +8% of capital and a market/capital ratio of 4.8. At the same time, K-Mart had free cash flow of −7% of capital, but had an EVA return of −3% and a market/capital ratio of 1.1. Because FCF fails to distinguish between poor performance and high investment, it does a poor job of explaining differences in market value. In an earlier study, I analyzed the relationship between operating performance and market value for the years 1985-1993 for the companies in the 1993 Stern Stewart Performance 1000 database and compared the explanatory power of free cash flow (FCF), net operating profit after tax (NOPAT), and EVA.[1] My results, which were based on a sample of 6,551 company/years and expressed in terms of the variance explained in the market/capital ratio, were as follows:

Variable/Model	Variance Explained
FCF	0%
NOPAT	17%
NOPAT (i.e., non-zero intercept)	33%
EVA	31%
EVA with positive and negative coefficients and with ln (capital) term	38%
	42%

The following example shows that the problem with FCF is that it fails to match the investment with the value it creates. Consider a restaurant chain where each new restaurant costs $500,000 to build and generates $100,000 in annual cash flow after the first year. If the chain has 20 restaurants in operation and

---

[1] Stephen F. O'Byrne, "EVA and Market Value," *Journal of Applied Corporate Finance* (Spring 1996), pp. 116-125.

builds two more during the year, it will have cash flow of $1 million [= 20 × $100,000 − 2 × $500,000]. If a second chain also has 20 restaurants in operation, but builds eight more restaurants during the year, it will have cash flow of −$2 million [= 20 × $100,000 − 8 × $500,000].

As shown below, the second restaurant chain has lower current cash flow, but a higher DCF value (using a discount rate of 10%, and assuming no new units for both chains after year 1):

Year	Chain 1 Cash Flow	PV Of Chain 1 Cash Flow	Chain 2 Cash Flow	PV Of Chain 2 Cash Flow
1	1,000	909	−2,000	−1,818
2	2,200	1,818	2,800	2,314
3+	2,200	18,182	2,800	23,141
Total		20,909		23,637

The second chain spends an extra $3 million in year 1, but has additional cash flow of $600,000 in each subsequent year. The value, at the end of year 1, of the additional $600,000 per year is $6 million, or $3 million more than the additional cost in year 1. The present value of this $3 million, $2,727,000, is the difference in the value of the two companies. Cash flow is a poor measure of market value in this example because it subtracts the cash spent to build new restaurants in year 1 without adding the present value of the cash likely to be produced by the new restaurants in subsequent years.

ECONOMIC PROFIT

Economic profit differs from FCF by substituting, for the actual investment in the year, a capital charge based on book capital:

FCF = NOPAT − Δcapital

EP = NOPAT − c × capital

Economic profit can provide a better measure of period performance — while maintaining consistency with DCF valuation — because it *permits the recognition of expenditures to be deferred to the future periods they benefit*. Economic profit maintains consistency with DCF valuation because the total expense recognized under EP — depreciation and capital charge — is always equal, in present value, to the initial cash outlay regardless of the depreciation schedule. Economic profit defers the recognition of expenditures through the capitalization process. A capitalized expenditure is not charged against economic profit in the year in which it is made, only in the years in which depreciation and/or capital charge is recognized.

The total expense recognized under EP — depreciation or amortization, if any, plus the capital charge — is equal, in present value, to the initial cash outlay regardless of whether the cash outlay is (1) recognized as an expense in the year incurred, (2) capitalized and amortized over a finite life, (3) capitalized and kept on the balance sheet without amortization forever, or even (4) capitalized and accreted each year with "negative depreciation." The example in Exhibit 1 shows that the present value of the total asset cost is the same when a $100,000 outlay is depreciated over a 4-year life and when it is depreciated over a 7-year life.

It is not difficult to prove, in the general case, that the present value of the total expense recognized under EP is equal to the initial cash outlay. We will prove the result for a non-depreciable asset (and leave the depreciable asset case to the reader).

Let $EP_1 = NOPAT_1 - c \times Capital_0$ and $FCF_1 = NOPAT_1 - I_1$. Investment of I_1 reduces FCF by I_1 in year 1 and reduces EP by $c \times I_1$ in all subsequent years (for the simple case of a non-depreciable asset). The present value of the EP investment charge is equal to the FCF investment charge:

$$I_1 = c \times I_1/(1 + c)^1 + c \times I_1/(1 + c)^2 + c \times I_1/(1 + c)^3 + \ldots$$

Since EP also charges for beginning book capital (a sunk cost irrelevant to FCF), the fundamental EP valuation equation is:

PV of future FCF = $Capital_0$ + PV of future EP

Exhibit 1: Present Value of Total Asset Cost Using a 4-Year and 7-Year Life

4-Year Write-Off of $100,000 Outlay

Year	Depreciation	PV of Depreciation	Beginning Capital	Capital Charge	PV of Capital Charge
1	25,000	22,727	100,000	10,000	9,091
2	25,000	20,661	75,000	7,500	6,198
3	25,000	18,783	50,000	5,000	3,757
4	25,000	17,075	25,000	2,500	1,708
Total		79,247			20,753

PV of total asset cost = $79,247 + $20,753 = $100,000

7-Year Write-Off of $100,000 Outlay

Year	Depreciation	PV of Depreciation	Beginning Capital	Capital Charge	PV of Capital Charge
1	14,286	12,987	100,000	10,000	9,091
2	14,286	11,806	85,714	8,571	7,084
3	14,286	10,733	71,429	7,143	5,367
4	14,286	9,757	57,143	5,714	3,903
5	14,286	8,870	42,857	4,286	2,661
6	14,286	8,064	28,571	2,857	1,613
7	14,286	7,331	14,286	1,429	733
Total		69,549			30,451

PV of total asset cost = $69,549 + $30,451 = $100,000

Exhibit 2: Current Operations Value and Future Growth Value of Coca-Cola and Coca-Cola Enterprises (April 1998)

		Coca-Cola ($bil)	Coca-Cola Enterprises ($bil)
Market value =	Market value =	$194.7	$23.7
	Capital +	$15.0	$12.6
Current Operations Value + "COV"	Capitalized Current EP +	$29.5	$1.1
Future Growth Value "FGV"	PV of Expected EP Improvement	$150.2	$10.0
	EP ($mil)	$2,850	$99
	Cost of capital	9.65%	9.18%
	Stock Price (4/98)	$75.88	$37.75
	Shares Outstd (mil)	2,515	396

FUTURE GROWTH VALUE AND EXPECTED EP IMPROVEMENT

The fundamental EP valuation equation provides much more insight when we break the present value of future EP into two pieces: the perpetuity value of current EP and the present value of expected EP improvement:[2]

Market value = Capital + EP_0/c + PV of future $\Delta EP_{i,0}$

Market value = Current operations value + Future growth value

In this equation, $\Delta EP_{i,0}$ is the difference between EP_i and EP_0, i.e., $\Delta EP_{i,0} = EP_i - EP_0$. We can also express future growth value as $(1 + c)/c \times$ PV of future annual ΔEP_i where annual $EP_i = EP_i - EP_{i-1}$:[3]

Market value = Capital + EP_0/c + $[(1 + c)/c] \times$ PV of future ΔEP_i

Exhibit 2 illustrates these two components of value in the April 1998 valuations of Coca-Cola and Coca-Cola Enterprises.

The distinction between current operations value (COV) and future growth value (FGV) is critical to understanding the relationship between EP,

---

[2] Grant develops an EP valuation framework by unfolding the classic "Investment Opportunities Approach to Valuation" into (1) the contribution to market value generated by the firm's existing assets, and (2) the EP contribution to enterprise value generated by the firm's expected future assets (capital investments) not currently in place. The classic IOAV model can be found in Eugene F. Fama and Merton H. Miller, *The Theory of Finance* (New York: Holt, Rinehart, and Winston, 1972), while Grant's EP interpretation is covered in James L. Grant, *Foundations of Economic Value Added* (New Hope, PA: Frank J. Fabozzi Associates, 1997).

[3] O'Byrne, "EVA and Market Value."

which is a measure of return on book capital, and shareholder return, which is based solely on market value. Investors expect a cost of capital return on the *total* market value of the company. This means that they expect a cost of capital return on current operations value *and* a cost of capital return on future growth value:

$$c \times MV_0 = c \times COV_0 + c \times FGV_0$$

Future growth value is an extremely important concept because it can tell us (after considerable analysis) how much EP improvement is needed for investors to earn a cost of capital return on market value. If a company has no future growth value, it does not need any EP improvement to provide its investors with a cost of capital return on the market value of their investment. NOPAT, with no EP improvement, provides a cost of capital return on current operations value and hence, a cost of capital return on market value when future growth value is zero.[4]

When future growth value is positive, ΔEP and ΔFGV must provide a return of $c \times FGV_0$ for investors to earn a cost of capital return on market value. The return on future growth has only three sources:

- The contribution of ΔEP to cash flow, i.e., ΔEP,
- The contribution of ΔEP to current operations value, i.e., $\Delta EP/c$, and
- The change, if any, in FGV, i.e., ΔFGV.

These three sources of value must provide the required return:[5]

$$\Delta EP_1 + \Delta EP_1/c + \Delta FGV_1 = c \times FGV_0$$

In the simple cases where $\Delta FGV_1 = 0$ or ΔFGV_1 is a multiple of $\Delta EP_1/c$, the required return on future growth value depends only on ΔEP and we can speak unambiguously of "Expected EP Improvement," i.e., the EP improvement needed to provide a cost of capital return on future growth value. Exhibit 3 shows the calculation of expected EP improvement for Coca-Cola and Coca-Cola Enterprises under the assumption $\Delta FGV_1 = 0$.

---

[4] This NOPAT-cost of capital link follows from:

$NOPAT_1 = EP_1 + c \times Capital_0$ (from the definition of EP)
$NOPAT_1 = EP_0 + c \times Capital_0$ (since no EP improvement implies $EP_1 = EP_0$)
$NOPAT_1 = c \times (EP_0/c + Capital_0) = c \times COV_0$

[5] This formula follows from substituting the following expressions:

$MV_0 = Cap_0 + EP_0/c + FGV_0$
$MV_1 = Cap_1 + EP_1/c + FGV_1$
$FCF_1 = NOPAT_1 - \Delta Cap_1 = EP_1 + Cap_0 - \Delta Cap_1$

into the equation of the actual and expected returns:

$MV_1 + FCF_1 - MV_0 = c \times MV_0$

Exhibit 3: Expected EP Improvement for Coca-Cola and Coca-Cola Enterprises Assuming Change in Future Growth Value is Zero

	Coca-Cola	Coca-Cola Enterprises
Future Growth Value ($mil)	$150,221	$9,994
Required Return on FGV	$14,502	$917
Cost of Capital	9.65%	9.18%
EP Multiple [1 + (1/c)]	11.36	11.89
Expected ΔEP	$1,277	$77

If ΔFGV_1 is a multiple of $\Delta EP_1/c$, e.g., $\Delta FGV_1 = 0.8 \times \Delta EVA_1/c$, the expected return equation requires:

$$\Delta EP_1 + \Delta EP_1/c + 0.8 \times \Delta EP_1/c = (1 + (1.8/c)) \times \Delta EP_1 = c \times FGV_0$$

In this case, the EP multiple would be 19.65 [= 1 + (1.8/.0965)] for Coca-Cola and 20.61 for Coca-Cola Enterprises, and Expected ΔEP would be $738 = ($14,502/19.65) for Coca-Cola and $44 for Coca-Cola Enterprises.

The more general case is where ΔFGV depends on factors other than ΔEP. One factor that ΔFGV is often said to depend on is FGV_0. FGV_0 is said to decay, or "fade," to zero over a "competitive advantage period." My own empirical analysis of 5-year changes in FGV shows that ΔFGV is negatively related to FGV_0, i.e., there is a fade, but also that ΔFGV is positively related to sales (or capital) growth. When sales growth affects ΔFGV, there is not a unique expected EP improvement. Higher sales growth means a smaller EP improvement is needed to provide the required return on FGV, while lower sales growth means a larger EP improvement is needed to provide the required return on FGV.

THE STERN STEWART EVA BONUS PLAN DESIGN

Bonus plans based on economic profit have existed for many years. The most common plan design simply gave management a fixed percentage of each year's economic profit. For example, in 1922, General Motors adopted a bonus plan that provided for a bonus pool equal to 10% of profit in excess of a 7% return on capital. More recently, in 1984, the Walt Disney company gave Michael Eisner an annual bonus equal to 2% of net income in excess of a 9% return on equity. In both of these cases, a fixed percentage interest in economic profit worked quite well and the plan survived for a very long time. The General Motors bonus formula was used for 25 years without any change in the sharing percentage or cost of capital[6] and the Eisner formula was used for almost 15 years with only one change in the cost of capital. Despite its success at General Motors and Walt Disney, this simple bonus formula is rarely used today.

---

[6] Alfred Sloan Jr., *My Years With General Motors* (New York: Doubleday, 1963).

A fixed percentage interest in economic profit can lead to four significant problems. For companies with persistently negative economic profit, the bonus plan provides no incentive. For more average companies, where economic profit fluctuates from positive to negative, the bonus is, in effect, an option on the good years. This encourages management to shift revenue and expense across years to maximize incentive payouts and can also have the effect of making management's effective share of cumulative economic profit far greater than its nominal share. A third problem is that giving management a share of economic profit from the first dollar leads to very inefficient trade-offs between the strength of the incentive and the shareholder cost of the incentive. For example, if we apply Michael Eisner's formula of 2% of economic profit to a company, like Wal-Mart, with $1 billion in economic profit, the result is a $20 million bonus, which shareholders will rightly feel is far more than necessary to attract highly qualified managerial talent. The seemingly simple solution to this problem is to move the decimal point to the left, i.e., give an interest of 0.2% of economic profit instead of 2.0%. But this isn't really a good answer. When we cut management's share of economic profit from 2.0% to 0.2%, we reduce the incentive at the margin by a factor of 10. The more efficient solution is to give management a share of economic profit improvement.

The fourth problem is that the formulas make no provision for expected economic profit improvement and hence, can provide substantial payouts when the shareholders lose money. The recent history of Wal-Mart provides an example of the situation in which this can occur. In 1992, Wal-Mart had $957 million of economic profit and a future growth value of $55 billion (or $30 billion more than its current operations value of $25 billion). This future growth value implied investor expectations of substantial economic profit improvement. When Wal-Mart's economic profit went sideways over the next two years ($1,056 million in 1993 and $917 million in 1994), its future growth value dropped by $25 billion and its stock price declined from $32.00 to $21.25. In this situation, a fixed percentage of economic profit would provide substantial bonuses even though the shareholders were losing money.

The modern version of the economic profit bonus plan, the Stern Stewart EVA bonus plan[7] begins by making the performance measure economic profit improvement. There are three reasons for this. The first is that an interest in economic profit improvement provides a more efficient incentive/cost trade-off than an interest in economic profit. The second is that economic profit improvement is a measure that applies to all companies, not just companies with positive economic profit. The third is that economic profit improvement provides a mechanism for linking bonuses to the shareholders' return on market value. By making the bonus plan performance measure "excess EP improvement," i.e., the EP improvement in excess of the expected EP improvement required for investors to

---

[7] See the following articles: Stephen F. O'Byrne, "EVA and Management Compensation," *ACA (American Compensation Association) Journal* (Summer 1994), pp. 60-73; Stephen F. O'Byrne, "Total Compensation Strategy," *Journal of Applied Corporate Finance* (Summer 1995); and, Stephen F. O'Byrne, "Executive Compensation," Chapter E9 in *Handbook of Modern Finance* (New York: Warren, Gorham & Lamont, 1997).

earn a cost of capital return on market value, the plan can control the relationship between bonus payout and shareholder return. A fixed percentage, or ownership, interest in excess economic profit improvement is the heart of the Stern Stewart EVA bonus plan. The bonus earned is the sum of the fixed percentage of excess EP improvement (which can be negative) and a target bonus. The target bonus is the bonus earned for zero excess EP improvement, i.e., for achieving the expected EP improvement. The target bonus is used to provide a bonus for expected performance that is competitive with labor market norms. The bonus earned can be negative and is uncapped on both the upside and the downside. The bonus earned is credited to a bonus bank, and the bonus bank balance, rather than the current year bonus earned, determines the bonus paid. Typically, the payout rule for the bonus bank is 100% of the bonus bank balance (if positive), up to the amount of the target bonus, plus ⅓ of the bank balance in excess of the target bonus. Exhibit 4 shows the modern economic profit bonus plan.

The "EP interval" shown in Exhibit 4 is the shortfall in excess economic profit improvement that wipes out the target bonus. The slope of the bonus line is the ratio of the change in bonus to the change in excess EP and gives management's share of excess EP improvement. The slope, or management's share of excess economic profit improvement, can be expressed as the ratio of the aggregate target bonus to the EP interval since the target bonus is the change in bonus associated with an excess EP improvement equal to the EP interval. For a typical manufacturing company, management's share of excess economic profit improvement is 40%-60%. The calibration of an economic profit bonus plan requires the determination of three key parameters: (1) the target bonus, (2) the expected EP improvement, and (3) the EP interval, and bonus bank terms and payout rules. For each of these parameters, the calibration normally starts with a guiding concept:

Exhibit 4: The Modern Economic Profit Bonus Plan

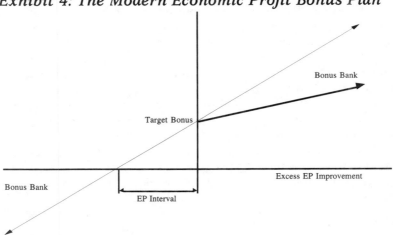

- *Expected EP improvement:* the EP improvement required for the company's investors to earn a cost of capital return on the market value of their investment,
- *The EP interval:* the EP shortfall that makes the investor (or shareholder return) return equal to zero, and
- *The target bonus:* a competitive bonus opportunity based on peer company compensation practices.

Expected EP improvement and management's share of excess EP improvement (the target bonus divided by the EP interval) are typically fixed for a 3- to 5-year period. Fixing the performance target and management's percentage interest eliminates the "performance penalty" inherent in competitive compensation policies and provides a stronger incentive. A policy of recalibrating annually to a competitive compensation level always penalizes performance because superior performance leads to higher targets and/or a smaller percentage interest and poor performance leads to reduced targets and/or a larger percentage interest.[8] Fixing the plan parameters for a multi-year period provides a stronger incentive, but also creates more retention risk and/or higher shareholder cost than a typical competitive compensation program. The guiding concept of making the bonus zero when the shareholder return is zero usually results in too much retention risk (i.e., too great a risk of a multi-year zero bonus) and leads to the use of a wider EP interval.

The need for a wider EP interval forces the company to make a difficult trade-off between the strength of the incentive and the cost of the incentive plan to the shareholders. If the wider EP interval is completely offset by an increase in the target bonus (i.e., the target bonus is increased proportionally), management can retain the same percentage interest in excess EP improvement with a lower risk of a zero bonus. In this case, the company achieves a stronger incentive with tolerable retention risk by providing compensation opportunities that are above competitive levels. In effect, the shareholders pay for a stronger incentive by providing higher compensation opportunities.

Alternatively, the company may decide to offset none, or only a part, of the wider EP interval by an increase in the target bonus and hence, accept a weaker incentive in order to limit shareholder cost. In some cases, after considering alternatives, the company will decide to keep a shorter EP interval and accept more retention risk. In these cases, management "pays" for a stronger incentive by accepting greater compensation risk. Most EVA companies I have worked with have adopted bonus plan parameters that provide stronger incentives than a typical competitive compensation program and "finance" the stronger incentive through a combination of higher shareholder cost and greater retention risk (relative to a typical competitive compensation program).

---

[8] See O'Byrne, "EVA and Market Value," for a much more extended discussion of this issue.

THE OBJECTIVES OF SHAREHOLDER VALUE ACCOUNTING

Economic profit is an effort to provide a better measure of period performance than FCF by recognizing cash outlays as expenses in different periods from the periods in which they are incurred. There are two basic techniques to shift the recognition of expense while maintaining consistency with DCF valuation: capital charge and present value. The recognition of a current cash expenditure can be deferred to future periods while maintaining consistency with DCF valuation through the use of a *capital charge*. The recognition of a future cash expenditure can be accelerated to the current period while maintaining consistency with DCF valuation through the use of *present value*. These two techniques make it *possible* to create an economic profit measure which is a better measure of period performance than FCF. However, these two techniques, by themselves, are not sufficient to create a better measure of period performance because they do not answer any of the following questions: Which outlays benefit future periods? What is the life of the future benefit? Is the benefit constant over time? Increasing? Or decreasing? Is the benefit constant (increasing/decreasing) over time: In absolute dollars? In EP? In ROIC?

The objective of expense, amortization, and accretion policies for economic profit accounting should be to make economic profit more consistent with discounted cash flow valuation and more highly correlated with price levels and returns. This objective is widely shared by financial economists and academic accountants. William Beaver writes:[9]

> When a "desirable" properties approach is pursued, financial accounting theorists have usually adopted an economic income approach. Under this approach, accounting alternatives are evaluated in terms of their perceived proximity to this "ideal"... Economic income is defined as the change in the present value of future cash flows, after proper adjustments for deposits (for example, additional common stock issues) or withdrawals (for example, dividends).

More specifically, expense, amortization and accretion policies should:

- Make accounting depreciation equal to economic depreciation, i.e., make accounting depreciation equal to the decline (or accretion) in the present value of the future cash flows from the asset,
- Make the accounting return on capital equal to the economic, or internal, rate of return, and
- Make current NOPAT and capital better predictors of current market value.

---

[9] William H. Beaver, *Financial Reporting: An Accounting Revolution* (Upper Saddle River, NJ: Prentice Hall, 1998).

Accounting policies that achieve these objectives are generally not permitted under GAAP. "Annuity," or sinking fund, depreciation, which makes the accounting return on capital equal to the economic return (when future cash flows are constant), is not permitted under GAAP (FAS 92, ¶37). While no official pronouncement explains why sinking fund depreciation is not permitted, the authors of a leading accounting text says that sinking fund depreciation has been attacked "because it yields an increasing charge to depreciation in each year of asset life, while accountants generally agree that the service potential of the asset actually decreases each year."[10]

Capitalizing R&D, which is only the first step in making accounting depreciation equal to economic depreciation for R&D, is not permitted under GAAP either (FAS 2). The FASB believes that a more objective approach, that provides greater certainty about the method of calculation used across companies, is more desirable than a more judgmental approach that may provide a better estimate of economic income. The benefits of R&D "cannot be measured with a reasonable degree of certainty," and "the relationship between current R&D costs and the amount of resultant future benefits to an enterprise is so uncertain that capitalization of any R&D costs is not useful in assessing the earnings potential of the enterprise." (FAS 2, ¶45, 50).

The unwillingness of GAAP to accept economic depreciation for PP&E, much less for R&D, forces companies that use EP for financial management and incentive compensation to decide whether the benefits of economic depreciation outweigh its complexity and the confusion of having GAAP and economic depreciation. The vast majority of EVA companies have decided that the benefits of economic depreciation do not outweigh its complexity. Only one EVA company (that the author is aware of) has adjusted GAAP depreciation for PP&E. Many EVA companies capitalize R&D, but none (that the author is aware of) depart from straight line depreciation of R&D. Almost all EVA companies add goodwill amortization back to NOPAT, but only one EVA company has used negative economic depreciation for acquisitions (and that company is only planning to use it for one year).

We will show later in this chapter that the failure of EVA companies to use negative economic depreciation for acquisitions has led to severe conflicts between EVA and shareholder value. In some cases, the conflict has caused the company to reject acquisitions that would increase shareholder value. More frequently, EVA companies have proceeded with acquisitions that appear to have positive net present value and sought other means to reconcile the conflict between EVA and shareholder value. In some of these cases, the conflict has been reconciled by abandoning EVA as a measure of performance. In other cases, the conflict has been reconciled by "metering in" the acquisition cost to capital, by recalculating EVA on a pro-forma basis, and by excluding non-interest bearing liabilities assumed in the acquisition from capital. The first two of these approaches, "metering in" the acquisition cost and recalculating EVA on a pro-forma basis (which requires recalibrating incentive plan targets), can replicate

---

[10] Richard G. Schroeder and Myrtle W. Clark, *Accounting Theory: Text and Readings* (New York: John Wiley & Sons, 1998), p. 374.

negative economic depreciation and hence, can truly reconcile the conflict between EP and shareholder value. To understand the conflicts between EP and shareholder value as well as the company responses, we need to look more closely at the problems created by straight line depreciation and acquisitions.

THE CONFLICT BETWEEN SHAREHOLDER VALUE AND EP USING STRAIGHT LINE DEPRECIATION

When a company adopts economic profit as an operating performance measure without adjusting GAAP (i.e., straight line) depreciation, the economic profit measure is not consistent with shareholder value. Consider the following project, which has a $2,000 cash operating margin each year for five years and an internal rate of return of 21.7%. If the company's cost of capital is less than 21.7%, the company should accept the project, otherwise it should reject the project. With straight line depreciation, assuming a 20% cost of capital, economic profit is negative in the first two years (−$240 in year 1 and −$60 in year 2), even though the cumulative EP improvement, on a present value basis, is $28 (which implies a cumulative EP, on a present value basis, of $(1 + c)/c \times 27.6, or $165). The big negative EP in year 1 results in negative cumulative ΔEP on a present value basis through year 2, so a manager with an EVA bonus plan would have no incentive to take the project unless the plan had a 3-year horizon before recalibration.

The project EP is negative in years 1 and 2 because the accounting return on capital in year 1 (14.7%) and year 2 (18.3%) is less than the economic, or internal, rate of return. This is illustrated in Exhibit 5.

Exhibit 5: Straight Line Depreciation Makes the Level and Trend of ROIC Misleading

Year	0	1	2	3	4	5	6
Cash operating margin		2,000	2,000	2,000	2,000	2,000	
Fixed capital (year end)	4,500	3,600	2,700	1,800	900	0	
Depreciation		900	900	900	900	900	
Operating profit		1,100	1,100	1,100	1,100	1,100	
Tax rate/taxes	40%	440	440	440	440	440	
NOPAT		660	660	660	660	660	
ROIC		14.667%	18.333%	24.444%	36.667%	73.333%	
Delta Capital	4,500	−900	−900	−900	−900	−900	
Free Cash Flow	−4,500	1,560	1,560	1,560	1,560	1,560	
IRR	21.660%						
EP (Cost of Capital = 20%)		−240	−60	120	300	480	0
EP Improvement		−240	180	180	180	180	−480
PV of EP Improvement		−200	125	104	87	72	−161
Cumulative PV of EP Improvement		−200	−75	29	116	188	28

Exhibit 6: Sinking Fund Depreciation Can Make ROIC Equal IRR

Year	0	1	2	3	4	5	6
Cash operating margin		2,000	2,000	2,000	2,000	2,000	
Fixed capital (year end)	4,500	4,041	3,426	2,599	1,490	0	
Depreciation		459	616	827	1,110	1,490	
Operating profit		1,541	1,384	1,173	890	510	
Tax rate/taxes	40%	617	554	469	356	204	
NOPAT		925	831	704	534	306	
ROIC		20.553%	20.553%	20.553%	20.553%	20.552%	
Delta Capital	4,500	−459	−616	−827	−1,110	−1,490	
Free Cash Flow	−4,500	1,383	1,446	1,531	1,644	1,796	
IRR	20.553%						
EP (Cost of Capital = 20%)		25	22	19	14	8	0
EP Improvement		25	−3	−3	−5	−6	−8
PV of EP Improvement		21	−2	−2	−2	−2	−3
Cumulative PV of EP Improvement		21	19	17	15	12	10

We can also use this example to show that straight line depreciation can lead to two false inferences about company performance. The first false inference is that company performance is improving. The accounting return on capital in this example is rising each year, but the annual cash flow is constant so there is no reason to say that performance is improving or to expect that a second identical project would have a higher internal rate of return. This false inference can lead to misguided stock recommendations by security analysts who base their buy and sell recommendations on changes in ROIC. The second false inference is that the company earns more (or less) than the cost of capital and hence, that growth does (or does not) add value. If the company has a 20% cost of capital, it appears that the company earns less than the cost of capital in the first two years even though its internal rate of return exceeds the cost of capital. This false inference can also lead operating managers to make misguided decisions about capital allocation.

To make the accounting return on capital equal to the internal rate of return, we need to use sinking fund depreciation based on the pre-tax internal rate of return. If we make the simplifying assumption that tax and book depreciation are the same, sinking fund depreciation, calculated from the pre-tax IRR, will make the accounting return on capital equal to the internal rate of return as shown in Exhibit 6.

The sinking fund depreciation eliminates the conflict between the EVA bonus plan and shareholder value in this example. The EP improvement is positive in the first year and the present value of the cumulative EP improvement is positive for all time horizons. Sinking fund depreciation is based on the same principles as the amortization of a home mortgage. To calculate sinking fund depreciation, determine the useful life of the asset, determine the appropriate discount rate, calculate the level payment needed to amortize the cost of the asset over its useful life, and split each year's level payment into principal (i.e., depreciation) and interest. Exhibit 7 illustrates the calculation of the sinking fund depreciation (assuming no salvage value at the end of the asset's useful life) for the first year.

Exhibit 7: Calculation of Year 1 Depreciation Using Sinking Fund Depreciation

Asset cost	$4,500
Useful life (years)	5
Discount rate	34.25%
Annuity factor	2.25
Level payment	$2,000
Year 1 interest	$1,541
Year 1 depreciation	$459
Year 1 end net asset value	$4,041

The formula for the annuity factor is $[1 - (1/(1 + r))^N]/r$
Year 1 interest is $4,500 × 0.3425

The level payment is equal to the cash operating margin. This shows that the sinking fund depreciation is splitting each year's cash operating margin into investment return and recovery of capital. Sinking fund depreciation eliminates the two false inferences we made with straight line depreciation. There is no change in the rate of return and hence, no false inference that company performance is improving or that the company earns more (or less) than the cost of capital. Sinking fund depreciation also eliminates the year 2 penalty in incentive compensation for undertaking the project. The cumulative present value of EP improvement, and hence, the cumulative present value of the bonus, is positive in every year.

In a more general case, where the cash operating margin is not constant or tax depreciation is independent of book depreciation, we need to use economic depreciation to make the accounting return on capital equal to the economic, or internal, rate of return. Economic depreciation is equal to the decline in the asset value (i.e., the decline in the present value of the future cash flows, from one period to the next). To ensure that the cumulative depreciation is equal to the historical cost of the asset, we need to calculate the present value of the future cash flows using the internal rate of return. The example in Exhibit 8 modifies the prior example by projecting a 10% annual increase in the cash operating margin.

The use of economic depreciation eliminates the conflict between the EVA bonus plan and shareholder value (with straight line depreciation, the EP improvement in year 1 is −$240). The EP improvement is positive in year 1 and the present value of the cumulative EP improvement is positive for all time horizons. We can use the IRR to make a shortcut calculation of economic depreciation. The expected total return on the asset in each period is equal to the expected cash received plus the change in the asset value. In depreciation terms, where a decline in asset value is positive depreciation, the expected total return on the asset in each period is equal to the expected cash received minus depreciation (i.e., the decline in the asset value). Thus, depreciation is equal to the expected cash received minus the expected total return on the asset. The expected cash received in year 1 is $1,560. The expected return on the asset is beginning capital

× IRR, or $4,500 \times 0.27501 = \$1,238$. This implies that the economic depreciation in year 1 is $\$1,560 - \$1,238 = \$322$.

While the conflict between economic profit and shareholder value created by straight line depreciation can be overcome by sinking fund or positive economic depreciation, only one EVA company (that I am aware of) has ever used sinking fund depreciation for an asset that is not leased! (When operating leases are capitalized by EVA companies and the lease expense is reduced by implicit interest, the net lease expense is equivalent to sinking fund depreciation.) Many EVA companies have considered sinking fund depreciation, but rejected it as too complicated to justify the benefit. Their rejection of sinking fund depreciation may be influenced by the fact that the built-in EVA improvement arising from straight line depreciation on the existing asset base more than offsets the benefit of sinking fund depreciation on new assets.

Eliminating the conflict between EP and shareholder value created by straight line depreciation requires a departure from normal GAAP depreciation, but does not require the abandonment of historical cost accounting because the economic depreciation is positive. A much more difficult problem arises for investments that have negative economic depreciation. Negative economic depreciation occurs whenever the expected cash return is less than the expected total return. Negative economic depreciation is commonplace for investments with "back-loaded" cash flows, e.g., acquisitions, R&D, training, developing a distribution network. Most of these investments with back-loaded cash flows are investments in "intangibles." Failure to recognize negative economic depreciation can lead to severe conflicts between EP and shareholder value when a company makes an acquisition or develops an intangible asset internally. We will see that EVA companies, while hardly bothered by depreciation problems, have struggled tremendously with the conflicts created by acquisitions.

Exhibit 8: Economic Depreciation Makes ROIC Equal IRR

Year	0	1	2	3	4	5	6
Cash operating margin		2,000	2,200	2,420	2,662	2,928	
Fixed capital (year end)	4,500	4,178	3,646	2,837	1,660	0	
Depreciation		322	531	809	1,177	1,660	
Operating profit		1,678	1,669	1,611	1,485	1,268	
Tax rate/taxes	40%	440	520	608	705	811	
NOPAT		1,238	1,149	1,003	780	457	
ROIC		27.501%	27.501%	27.501%	27.501%	27.501%	
Delta Capital	4,500	−322	−531	−809	−1,177	−1,660	
Free Cash Flow	−4,500	1,560	1,680	1,812	1,957	2,117	
IRR	27.501%						
EP (Cost of Capital = 20%)		338	313	274	213	125	0
EP Improvement		338	−24	−40	−61	−88	−125
PV of EP Improvement		281	−17	−23	−29	−35	−42
Cumulative PV of EP Improvement		281	264	241	212	177	135

Exhibit 9: Aquisition at 16× NOPAT Gives Negative EP

	0	1	2	3	4	5	6	7
Operating Forecast								
Capital Growth Rate		15%	15%	15%	15%	15%	15%	15%
Operating Capital	10,000	11,500	13,225	15,209	17,490	20,114	23,131	26,600
Return on Operating Capital		18%	18%	18%	18%	18%	18%	18%
NOPAT		1,800	2,070	2,381	2,738	3,148	3,620	4,164
Valuation								
Investment	10,000	1,500	1,725	1,984	2,281	2,624	3,017	3,470
Free Cash Flow		300	345	397	456	525	603	694
PV of Free Cash Flow		273	285	298	312	326	341	356
Cumulative PV of FCF	2,190							
Terminal Value	54,126							
PV of Terminal Value	27,775							
Market Value	29,965	32,662	35,583	38,744	42,162	45,854	49,836	54,126
Conventional EP Analysis								
Book Capital With Acquisition		32,662	34,387	36,370	38,652	41,275	44,292	47,762
Return on Acquisition Book Capital			6.3%	6.9%	7.5%	8.1%	8.8%	9.4%
Capital Charge			3,266	3,439	3,637	3,865	4,128	4,429
Economic Profit			−1,196	−1,058	−899	−717	−507	−266
Economic Profit Improvement			−1,196	138	159	183	210	241
PV of EP Improvement			−1,087	114	119	125	130	136
Cumulative PV of EP Improvement			−1,087	−973	−854	−729	−599	−463
EP With Economic Depreciation								
Decline in Market Value			−2,921	−3,162	−3,418	−3,692	−3,982	−4,290
Add Back New Investment			1,725	1,984	2,281	2,624	3,017	3,470
= Economic Depreciation			−1,196	−1,178	−1,137	−1,068	−965	−820
Adjusted Acquisition Book Capital			35,583	38,744	42,162	45,854	49,836	54,126
Adjusted NOPAT			3,266	3,558	3,874	4,216	4,585	4,984
Adjusted Capital Charge			3,266	3,558	3,874	4,216	4,585	4,984
EP With Economic Depreciation			0	0	0	0	0	0

THE SEVERE CONFLICT BETWEEN EP AND SHAREHOLDER VALUE CREATED BY ACQUISITIONS

The example shown in Exhibit 9 shows an acquisition forecast that projects 15% capital growth and an 18% return on capital for seven years. In year 1, NOPAT is $1,800 on an investment of $10,000. By year 7, NOPAT increases to $4,164 and book capital increases to $26,600 with an investment of $3,470 in year 7. The terminal value at the end of year 7, $54,126, is 12 times projected year 8's NOPAT assuming a cost of capital (10%) return on the new investment in year 7: $54,126 = 12 × ($4,164 + 10% × $3,470). The DCF value of the forecast at the end of year 0 is $29,965, which is the sum of the present value of free cash flow for years 1-7, $2,190, plus the present value of the terminal value, $27,775. The "back-loading" of the cash flows is evident in the first year cash and income yields. The cash yield is only 1% (= $300/$29,965) and the earnings yield only 6% (= $1,800/$29,965), while the cost of capital is 10%. Despite these low yields, the back-loading of the forecast is not extreme for an acquisition or R&D investment. The DCF value at the end of year 0 is only 16.6 times year 1 NOPAT, which is not an unusually high multiple for an acquisition. The first year cash and earnings yields are much higher than a typical R&D investment, which usually has no cash or earnings contribution for several years.

To demonstrate the conflict between EP and shareholder value, we will assume that we purchase the company at the end of year 1 for its DCF value, $32,662. The purchase price, under normal EP accounting, becomes our book capital at the end of year 1. If we assume that the operating assets, after only one year, are still worth their book value, 65% of the purchase price, or $21,162, will be goodwill. To make it clear that goodwill amortization is only a small part of the conflict between EP and shareholder value, we will assume that there is no goodwill amortization. (We also assume, for simplicity, that there are no additional tax savings from the acquisition.)

Since the acquisition price is the DCF value of the forecast, realizing the forecast will not create or destroy any value for the shareholders (i.e., they are no better or worse off than if the acquisition had not been made and the cash had been returned to the shareholders). Since the acquisition is value neutral, economic profit should be zero every year, but, with conventional EP accounting (i.e., adding back goodwill amortization to NOPAT), economic profit is −$1,196 in year 2 and remains negative through year 7. The economic profit in year 2 is negative because year 2's NOPAT is only 6.3% of capital when the cost of capital is 10%. If this acquisition is added to an existing business, it will reduce bonuses under the EVA bonus plan for at least six years unless the bonus plan is recalibrated. The EP improvement in year 2 is negative (−$1,196) and the cumulative present value of EP improvement remains negative through year 7.

The bottom panel of Exhibit 9 shows that economic depreciation eliminates the conflict between EP and shareholder value. The calculation of economic depreciation in this case is a little more complicated than in the previous example because new capital is being invested each year. Since the new capital is not part of the original asset cost, the economic depreciation is the decline in the present value of future cash flows net of new capital invested. In the prior example, economic depreciation was the expected cash return minus the expected total return. In this case, the difference between the expected cash return in year 2, $345, and the expected total return, $3,266 (= 10% × $32,662) is −$2,921. The appreciation in the value of the business is $2,921, but −$2,921 is not the economic depreciation of the original acquisition asset because the expected cash return was reduced by $1,725 of new investment. When we subtract the new investment from the gross economic depreciation, we get the correct economic depreciation of −$1,196.

THE RESPONSES OF EVA COMPANIES TO THE CONFLICT BETWEEN SHAREHOLDER VALUE AND EP

While negative economic depreciation can provide an accounting result that is consistent with maximizing shareholder value, only one EVA company (that I am aware of) has used negative economic depreciation and that company plans to use it for only the first year of an acquisition. A major reason that few EVA companies recognize negative economic depreciation is that Stern Stewart has generally placed little emphasis on depreciation, amortization, and accretion issues. Stern Stewart has been far more concerned about the understatement of investment than depreciation policy as indicated by the following:

> Capital employed can be estimated by taking the standard accounting book value for a company's net assets and then grossing it up three ways:
>
> - To convert from accrual to cash accounting (by adding accounting reserves that are formed by recurring, non-cash bookkeeping provisions such as the deferred tax reserve)
> - To convert from the liquidating perspective of lenders to the going-concern perspective of shareholders (as by capitalizing R&D outlays and market-building expenditures)
> - To convert from successful-efforts to full-cost accounting (as by adding back cumulative unusual losses, less gains, after taxes). [11]

The responses of EVA companies to the conflict between shareholder value and EVA for positive NPV acquisitions can be grouped in three broad categories:

- *The company rejects the acquisition* because it does not contribute positive EVA within the incentive plan cycle. This is not a good outcome for the shareholders because positive NPV implies that the acquisition increases shareholder value. However, it does not appear (based on the number of negative EVA acquisitions that they have undertaken) that EVA companies reject positive NPV acquisitions very often. The problem is probably more severe at the business unit level where the managers evaluating the acquisition are not in a position to control the accounting treatment of the acquisition for EVA calculation.
- *The company drops EVA* because it cannot show that the acquisitions increase EVA. This is what has happened at Monsanto.

---

[11] Bennett G. Stewart III, *The Quest For Value: A Guide For Senior Managers* (New York: Harper Business, 1991), p. 70.

- *The company makes an accounting adjustment to make the acquisition EVA positive or neutral.* There are at least four different accounting adjustments that EVA companies have adopted to make the acquisition EVA positive or neutral:
  - "Metering" the acquisition cost into capital,
  - Making a "dilutive" adjustment to NOPAT (this is really negative economic depreciation although the company does not label it as such),
  - Using a pro-forma base year to measure EVA improvement and recalibrating EVA incentive compensation targets, and
  - Excluding non-interest bearing liabilities from capital.

The first two responses are really failures to reconcile the conflict between shareholder and EP. Since rejected opportunities are difficult to track and document, we are not able to present a case study of a rejected acquisition. The second response, dropping EVA, can be viewed with much better perspective if we first consider the accounting adjustments that EVA companies have made to reconcile the conflict and maintain their commitment to value-based management. We now cover economic profit adjustments for acquisitions including (1) "metering" the acquisition cost into capital, (2) making a "dilutive" NOPAT adjustment, (3) using a pro-forma base year, and (4) excluding non-interest bearing liabilities —such as accounts payable and future environmental liabilities — from acquisition capital.

"Metering" The Acquisition Cost Into Capital

Some EVA companies "meter" the acquisition cost into capital at a rate that provides zero EVA improvement for achieving the zero NPV acquisition forecast, as Exhibit 10 illustrates. The capital recognized is just sufficient to wipe out the EVA improvement computed on operating capital. Let's use year 2 for an example. The projected operating capital EVA for year 2 is $920 = $2,070 - 10\% \times $11,500$. This represents an increase of $120 over year 1's EVA of $800. The projected EVA improvement will cover the capital charge on $1,200 = $120/10\%$ of acquisition goodwill, so $1,200 of acquisition goodwill is recognized in year 1 ending capital and $19,962 of acquisition goodwill is kept off the books in a "suspense" account. The exclusion of $19,962 from capital creates a deferred capital charge of $1,996 that must be added to the suspense account to maintain consistency with DCF valuation. The size of the deferred capital charge keeps the suspense account growing until year 6 and leaves $20,419 of deferred goodwill, or 96% of the original acquisition goodwill, in the suspense account at the end of year 7. It is unlikely, however, that the suspense account would remain for seven years. When the incentive plan targets are recalibrated (typically three to five years after the initial calibration), the prior year EVA, used to determine EVA improvement, would be recalculated on the basis of actual capital (including all goodwill) and the suspense account would be eliminated. Thus, this approach ultimately becomes another case of using a pro-forma base year.

Exhibit 10: "Metering" the Acquisition Cost into Capital

Operating Forecast	0	1	2	3	4	5	6	7
Operating Capital Growth Rate		15%	15%	15%	15%	15%	15%	15%
Operating Capital	10,000	11,500	13,225	15,209	17,490	20,114	23,131	26,600
Total Goodwill		21,162	21,162	21,162	21,162	21,162	21,162	21,162
Recognized Goodwill		1,200	2,580	4,167	5,992	8,091	10,504	13,280
Deferred Goodwill		19,962	20,578	21,049	21,329	21,363	21,086	20,419
Total Capital	10,000	12,700	15,805	19,376	23,482	28,204	33,635	39,880
Return on Operating Capital		18%	18%	18%	18%	18%	18%	18%
NOPAT		1,800	2,070	2,381	2,738	3,148	3,620	4,164
Capital Charge		1,000	1,270	1,581	1,938	2,348	2,820	3,364
Economic Profit		800	800	800	800	800	800	800
Economic Profit Improvement			0	0	0	0	0	0	0

A major weakness of this approach is that it is completely dependent on management's acquisition forecast and thus, creates an incentive for management to justify the acquisition on a heavily backloaded basis. With a backloaded forecast, quite modest EP improvement targets can be justified for the remaining term of the current incentive plan term, while the burden of the more substantial EP improvements projected for the long term is avoided through recalibration at the end of the plan term.

Adding a "Dilutive" Adjustment to NOPAT

One EVA company makes a "dilutive" adjustment to NOPAT in the first year of an acquisition. The dilutive adjustment offsets the projected decline in first year EVA caused by the acquisition. The company's intention is to limit the dilutive adjustment to the first acquisition year. Under this policy, positive year 2 EVA rather than positive NPV becomes the company's acquisition standard. If the company adheres to this policy, it may miss out on many attractive acquisition opportunities.

Using a Pro-Forma Base Year and Recalibrating Incentive Plan EVA Improvement Targets

Some companies reconcile the conflict between EP and shareholder value by using a pro-forma base year for the EP improvement calculation. The pro-forma calculation adds the acquisition goodwill to capital before computing the prior year EP. In this case, beginning capital for the pre-acquisition year (year 1) would be $10,000 + $21,162 = $31,162, and make pro-forma EP for the base year (year 1) equal to $1,800 − 10% × $31,162 = −$1,316. The pro-forma calculation makes current operations value equal to $19,500 (= $32,662 + (−$1,316.2/10%)) and future growth value equal to $13,162 (= $32,662 − $19,500). The pro-forma calculation changes the first year EP improvement from −$1,196 to + $120 (= −$1,196 − (−$1,136)). The pro-forma calculation can make the bonus plan measure of excess EP improvement completely consistent with shareholder value if the "expected EP improvement" target in the bonus plan is adjusted to reflect the required return on the acquired future growth value of $13,162.

Excluding Acquisition Liabilities from Capital

Another approach to reconciling the conflict between EP and shareholder value in acquisitions is the exclusion from capital of non-interest bearing long-term liabilities assumed by the acquirer. This approach has the effect of increasing post-acquisition EP, but is not correct because it destroys the equality of operating and financing free cash flow, and hence, destroys the linkage between excess EP improvement and shareholder return. It is based on an incorrect belief that it is appropriate to exclude liabilities from capital because they are not interest bearing.

Capital is often defined as total assets minus non-interest bearing liabilities. This is an extension of Bennett Stewart's use of "current non-interest bearing liabilities" in the operating definition of capital.[12] The term "non-interest bearing" is a frequent source of confusion because it does not accurately describe the liabilities that can be subtracted from capital without destroying the equality of financing and operating FCF. "Hidden interest liabilities" is a more accurate description of the liabilities that can be subtracted from capital without destroying the equality of financing and operating FCF. Some companies have significantly improved their post-acquisition EP by excluding from capital substantial environmental liabilities that are not stated on a present value basis and hence, do not bear interest. It will be easier to show why it is inappropriate to exclude these liabilities if we first consider accounts payable, which can be excluded from capital without destroying the equality of financing and operating free cash flow.

The example in Exhibit 11 shows that the present value of future free cash flow when accounts payable are deducted from capital is exactly equal to the present value of future free cash flow when accounts payable are treated as debt as long as cost of goods sold is reduced by the implicit interest on account payable. In this example, we assume that the implicit interest rate is equal to the pre-tax cost of capital since this is the simplest way of assuming that the weighted average cost of capital is unaffected by the accounting treatment of accounts payable. In the first case, capital is equal to total assets minus accounts payable, and the implicit interest in cost of goods sold is a deduction against operating profit. In the second case, capital is equal to total assets since accounts payable are considered debt and no implicit interest is charged against operating profit. In year 4 in both cases, inventory is liquidated, accounts payable are paid off, and PP&E is sold for book value at the end of the year. In the first case, where accounts payable is treated as a reduction in investment (i.e., capital), the present value of future free cash flow is $9,626. In the second case, where accounts payable is treated as a debt, the present value of future free cash flow is $10,694. But this implies, since the beginning accounts payable is $1,068, that the equity value is $10,694 minus $1,068, or $9,626, which is exactly the present value of free cash flow in the first case.

---

[12] Stewart, *The Quest for Value: A Guide For Senior Managers.*

Exhibit 11: Valuation with Alternative Treatments of Accounts Payable

Accounts Payable Deducted From Capital

	0	1	2	3	4
Operating Forecast					
Sales		10,000	11,500	13,225	15,209
Cash Cost of Goods Sold		6,500	7,475	8,596	9,886
Interest in Cost of Goods Sold		164	189	217	250
Gross Margin		3,336	3,836	4,411	5,073
SG&A		2,000	2,300	2,645	3,042
Operating Profit		1,336	1,536	1,766	2,031
Taxes		467	538	618	711
NOPAT		868	998	1,148	1,320
PP&E	10,000	11,000	12,650	14,548	0
Inventory	1,083	1,246	1,433	1,648	0
Accounts Payable	1,068	1,229	1,413	1,625	0
Capital	10,015	11,017	12,670	14,570	0
Valuation					
Investment	10,015	1,002	1,653	1,900	−14,570
Free Cash Flow		−134	−654	−752	15,890
PV of Free Cash Flow		−122	−541	−565	10,853
Cumulative PV of FCF	9,626				
Terminal Value	0				
PV of Terminal Value	0				
Market Value	9,626				

Accounts Payable Treated As Debt

	0	1	2	3	4
Operating Forecast					
Sales		10,000	11,500	13,225	15,209
Cash Cost of Goods Sold		6,500	7,475	8,596	9,886
Gross Margin		3,500	4,025	4,629	5,323
SG&A		2,000	2,300	2,645	3,042
Operating Profit		1,500	1,725	1,984	2,281
Taxes		525	604	694	798
NOPAT		975	1,121	1,289	1,483
PP&E	10,000	11,000	12,650	14,548	0
Inventory	1,083	1,246	1,433	1,648	0
Accounts Payable	1,068	1,229	1,413	1,625	0
Capital	11,083	12,246	14,083	16,195	0
Valuation					
Investment	11,083	1,163	1,837	2,112	−16,195
Free Cash Flow		−188	−716	−823	17,678
PV of Free Cash Flow		−170	−591	−618	12,074
Cumulative PV of FCF	10,694				
Terminal Value	0				
PV of Terminal Value	0				
Market Value	10,694				
Less Debt =	1,068				
Market Equity Value	9,626				

Confusion and inaccuracy arises when this example is falsely generalized to the conclusion that liabilities recognized on a future value basis may be excluded from capital without harm. One company has excluded from capital more than $1 billion of environmental liabilities assumed in an acquisition. These liabilities should be recognized on a present value basis, but they should also be included in capital because they represent real liabilities for future cash payments by the company's shareholders and the implicit interest on the liabilities is not being charged against operating profit. Since the payment of the liability is tax deductible, it should be included in capital on an after-tax present value basis. If we assume that the present value of these liabilities is $1.0 billion, the addition to capital would be the after-tax value of the liabilities, or $650 million (assuming a 35% tax rate). Their exclusion from capital reduces the capital charge in the EP calculation by $65 million (based on a 10% cost of capital). This difference is large enough to change the EP impact of the company's acquisition from positive to negative. To demonstrate that it is not appropriate to exclude the present value of these liabilities from capital, let's make two modifications to our example in Exhibit 11. We eliminate the accounts payable (so we can focus on just one liability) and assume that there is an environmental liability that is settled at the end of year 3 for $2,000.

Exhibits 12 and 13 show that the environmental liability can be treated as debt or deducted from capital as long as the implicit after-tax interest expense on the liability is charged against NOPAT. In both cases, the liability is recognized on an after-tax present value basis using a 35% tax rate. The initial liability is $977 $[= (1 - 0.35) \times \$2,000/(1.1)^3]$ and interest expense is computed using the 10% cost of capital. In both cases, the equity value is $9,717.

As can be seen in Exhibit 14, when the environmental liability is recognized on a future value basis and deducted from capital without charging any implicit interest against NOPAT, the operating definition of free cash flow is not correct and economic profit is overstated. In year 2, for example, economic profit appears to be +$97 when it should be −$103.

ABANDONING EVA AS A PERFORMANCE MEASURE

Now that we have seen the complexity of the accounting adjustments needed to reconcile EP with shareholder value, it is easier to appreciate that the accounting and target setting effort required might overwhelm companies with a limited commitment to economic profit as financial management system and basis for incentive compensation. Let's look at a couple of case studies.

Monsanto

Monsanto announced its adoption of EVA in its 1996 annual report:

> In 1996, Monsanto put in place a new performance measurement system called economic value added (EVA). The company will begin measuring its performance against EVA targets in 1997.

Exhibit 12: Environmental Liability Treated As Debt

	0	1	2	3	4
Operating Forecast					
Sales		10,000	11,500	13,225	15,209
Cash Cost of Goods Sold		6,500	7,475	8,596	9,886
Gross Margin		3,500	4,025	4,629	5,323
SG&A		2,000	2,300	2,645	3,042
Operating Profit		1,500	1,725	1,984	2,281
Taxes		525	604	694	798
NOPAT		975	1,121	1,289	1,483
PP&E	10,000	11,000	12,650	14,548	0
Inventory	1,083	1,246	1,433	1,648	0
After-tax Environmental Liability	977	1,074	1,182	1,300	0
Capital	11,083	12,246	14,083	16,195	0
Valuation					
Investment	11,083	1,163	1,837	2,112	−16,195
Free Cash Flow		−188	−716	−823	17,678
PV of Free Cash Flow		−170	−591	−618	12,074
Cumulative PV of FCF	10,694				
Terminal Value	0				
PV of Terminal Value	0				
Market Value	10,694	11,951	13,862	16,071	0
Less Debt =	977				
Market Equity Value	9,717				
Economic Profit Analysis					
Beginning Capital		11,083	12,246	14,083	16,195
Return on Capital		8.8%	9.2%	9.2%	9.2%
Capital Charge		1,108	1,225	1,408	1,620
Economic Profit		−133	−103	−119	−137
PV of Economic Profit		−121	−85	−89	−93
Cumulative PV of EVA	−389				
Capital + PV of EVA	10,694				

In 1997, Monsanto spun off its chemicals business and significantly increased its spending on agricultural bio-technology and pharmaceuticals. The annual report said:

> Although there's no universally accepted definition of "growth" spending, our calculations — which include technology, infra-structure costs and the income effects of recent acquisitions — show...we spent more than $1.3 billion pretax on growth in 1997, an increase of more than $500 million, or about a 60 percent increase, from our growth spending in 1996.

In February 1997, a portion of the new EVA bonus was replaced by a performance stock option grant. In the annual report for 1997, the company praised future EVA, but highlighted the shortcomings of current income (which implies, with rising capital, an even greater shortcoming in current EVA): "Our value-based metrics, such as Economic Value Added (EVA), incline us to make economically attractive investments, even when they depress current income, as they often do." The current performance measure the company highlighted in the 1997 annual report was "Earnings Before Interest, Taxes, Amortization and Technology". In its first quarterly earnings report for 1998, Monsanto said:

> We have an extremely attractive new product pipeline and a growing position in critically important technologies. We've been very clear about our commitment to make the investments necessary to take full advantage of these opportunities, recognizing that they have had and will have an increasing effect on near-term quarterly earnings.

Exhibit 13: Environmental Liability Deducted from Capital/Expense Recognized

	0	1	2	3	4
Operating Forecast					
Sales		10,000	11,500	13,225	15,209
Cash Cost of Goods Sold		6,500	7,475	8,596	9,886
Gross Margin		3,500	4,025	4,629	5,323
SG&A		2,000	2,300	2,645	3,042
Operating Profit		1,500	1,725	1,984	2,281
Taxes		525	604	694	798
NOPAT		975	1,121	1,289	1,483
Implicit A-T Interest on Environmental Liability		98	107	118	0
Adjusted NOPAT		877	1,014	1,171	1,483
PP&E	10,000	11,000	12,650	14,548	0
Inventory	1,083	1,246	1,433	1,648	0
After-tax Environmental Liability	977	1,074	1,182	0	0
Capital	10,107	11,171	12,901	16,195	0
Valuation					
Investment	10,107	1,065	1,729	3,294	−16,195
Free Cash Flow		−188	−716	−2,123	17,678
PV of Free Cash Flow		−170	−591	−1,595	12,074
Cumulative PV of FCF	9,717				
Terminal Value	0				
PV of Terminal Value	0				
Market Value	9,717	10,877	12,680	16,071	0
Economic Profit Analysis					
Beginning Capital		10,107	11,171	12,901	16,195
Return on Capital		9.6%	10.0%	10.0%	9.2%
Capital Charge		1,011	1,117	1,290	1,620
Economic Profit		−133	−103	−119	−137
PV of Economic Profit		−121	−85	−89	−93
Cumulative PV of EVA	−389				
Capital + PV of EVA	9,717				

Exhibit 14: Environmental Liability Deducted from Capital/No Expense Recognized

	0	1	2	3	4
Operating Forecast					
Sales		10,000	11,500	13,225	15,209
Cash Cost of Goods Sold		6,500	7,475	8,596	9,886
Gross Margin		3,500	4,025	4,629	5,323
SG&A		2,000	2,300	2,645	3,042
Operating Profit		1,500	1,725	1,984	2,281
Taxes		525	604	694	798
NOPAT		975	1,121	1,289	1,483
Implicit A-T Interest on Environmental Liability		0	0	0	0
Adjusted NOPAT		975	1,121	1,289	1,483
PP&E	10,000	11,000	12,650	14,548	0
Inventory	1,083	1,246	1,433	1,648	0
After-tax Environmental Liability	2,000	2,000	2,000	0	0
Capital	9,083	10,246	12,083	16,195	0
Valuation					
Investment	9,083	1,163	1,837	4,112	−16,195
Free Cash Flow		−188	−716	−2,823	17,678
PV of Free Cash Flow		−170	−591	−2,121	12,074
Cumulative PV of FCF	9,191				
Terminal Value	0				
PV of Terminal Value	0				
Market Value	9,191	10,298	12,044	16,071	0
Economic Profit Analysis					
Beginning Capital		9,083	10,246	12,083	16,195
Return on Capital		10.7%	10.9%	10.7%	9.2%
Capital Charge		908	1,025	1,208	1,620
Economic Profit		67	97	81	−137
PV of Economic Profit		61	80	61	−93
Cumulative PV of EVA	108				
Capital + PV of EVA	9,191				

In 1998, the retreat from EVA continued:

- In the first quarter earnings press release, Monsanto devoted a paragraph to its EVA performance and reported EVA results just below earnings per share.
- In the second quarter earnings press release, Monsanto dropped the paragraph about its EVA performance, but continued to report EVA results just below earnings per share.
- In the third quarter earnings press release, Monsanto omitted any discussion of its EVA performance, but continued to report EVA results just below earnings per share.
- In the fourth quarter earnings press release, Monsanto dropped its reporting of EVA and substituted EBIT where it had previously reported EVA.

In 1999, Monsanto's EVA Director was given new responsibilities. He is now "Director of Y2K Planning."

AT&T

AT&T's 1992 annual report expressed strong support for economic profit as a basis for performance measurement and incentive compensation:

> In 1992 we began measuring the performance of each of our units with an important new management tool called "Economic Value Added" — "EVA" for short....EVA gives our managers a way to also track the creation of shareowner value in individual AT&T units....We have made it the centerpiece of our "value based planning" process. And we are linking a portion of our managers' incentive compensation to performance against EVA targets for 1993....In summary, our performance planning, measurement and reward programs are now fully aligned with the interests of the shareowners."

The company remained enthusiastic about EVA for two years. In 1993 and 1994, it exceeded its EVA targets. Then, in September 1995, CEO Bob Allen announced the spin-offs of Lucent Technologies and NCR. For the fourth quarter of 1995,

> the bonus plan "was adjusted to provide 50% of the incentive on the EVA level of achievement and 50% based on successful accomplishment of the restructuring transition work, including the impact on PVA [People Valued Added] and CVA [Customer Value Added]....Because of adjustments for NCR (formerly AT&T Global Information Solutions) writedown, the 1995 EVA target was not met and the portion of the Chairman's annual bonus which relates to this target was reduced accordingly. The 1995 results for the PVA, CVA, and restructuring transition measurements were met."
> (1996 proxy)

In the same year, the Compensation Committee said:

> The committee recognizes that the Company's impending restructure will render obsolete the performance criteria established for the long-term cycles 1994-96 and 1995-97. To address this transition period, and the difficulty of setting long-term financial targets while the restructure is in process, the committee has recommended and approved that the criteria for performance periods 1994-1996 and 1995-97 are deemed to have been met at the target level." (1996 proxy)

In 1996, the company started to abandon EVA:

> The Company achieved its EVA target, but the Committee noted
> that it did so, in part, by modifying spending plans, resulting in
> lower average capital deployed. The Committee therefore deter-
> mined that, with respect to financial performance, the additional
> metric of Earnings Per Share results should be considered....The
> Company achieved its EVA target, but...shareholders experienced a
> 9% decrease in the value of their AT&T-related holdings during
> 1996, though the broad market rose 20%.....In 1997, the Company
> will re-institute a performance share program tied to three-year rel-
> ative total shareholder return ('TSR') as measured against a peer
> group of industry competitors. (1997 proxy)

In 1997, the company dropped EVA completely and adopted earnings per
share and expense to revenue ratio as its financial performance measures. While
AT&T's decision to drop EVA took five years, evidence from its investor relations
website suggests that it lost its enthusiasm for EVA early on. A search for "EVA"
in the website, which includes 718 documents, identifies only two documents –
the 1992 annual report and the 1993 mission statement.

Other Examples

A number of other companies have dropped EVA after encountering difficulties in
adjusting for spin-offs and divestitures. Premark provides an example:

> The financial objectives for the 1995-97 and 1996-98 long-term
> incentive programs were originally established as a certain level of
> EVA. However, due to the difficulties and complexities of adjusting
> EVA fairly in order to exclude the effects of the spin-off and Hartco
> divestiture on capital, tax rates and corporate office expense, the
> financial objectives have been restated by the Committee as seg-
> ment profit. (1997 proxy)

For other companies, the complexity of economic profit was more than
they could handle. Grancare's compensation committee, in explaining its decision
to drop EVA as a performance measure, said:

> The Committee believes that fulfilling EPS expectations is the most
> essential short-term object for those having corporate responsibili-
> ties. It also is simple for participants, members of the Company's
> Board of Directors and the investment community to understand
> and is a prevalent measure in the healthcare management industry.

SUMMARY AND CONCLUSIONS

It is not easy to make economic profit consistent with shareholder value despite the facile claims that shareholder value is just a matter of "getting to cash." Many, if not most, of the companies that embrace economic profit as an approach to financial management and incentive compensation are unprepared for the accounting complexity and effort required to make economic profit consistent with shareholder value. Very few companies are willing to adopt the non-GAAP accounting concepts, such as sinking fund depreciation and negative economic depreciation, that are needed to reconcile economic profit with shareholder value "on the books." Without these concepts, or equivalent "off the books" adjustments, incentive plans based on economic profit improvement discourage value creating investments that don't provide a current cash return equal to the cost of capital. This is the standard profile of investments in intangibles, such as R&D and acquisition goodwill, so there is no doubt that economic profit, as normally calculated, does discourage investment in intangibles. A number of companies have adopted "off the books" adjustments that do substantially reconcile economic profit with shareholder value. The two adjustments that have been used most often are "metering" the acquisition cost into capital and using a pro-forma base year combined with recalibration of the incentive plan targets. The difficulty and complexity of the effort needed to reconcile economic profit with shareholder value is evident in the companies that have failed to carry through the effort and decided instead to drop economic profit as a performance measure.

What distinguishes the companies that persevere from those that give up? It is my judgment, based on the case studies and my broader experience, that companies that take a contractual approach to management compensation, by making multi-year commitments to sharing percentages and performance targets, are much more willing to invest the time and effort required to address accounting issues that must be resolved to make economic profit consistent with shareholder value. For these companies, the accounting issues have important compensation consequences. The companies that provide the basis for the examples of accounting adjustments that reconcile acquisition EP with shareholder value all use the Stern Stewart EVA bonus plan design with multi-year commitments to sharing percentages and expected EVA improvement. Several of them also make multi-year commitments to fixed share stock option grant guidelines. The companies that have abandoned EVA, on the other hand, take a very discretionary approach to executive compensation. The Premark compensation committee says:

> The Committee verifies the actual performance achieved as a pre-
> condition to approving awards, and reserves the right to adjust any
> formula-based award that, in its judgment, is inappropriate in light
> of overall results and circumstances.

The Quaker Oats compensation committee says:

Company and unit financial performance is measured primarily by Controllable Earnings targets…The Committee also considers performance against other key financial measures such as sales, earnings per share, return on assets, return on equity and operating income. In order for the full financial portion of the target bonuses to be paid, the Company must meet its internal financial targets and the Committee also considers how that performance relates to other comparable companies.

The experience of these companies suggests that there are two good reasons why companies should take a more contractual approach to executive compensation: stronger incentives and better accounting!

Chapter 6

Integrating EVA® into the Portfolio Management Process

Jason L. Wolin
Director
CDC Investment Management

Steven Klopukh, CFA
Equity Research Analyst
CDC Investment Management

INTRODUCTION

Economic Value Added (EVA®)[1] has been adopted by many corporations as a tool for maximizing shareholder value. Yet the same EVA principles that have lead companies to focus on value creation, have not been readily applied to investment management.[2] In fact, most active managers have underperformed their benchmarks, thereby destroying investor value. For the most part, investment managers are not necessarily focused on, nor compensated for, generating risk-adjusted excess return above an appropriate benchmark.

We believe that the EVA methodology enhances active equity management for three major reasons. First, EVA sets the overall investment objective: to produce a strong risk-adjusted excess return over an appropriate benchmark, or alternatively, to create "investor value added." Risk management is critical to creating investor value. Managers should actively seek to minimize exposures to a range of incidental factors that can harm investor returns and increase risks. Second, EVA can be used to perform rigorous fundamental analysis on corporations, thereby improving security selection in the portfolio. Third, if properly constructed, performance fees align the interests of investment managers with their investors by rewarding managers for creating "investor value added."

---

[1] EVA® is a Trademark of the Stern Stewart Company

[2] The good news however is that the economic profit (EVA) approach to equity management is growing rapidly. For an in depth discussion of theory, application, and EVA-based players in investment management, see Frank J. Fabozzi and James L. Grant, *Equity Portfolio Management* (New Hope, PA: Frank J. Fabozzi Associates, 1999).

Exhibit 1: EVA Definitions

$$EVA_t = (ROIC_t - WACC_t) \times Capital_{t-1}$$

$$MVA_{t-1} = \sum_{t=1}^{T} \frac{EVA_t}{(1 + WACC)}$$

$$MV_{t-1} = MVA_{t-1} + Capital_{t-1}$$

where

ROIC	=	Return on Invested Capital or NOPAT/Capital
NOPAT	=	Net Operating Profit After Taxes
WACC	=	Weighted Average Cost of Capital
MVA	=	Market Value Added
MV	=	Market Value of the Firm

EVA Defined

It is helpful to define EVA and review a few concepts before discussing its applications in investment decision making. As explained in Chapter 1, EVA is a measure of corporate performance developed by the consulting firm Stern Stewart. The origins of EVA are rooted in the theory of firm valuation originally developed by Nobel laureates Franco Modigliani and Merton Miller in the late 1950s. Their work on corporate financial structure and its effects on firm value lead to the development of the discounted cash flow model (DCF) of firm valuation. The DCF model simply equates a firm's value to the net present value of its future cash flows.

EVA is a modified version of the DCF. The modifications where developed by Stern Stewart with a specific goal in mind: to align management's interests with those of its shareholders.[3] Like the DCF, EVA equates the firm's value to discounted future cash flows. The two methods differ in that EVA attempts to measure whether a firm's management creates value (or positive EVA) over a specific period of time. This enables EVA measures to be tied directly to executive compensation, ensuring that management is focused on creating value for the firm's shareholders. Exhibit 1 presents how EVA is calculated and its relationship to firm value.

Exhibit 1 shows that a specific period's dollar EVA is equal to the spread between the firm's return on invested capital (ROIC) and weighted average cost of capital (WACC) times the dollar capital employed in the business to generate the return. ROIC is defined as net operating profit after taxes (NOPAT) divided by capital. The next equation in Exhibit 1 defines market value added (MVA). MVA is equal to the sum of all future EVA that the firm is expected to generate discounted by the WACC. Finally, MVA plus the total capital invested in the firm is equivalent to the firm's market value (MV).

There are two major advantages to EVA over traditional measures of corporate performance that are relevant to investment decision making. One advantage can be found in the calculation of net operating profit after taxes (NOPAT).

---

[3] For a full discussion of the EVA methodology, see G. Bennett Stewart III, *The Quest for Value* (Harper-Collins, Publishers Inc.,1990). See also Chapters 2 and 4 in this book.

The benefit of NOPAT is that it adjusts standard accounting statement earnings to represent firm profit independent of financing decision or accounting convention. This allows management performance to be evaluated without the effects of financial gimmicks. For example, a performance measure based on return on equity (ROE) can easily be gamed by taking on more debt. By leveraging a firm's operation with debt, ROE can be increased without adding incremental value to shareholders. Despite the benefits of a higher interest tax shield, it is possible for an increase in leverage to destroy shareholder value due to increased risk of future earnings and the cost associated with financial distress.

The second advantage of EVA is the assignment of a capital charge to earnings. Unlike common performance measures such as earnings per share or ROE, EVA compares the profitability of the firm relative to a benchmark. The benchmark is the cost associated with the capital used to generate NOPAT. The cost of capital represents the price management must pay for taking risk to generate return. Alternatively, the cost of capital represents the opportunity cost associated with choosing one investment opportunity over another. Consistent with financial theory, the cost of capital varies with the risk of creating future economic earnings. The more risk perceived in future earnings, the higher is the cost of capital.

Now, let's apply these EVA concepts to investment decision making. It is important to note that the purpose of EVA is not simply to measure corporate performance but to focus corporate managers on making the most economically efficient capital allocation decisions targeted at producing value for shareholders. This same goal can be applied to portfolio managers whose charge is to create value for investors.

CREATING INVESTOR VALUE

EVA principles applied to investment management establish the following objective: the active manager creates value by producing a risk-adjusted return above a passive benchmark. To illustrate, consider the following alternatives. An investor interested in the return of the U.S. equity market has the option of putting money into an active strategy (managed equity fund) or a passive strategy (S&P 500 Index fund). In this context, the active manager can only add value by outperforming the passive alternative net of fees and expenses. It is not sufficient to produce a positive return. The portfolio manager must outperform the passive alternative to create value. This implies the following two links to EVA principles: the risk-adjusted benchmark return represents the cost of capital of the managed portfolio; and, the managed portfolio's return above the risk-adjusted benchmark represents investor value added.[4]

---

[4] We recognize the similarity between the EVA concept of investor value added and the traditional "alpha" measure of abnormal equity performance.

Exhibit 2: Active Risk versus Total Risk

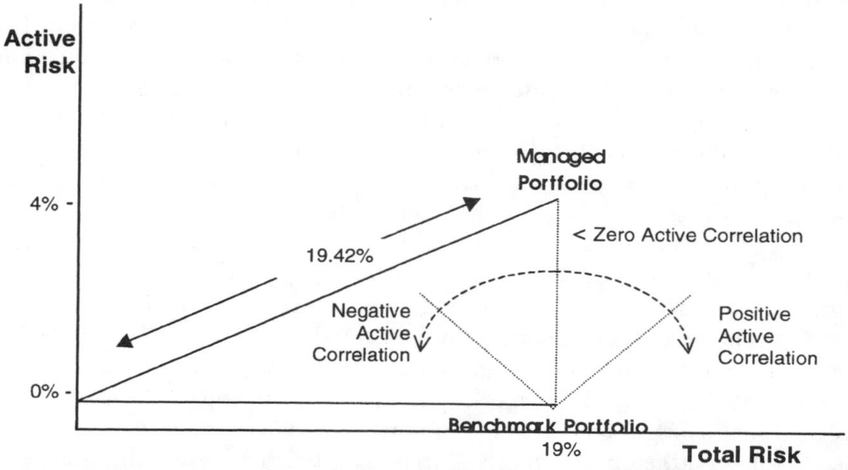

Measuring Active Investment Performance and Risk

It is possible for the active manager to outperform without creating value for the investor. Similar to the gaming issues of firm ROE and leverage, a portfolio manager can simply increase the portfolio's leverage to outperform the benchmark. This is why it is necessary to adjust the benchmark return for risk. One should pay careful attention to the risk characteristics of the managed portfolio when evaluating excess return.

To measure risk, one can separate a managed portfolio into two distinct components. The first component is the benchmark portfolio against which the managed portfolio is measured. The second component is the active overlay portfolio that differentiates the managed portfolio from the benchmark. In order to produce excess return (that is above the benchmark), the portfolio manager must take active risk. Active risk is defined as the variance of excess returns of the managed portfolio over the benchmark. It is possible to incur active risk and still have the same total risk as the benchmark. Exhibit 2 illustrates this point.

Exhibit 2 compares the relationship between active portfolio risk and total portfolio risk. In the exhibit, the managed portfolio has a total risk of 19.42%.[5] This risk is very similar to the total risk of the benchmark portfolio at 19%. However, the managed portfolio has an active risk relative to the benchmark of 4%. The diagram suggests that the active portfolio[6] must be uncorrelated with

---

[5] The managed portfolio's total risk of 19.42% is measured by the length if the hypotenuse of the right triangle in Exhibit 1. Given the total risk of the benchmark is 19% and the active risk of the managed portfolio is 4% (plus the assumption that the active portfolio is zero correlated with the benchmark), we find the length of the hypotenuse given as $c^2 = a^2 + b^2$ or $19.42\%^2 = 19\%^2 + 4\%^2$.

[6] The active portfolio is defined as the difference between the managed and benchmark portfolio constituent's weights.

the benchmark portfolio in order for the total risk to be similar for both portfolios.[7] In the case where the active portfolio is uncorrelated with the benchmark, only a slight risk adjustment to the benchmark portfolio is necessary. If the active portfolio is correlated with the benchmark, the managed portfolio will have more total risk than the benchmark portfolio.

For example, an active portfolio constructed only with leverage has a correlation of one with its benchmark. This would be the equivalent of the active manager borrowing money and investing in the benchmark to generate an excess return. This does not create value for investors since the investor can replicate this strategy on their own. Another form of leverage is for the active manager to buy companies with high risk relative to the benchmark. Again, the managed portfolio will have more total risk than the benchmark. Therefore, the return of the benchmark portfolio return must be adjusted for the additional risk when evaluating excess return.

The following techniques can be employed to calculate risk-adjusted benchmark returns. One way is to multiply the benchmark return by the beta of the managed portfolio. This would increase (or decrease) the benchmark return for the level of risk being taken by the managed portfolio as measured by beta. Similarly, one can lever the benchmark return until its volatility is equivalent to that of the managed portfolio. Alternatively, a Sharpe ratio[8] compares the efficiency of both the managed and benchmark portfolio. The Sharpe ratio relates a portfolio's excess return above the risk-free rate to its total volatility. The managed portfolio creates value when its Sharpe ratio is greater than that of the benchmark.

Risk Management Discipline

We believe stock selection to be the major source of investor value. This is an important statement in that most investment managers base their investment decisions on a particular investment style. There is empirical evidence that investment style explains 90% of U.S. equity portfolio returns.[9] A first step towards reaching the goal of creating investor value is to identify how common investing styles can result in bias and destroy value. In this regard, EVA principles serve as a guide to implement stock selection strategies that create investor value and avoid those that destroy value.

The investment management community recognizes several strategies that are employed to generate return for investors (we refer to "generate return" instead of "generate value" since most managers fail to outperform their passive benchmarks). Strategies widely accepted by the industry include buying companies based on growth, value and/or size characteristics. Other strategies include industry and market timing. Industry timing is an attempt to overweight industry

---

[7] This model assumes unlimited liquidity in the active portfolio.

[8] For an application of the single-index Sharpe ratio — as well as multiple-index Sharpe ratio benchmarks — see Fabozzi and Grant, *Equity Portfolio Management*.

[9] William F. Sharpe, "Asset Allocation: Management Style And Performance Measurement," *Journal of Portfolio Management* (Winter 1992), pp. 7-19.

groups that appear attractive. Market timing involves buying and selling companies in anticipation of general market movements.

Relying exclusively on a particular investment strategy can destroy value due to the potential for stock selection bias. For example, it has been widely accepted that over time, value stocks outperform growth and that small capitalization stocks outperform large ones. If this were the case, then overweighting value and small capitalization companies would create investor value[10] since the passive benchmark contains all types of companies.[11] In the bull market of 1995-1999, the opposite occurred. Large capitalization growth stocks have dominated the market. The investment manager may pick excellent companies within the target universe but the bias towards small capitalization and/or value stocks dominates the investment returns.

The bias example highlights the main problem with depending on any one strategy to generate investor value. A particular investment style is like a hot fashion trend, which can fall in and out of favor over time. To illustrate, Exhibit 3 demonstrates the cyclical nature of value and growth strategies.

Exhibit 3: Excess Return of Barra S&P 500 Value and Growth Indices from October 1993 to May 1999

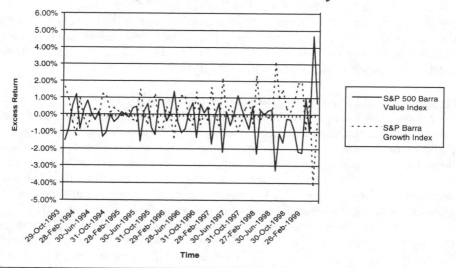

---

[10] It is important to realize that creating investor value and the value strategy of investing are two separate ideas. The value investing strategy is commonly defined as buying companies with characteristics such as low price to earnings, low price to book ratios and/or high dividend yields. We have defined investor value as the creation of excess return above a risk-adjusted benchmark.

Moreover, Grant emphasizes the importance of discovering the "real value" in common stocks using economic profit principles. See James L. Grant, *Foundations of Economic Value Added* (New Hope, PA: Frank J. Fabozzi Associates, 1997).

[11] We are aware that the passive benchmark may actually be a style-based benchmark, such as the Barra S&P 500 Value or Growth indexes.

Exhibit 3 demonstrates that the persistence of a particular style is short lived and follows a random path.[12] By construction, when the Barra S&P 500 Value index outperforms the S&P 500, the Barra S&P 500 Growth index must underperform and vice-versa. This condition exists because both indices combine to equal the S&P 500 index.[13] If a particular style of investing is relied on, it is inevitable that opportunities outside the investment focus are ignored. This bias results in value destruction since it is nearly impossible to generate excess return against a broad market index (such as the S&P 500) when the style is out of favor. The following highlights some common portfolio biases that can destroy value if left unchecked.

Too Much Cash

Typically, equity portfolios will hold anywhere from 3% to 8% cash. Since equity markets are on average rising over time, cash positions will be a drag on performance. To illustrate, say the average portfolio holds 100 stocks. Then the average stock holding would be 1% (if you were fully invested). Given this scenario, a 3% to 8% cash position would be the largest active position in the portfolio, dominating any individual stock selection decision.

Beta Bias

Buying companies that carry more relative risk than the average company in the benchmark causes a beta bias. This bias results in general market movements dominating portfolio returns. A beta bias can result in increased portfolio risk as well.

Industry Bias

Value investors are notorious for avoiding the technology sector whose members often carry a valuation multiple higher than the market. This bias will result in an underweight in technology issues and an overweight in industries such as finance, utilities or cyclicals whose multiples tend to be lower than the market. In this situation, the portfolio is more dependent on industry performance than individual company performance.

Size Bias

Having small or middle capitalization companies dominate portfolio stock selection results in size bias. This is certainly appropriate when the investment mandate is for a small or mid cap return. However, size bias will cause trouble when the mandate is to outperform a general market index that is capitalization weighted (such as the S&P 500). In this case, the portfolio will only add value when small companies outperform larger ones. Although financial theory suggests that small companies

---

[12] This view that abnormal style (and size) benefits may vary considerably over time is also recognized by Jacobs and Levy. See Bruce I. Jacobs and Kenneth N. Levy, "Investment Management: An Architecture for the Equity Market," Chapter 1 in Frank J Fabozzi (ed.), *Active Equity Portfolio Management* (New Hope, PA: Frank J. Fabozzi Associates, 1998).

[13] The Barra S&P 500-value index contains the cap-weighted (up to 50%) companies in the S&P 500 with the lowest price-to-book score. The Barra S&P 500-growth index contains the cap-weighted companies with the highest score (or lowest book-to-price ratio).

should outperform larger companies over time, the evidence is mixed. During the most recent bull market, small capitalization companies performed terribly.

Understanding the components of active risk is critical for identifying and controlling portfolio bias and minimizing value destruction. By applying EVA concepts to portfolio management, we view active risk in the context of the cost of capital that one must incur to generate excess return. A number of companies provide risk models that measure and quantify active risk in regard to the potential biases discussed above. Barra and Northfield Information Services, Inc. are two companies whose models we have used in our investment process.

Performance Fees

The investment management fee structure is another area where EVA principles can be applied in the best interest of investors. In the funds management industry, it is standard for traditional active fund managers to charge fixed fees for their services. These fees can be upwards of 50 basis points of assets under management, annually. The fee is paid regardless of the performance of the investment portfolio.

Standard management fees are a drag on performance. Management fees plus normal fund expenses can reduce returns by more than 1%. It is no wonder that far more than 50% of active managers underperform the S&P 500 when one considers fees and expenses.

EVA dictates that managers should be paid in line with performance. Performance fees pay the investment manager based on a scale relative to return they generate above the passive benchmark. When managers outperform, they participate in the upside of their good work. When managers underperform, they help cushion the downside by giving a portion of their fee back to the investor.

EVA APPLIED TO STOCK SELECTION

EVA methodologies can be an effective tool for stock selection.[14] We believe that identifying mis-priced companies and the catalysts that drive return is an effective way to generate investor value consistently. EVA provides for a stronger relationship between corporate performance and valuation. Exhibit 4 shows the relationship of EVA return on invested capital (ROIC) to the ratio of firm enterprise value[15] (EV) to invested capital for the S&P 500.

As can be seen in Exhibit 4, EVA ROIC explains about 50% of the variance of the Enterprise Value/Invested Capital ratio. This can be compared to Price to Book versus Return on Equity and Price to Earnings versus Return on Equity, which, from our analysis, have a R^2 of 37% and 0.65% respectively. This example demonstrates that EVA adjustments provide a more accurate picture of historical

---

[14] For example, Grant provides several quantitative applications of EVA in common stock and industry selection. See Grant, *Foundations of Economic Value Added*.

[15] Enterprise value is defined as the market value of equity plus all outstanding debt less excess cash.

corporate performance than do more traditional methods. However, we must point out that this historical analysis proves to be a poor proxy for whether a stock is mis-priced and therefore is a good or bad investment.

An EVA Illustration: The Dayton Hudson Corporation

To demonstrate the benefits of EVA as a stock selection tool, we perform an analysis of the Dayton Hudson Corporation (DHC). First, we calculate NOPAT and implement the major EVA adjustments required to map GAAP accounting to economic earnings. Next, we compare DHC's recent EVA-adjusted financial performance to its competitors in an effort to explain DHC's value drivers. Finally, we demonstrate how separating EVA into economic book value and future growth opportunities provides insights into DHC's intrinsic value as well as highlight the importance of the competitive advantage period.[16]

DHC has adopted EVA to evaluate capital investment decisions and financial performance. Moreover, DHC's management incentive compensation is tied to achieving certain EVA objectives. We have provided DHC's income statement and balance sheet from its 1998 annual report for reference in Exhibits 5 and 6, respectively.

For a quick company description, DHC is the fifth largest retailer in the United States. The company operates over 1,100 department stores in 39 states. DHC's Target division represents 75% of the company revenues and pre-tax profits. Target is one of the fastest growing upscale discount retailers in the United States and has delivered compound annual revenue growth over the past 10 years of 14%, of which comparable-store sales increased 5%. Over that same time period, DHC's stock increased over 8 fold for a 25.5% compounded annual return — twice the market's return.

Exhibit 4: Regression of Enterprise Value/Invested Capital versus ROIC (S&P Industrials as of June 30, 1999)

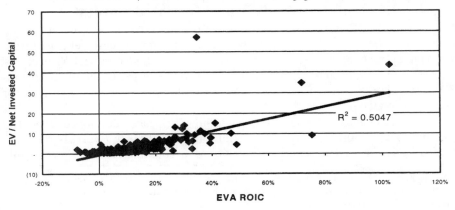

---

[16] The competitive advantage period is an EVA term that is defined as the number of years a company will generate above average returns for its investors.

Exhibit 5: DHC Income Statement

Dayton Hudson Corporation Consolidated Results of Operations			
(Millions of dollars, except per share data)	1998	1997	1996
Revenues	$30,951	$27,757	$25,371
Cost and Expenses			
Cost of retail sales, buying and occupancy	22,634	20,320	18,628
Selling, publicity and amortization	5,077	4,532	4,289
Depreciation and amortization	780	693	650
Interest expense	398	416	442
Taxes other than income taxes	506	470	445
Real estate repositioning	-	-	134
Total costs and expenses	29,395	26,431	24,588
Earnings before income taxes and extraordinary charges	1,556	1,326	783
Provision for income taxes	594	524	309
Net earnings before extraordinary charges	962	802	474
Extraordinary charges from purchase and redemption of debt, net of tax	27	51	11
Net earnings	935	751	463
Basic Earnings Per Share			
Earnings before extraordinary charges	$2.19	$1.84	$1.09
Extraordinary charges	(0.06)	(0.12)	(0.03)
Basic Earnings Per Share	$2.13	$1.72	$1.07
Diluted Earnings Per Share			
Earnings before extraordinary charges	$2.13	$1.72	$1.07
Extraordinary charges	(0.06)	(0.11)	(0.02)
Diluted Earnings Per Share	$2.07	$1.61	$1.04
Weighted Average Common Shares Outstanding (millions)			
Basic	440.0	436.1	433.3
Diluted	467.3	463.7	460.9

Calculating NOPAT and Invested Capital

EVA defines NOPAT as after-tax operating income net of depreciation and excluding the effects of financing. NOPAT is a proxy for the cash generated from recurring business activities. The one non-cash item included in NOPAT is depreciation since it represents the best *available* estimate of the economic deterioration in invested assets. In Exhibit 7, we provide two equivalent methods for calculating NOPAT.[17]

To calculate NOPAT, Stern and Stewart[18] have developed over 160 potential accounting adjustments, which they call *Equity Equivalents* (EE). Equity Equivalents are necessary to map GAAP accounting earnings to economic

---

[17] See Pamela P. Peterson and David R Peterson, *Company Performance and Measures of Value Added* (Charlottesville, VA: The Research Foundation of the Institute of Chartered Financial Analysts, 1996) and Chapters 2 and 4 in this book for additional background reading.

[18] See Stewart's, *The Quest for Value* for a more complete discussion on the many EVA-based accounting adjustments. Also, see Chapter 5 by Stephen O'Byrne on the proper EVA treatment of economic depreciation and acquisition goodwill.

earnings. The exercise of applying EE in the calculation of NOPAT can be quite revealing as to whether a firm is conservative or aggressive in managing its earnings. It is important to note that every EE adjustment applied to NOPAT has a corresponding adjustment to capital. The major EE are highlighted in Exhibit 8.

The identification and calculation of equity equivalents can be quite involved. The following provides a description of those appropriate for DHC.

Exhibit 6: DHC Balance Sheet

Dayton Hudson Corporation Consolidated Statements of Financial Position		
(Millions of dollars)	January 30, 1999	January 31, 1998
Assets		
Current Assets		
Cash and cash equivalents	$255	$211
Retained Securitized Receivables	1,656	1,555
Merchandise inventories	3,475	3,251
Other	619	544
Total Current Assets	6,005	5,561
Property and Equipment		
Land	1,868	1,712
Buildings and improvements	7,217	6,497
Fixtures and equipment	3,274	2,915
Construction-in-process	378	389
Accumulated depreciation	(3,768)	(3,388)
Property and Equipment, net	8,969	8,125
Other	692	505
Total Assets	$15,666	$14,191
Liabilities and Shareholders' Investment		
Current Liabilities		
Accounts payable	$3,150	$2,727
Accrued Liabilities	1,444	1,346
Income taxes payable	207	210
Current portion of long-term debt and notes payable	256	273
Total current liabilities	5,057	4,556
Long-Term debt	4,452	4,425
Deferred income taxes and other	822	720
Convertible preferred stock, net	24	30
Shareholders' Investment		
Convertible preferred stock	268	280
Common stock	74	73
Additional paid-in-capital	286	196
Retained earnings	4,683	3,930
Loan to ESOP	-	19
Total Shareholders' Investment	5,311	4,498
Total Liabilities and Shareholders' Investment	$15,666	$14,229

Exhibit 7: NOPAT Calculation

Operating Approach
  Sales
  Less Cost of Goods Sold
  Less SG&A
  Less Depreciation
  Plus Implied Interest on Operating Leases
  Less Equity Equivalents*
  = Adjusted Operating Profit Before Taxes
  Less Cash Operating Taxes
  = NOPAT
* when included as expenses in NOPAT calculation

Financing Approach
  Net Income Before Extraordinary Items Available to Common
  Plus Preferred Dividend
  Less Minority Interest
  Plus After-tax Interest Expense
  Plus Equity Equivalents
  = NOPAT

Exhibit 8: Major Equity Equivalents

The following are added to capital and the increase is added to NOPAT:

Deferred Tax Reserve
LIFO Reserve
Cumulative Goodwill Amortization
Unrecorded Goodwill
(Net) Capital Intangibles
Full-Cost Reserve
Cumulative Unusual Loss (Gain) After-tax
Other Reserves, such as:
  Bad debt reserve
  Inventory obsolescence reserve
  Warranty reserve
  Deferred income reserve

Operating Leases

Accountants have adopted conventions regarding when to capitalize lease obligations. In essence, leasing an asset is the equivalent of buying an asset and financing the purchase through a third party. Regardless of how a company accounts for the lease, the future operating lease payments represent non-cancelable obligations and have an interest cost embedded in the payment. Therefore all leases should be capitalized.

Exhibit 9: Present Value of Operating Leases

Year	Operating Leases (in millions)	
	January 31, 1999	January 30, 1998
1998		$111
1999	$115	105
2000	94	82
2001	86	75
2002	78	70
2003 (and thereafter for 1998)	63	617
2004 and thereafter	564	
Total Minimum Payments	1,000	1,060
Present Value at 9% and 9.1% interest rate, respectively	593	621
Interest Expense	53	57

To capitalize DHC's operating leases, we take the present value of future payments at the rate the company pays on debt. DHC provides the weighted average interest rate on lease obligations in its financial statements. When companies do not provide the interest rate paid on leases, the interest cost can be estimated from leases that the firm has capitalized, or alternatively, from the firm's general borrowing rate. Since we know the actual payments for only the first five years, we also need to estimate how long the remaining stream of payments will last. To estimate the number of payments remaining, we divide the remaining payments ($564 million in 2004 and thereafter) by the payment in the fifth year ($63 million in 2003) which is approximately 9 years. Finally, we take the present value of the 14 years of lease payments, which results in $593 million at January 31, 1999. Exhibit 9 illustrates the calculation of the present value of lease obligations.

Deferred Taxes
We add back DHC's deferred tax liability of $437 million to capital and subtract the $13 million increase in net deferred tax assets to NOPAT.[19] We add the deferred tax liability to capital since as long as the company is a going concern, it will continue to reinvest in the assets that gave rise to the tax deferral in the first place. Moreover, we add back the change in deferred tax reserves (i.e., the net amount of deferred tax assets and liabilities) to NOPAT since deferred taxes represent the difference between GAAP accounting provision for taxes and current taxes actually paid. An increase in net deferred tax assets understates current taxes and therefore the increase should be subtracted from NOPAT. For a liability, we would add back the increase.

LIFO Reserve
We add DHC's LIFO reserve of $60 million to capital and the $32 million decrease in the LIFO reserve is subtracted from NOPAT. The LIFO reserve is the

---

[19] Deferred taxes and reserve accounts described herein are provided in notes to DHC's financial statements.

difference between the LIFO and FIFO value of inventory. Under LIFO, a company's costs of goods sold reflect most recent market prices, which in inflationary periods will decrease gross margins and therefore taxes. In addition, inventories will be understated since LIFO accumulates costs from many prior periods. Therefore, we add back the LIFO reserve to inventory to provide a better approximation of the inventory's replacement value and add back the increase in LIFO reserve to NOPAT to recognize the unrealized gain attributable to holding inventories that appreciated in value.

Goodwill

If DHC had goodwill on its balance sheet, we would add the accumulated amortization back to capital and add back the annual amortization to NOPAT. To make the non-cash, arbitrary amortization of goodwill a non-issue and provide a rate of return that reflects a true cash-on-cash yield, we undo the effects of goodwill amortization. A potentially more difficult measurement problem arises when mergers are accounted for under pooling-of-interests. In a pooling, the buyer only recognizes the seller's accounting book value and nowhere is the actual cost of the securities offered recognized. To record the true cost of an acquisition and more accurately measure the rate of return the acquirer is earning, we need to add back unrecorded goodwill (i.e., the difference between the market value purchase price and the seller's book value) to capital.

Intangibles Assets

Under GAAP accounting conventions intangible assets, such as research and development, are expensed as incurred. EVA considers such costs as capital investments that provides future benefits — analogous to investing in plant and equipment. Therefore, we capitalize R&D outlays and other similar intangible assets on the balance sheet and amortize the costs in NOPAT over the intangible asset's useful economic life. When we add the change in net capitalized intangible asset to NOPAT, the expense is replaced with the amortization of the capitalized intangible.

To illustrate how intangibles would be capitalized, we assume DHC's advertising activities provide the company on-going economic benefits. DHC spent $745 million and $679 million in 1998 and 1997, respectively, on advertising to promote its brand name and image. Since we believe that consumers are by nature fickle, the useful life of advertising is fairly short.[20] Therefore, we used an amortization period of two years and, as a result, added back $1,085 million to capital and decreased advertising expenses by $89 million. Exhibit 10 details this treatment.

---

[20] We capitalized and amortized advertising expenses over a two-year period. For year-end 1998, net capitalized advertising expense would equal the advertising expense in 1998 of $745 million plus one-half of the previous year's advertising expense of $679 million.

Exhibit 10: Intangible Assets

Advertising Expense (in millions)	
Year	Expensed
1998	$745
1997	679
1996	634
Capitalized Over 2 Years	
Year	Capitalized
1998	$1,085
1997	996
Change in Advertising Expense	$89

Exhibit 11: Non Recurring Income (Loss)

One-time write-offs (in millions)	Pre-tax	After-tax
Mainframe outsourcing write-down and expenses (1998)	$42	$25
Real estate repositioning (1996)	134	81
IRS Tax Judgment Reversal (1998)	(20)	(20)
Total Non-recurring items	$196	$126

Exhibit 12: Accounts Receivable

Gains/Losses on Sales of Securitized Receivables (in millions)	After-tax
Gain on Sale of Receivables (1998)	$21
Loss on Maturity of 1995 Receivables Sale (1998)	23
Gain on Sale of Receivables (1997)	19
Retroactive Gain on 1995 Sale of Receivables (1997)	8

Non-Recurring Income (Loss)

From 1996 to 1998, DHC has written off $106 million (after tax) in assets and received a favorable tax ruling for $20 million (after tax). In addition, DHC operates a finance subsidiary for its private-label credit card and, from time to time, monetizes its account receivables resulting in accounting gains (losses). These non-recurring, non-cash events should be added back to NOPAT and the cumulative effect should be added back to capital. These adjustments normalize earnings and better reflect a company's actual cash receipts and disbursements (illustrated in Exhibits 11 and 12).

Other Reserves

EVA deals with other reserves on a case-by-case basis, but the same theme holds true: reverse accruals to reflect cash consequences. For DHC, the major reserves include allowance for doubtful accounts, pension and post-retirement health benefits expense (pension expense), and ESOP accrual. We add back the change of $5 million in the allowance for doubtful accounts to NOPAT since it represents a non-cash provision above actual net charge-offs. We replace the reported pension expense of $31 million with the actual service cost of $36 million since the difference represents financing effects and actuarial assumptions; and, we add the net pension liabilities of $45 million to capital. Finally, we subtract the ESOP accrual of $19 million from NOPAT since it reflects employees' cash contribution and dividends on common stock held in the ESOP trust.

Cash Operating Taxes

Finally, we calculate DHC's cash operating taxes from recurring operating activities as if the firm had no leverage. We add back the increase in deferred tax assets, remove the tax benefit of interest expense (including operating leases), and eliminate the tax effect from non-operating and non-recurring activities. As highlighted in Exhibit 13, DHC's income tax expense increases from a reported $594 million to $802 million.

Investments and Excess Cash

It is important to discuss how EVA deals with equity investments, other income, and excess cash. We carefully look at equity investments to decide whether they should be consolidated or valued separately. If the firm exercises significant control of its equity investment, then the controlled entity should be consolidated. Also, we tend to exclude other income from NOPAT unless the income is directly related to the firm's operations. Finally, firms with excess cash on their books are implicitly making a financing decision since the cash could be used to reduce debt or to buyback stock. Thus we subtract excess cash from capital.

NOPAT Calculation

We now bring all the individual adjustments together to calculate NOPAT. We present the NOPAT calculation using two equivalent methods: the financing approach and the operating approach. In Exhibit 14, we present in detail both methods for DHC with the EVA adjustments italicized.

Similarly, we present calculations for invested capital under the financing or operating approaches in Exhibit 15.

Exhibit 13: Cash Operating Taxes

Cash Operating Taxes (in millions)	1998
Income Tax Expense	$594
Plus: Increase in Deferred Tax Assets	13
Plus: Tax Benefit from Adjusted Interest Expense	178
Less: Taxes on Non-Operating Income	—
Plus: Tax Benefit on One-Time Items	17
Cash Operating Taxes	$802

Exhibit 14: Calculation of NOPAT for DHC

Dayton Hudson Corporation
NOPAT Calculation

Operating Method (In millions)	1998
Revenues	$30,951
Cost and Expenses	
Cost of Retail Sales, Buying and Occupancy	22,634
Selling, Publicity and Amortization	5,077
Depreciation and Amortization (excluding Goodwill)	780
Interest Expense on Non-Capitalized Operating Leases	*(53)*
Decrease in LIFO Reserve	*32*
Increase in Doubtful Accounts	*(15)*
Increase in Capitalized Advertising Expense	*(89)*
Non-recurring Items	*(22)*
Loss on Sales of Securitized Receivables	*(2)*
Pension and Post-Retire. Healthcare Expense Less Service Cost	*(5)*
ESOP Accrual	*19*
Adjusted Operating Expenses	28,356
Adjusted Net Operating Profit	2,595
Taxes other than income taxes	506
Net Operating Earnings Before Income Taxes	2,089
Cash Operating Taxes	*802*
NOPAT	*1,287*

Dayton Hudson Corporation
NOPAT Calculation

Financing Method (In millions)	1998
Net Earnings Before Extraordinary Charges	962
Equity Equivalents	
Increase in Deferred Taxes Assets	*(13)*
Decrease in LIFO Reserve	*(32)*
Increase in Doubtful Accounts	*15*
Increase in Capitalized Advertising Expense	*89*
Non-recurring Items (net of taxes)	*5*
Loss on Sales of Securitized Receivables	*2*
Pension and Post-Retire. Healthcare Expense Less Service Cost	*5*
ESOP Accrual	*(19)*
Adjusted Earnings Before Extraordinary Charges	1,014
Interest Expense	398
Interest Expense on Operating Leases	*53*
Adjusted Interest Expense	451
Tax Benefit of Interest Expense	(178)
Interest Expense After Taxes	*273*
NOPAT	*1,287*

Note: EVA adjustment italicized.

Exhibit 15: Calculation of Invested Capital for DHC

Dayton Hudson Corporation
Invested Capital Calculation

Operating Method (In millions)	January 30, 1999	January 31, 1998
Cash and Cash Equivalents	$255	$211
Retained Securitized Receivables	1,656	1,555
Merchandise Inventories	3,475	3,251
LIFO Reserve	*60*	*92*
Other	619	544
Adjusted Total Current Assets	6,065	5,653
Accounts Payable	$3,150	$2,727
Accrued Liabilities	1,444	1,346
Income Taxes Payable	207	210
Non-Interest Bearing Liabilities	4,801	4,283
Net Working Capital	1,264	1,370
Property and Equipment, net	8,969	8,125
Capitalized Operating Leases	*593*	*621*
Adjusted Property and Equipment, net	9,562	8,746
Capitalized Advertising Expense	*1,085*	*996*
Cumulative Non-Recurring Items (net of taxes)	*5*	*81*
Other Assets	692	505
Adjusted Other Assets	1,782	1,582
EVA Capital	$12,608	$11,698

Dayton Hudson Corporation
Invested Calculation

Financing Method (In millions)	January 30, 1999	January 31, 1998
Current Portion of Long-Term Debt and Notes Payable	256	273
Long-Term Debt	4,452	4,425
Capitalized Operating Leases	*593*	*621*
Total Debt & Leases	5,301	5,319
Total Shareholders' Investment	5,311	4,460
Deferred Income Taxes and Other	*822*	*720*
Convertible Preferred Stock, net	24	30
LIFO Reserve	*60*	*92*
Capitalized Advertising Expense	*1,085*	*996*
Cumulative Non-Recurring Items (net of taxes)	*5*	*81*
Adjusted Shareholders' Investment	7,307	6,379
EVA Capital	$12,608	$11,698

Note: EVA adjustment italicized.

To highlight the impact of making EVA adjustments on financial ratios, in Exhibit 16 we compare EVA-based return on invested capital (ROIC) to return on invested capital calculated from "as reported" financial statements. EVA adjusted ROIC is 1.9 percentage points less than the 12.5% reported ROIC, or a $130 million difference in value creation. Given this substantial difference, implementing EVA adjustments appears well worth the additional effort.

Exhibit 16: Financial Ratio Comparisons

Dayton Hudson Corporation EVA ROIC vis-à-vis Reported ROIC		
For the Year Ended 1999	EVA	Reported
Net Operating Profit	4.2%	3.9%
× Net Invested Capital Turnover	2.5×	3.2×
= Return on Invested Capital	10.6%	12.5%
Less Weighted Avg. Cost of Capital	8.5%	8.5%
= Excess Return	2.1%	4.0%
Average Invested Capital	12,153	9,635
Net Value Created Effect for Year	255	385
Difference from Reported	(130)	
% Difference from Reported	−34%	

EVA-Based Competitive Analysis

In the 12 months ended January 31, 1999, DHC generated a 12.4% ROIC, which was not only higher than its competitors but also higher than its 3-year average. How did DHC manage to generate such superior returns? What strategies has DHC pursued to differentiate itself from competitors?

In this section, we compare DHC's recent financial performance to its competitors to uncover how DHC has been able utilize its competitive advantages to drive returns. By isolating DHC's value drivers and sources of differentiation, we can better assess the sustainability of past performance and quantify their value implications. Exhibit 17 provides an EVA ratio analysis of DHC versus its competitors.

The EVA ratio tree in Exhibit 17 breaks down the sources of DHC's return on invested capital relative to its competitors. In the 12 months ending January 31, 1999, DHC generated a 6.5% NOPAT margin, slightly higher than the 3-year average and substantially higher than the average generated by its competitors. DHC's higher margin can be attributed to a richer product mix. DHC offers more upscale merchandise, which typically carry higher margins. DHC's higher gross margins are offset by higher depreciation and SG&A expense, while its cash tax rate has been in-line with its peers. DHC's higher depreciation expense is a result of building more expansive, elaborate stores and generating lower average sales per square foot, while higher SG&A reflects higher operating costs associated with DHC's department store division.

In 1997 and 1998, DHC's invested capital turnover of 2.8 times was significantly lower than its competitors, although it has improved from its 3-year average. DHC's lower capital turnover results from higher working capital levels and higher investments in stores. DHC operates with higher working capital due to its capital-intensive private-label credit card operation, whereas its competitors rely on third-party providers. As the higher depreciation charge indicates, DHC's strategy is to spend more on stores than its competitors, but its PP&E turnover trend is positive.

Finally, combining DHC's NOPAT margin and invested capital turnover produces DHC's superior ROIC relative to its peers and reveals a positive trend.

Exhibit 17: EVA Ratio Analysis for Dayton Hudson Corp
EVA-Based Financial Ratio Tree

	LTM 1/99	3 Year Avg.
Gross Margin		
DH	25.1%	25.0%
Comps	19.6%	19.4%

Less

	LTM 1/99	3 Year Avg.
Depreciation/Sales		
DH	2.5%	2.5%
Comps	1.4%	1.4%

Less

	LTM 1/99	3 Year Avg.
SG&A/Sales		
DH	16.1%	16.2%
Comps	14.4%	14.3%

× 1 −

Cash Tax Rate		
	31.4%	32.1%
	31.3%	30.5%

NOPAT Margin		
	6.5%	6.4%
	3.9%	3.7%

	LTM 1/99	3 Year Avg.
Net Working Capital/Sales		
DH	4.3%	5.3%
Comps	3.4%	−1.3%

+

	LTM 1/99	3 Year Avg.
Net PP&E/Sales		
DH	29.7%	30.7%
Comps	19.4%	20.3%

/1 =

Net Invested Capital Turnover		
	2.8	2.6
	3.7	3.7

+

	LTM 1/99	3 Year Avg.
Other Assets/Sales		
DH	2.3%	2.0%
Comps	2.2%	2.0%

× =

ROIC		
	LTM 1/99	3 Year Avg.
	12.4	11.3
	9.7	9.0

Notes: 1. Comps include COST, KM, and WMT, and based on the mean ratio.
2. Advertising expenses are not capitalized. While we illustrate that advertising expense can be capitalized, we prefer not to capitalize them for this analysis. Retailers need to continually advertise to sustain sales. Therefore, we believe that the economic life of advertising is short lived.

EVA-Based Valuation Measures

In addition to aiding in fundamental analysis, EVA principles provide an intuitive framework for understanding key value drivers and estimating firm intrinsic value. Equation (1) separates value into two components: existing value and future value.[21]

$$EV_t = \frac{NOPAT_1}{WACC_1} + \sum_{t=2}^{n} EVA_t / (1 + WACC)^t \tag{1}$$

[21] See Thomas Copeland, Timothy Koller, and Jack Murrin, *Valuation: Measuring and Managing the Value of Companies, Second Edition* (New York: John Wiley & Sons, 1994), for a similar discussion on applying residual income approach to valuation. EVA valuation models are also covered by Fabozzi and Grant, *Equity Portfolio Management*, and in Chapters 2 and 5 of this book.

Exhibit 18: % PVGO

Financial data LTM ended January 31, 1999 Price as of June 11, 1999	%PVGO
DHC	73%
Costco	53%
K-Mart	47%
Wal-Mart	84%
Comps – Mean	61%

We refer to the first term NOPAT/WACC as the firm's economic book value. It represents the firm's value as a going concern that does not invest in new projects. We refer to the second term, as the *present value of future growth opportunities*, which represents how much value the firm will create from new investments.

Present Value of Future Growth Opportunities

The present value of future growth opportunities provides a single measure that reflects current operating performance and market expectations for future value creation. Applying equation (1) to current financial data and market prices, we can infer what percent of the current stock price represents investor expectations for future growth (i.e., %PVGO). A historical and relative comparison of %PVGO can provide insight as to whether a particular company is appropriately valued.

We apply this approach for DHC and its competitors in Exhibit 18. We would expect that the fastest growing retailers be accorded the highest %PVGO. Wal-Mart has historically been the fastest growth story in the industry and trades at the highest ratio, while K-Mart has been restructuring and trades at the lowest ratio. Both DHC and Costco have high growth rates, but trade at a discount to Wal-Mart.

EVA Valuation Techniques

We can also apply the EVA-model to derive an intrinsic value since EVA is essentially a residual income model.

$$EV_{t-1} = \text{Invested Capital}_{t-1} + \sum_{t=1}^{n} EVA_t / (1 + WACC)^t \qquad (2)$$

With a slight modification to equation (1), the EVA-model can be expressed as a residual income model in equation (2). The firm's enterprise value is equal to its invested capital plus the present value of all future EVA (including existing and new projects) discounted at the firm's weighted average cost of capital. To derive a value applying equation (2), we need to make three explicit assumptions:

1. The growth rate for invested capital
2. How long a firm is able to generate excess returns
3. The rate used to discount future earnings

Exhibit 19: Weight Average Cost of Capital Calculation for DHC

Book Weights (in millions)	Average Balances	Weight
Total Debt and Leases, net of excess cash	$5,310	43.7%
Convertible Preferred Stock – assumes full conversion into common	-	0.0%
Common Equity	6,843	56.3%
Total Invested Capital	$12,153	
Cost of Capital	Cost	
Debt		
Interest Expense	$451	
Average Total Debt and Leases, net of excess cash	5,310	
Cost of Debt	8.5%	
After-Tax Cost of Debt	5.4%	
Common Equity		
Northfield Predicted Beta	0.97	
Assumed Market Risk Premium	5.0%	
10 Year Treasury Bond Yield	6.0%	
CAPM Predicted Cost of Equity	10.9%	
Weighted Average Cost of Capital	Weight	Cost
Total Debt and Leases, net of excess cash	43.7%	5.4%
Common Equity	56.3%	10.9%
WACC		8.5%

The growth rate can be expressed as the firm's ROIC times the earnings retention rate. The other two assumptions require more analysis.

To address the second unknown, EVA introduces a key concept called the *competitive advantage period* (CAP). Investors have well appreciated the fact that over time competition should drive economic profits to an industry's cost of capital and therefore drive economic profits to zero. CAP addresses the length of time it will take to reach equilibrium. As a result, CAP can be interpreted in the same context as %PVGO and compared across firms and over time.

The discount rate is represented by the weighted average cost of capital (WACC). We estimated DHC's equity cost of capital based on a predicted equity beta,[22] a market risk premium of 5%, and a 10-year Treasury yield of 6%. The after-tax cost of debt was based on DHC's weight average interest expense, including operating leases. Finally, the EVA model requires that book value weights be used in deriving a WACC. We present a detailed calculation in Exhibit 19.

We estimate DHC's value by applying equation (2) and in the process derive an implied CAP. We use Value Line estimates to forecast ROIC over the first 5 years and then assume returns will approach DHC's cost of capital over time. We also held DHC's dividend payout ratio constant to derive an internal growth rate for capital. In

---

[22] The predicted beta is estimated from a fundamental risk factor model. Northfield Investor Services estimated the particular model used. Risk models estimate market betas controlling for the variability of common factors such as price to book ratio or firm size.

order to justify DHC's enterprise value of $32.2 billion on June 11, 1999, we need a CAP of 40 years. That is a relatively long time period for any company to sustain its competitive advantage. To reduce the CAP, DHC must generate higher returns, accelerate its growth rate, or reduce its cost of capital. Exhibit 20 details the results.

In summary, DHC's stock appears to reflect its strong current and anticipated operating performance. Given the superior operating performance and a high growth rate, DHC should trade in the upper range within its industry. As of June 11, 1999, DHC's %PVGO suggests that the firm is trading in an upper range relative to its competitors. At the same time, DHC's long CAP period may be of some concern, but that observation holds true for its peers as well — since they generate lower ROICs and possess a similar cost of capital, their CAP must be longer as well. Given these conclusions, DHC appears to be fairly valued. Due to its strong operating performance, we would hold DHC in our portfolio at a neutral to moderate overweight.

CONCLUSION

Most discussions of EVA focus on its value as a measure of corporate performance. We take the position that EVA is more than a performance metric. EVA provides structure and discipline to the investment decision making process.

The EVA methodology in a corporate setting seeks to change behavior so that employee's are empowered to focus on what is best for shareholder. Similarly, we seek to focus the active investment manager on providing value relative to the investor's alternatives. In achieving this goal, we acknowledge the importance of risk management in identifying common practices that can destroy investor value. Furthermore, we suggest the use of performance fees to further align the manager's interests with that of the investor.

Exhibit 20: EVA Valuation and CAP for DHC

Period	1	2	3	....	39	40	41
Year	1999	2000	2001	....	2037	2038	2039
Invested Capital* – Beg. of Year	$11,523	12,701	14,052	....	429,633	460,817	493,565
ROIC	12.5%	13.0%	13.5%	....	8.9%	8.7%	8.5%
Retention Rate	82%	82%	82%	....	82%	82%	82%
Growth in Invested Capital	10.2%	10.6%	11.0%	....	7.3%	7.1%	7.0%
WACC	8.5%	8.5%	8.5%	....	8.5%	8.5%	8.5%
Excess Return	4.0%	4.5%	5.0%	....	0.4%	0.2%	0.0%
EVA	461	572	703	....	1,596	856	-
PV of Future EVAs	21,047	22,375	23,705	....	2,198	789	-
Enterprise Intrinsic Value	32,570						
Less: Debt & Leases	5,301						
Equity Value	27,269						
Competitive Advantage Period	40 years						

* Excludes capitalized advertising expenses.

Finally, we demonstrate how EVA can be used to perform rigorous fundamental analysis. The key findings to take away from our implementation of EVA in stock selection is the following: The information content of EVA metrics is found in the detailed analysis of a firm relative to its competitors. Although this analysis requires far more work than simply calculating and ranking firms by EVA, the effort is well worth it and enables far better investment decisions.

Chapter 7

Economic Margin: The Link Between EVA and CFROI

Daniel J. Obrycki
Co-Founder
The Applied Finance Group, Ltd.

Rafael Resendes
Co-Founder
The Applied Finance Group, Ltd.

During the past ten years, great strides have been made to educate corporate executives and institutional investors regarding the benefits of value-based metrics. In general, Economic Value Added (EVA) has emerged as the standard for corporate governance, while Cash Flow Return on Investment (CFROI) has been the most popular value-based management (VBM) metric among institutional investors. Given that each of these metrics attempts to accomplish the same goal, which is to convert accounting data into economic information, the questions each VBM user should ask are:

1. Why have corporations and money managers needed to utilize different metrics?
2. What strengths and weaknesses are inherent in each framework?
3. Most importantly, is there a single measure that can satisfy the needs of all VBM users?

This chapter introduces a new performance measurement and valuation system called the *Economic Margin framework*. This value-based measurement system is designed by The Applied Finance Group, Ltd. (AFG)[1] to develop an economic profit measure that is comparable across companies, industries, and time. The Economic Margin Framework is more than just a performance metric as it encompasses a valuation system that explicitly addresses the four main drivers of enterprise value: profitability, competition, growth, and cost of capital. This chapter concentrates on the first two drivers of firm value, profitability and competition.

---

[1] The Applied Finance Group is a Chicago based capital markets advisory firm. AFG's research specializes in linking economic profits to market values and is used by corporations, money managers, and retail investors.

Exhibit 1: No Correlation Between EPS Growth and P/E

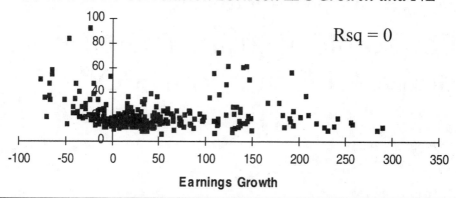

THE NEED FOR VALUE-BASED METRICS

Since the motivation for value-based metrics has been explained in other chapters of this book, we will not dwell on the subject beyond a few paragraphs. In short, value-based metrics have become popular for two reasons. First, capital markets have forced money managers and corporations to have a renewed focus on the balance sheet. In other words, corporations are not only expected to generate positive earnings and sales growth, they also must provide an adequate return on the money they have invested. Second, accounting information, although necessary, does not by itself adequately explain market valuations nor provide comparability between firms. Exhibit 1 examines the link between earnings growth and P/E multiples for the industrial companies within the S&P 500.

Ideally, a corporate performance metric (earnings growth) should provide insights into what a firm is worth (P/E multiple). In this case we would expect that higher earnings growth rates would correspond to higher P/E multiples. In Exhibit 1, however, there is only a very weak correlation. Indeed, notice that regardless of how well a firm performs as measured by earnings growth, the market appears indifferent to such growth in assigning a firm's P/E.

This lack of relation between earnings growth (performance) and P/Es (valuation) raises the question as to why are accounting measures inadequate? Exhibit 2 provides an overview of the common accounting distortions that prevent accounting data from reliably capturing a firm's true economic performance.

In the end, the goal of any value-based metric is to remove these and other accounting distortions to provide comparability over time, firms, and industries; plus help answer the following questions:

- How well is this firm/project managed? (corporate performance)
- What is this firm/project worth? (valuation)

Exhibit 2: Common U.S. GAAP Distortions

Earnings as a proxy of economic profitability does not account for:

Investment to Generate the Earnings
Cost of Capital
Inflation
Cash Flow

Accounting ratios/multiples are not comparable because each company has a different:

Asset Life
Asset Mix
Asset Age
Capital Structure
Growth Potential

Accounting rules distort economic reality due to:

Off Balance Sheet Assets/Liabilities such as:
 • Operating Leases
 • Research & Development
Pooling versus Purchase Accounting
Inventory Policies

MONEY MANAGERS VERSUS CORPORATE EXECUTIVES

You may ask, "If all value-based metrics have similar goals, then why are there different metrics?" A cynic might answer that it gives all the consultants something to argue about. Although this hypothesis has merit, the reality is that different metrics serve different purposes.

The principal users of value-based metrics are money managers/analysts and corporate executives. Each party has unique needs and access to information when carrying out their daily activities. For instance, money managers need a metric that allows them to quickly evaluate hundreds and even thousands of companies on the basis of publicly available information. They evaluate management's skill by looking at management's historic and forecasted track record relative to peers, and then determine whether the firm is over or undervalued based on their expectations. Once they complete their analyses, money managers purchase the stock(s) and the market tells them if their assumptions were wrong or right.

Contrast this to corporate executives who have almost limitless information on a single firm. The firm, however, is made up of several business units, hundreds of projects and thousands of employees. Corporate executives must not only make strategic decisions to help the firm create shareholder value, they must also promote and instill value-based management principles throughout the organization down to the lowest levels. In addition, they must design and maintain internal management systems to ensure that the firm does not stray from the designated path. Although always aware of the external demands of the market and pressure from competition, the corporate executive's predominate focus is internal, with a primary emphasis on managing the operational details of running a business.

Exhibit 3: Economic Margin Calculation

$$EM = \frac{\text{Operating Cash Flow - Capital Charge}}{\text{Invested Capital}}$$

Operations Based Cash Flow: — **Capital Charge:**

+ Net Income   + Return on Capital
+ Depreciation and Amort.   + Return of Capital
+ After Tax Interest Expense
+ Rental Expense Net Int. Adj.
+ R & D Expense
± Non-Recurring Items

Inflation Adjusted Invested Capital:
+ Total Assets
+ Accumulated Depreciation
+ Gross Plant Inflation Adjustment
+ Capitalized Operating Rentals
+ Capitalized R & D
- Non Debt Current Liabilities

In short, money managers want a performance metric that is comparable across a large number of firms and a valuation system that objectively sets target values. Corporate executives want the same properties, but are much more interested in a simple measure that is easy to communicate and administer throughout the firm. Can one framework meet the needs of both parties?

THE ECONOMIC MARGIN

Exhibit 3 contains the basic Economic Margin (EM) calculation and its three components — Cash Flow, Invested Capital, and a Capital Charge. We have included only the most common adjustments, although more are available if a firm requires special consideration. Sharing similarities individually with both EVA and CFROI, Economic Margin is a unique mixture of the two metrics designed to capture the best qualities of each measurement. Similar to EVA and CFROI, the Economic Margin Cash Flow component is meant to capture all the cash generated by a firm's capital base. From an investment perspective, EVA, CFROI, and Economic Margins all seek to measure the total capital investors have entrusted to a company's managers. In general, the metrics have more in common than not.[2]

---

[2] In a perfect world — where everybody makes the same correct accounting adjustments — EVA, CFROI, and EM must all lead to the same economic profit and intrinsic worth of the firm. In this theoretical context, the Economic Margin is equivalent to the "residual return on capital" or the "EVA spread" explained by Fabozzi and Grant in Chapter 2.

Exhibit 4: Calculating IBM's 1998 Operating Cash Flow and Invested Capital (in $ millions)

Operations Cash Flow Calculation		Invested Capital Calculation	
Inc. Before Pref.,Extraord.,& Disc. Ops.	$6,329	Total Assets	$50,269
+ Total D&A Expense	$2,224	+ Accumulated Depreciation	$17,958
+ Interest Expense AFIT	$25	+ Inflation Adjustment	$4,219
+ Normalized Rental Exp. Net Interest Adj	$1,290	+ Capitalized Rentals	$9,194
+ Normalized R&D Exp.	$4,411	+ Capitalized R&D	$18,188
+/- Non-Recurring Items	$0	- Non-Debt Current Liabilities	$14,845
+/- Monetary Gain/Loss	-$221		
= Operations Cash Flow	$14,059	= Invested Capital	$84,983

Non-Depreciating Assets Calculation	
Current Assets	$31,007
+ Other Assets	$4,349
- Non-Debt Current Liabilities	$14,845
= Non-Depreciating Assets	$20,511

Beyond the pure mechanical nature of any equation, several things should stand out when viewing the Economic Margin calculation. First, the numerator of the Economic Margin, like EVA, is based on economic profit, which helps focus managers on value creation. Unlike EVA, however, Economic Margin adds depreciation (and amortization) to cash flow and instead incorporates the return of capital explicitly in the capital charge. Second, like CFROI, Economic Margin is based on gross assets, which helps to avoid the growth "disincentive" typically associated with net asset based measures. Unlike CFROI, however, the Economic Margin's cash flows are unlevered (i.e., all equity financed) and do not mix operating and financing decisions. These similarities and differences will be expanded on later in this chapter.

Exhibits 4 through 7 step through the Economic Margin calculation for IBM[3] in 1998. Exhibit 4 provides the numeric detail to calculate cash flow, invested capital, and non-depreciating assets. Exhibit 5 graphically lays out the logic behind calculating the capital charge embedded in an Economic Margin. In principle, the capital charge is identical to a mortgage payment. The key difference between an Economic Margin capital charge and a mortgage payment is that when calculating a mortgage payment, the entire investment amount due to the bank is treated as a depreciating asset. For most companies, however, part of their assets are non-depreciating (such as working capital) and can be returned to investors if the company were liquidated when its existing assets wear out. Exhibit 6 provides a capital charge sensitivity based on asset life and non-depreciating assets and finally, Exhibit 7 brings everything together by calculating IBM's 1998 Economic Margin.

---

[3] The IBM example has IBM's Global Finance subsidiary stated on an equity basis.

Exhibit 5: Calculating IBM's 1998 Capital Charge
Capital Charge (in $ millions): Required Return On and Of Capital

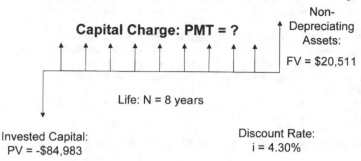

Capital Charge: PMT = ?

Non-Depreciating Assets:

FV = $20,511

Life: N = 8 years

Invested Capital:
PV = -$84,983

Discount Rate:
i = 4.30%

Annual Capital Charge = PMT(.043, 8, -$84,983, $20,511) = $10,577

Return On Capital = 0.043 * $84,983 = $3,654

Return Of Capital = $10,577 - $3,654 = $6,923

Exhibit 6: Calculating IBM's 1998 Capital Charge Sensitivity
Capital Charge: Sensitivity

Non-Depreciating Assets/Invested Capital (%)

		0%	24%	48%
	6	$16,370*	$13,301	$10,232
Life	8	$12,779	$10,577	$8,375
	10	$10,635	$8,950	$7,265

* in $ millions

Exhibit 7: Calculating IBM's 1998 Economic Margin

Economic Margin

Operations Cash Flow	$14,059
– Capital Charge	$10,577
= Economic Profit	$3,482

Economic Profit	$3,482
/ Invested Capital	$84,983

| = Economic Margin | 4.10% |

Exhibit 8: Simple Project Assumptions

Capital	$100	Deprec./Year	$10
Working Cap.	$0	NOPAT/Year	$9
Life	10 yr.	Cash Flow/Year	$19
No Inflation		Discount Rate	10%

Exhibit 6 overviews how important it is to understand asset characteristics. For example, given two firms with identical investment bases and cash flows, whether they create or destroy value will depend on their economic make-up. As the proportion of non-depreciating assets and viable asset lives change, so does the minimum cash flow hurdle to create value. By making this capital sensitivity an explicit aspect of the Economic Margin calculation, our experience has demonstrated that managers become much more aware of the economic ramifications of alternative project choices. Furthermore, it allows accurate comparisons across companies in different industries, or business units with different operating characteristics.

ECONOMIC MARGIN AND EVA

As discussed earlier, a primary goal of value-based metrics is to eliminate the numerous distortions in accounting data to provide comparability across time, firms, and industries. Once we have "cleaned" up the accounting data, we can evaluate if companies are creating or destroying shareholder wealth, and provide more insightful valuations. An issue that arises with basic EVA calculations is the use of historic net plant in its invested capital base and GAAP depreciation expense in its NOPAT calculation.[4] Utilizing these items in a performance metric can cause many difficulties for a money manager who is trying to compare firms across time and industries to determine the best investment opportunity. For example, how does a manager compare EVA for two firms when one firm uses accelerated depreciation and the other straight-line? Or what about firms having similar fixed assets that were purchased at different times? In addition, the manager must determine if the net asset base adequately accounts for the money the firm has invested to generate its cash flows (e.g. the firm may have fully depreciated, but not retired fixed plant) and whether GAAP depreciation expense is sufficient to replace the existing fixed assets.

These issues have additional implications for the corporate executive. Exhibits 8 and 9 demonstrate how the basic EVA calculation's reliance on Net Plant can lead corporations to confusing conclusions regarding wealth creation and optimal strategy. We call this effect "The Old Plant Trap." Exhibit 8 contains the assumptions for a simple project that will form the basis for many of the following discussions. Exhibit 9 presents the basic EVA calculation for this project.

---

[4] For a rigorous discussion on how to estimate economic depreciation in an EVA context, see Chapter 5 by Stephen O'Byrne.

Exhibit 9: Basic EVA Falls into "The Old Plant Trap"

Years	1	2	3	...	9	10
Gross Plant	100	100	100		100	100
Acc. Dep.	10	20	30		90	100
Net Plant	90	80	70		10	0
Net Income	9	9	9		9	9
B.O.Y. Net Inv. Cap.	100	90	80		20	10
C.O.C.	10	10	10		10	10
EVA Cap. Chrg.	10	9	8		2	1
EVA	-1	0	1		7	8
EVA/B.O.Y. Net Inv. Cap.	−1%	0%	3%		35%	80%

Compare the project's EVA in year 1 against year 10. As the project gets older, EVA increases from negative $1 to positive $8. Why? Has the project's economics changed? No, the basic EVA calculation increased only because the plant was depreciated, which decreased the capital charge each year. In addition, which EVA is the "correct" EVA, and how does a manager know whether to accept or reject the project?

While it is easy to dismiss such a problem as a "calculation issue," its implications are much more serious. For example, if a company has adopted a compensation system that rewards improvement in EVA, the manager of the above project is likely to resist growing since each new project will incrementally decrease his EVA, while doing nothing increases it. Inflation makes the problem even worse. Adding new plant at current costs increases the manager's invested capital base (relative to older plant at historic costs) and decreases NOPAT via a larger depreciation expense.[5]

Can EVA deal with the "Old Plant Trap"? Yes, of course. By replacing the accounting depreciation used to calculate NOPAT in a basic EVA calculation with sinking fund depreciation, the "Old Plant Trap" problem can be eliminated. Obviously, a corporate manager must determine whether the added complexity is worth the additional benefit. For institutional investors, however, such a solution is not as easy. Calculating sinking fund depreciation using only publicly available information is difficult since you must consider how old the assets are and how long they will last to reasonably estimate the current year's sinking fund depreciation.

The natural question is, "How does Economic Margin handle the Old Plant Trap?" Exhibit 10 illustrates the Economic Margins generated by our simple project.

---

[5] This disincentive to grow was made clear in a discussion we had with the CEO of a Midwestern manufacturing firm that implemented EVA. As part of the EVA system, the CEO gave out two types of awards, one for increasing EVA and the other for growth. The CEO said that while the system was in place, he never gave an award for growth.

Exhibit 10: Economic Margins Solve "The Old Plant Trap"

Years	1	2	3	...	9	10
Net Income	9	9	9		9	9
Depreciation	10	10	10		10	10
Cash Flow	19	19	19		19	19
Gross Investment	100	100	100		100	100
C.O.C.	10	10	10		10	10
EM Cap. Chrg.	16.27	16.27	16.27		16.27	16.27
Economic Profit	$2.73	$2.73	$2.73		$2.73	$2.73
Economic Margin	2.73%	2.73%	2.73%		2.73%	2.73%

Economic Margin, defined as:

(Operating Cash Flow – Capital Charge)/Gross Invested Capital

avoids the pitfalls inherent to the basic EVA calculation and solves "The Old Plant Trap." Based on cash flow and gross plant, EM yields a consistent answer of 2.73% (or $2.73 measured in dollar amounts) and does not change with time. A project manager rewarded on EM has no conflict regarding growth since new projects are added to the capital base at gross costs, like the other investments, and depreciation is added to net income to obtain cash flow. A corporate executive/money manager clearly knows this project/firm increases shareholder value and because the economic profit has been standardized by invested capital, the metric has no size bias. EM is a consistent, reliable measure that a value-based manager can compare across time, companies, and industries.[6]

ECONOMIC MARGIN AND CFROI

CFROI takes a very different approach relative to EM and EVA. Instead of being a measure of economic profit, CFROI is an internal rate of return (IRR). As a rate of return, it provides a consistent basis from which to evaluate companies regardless of their size, which a dollar based measure of economic profit cannot do. This characteristic of CFROI has made it very popular in the money management community, as investors need to compare many companies against each other to make investment decisions.

---

[6] AutoZone is one example of the potentially different insights obtained from a basic EVA calculation and EM. For the period between 1994 and 1997, EVA improved from $18 million to $75 million, and EVA/Net Invested Capital increased from 3% to 6%. EM, however, declined from 12.8% to 9.6%. Over the period, AutoZone's share price remained flat at $29/share, underperforming the market by nearly 50%.

Exhibit 11: Unlevered and Levered Financial Statements for Our Simple Project

Company	Unlevered	Levered		Unlevered	Levered
Sales	95	95	Gross Plant	100	100
Operating Expenses	70	70	Acc. Dep.	10	10
Depreciation	10	10	Net Plant	90	90
Operating Income	15	15			
			Total Assets	90	90
Interest Expense	0	5.6			
PreTax Income	15	9.4	Debt	0	80
			Equity	90	10
Income Tax (40%)	6	3.76			
Net Income	9	5.64	Total Liab & Equity	90	90

It is, however, important to understand the limitation that ratios have when used to measure wealth creation. First, internal rate of return measures by themselves do not provide any indication as to whether a firm is destroying or creating shareholder value. Is an IRR of 8% good or bad? How much shareholder value has the firm created or destroyed? Without reference to a company's cost of capital, it is impossible to answer these questions. Second, an IRR is a non-linear measure, which creates communication issues among non-financial managers. For instance, how much would a manager need to improve cash flow to obtain a 10% increase in IRR? As a form of an IRR, CFROI faces these issues. For example, using our simple project the CFROI, which we calculate later in Exhibit 12, is 13.77%. A 10% increase in CFROI implies a CFROI of 15.15% (= 13.77% × 1.1). To determine the incremental cash flow, you must first solve the following payment function, PMT (0.1515, 10, −100, 0) where 0.1515 = return, 10 = life, −100 = invested capital, 0 = working capital, and then subtract the previous cash flow from the result. The answer is irrelevant, but what is relevant is that this concept must be explained and made meaningful to all levels of an organization.

Beyond any difficulties in managing to an internal rate of return, the CFROI also mixes operating and financing decisions exactly like a Return on Equity (ROE) calculation. Let's remember that the primary goal of a value-based metric is to provide comparability over time, firms, and industries. Given that, what is undesirable about mixing operating and financing decisions? The answer is that by mixing operating and financing, CFROIs can change when there has been no change in a firm's underlying operating performance. This is identical to the behavior of a ROE. Exhibits 11 and 12 illustrate the similarity between the two measures.

Exhibit 11 contains balance sheets and income statements for our simple project assuming two cases, all equity financing and 89% debt financing. We have also assumed a 40% tax rate. Exhibit 12 calculates each firm's CFROI and ROE. Notice that for each firm the assets and operating income are identical. Yet the CFROI and ROE for the levered firm are dramatically higher than for the unlevered firm. This is a very important point and worth repeating. There has been no change in operating performance, but CFROI and ROE have increased as a result of financing.

Why does this happen? Because CFROI adds the entire interest expense, including the tax benefit ($5.6 × 40% = $2.24), back to cash flow. Consequently, a levered firm will always show higher cash flows and CFROIs compared to an unlevered firm. A portfolio manager or corporate executive, therefore, cannot compare CFROIs across time, companies or industries, and cannot forecast CFROIs without explicitly addressing leverage.[7]

How does Economic Margin improve upon IRR type metrics? First, since an EM incorporates the investors required return on capital within its capital charge, an EM is a direct measure of shareholder wealth creation. A company with a positive EM creates wealth, a zero EM maintains wealth, and a negative EM destroys wealth. Second, since the EM concept is derived from economic profit, it is easier to communicate and set goals. If a money manager or corporate executive wants to know the incremental cash flow required to obtain a 10% increase in the EM for our simple project (see Exhibit 10), he does the following multiplication: EM × Percent Increase × Gross Investment (2.73% × 10% × $100 = $0.27). Finally, EM does not mix operating and financing decisions in its cash flows. As shown in Exhibit 13, EM tax adjusts interest expense before adding it to cash flow. While the tax deductibility of interest expense is a valuable asset, the Economic Margin framework incorporates it in the valuation process within the weighted average cost of capital. This leaves the EM cash flow as a true measure of the cash generated by the firm's operating assets, undistorted by financing choices.

Exhibit 12: CFROI and ROE Change Due to Leverage

Company	Unlevered	Levered
Net Income	9	5.64
DDA	10	10
Interest Expense	0	5.6
Cash Flow	19	21.24
Gross Investment	100	100
Life	10	10
CFROI	13.77%	16.71%
ROE	10.0%	56.4%

[7] Kroger demonstrates how CFROI and leverage can combine to provide potentially ambiguous information to a portfolio manager. In 1990, Kroger had leverage at market of 83% and a CFROI of 13.4%. By 1998, the company had cut its leverage to 30%, while its CFROI declined to 11.5%, nearly 2%. Was Kroger's operating performance truly down for this period? Or had CFROI missed the improvement in operating performance as the benefit from the interest tax shield decreased with leverage? In the end, the market is the true judge of performance, and from 1990 to 1998, Kroger outperformed the market by 58%. Kroger's Economic Margins over the period increased from 1.3% to 3.8%.

Exhibit 13: EM Cash Flow's are Unaffected by Leverage

Company	Unlevered	Levered
Net Income	9	5.64
DDA	10	10
After Tax Interest Expense	0	3.36
Cash Flow	19	19
Gross Investment	100	100
Capital Charge	16.27	16.27
EM	2.73%	2.73%

VALUATION ISSUES

Similar to VBM metrics attempting to correct the distortions in accounting data for performance measurement purposes, EM, EVA, and CFROI also attempt to make traditional discounted cash flow (DCF) models more useful. The problem with most DCF valuations is that the majority of a firm's value is embedded within the perpetuity attached to the end of the forecast period. How can value-based metric frameworks solve the perpetuity problem? The answer is by focusing on forecasting economic profits (i.e., the amount of cash a firm earns in excess of the cash required by investors for using their money)!

In general, the advantages of value-based metric frameworks, relative to Free Cash Flow and Dividend Discount Models, are that they explicitly:

1. link how well a company is performing to what it is worth,

2. distinguish between the value of a firm's existing assets and future investments, and

3. incorporate a decay concept that recognizes competition will eliminate returns above/below the cost of capital over time.

Together these advantages form the basis for developing valuation models that provide true insights into what a company is worth.

BASIC EVA VALUATIONS AND "T"

EVA has made a tremendous impression in boardrooms and is just now starting to enter into the equity analyst's toolbox. For example, CS First Boston utilizes EVA concepts in its analyst reports.[8] As a result, this type of framework will gain increas-

---

[8] For a discussion of EVA and other VBM players in today's rapidly evolving world of value-based management, see Chapter 1.

ing attention in the market, and its valuation strengths and weaknesses should be clearly understood. The following is a generic EVA valuation formula:

$$\text{Firm value} = \underbrace{\frac{\text{NOPAT}}{c^*}}_{\text{Existing Assets}} + \underbrace{\frac{\text{Avg. EVA Fut.}}{c^*} \times \frac{1}{(1 + c^*)} \times T}_{\text{Future Investments}}$$

where

c^* = Compay weighted average cost of capital

T = Time period over which management can initiate positive EVA projects

This economic profit model says that a firm will:

1. earn its NOPAT on its existing assets forever (i.e., NOPAT/c^*),
2. earn positive EVA forever on new investments made over period "T" (i.e., Avg. EVA Fut./c^*), and
3. earn zero EVA on any new investments made after period "T."

The EVA model is very compact and mathematically elegant leading to the ability to generate quick insights into a valuation problem. This can be useful when communicating a particular point of view, or getting agreement from a diverse group of people. The price paid for immediate insights and computational ease, however, is the potential to oversimplify.

For example, the basic EVA model assumes that competition has no effect on the existing assets or the new investments made through period "T," but competition does effect investments made after "T." In other words, if Wal-Mart has 1,000 existing stores, these stores will generate their existing level of profitability forever; plus any new stores added during the first "T" years will also generate economic profits into perpetuity. All stores added after "T," however, will generate zero economic profits. Unfortunately, this is a very unrealistic model of how business works. Competition reduces the earning power of all assets, existing and future.

The basic EVA model's other shortfall is that it does not provide guidance regarding "T." Instead, the model tries to find insight into competition by using a firm's market value to solve for "T" and asking if the number is reasonable. The first thing that should strike you as odd is that the model uses its own set of perpetuities to solve for "T," whose purpose is to get us away from the perpetuity assumptions inherent in a DCF valuation. Putting this aside, let's examine the potential results. Solving the EVA valuation formula for "T" we get:

$$T = \left(\text{Firm Value} - \frac{\text{NOPAT}}{c^*}\right) \times \frac{c^* \times (1 + c^*)}{\text{Avg. EVA Fut.}}$$

Looking at the equation, notice that as NOPAT/c^* becomes large, "T" approaches zero or goes negative. In addition, if NOPAT/c^* or the Average EVA Future is small, "T" becomes extremely large. Finally, if we can calculate "T" and it is a reasonable number, what do we compare it to? Is a "T" of 5 good or bad? A portfolio manager or corporate executive cannot use "T" to make a decision without having some guidance as to a reasonable value for "T."

In summary, the basic EVA valuation model provides an easy and quick approach to valuing a company and provides some insights into competition. However, because the approach relies heavily on perpetuity assumptions and gives little to no guidance on "T," it has limited application when trying to systematically and objectively value companies.

CFROI VALUATIONS, FADE, AND FADE TO LEVELS

Like the basic EVA model's "T," the CFROI valuation model provides insights into competition through a concept called *fade*. In general, fade refers to the notion that all firms' levels of performance will over time converge to the same economy wide value. Where the CFROI valuation model improves over the basic EVA valuation model is that it utilizes the fade to avoid the perpetuity problem by explicitly forecasting out returns and discount rates. Exhibit 14 illustrates one of many CFROI fade patterns.

To understand Exhibit 14, it is helpful to understand what the CFROI valuation model and fade concepts are trying to accomplish. Simply put, the key to avoiding perpetuity problems is to determine when a company's return on capital is equal to its cost of capital (i.e., discount rate). Afterward, no matter how much a firm grows, the net present value of future investments is zero. This is the model's objective.

Exhibit 14: CFROI Fade Pattern – CFROI > Fade To, Discount Rate < Fade To

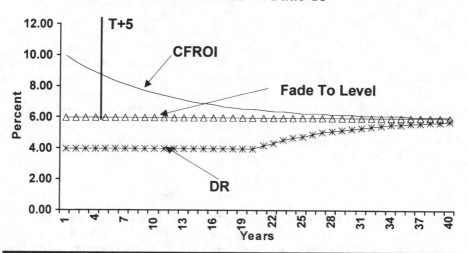

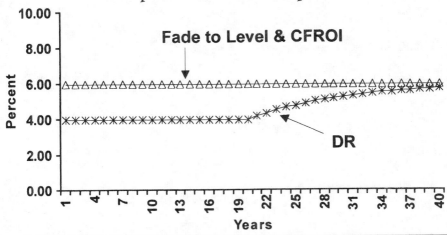

Exhibit 15: CFROI Fade Pattern – Forecasting No Competition & Positive Spread

Looking at Exhibit 14, there are many pieces to the CFROI fade concept to examine. To begin, the CFROI model utilizes one level of return (in general 6%) that all firms will fade to by year 40. As shown in Exhibit 14 and later exhibits, we will call this the "Fade to Level." Once the "Fade to Level" is set, the next issue is how to make the CFROI and discount rate (DR) converge to this value. On or before year 40, the CFROI and discount rate must be equal or the company would still be making excess profits/losses. The CFROI is brought to the "Fade to Level" in two stages, an initial 5-year window where CFROI fade rate research (based on CFROI level, CFROI variability, and growth) is applied and the remaining period where a 10% exponential decline is used. The discount rate is held constant for 20 years and afterward also faded to the "Fade to Level" at a 10% exponential rate. In essence, we have two converging fades, one for the CFROI and another for the discount rate.[9]

The main assumption behind the CFROI model is that over time a company's performance regresses towards an average level. Historically, this value is relatively stable at approximately 6% and appears to be a reasonable rate to forecast as a long-term, company profitability level. Upon further inspection, however, fixing the "Fade to Level" can lead to some unintuitive valuation assumptions. Exhibits 15, 16, and 17 capture a few of the issues associated with fixing a "Fade to Level."

Exhibit 15 is a simple example of the CFROI fade concept. It assumes that the CFROI equals the "Fade to Level" which equals 6%. The current discount rate, however, is at 4%. Since the CFROI equals the "Fade to Level," it remains unchanged over the next 40 years. The discount rate also remains unchanged until year 21 when it begins fading to the "Fade to Level."

[9] Bartley J. Madden, *CFROI Valuation: A Total System Approach to Valuing the Firm* (Woburn, MA: Butterworth-Heinemann, 1999), pp. 173-175 provided the background for the explanation of Exhibit 14.

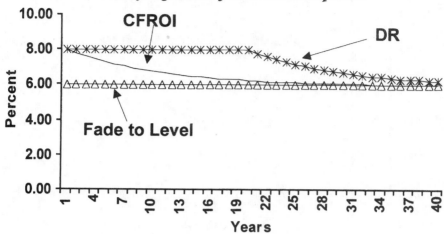

Exhibit 16: CFROI Fade Pattern –
Destroying Value from a Zero Spread

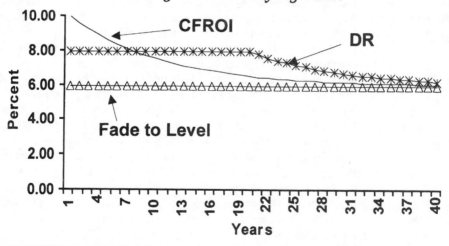

Exhibit 17: CFROI Fade Pattern –
Creating then Destroying Value

How has fade captured competition in this example? For the first 20 years it does not. When the spread between the CFROI and discount rate remains steady, there is no competition and economic profits remain constant. In fact, in year 21 and beyond, the spread only dissipates because the firm's discount rate begins fading up to the "Fade to Level." This behavior implies that cash flows are becoming more risky. The question, however, is "Why?" Why is the firm's discount rate changing starting in year 21? Why do all firms fade to the same discount rate? Specifically, why should Coca-Cola have the same discount rate as a start-up biotech?[10]

With the initial discount rate above the "Fade to Level," Exhibit 16 is nearly the mirror image of Exhibit 15. The significant difference, however, is that here the initial CFROI is equal to the discount rate and not the "Fade to Level." Afterward, the CFROI and discount rate take their own path to the "Fade to Level" (utilizing the CFROI standard methodology) until they are equal once again in year 40. As previously discussed, the key to avoiding perpetuity problems is to determine when a company's return on capital is equal to its discount rate. Afterward, no matter how much a firm grows, the net present value of future investments is zero. In Exhibit 16, however, this is not the case. The CFROI and discount rate start out equal, but as a result of the "Fade to Level" assumption, the CFROI falls below the discount rate destroying value with future investment. In EVA terms, the "Fade to Level" basically forces all firms to have a "T" of 40 years. It also forecasts all firms with zero economic profits to destroy future value if their CFROI/discount rate start above the "Fade to Level".

Finally, Exhibit 17 is an extension of Exhibit 16 with the initial CFROI > discount rate > "Fade to Level." In this case, the firm first creates (CFROI > discount rate) then destroys (CFROI < discount rate) value as the CFROI and discount rate follow their separate paths to the "Fade to Level." Although this is a feasible outcome, most firms do not systematically forecast destroying value. Instead, a more intuitive assumption is that once the CFROI and discount rate are equal, future investments neither create nor destroy value.

To summarize, just as the basic EVA valuation model is very valuable to analysts that understand it, so is the CFROI valuation model valuable to its proponents. Utilizing fade rates to forecast CFROIs and discount rates to converge to a "Fade to Level" will eliminate the perpetuity problem inherent in most DCF valuations. It is important, however, not to focus solely on the "Fade to Level," but rather to adhere to the basic VBM principle that firms continuously face competition, forcing excess profits to zero and once at zero, future investments add no incremental value. Otherwise, the portfolio manager or corporate executive must look at each company/business unit individually to understand the "Fade to Level" valuation implications.

ECONOMIC MARGIN VALUATION AND DECAY

The Economic Margin framework contains the advantages of an economic profit measure and incorporates the insights gained from understanding fade. Like EVA, the numerator of the Economic Margin consists of economic profit. In addition, similar to the CFROI valuation model's fade, the EM framework utilizes a concept

---

[10] Note that fading the discount rate towards the 6% average creates a valuation model that literally incorporates over 20 company specific costs of capital.

called *decay*. The key difference, however, is that instead of decaying IRRs (i.e., returns), the EM framework decays economic profits (positive or negative) to zero over time. These discreet economic profit forecasts can be converted to cash flows from existing assets and future investments to value the company/business unit without the "perpetuity" problem associated with traditional DCF models.

Decay is defined as the percent per year of Economic Margin that is lost (positive margins) or gained (negative margins) due to competition. For example, the EM for our previous simple project (see Exhibit 10) was constant at 2.73% per year. If the project began with a 2.73% EM and afterward had a 25% decay/year, the EM profile would look like Exhibit 18. Similarly, Exhibit 19 illustrates the EM profile if the EM began with a −2.73%.

Exhibit 18: Positive EM Decaying to Zero Economic Profit

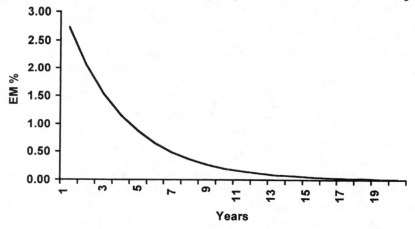

Exhibit 19: Negative EM Decaying to Zero Economic Profit

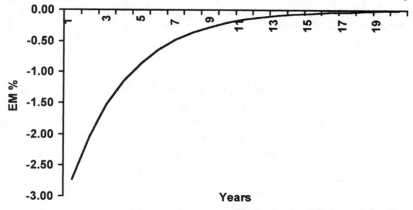

The EM framework utilizes decay rates derived from empirical research that relate EM level, EM variability, EM trend, and firm size to the decay rate. In general, a company has a high decay if its:

1. EMs are very positive or negative
2. EMs vary greatly from year to year
3. EM change is negative
4. size (defined by invested capital) is small

The intuition behind the four factors is straightforward. First, firms with very high (positive) EMs face stiffer competition than firms with EMs near zero, while firms with very low (negative) EMs must fix their businesses quickly or be forced out of business. Therefore, firms with "extreme" EMs (i.e., very positive or very negative) have greater decay rates than those with EMs closer to zero. Second, if a firm has had a very unstable/cyclical EM pattern and is at a peak or valley, the investor will be unwilling to assume that the peak or valley will persist very long and will assign the firm a high decay rate. If the company has a very steady EM history, however, the investor is more likely to believe that management can maintain this EM level over a longer period and will assign it a low decay rate. Third, if there are two firms, the first with EMs going from 6 to 4 and the second with EMs moving from 2 to 4, the second firm has "momentum" in its favor and will have a lower decay rate. Finally, it is more difficult to turn an ocean liner than a speedboat. Similarly, a small firm can see its profitability increase or decrease rapidly relative to a larger firm that has either built up (1) barriers to entry that enhance profitability, or (2) large fixed costs that are hard to restructure in difficult times. Consequently, larger firms have lower decay rates than smaller firms.

Given an initial EM level, investment, discount rate, and decay rate, it is very simple to value a future investment or an existing asset. For our previous simple project having an initial EM of 2.73%, investment of $100 lasting 10 years, and a discount rate of 10%, let's assume a decay rate of 25% as in Exhibit 18. To calculate the net present value of this future investment, you simply discount the forecasted economic profits. Exhibit 20 illustrates how easy it is to calculate the net present value for this future investment. It also illustrates another point that we have been repeating throughout the chapter. When the EM (or economic profit) equals zero, the contribution of any future investments to value is zero and the perpetuity problem associated with typical DCF forecasts is eliminated. This is why it is so important to understand decay.

A firm, however, consists of future investments and existing assets. We value existing assets similar to future investments except that we add back the capital charge to the economic profits to obtain the cash flow from the existing assets. Since the existing assets have already been purchased, the initial investment is a sunk cost and only the cash flow from the investment is relevant. Exhibit 21 illustrates how we would value our previous simple project if we had just spent the $100. Notice that the PV is $107.62, exactly $100 more that the future investment case in Exhibit 20. This means that the PV of the capital charge exactly equals the investment, which in turn is why the discounted value of the economic profits on future investments provides the correct NPV. The capital charge holds management accountable for their investments!

How would the EM framework handle the cases discussed in the CFROI valuation section (see Exhibits 15 through 17)? For Exhibit 15, rather that assuming no competition for 20 years, the EM framework would begin decaying the spread immediately (see Exhibit 18) since competition continuously works to eliminate excess profits or losses. For Exhibit 16, the CFROI model has the firm destroying value with future investments despite it having an initial zero spread business. In the EM framework, the future investment value for a zero spread business is zero. There simply is no economic profit to decay! Finally, in Exhibit 17, the CFROI valuation concepts have an initially positive spread firm later destroying value. The EM framework does not follow this pattern. Instead, once the spread (whether positive or negative) reaches zero, future investments add no value.

Exhibit 20: Using EMs and Decay Rates to Value Future Investments

Year	EM	Investment	Econ. Profit	Disc. Factor @ 10%	Disc. Cash Flow
1	2.73%	100	$2.73	1.10	$2.48
2	2.04%	100	$2.04	1.21	$1.69
3	1.53%	100	$1.53	1.33	$1.15
4	1.15%	100	$1.15	1.46	$0.79
5	0.86%	100	$0.86	1.61	$0.54
6	0.65%	100	$0.65	1.77	$0.37
7	0.49%	100	$0.49	1.95	$0.25
8	0.36%	100	$0.36	2.14	$0.17
9	0.27%	100	$0.27	2.36	$0.12
10	0.20%	100	$0.20	2.59	$0.08
				NPV	$7.62

Exhibit 21: Using EMs and Decay Rates to Value Existing Assets

Year	EM	Investment	Econ. Profit	Cap. Charge	Cash Flow	Disc. Factor @ 10%	Disc. Cash Flow
1	2.73%	100	$2.73	$16.27	$19.00	1.10	$17.27
2	2.04%	100	$2.04	$16.27	$18.32	1.21	$15.14
3	1.53%	100	$1.53	$16.27	$17.81	1.33	$13.38
4	1.15%	100	$1.15	$16.27	$17.42	1.46	$11.90
5	0.86%	100	$0.86	$16.27	$17.14	1.61	$10.64
6	0.65%	100	$0.65	$16.27	$16.92	1.77	$9.55
7	0.49%	100	$0.49	$16.27	$16.76	1.95	$8.60
8	0.36%	100	$0.36	$16.27	$16.64	2.14	$7.76
9	0.27%	100	$0.27	$16.27	$16.55	2.36	$7.02
10	0.20%	100	$0.20	$16.27	$16.48	2.59	$6.35
						NPV	$107.62

CONCLUSION

Corporate executives and portfolio managers have increasingly utilized value-based metrics, such as EVA and CFROI, to help them understand a firm's performance and determine its value. Each measure provides unique advantages over traditional non-economic metrics such as EPS and ROE. Economic Margin is a new metric that links the two VBM metrics, combining their strengths and minimizing their weaknesses.

The EVA framework, as a subset of economic profit measures, provides managers a single metric that summarizes wealth creation, and avoids the goal setting problems found with ratio based and IRR measures. For example, with ratio and IRR based measurement systems managers often struggle with taking on new profitable projects because they may have a lower IRR than their existing projects and make their divisions look bad in the eyes of the CEO. By measuring wealth creation, economic profit measures fix this problem. Thus any project that generates positive economic profits will be accepted as it will raise the division's overall economic profits and make a manager look good in the CEO's eyes.

The CFROI framework's core strength is its fade concept that gives it a strong link to market values. This allows portfolio managers the ability to understand the performance expectations built into a company's market valuation. Armed with such information, money managers can ask managers more intelligent questions than just what will be next quarter's EPS. Instead, money managers and analysts can engage management about strategic issues and more thoughtfully evaluate how those strategies link back to wealth creation.

The Economic Margin framework is unique in that it marries the advancements in VBM made by economic profit and IRR based metrics. The Economic Margin is a cash flow based economic profit measure. Unlike most economic profit metrics, Economic Margins use gross assets to avoid the "old plant" accounting distortions inherent in most economic profit measures. Since the metric begins as a dollar measure of profit, it ensures that managers always pursue opportunities that create wealth. This eliminates the conflicts created by IRR based frameworks that put managers in the awkward position of accepting opportunities that reduce the average IRR of their division.

Similar to CFROI and other IRR based frameworks, the Economic Margin framework directly incorporates a decay/fade concept that provides guidance as to how to systematically eliminate economic profits. This feature allows the measure to create a valuation framework that directly avoids the perpetuity assumptions embedded in most basic economic profit valuation models. Similarly, by decaying/fading the economic profit, the Economic Margin framework avoids the need to force all company's to the same "Fade to Level," which characterizes IRR based frameworks.

Because the Economic Margin framework combines these powerful features, it represents a unique tool that is usable for both corporate managers and investment professionals. Corporate managers can use the tool knowing that conflicts inherent to ratio and IRR based systems do not exist and the disincentives to grow often found with economic profit systems have also been handled. Investment managers can use the system knowing that they will not have to rely on the perpetuities embedded in traditional DCF and the basic economic profit valuation models or force every company to an identical cost of capital and return level required in IRR valuation frameworks.

Finally, an obvious question that arises when evaluating different VBM frameworks is what are their inherent limitations. The simple answer is that no VBM tool is a panacea, or a substitute for good business judgment. This means that while these measures can provide the tools for a manager or analyst to get an answer consistent with value creation, these metrics say nothing about the quality of the assumptions going into the calculations. In addition, it is critical to really understand the assumptions behind each metric to avoid conclusions driven by a model's assumptions rather than the economic facts of the problem. Although every correct VBM framework yields the same answer with "laboratory data," each framework will generate very different answers when applied to real world information.

Chapter 8

Value-Based Management and Economic Value Added: A Global Perspective

S. David Young
Professor
INSEAD

INTRODUCTION

We hear a lot these days about the shareholder value revolution sweeping the globe. As a professor at INSEAD, an international business school based in France, and from my personal experiences as a consultant, I can testify to the enormous interest expressed by European and Asian managers in economic value added (EVA®) and other instruments of value-based management.[1] The world's major consulting firms (McKinsey, BCG, KPMG, Deloitte and Touche, etc.) all have fast-growing, value-oriented practices, and shareholder value concepts now receive unprecedented levels of coverage in business periodicals such as France's *L'Expansion* and Germany's *Capital*. Still, in general, Europe and Asia are years behind the United States in value-based thinking. And even when European and Asian managers attempt to promote such thinking in their companies, the implementation and practice of value-based management differs in important ways from the American experience. This chapter explores the application of EVA and value-based management in the non-American context. Most of the discussion focuses on recent experiences in Europe but Asia will be considered as well.

THE SHAREHOLDER VALUE REVOLUTION: THE GLOBAL CONTEXT

A generation ago, capital markets were both highly segmented and heavily regulated. Limits on capital flows, combined with low liquidity in most of the world's securities markets, meant that capital resources tended to stay put. Corporate man-

---

[1] EVA® is a registered trademark of Stern Stewart & Company.

agers liked it that way because pressures for performance were restrained. Even when companies underperformed, senior managers were rarely fired. Despite the absence of capital market pressure, many companies fared well, making a lot of money for their investors, thanks largely to robust economic growth. In the 30 years after World War II growth rates of 4%, 5%, or even higher, were common in several European economies. Some Asian countries did even better. In such a world, companies didn't have to be especially good to be profitable, they only had to be there. Ties to the political, commercial, and financial elites of the day were often more critical to corporate success than strategic vision or managerial excellence.

But this world underwent profound changes in the 1970s and early 1980s, beginning with the collapse of Bretton Woods and the post-War financial order, the advent of free floating exchange rates, the OPEC oil crisis, a growing climate of deregulation that forced its way into many sectors of the global economy, the election of Margaret Thatcher in the U.K. and Ronald Reagan in the U.S., and the start of a massive worldwide wave of privatization. The General Agreement on Tariffs and Trade, or GATT, played an important role too, as did the gradual strengthening of the European Economic Community (later the European Community, and now the European Union).

The 1980s saw a staggering increase in the power and accessibility of computing power, and a growth of investment capital brought on by several years of solid, worldwide economic expansion. Meanwhile, stock exchanges, eager to promote the interests of local companies in increasingly competitive commercial markets, strove to improve the attractiveness of these companies to foreign investors by lifting restrictions on foreign brokers, adopting technologically advanced trading systems, and boosting the depth and liquidity of local stock exchanges to reduce transaction costs. Attitudes towards regulation changed too. Instead of the protectionist variety designed to stifle markets, the emphasis shifted to making stock market investing a fairer game for small investors. The strengthening of regulation on insider trading and more extensive corporate disclosure requirements are examples of this trend.

Meanwhile, a new generation of young investors emerged, flush with surplus income to invest and more favorable attitudes toward stock markets than earlier generations. Governments in Britain, France, and elsewhere encouraged stock market investment with ambitious privatization campaigns. Interest in stocks, and in investing generally, grew in ways unimaginable to finance professionals in the 1970s. The result was a veritable, worldwide explosion in mutual funds, unit trusts, and other forms of institutional investment. Not only do many more people have financial stakes in companies, typically through mutual funds or pension funds, but of particular importance to corporate managers is that these funds are run by professional managers who care only about performance and delivering the highest returns possible to the people who hired them.

When these capital market developments are taken together, the principle lesson to corporate managers should be clear: Capital has attained a degree of mobility that is unprecedented in human history, and it will go to where is it most appreciated. In other words, capital isn't "sticky" anymore; capital can move. And move it will, whenever investors believe their capital will be more productively employed somewhere else. In this new world, companies must not only be competitive in commercial markets, but they must also be competitive in capital markets. Otherwise, their cost of capital will be higher than their competitors', a problem that is corrected either by improved performance or by takeover. In the worst cases, companies will go on bankrupt. All managers understand that for their companies to survive and grow they must be competitive in terms of operating costs — such as labor, materials, administrative costs, etc. What's changed is that survival also requires competitive *capital* costs, a reality still not fully appreciated by too many corporate managers.

A CASE IN POINT: EUROPE AND SHAREHOLDER VALUE

Because the impact of these developments was felt first in the United States, observers sometimes make the mistake of assuming that this change process is driven by the U.S. and the powerful American investment banks. The reality is very different, however. In the 1980s American corporate executives often resisted the performance demands imposed by capital markets with all the ferocity of European and Asian managers in the 1990s. These changes began in the U.S., but they arise from the confluence of the above factors, not because American bankers have sought out new markets. Crediting (or blaming) American investment houses for the spread of the shareholder value revolution is to confuse cause and effect.

Consider recent developments in Europe. Until the 1980s, most European countries heavily protected national champions from American and Japanese competitors. But with growing European integration, and a secular, worldwide trend towards freer trade, European companies have been subjected to an unprecedented degree of competition, from non-Europeans and from each other. Liberalized trade gives customers choices that they did not have before. In this environment, companies either deliver value to their customers, or they lose market share and fail. As a result of deregulation in the world's capital markets, investors too can go elsewhere whenever companies fail to deliver. The end of most capital controls, more liquid currency and securities markets, advances in information technology, and the growing importance of institutional investors have all played a role in creating massive pools of investment capital that can flow from one market to the next practically in an instant. Other important developments have occurred too.

These developments have led to the gradual erosion of "relational" capitalism, in which many business activities are conducted according to "old school ties" or other devices for social and cultural cohesion which place little emphasis on value creation and more on the preservation of privilege and the *status quo*. French *noyaux dur* and German universal banks have been notoriously undemanding of their shareholdings, because of long-standing business practices and strong personal relations between shareholders and company managers.

Europe's impressive response to the challenges of free trade, evidenced by the strong export performance of many European companies, offers some hope that they can make similar strides in the capital markets. The French, for example, have responded to increased commercial competition by becoming world class retailers and luxury-brand managers. But just as Europeans have learned to cope with deregulated *commercial* markets in the last 15 years, in the next 15 years they must learn to cope with deregulated *capital* markets and the relentless demands from shareholders and their representatives for performance. They must learn to communicate with, and satisfy the demands of, their capital providers, just as they have learned to communicate with their customers. EVA and similar value-based metrics are emerging as important tools for European managers, and for managers everywhere, to cope with the dramatic changes taking place in corporate finance.

This trend will only be intensified by what may be the most important development in European capital markets: The growth of capitalized pension funds. With aging populations and an unsustainable safety net, a growing number of Europeans now recognize that unfunded social security programs will be unable to serve the retirement needs of today's workforce. To provide for those needs, and to stimulate savings and corporate investment, many countries have implemented, or are planning to implement, tax-advantaged pension and savings plans that are already beginning to channel unprecedented amounts of equity capital to Europe's stock exchanges. These funds are invested by professional portfolio managers, competing aggressively against each other for the right to manage pension assets. Such money managers are interested only in performance, because that is how they are judged by their clients. The *noyaux durs* of stable, undemanding shareholdings that have characterized so much of French corporate governance are coming under enormous pressure, as professional money managers "vote with their feet" and withdraw support from any company that does not offer the prospect of competitive returns. German companies, which to date have enjoyed the relatively relaxed performance standards imposed by Deutsche Bank and its sister institutions, are finding themselves under similar pressure.

The trend toward ever greater institutional investment has been intensified by profound changes in the savings behavior of individuals. In the U.S., more people than ever participate in equity markets, mainly through mutual funds and personal pensions. And unlike past participation in stock markets by middle class investors, accumulations sometimes runs into the hundreds of thousands of dollars, sometimes even more. Attitudes among young European professionals have changed too. Their parents, many of whom suffered through wars and hyperinflation put their savings in the safest vehicles they knew, including large banks, government bonds, and sometimes under their mattresses. But young professionals are more sophisticated about markets, and have a better understanding of the risk and rewards of stock market investing. They know that if their investment horizon is long enough, long-term future wealth will be far higher if they invest in stocks instead of leaving their savings in bank accounts, like their parents would. The result is an enormous growth in demand outside the U.S. for pension funds and similar investment vehicles. Indeed, many of the largest American fund managers are now aggressively promoting their services all over the world, especially in Western Europe.

European managers are now feeling the pressure to deliver value but often lack the necessary diagnostic tools. Moreover, they lack the *language* of value creation, that is, a means of convincing capital providers that funds will be productively and profitably employed in their companies. Managers who fail in this task will find their companies at a competitive disadvantage in the race for global capital resources. Either they learn to navigate the rough seas of competitive capital markets or find themselves replaced by managers who can.

Still, there is widespread resistance in Europe to the idea that creating value for shareholders should be management's top priority. Value-based management is often criticized on the grounds that it ignores important constituencies other than the firm's shareholders, such as employees, customers, suppliers, the environment, and the local community. But encouraging counter-evidence can be seen from a recent Boston Consulting Group (BCG) study of German companies that reveals a strong link between investing in employees and stock market performance.[2] It found that companies with relatively high "employee focus" produced higher long-term returns for shareholders than industry peers. Such research is crucial because it counters the widely held belief, nurtured by the popular press in Germany, that shareholder value means job losses.

The BCG study examined ten industrial sectors from 1987 to 1994. Employee focus was defined in two ways, traditional human resources (HR) policies and "intrapreneurship." Traditional HR policies included training expenditures per employee, the number of layoffs relative to the industry average, and the extent to which the contribution of employees is reflected in corporate mission statements and publications. Intrapreneurship, a notion similar to empowerment, was defined in terms of flexible working hours, the prevalence of teams, the independence of working units, opportunities for employees to learn skills in new areas, and pay for performance.

In every industry, those companies which scored highest on these criteria produced superior shareholder returns than their competitors. In addition, the employee-focused companies also created the most jobs. This finding turns conventional wisdom in Europe on its head. It is widely assumed that companies deliver superior stock market returns by sacrificing the interests of their employees. Nevertheless, BCG found that more than three-quarters of the companies with above average shareholder returns produced a net increase in jobs over the observation period. Contrast this record with the rest of German industry and it becomes plain that shareholder returns need not put millions of workers out of their jobs.

The example of Bilfinger + Berger, a large German construction company, is particularly instructive. In the late 1980s, in response to years of medio-

---

[2] L. Bilmes, K. Wetzker, and P. Xhonneux, "Value in Human Resources," *Financial Times* (February 10, 1997), p. 10.

cre performance, the company embarked on a radical change program. Operations were decentralized, with employees down to the level of site foreman sharing in project risks and rewards. The company invested heavily in training and in the development of work teams. Compensation, performance reviews, and promotion policies were also overhauled. As a result, the company's sales grew at an annual rate of more than 20% and share price performance was dramatically reversed. A laggard before the change program was implemented, Bilfinger + Bilger's performance in the next seven years placed it at the very top of its industry.

EVA, MVA, AND SHAREHOLDER VALUE

Firms create value for their shareholders when they invest in projects, products, technologies, or strategies that are expected to earn returns greater than the cost of capital. In other words, shareholders become richer whenever companies undertake positive net present value (NPV) projects. Although total shareholder return has come to be viewed as the ultimate indicator of performance, it does not *directly* measure management's success in making positive NPV investments. *Market value added* (MVA) — a popular term used to describe a firm's NPV — does.

MVA is the difference between the total value of the firm (including equity *and* debt) and the total capital invested in the firm:

MVA = Total value − Invested capital

The aim of the firm's managers is to create as much MVA as possible. MVA increases only when invested capital earns a rate of return greater than the cost of capital. When newly raised capital is invested in value-creating projects (i.e., those with a positive net present value), MVA increases. When that capital is invested in value-destroying projects (i.e., those with a negative net present value), MVA decreases. In short, MVA is just the aggregate NPV for all of the firm's activities and investments.

But despite MVA's obvious appeal at the corporate level, it has important weaknesses in terms of motivating and evaluating managers. First, MVA is ineffective in motivating managers below the top management ranks. MVA can be calculated only for publicly traded entities; operating divisions do not have share prices. In other words, MVA can only be observed at the group level; MVA is not observable for operating divisions. For subordinate managers, the relationship between their actions and MVA is too remote for MVA to effectively motivate value creating behavior from these managers, or to serve as a reliable indicator of their contribution to shareholder value. In such cases, MVA fails to provide "line of sight." The remoteness of corporate MVA to divisional managers means that managers cannot directly observe the impact of their investment and operating decisions on the metric for which their performance is judged and compensated. But while any given subordinate manager's impact on MVA is small, when taken collectively, the impact of such managers on a company's MVA is profound. It is the actions of all company employees which ultimately determine the ability of a company to systematically deliver value to its shareholders and create lots of MVA. After all, top managers may provide strategic direction for the company, but they don't produce or sell anything. It's their subordinates who actually produce the company's products and services, and it's these same managers who interact most closely with the company's customers.

Another problem with MVA is that it is a wealth or "stock" measure. A stock measure is a term used by economists to denote the wealth that has been accumulated as of a certain point in time. It's a snapshot measure, and by itself says nothing about performance or the creation of value *over a period of time*. The problem is that managerial performance must be evaluated over periods of, say, three months, six months, or a year. We need flow measures, not stock measures. We could use changes in MVA as an indicator of performance over the last year, but as we have already noted MVA is observable only for publicly traded entities. We can calculate change in MVA for the corporate group, but not for divisions inside the company. Also, when measured over short time horizons, such as one year or less, much of share price movement may be driven by noise which has nothing to do with economic fundamentals or managerial performance. The noise problem gradually dissipates as the time horizon expands, but this fact does us no favors in evaluating managerial performance in the short term.

What we need, therefore, are measures of performance that:

1. can be calculated at divisional levels, thus providing line of sight for divisional managers;
2. are flows, not stocks, and thus are amenable to performance evaluation over periods of time;
3. are relatively immune to stock market volatility; but
4. which, nevertheless, are significantly and positively correlated with share price movements.

That's where EVA comes in. EVA is a short-term performance measure too, but unlike more conventional profit figures, accounting distortions can be reversed. The result is a short-term measure that, in theory at least, should be more highly correlated with shareholder returns than, say, net income or operating profit.[3] In addition, EVA shares the advantages of other profit measures, namely, that it can be calculated at divisional levels, it is a flow measure, and it is immune to stock market volatility. In short, say its advocates, EVA offers all of the advantages of other profit measures, in addition to some of its own, including close

---

[3] Whether this is true, in fact, is a subject of heated controversy. Recent academic evidence suggests that conventional earnings do just as well as, and perhaps even better than, EVA in explaining contemporaneous stockholder returns. For example, see Gary Biddle, Robert Bowen, and James Wallace, "Does EVA® Beat Earnings: Evidence on Associations with Stock Returns and Firm Values," *Journal of Accounting and Economics* (December 1997).

links with modern corporate valuation theory. This link becomes clear when we examine the relationship between MVA and EVA.

EVA is calculated as follows:

> Net Sales
> − Operating Expenses
> ————————————
> = Operating Profit (or Earnings before Interest and Tax, EBIT)
> − Taxes
> ————————————
> = Net Operating Profit After Tax (NOPAT)
> − Capital Charges (Invested Capital × Cost of Capital)
> ————————————
> EVA

NOPAT is the company's operating profit, net of tax, and measures the profits the company has generated from its ongoing operations.

Capital charges equal the company's "invested capital" times the weighted average cost of capital (WACC). The WACC equals the sum of the cost of each component of capital — short-term debt, long-term debt, and shareholders' equity — weighted for their relative proportions, at market value, in the company's capital structure. "Invested capital" is the sum of all of the firm's financing, apart from short-term non-interest-bearing liabilities, such as accounts payable, accrued wages, and accrued taxes. That is, invested capital equals the sum of shareholders' equity and all interest-bearing debt, both short-term and long-term.

How does EVA relate to NPV? The present value of future EVAs equals MVA. And because MVA and NPV are equivalent, the present value of future EVAs must also equal the NPV. Very simply, *EVA is a device for turning the stock measure of MVA (or NPV) into a flow*. Also, because it does not depend on share price, we can calculate EVA for divisions. Therefore, we can use it, at least in theory, to evaluate the performance of managers and employees at lower levels of the company, not just at the most senior levels.

In theory, EVA can be calculated for any division or unit as long as there are measures of operating profit and invested capital (or assets). We need only determine the appropriate cost of capital to determine the EVA. In addition, EVA is a flow measure, not a stock measure, and therefore is more amenable to performance evaluation than MVA or share price. In short, EVA provides the line of sight that is lacking when we try to use MVA or share price to motivate value creating behavior from divisional managers. By linking performance evaluation and compensation to EVA, companies can create stronger incentives for value creation.

EVA AND MANAGEMENT COMPENSATION

To illustrate the theory of EVA-linked compensation, consider the following scenario. Imagine yourself the managing director of a large division in a multinational company, and you want to take your division private. You and your management team aren't rich enough to buy the firm with your personal wealth, but your reputation in the industry has attracted a firm of buyout specialists who, in exchange for some of the equity, will arrange the necessary bank loans to pay off your employers' shareholders. When the dust settles, you and your colleagues are the proud owners of the business, but are saddled with a staggering debt burden. What do you do now?

From the moment you bought the company, your life has changed. When you were someone else's employee, you arrived at your office at 8:30 every morning, returning home by 7:00. You worked hard, but still had Sundays off, and maybe most Saturdays. Life was good, so was the pay, and you had time for your family and other personal pursuits. Not anymore.

The day after the buyout you are at your desk by 7:00 and you won't leave until late that evening. The next day, more of the same. Saturdays are workdays now, and maybe Sundays too. What do you do all day, day in, day out? Search for value. Period. There's an old saying in corporate finance: "Debt gets you out of bed, with equity you sleep in." This old saw speaks of the discipline that debt imposes on managerial behavior.[4] It would seem that merely owning the company provides enough incentive for you and your fellow managers to create value for the shareholders, because now you are the shareholders. When you the manager are now the shareholder you stop undertaking activities that might destroy value, like growing the firm without regard to whether the incremental returns justify the added capital costs. But does this mean that you become a relentless value creator? Not necessarily. Removing incentives to destroy value and establishing incentives that create value are not necessarily the same thing. An important virtue of debt, besides the tax shield, is that it galvanizes managers, and focuses attention on the need for continuous value creation in ways that more conservative capital structures cannot.

Firms with a highly levered capital structure have more transparent capital costs than firms with relatively small amounts of debt. The reason is that the dominant capital cost for the former is interest paid on bonds and bank borrowings, and these costs appear on company income statements. Indeed, as a firm's leverage increases, its net income begins to converge to its EVA. One of the well-known advantages of leveraged buyouts is that they make capital costs more explicit, and therefore it is harder for managers to hide from them.

Now that you have taken your company private with a staggering debt burden, your energies are consumed with a seemingly never ending search for value — whether in the form of cost cutting, working capital efficiencies, profitable growth, divestitures of underperforming assets, or any other way that managers can squeeze value out of their companies. Without this value creation it is simply impossible for the manager-owners to raise sufficient cash flow to service the debt. Enormous wealth awaits those who succeed, but failure beckons for those who don't.

---

[4] The notion that levered capital structures give managers an incentive to create wealth is also recognized by Michael Jensen in "Eclipse of the Modern Corporation," *Harvard Business Review* (September-October 1989).

Management buyouts (MBOs) are extraordinarily efficient vehicles for promoting value creation, which is why they have proven so popular in recent years. The movement started in the U.S., but is now spreading quickly in Europe. But what can we do when management buyouts are not feasible, perhaps because of genuine synergies among divisions? The short answer is to develop compensation systems that mimic the payouts that managers can expect in an MBO, thereby creating similar incentives for value creating behavior.

In short, management buyouts are powerful tools for promoting value creation because they combine ownership by managers with high levels of debt. The principle idea of management compensation in a value based company, therefore, is to get managers to think and act like owners of highly levered firms without actually going through the trouble of a real management buyout. This is not to say that firms have to become highly levered. It just means that EVA focuses attention on *all* invested capital, not just the bank debt. When managers are assessed capital charges on equity too, it is hoped, they have the same sorts of incentives as managers of LBO firms to utilize capital as efficiently as possible. EVA is a means of making all capital costs explicit, just as they are in a highly levered company.

But despite its obvious appeal, there are several drawbacks and limitations to compensation systems that draw on EVA to mimic the payoffs and risks of highly levered management buyouts.[5] Some drawbacks are universal, affecting companies everywhere. For example, because executives have large undiversified human capital investments in the companies they manage, they tend to be more risk averse than the companies' shareholders. In other words, senior managers and shareholders have different risk preferences. Subordinate managers are typically even more risk averse than their bosses. In the case of CEOs and other top managers, combining high personal (financial) wealth with stock options and other equity participation schemes leads to at least some convergence in risk preferences between them and their shareholders. For their subordinates, however, the monetary amounts at risk in their compensation program may appear modest, but the impact of variable pay on their standard of living is usually far greater than for top managers. The danger in any variable pay scheme, especially one that tries to create owner-like incentives, is that valued employees are scared off by the volatility of their future income stream, and choose to work for other firms.

Other limitations to the EVA/MBO model are country- or region-specific, and are of particular relevance in Europe and Asia. To illustrate, national culture can have a profound influence on the acceptance of shareholder value creation as the paramount corporate goal, and also on the acceptance of EVA-sensitive compensation plans. National culture refers to the values, beliefs, and assumptions that differentiate one group of people from another. This culture tends to be rela-

---

[5] To create MBO-like incentives, EVA bonuses are typically complemented with stock options. The main contribution of stock options is that they provide long-term incentives for value creation. By contrast, EVA provides incentives of a short-term and, through the use of deferred bonuses, medium-term nature.

tively stable, is deeply embedded in everyday life, and is fairly resistant to change. As Professors Schuler and Rogovsky argue, global companies that ignore these cross-cultural differences in human resources and compensation practices do so at their own peril.[6] They cite the example of Lincoln Electric, a success story in the U.S., but unable to duplicate that success internationally because of its lack of understanding of differences in expectations regarding compensation policies and practices.

In their empirical work on the influence of national culture on compensation practices, Schuler and Rogovsky draw heavily on the work of sociologist Geert Hofstede.[7] His work led to a widely-accepted framework based on four fundamental dimensions that characterize national value systems:

- Power distance
- Uncertainty avoidance
- Individualism vs. collectivism
- Masculinity vs. femininity

Power distance indicates the extent to which the unequal distribution of power is accepted by those who have it and those who don't. In cultures with small power distance, inequalities (whether in a company or in society) should be minimized. Hence, management practices in small power distance countries like the U.S. emphasize employee participation, while those in the large power distance countries of Southeast Asia and Latin America are more likely to be authoritarian. Accepting sharp inequalities in the distribution of power, a hallmark of countries with large power distance, also implies tolerance for large discrepancies in the rewards of top management versus those of workers. This is exactly what compensation consultants Towers Perrin discovered in their global survey of chief executive compensation as a multiple of the pay received by manufacturing employees.[8] Among the 23 countries surveyed, the seven highest scores all came from either Southeast Asia or Latin America (× denotes times):

Venezuela	84×
Brazil	48×
Hong Kong	43×
Mexico	43×
Malaysia	42×
Singapore	35×
Argentina	30×

Uncertainty avoidance represents the degree to which uncertainty and unpredictability are tolerated in a culture. In countries with higher uncertainty

---

[6] R.S. Schuler and N. Rogovsky, "Understanding Compensation Practice Variations Across Firms: The Impact of National Culture," *Journal of International Business Studies*, First Quarter, 1998, pp. 159-77.

[7] G. Hofstede and M.H. Bond, "The Confucius Connection: From Cultural Roots to Economic Growth," *Organizational Dynamics* (1988), pp. 4-21.

[8] T. Jackson, "The Fat Cats Keep Getting Fatter," *Financial Times* (August 1&2, 1998), p. 7.

avoidance, people are loath to take risks, preferring predictability and structure. In lower uncertainty avoidance countries like the U.S., people are more willing to take risk and actually welcome the discretion that comes with ambiguity.

Individualism is the degree to which people are inclined to put their own interests and those of their immediate family above those of others. High individualism is common among the English-speaking countries, including the U.S. In collectivist societies, such as Korea or Taiwan, first loyalties are to one's in-groups, which may be defined as clan, work team, company, community, or country. In exchange, one expects the group to look after them in case of need. In such societies, responsibilities tend to be group-based, and not individual-based as they are in more individualistic societies.

Masculinity is defined as assertiveness and acquisitiveness (i.e., coveting money and material goods). The U.S. and Japan are said to be "masculine" societies while those of the Scandinavian countries are "feminine," in that they place a high value on caring for others.

As Schuler and Rogovsky demonstrate, these cultural traits have profound implications for the design of corporate compensation programs. They begin by identifying four distinct compensation types:

- Compensation practices based on status
- Compensation practices based on individual performance
- Social benefits and programs
- Employee ownership programs

The results of their study confirm, for example, that because compensation practices based on seniority are predictable, we are more likely to observe them in countries with high levels of uncertainty avoidance. Pay-for-performance, focus on individual (as opposed to group) performance, and individual bonus practices are more likely in countries with high levels of individualism. On the other hand, pay for performance is less common in countries with high levels of uncertainty avoidance. Social benefits play a more active role in total compensation in countries exhibiting low degrees of masculinity (or high degrees of femininity) and in countries with high levels of uncertainty avoidance. And finally, employee ownership plans are less prevalent in countries with high levels of power distance and in countries with low levels of individualism.

What these findings demonstrate is that differences in compensation practices across companies and across countries are not just an accident or even necessarily a consequence of differing attitudes over the importance of value creation (although it certainly plays a part). But they do tell us that culture matters. In countries exhibiting high levels of power distance, high levels of uncertainty avoidance, low levels of individualism, and low degrees of masculinity, implementation of value-based compensation schemes will be considerably more difficult than in countries exhibiting the opposite characteristics.

WHAT DO MANAGERS REALLY THINK ABOUT SHAREHOLDER VALUE?

Although the pressure for performance from the capital markets has intensified in recent years, do managers really believe that value creation is the firm's primary mission? The evidence is mixed, and little research has been done of late on attitudes of managers outside the United States and the British Isles.

PA Consultancy Group recently surveyed British and Irish managers on their attitudes toward shareholder value.[9] Support for general propositions, such as "We believe that the key objective of our senior management is to manage for shareholder value," was high, which should be encouraging to observers who would like to see a stronger value-oriented culture in Europe. Nearly all respondents (chairmen, chief executive officers, and finance directors from 132 of the largest firms in the U.K. and Ireland) agreed with the statement, and over half strongly agreed. But support for value-based policies decreased as questions became more specific. For example, less support was expressed for the idea that "compensation at all levels of the company should include high variable elements which are driven by the level of shareholder value created."

This evidence suggests that while managers widely accept the importance of shareholder value in principle, they continue to resist implementation of the policies and systems required to create a strong value-based culture in their companies. Even managers themselves admit that integration of value-based principles with company systems and processes has been spotty and incomplete at best. Unfortunately, companies that implement shareholder value principles in a haphazard or piecemeal fashion are unlikely to achieve significant improvement in results. The risk is that value based management may be discredited in the minds of employees, who then come to view it as just another management fad, without the principles having been given a fair chance to succeed.

In an attempt to draw a link between stock market performance and value-based principles, PA Consulting isolated support for broad principles from processes and actions. Examples of processes include:

- A strategic planning process that focuses on deploying capital to maximize shareholder value
- The use of discounted cash flow techniques to evaluate capital investments
- Monthly or quarterly management reports that focus on value-based measures, such as EVA
- Variable pay driven by shareholder value creation
- Communications with capital markets that emphasize value creation instead of earnings per share
- Selecting board members on their willingness to be substantial shareholders

---

[9] *Managing for Shareholder Value* (London, PA: Consultancy Services Limited, 1997).

Actions include:

- Share buybacks when excess cash is created
- Many or most senior managers as substantial shareholders
- Value-destroying businesses closed or divested
- Focus on core competencies and the outsourcing of everything else
- Low base salary but high variable pay
- Identifying and maintaining a target capital structure which maximizes shareholder value

Companies in the PA survey fall into one of four categories: (1) generally negative about managing for shareholder value (MSV) principles, (2) positive about MSV principles but not processes, (3) positive about principles and processes but not actions, and (4) positive about principles, processes, and actions. Annualized total shareholder returns were calculated over a 4-year period, 1993 to 1996. While the average return for the FTSE 500 was 16% over this period, returns averaged 13%, 15%, 18%, and 21% for groups 1, 2, 3, and 4, respectively. Hardly scientific, but the results do suggest that while approving of value-based principles has a positive effect on performance, the greatest benefits go to those firms which go to the greatest lengths to ensure that the principles guide internal processes, systems, and managerial actions.

A similar attempt to gauge corporate attitudes towards shareholder value in medium- and large-sized Swiss companies was conducted by Price Waterhouse, a rare example of a survey on value-based management done outside the English-speaking world. Although companies in Continental Europe are thought to badly lag Anglo-American firms in the implementation of shareholder value principles, it is encouraging to note that over 60% of the respondents report implementing value-based management "to some degree," while nearly one in five claim to have implemented it even further. Also, just under 60% refer to maximizing shareholder value either explicitly or implicitly in the corporate mission statement. However, earnings per share, return on equity, and other accounting-based measures tend to dominate performance appraisal. Fewer than one in five use EVA or similar metrics. One discouraging piece of news is that only one in eight respondents uses financial performance measures (whether accounting, cash flow, or value-based) below the senior management level.

CONCLUDING REMARKS

The shareholder value revolution has reached Europe and, to a lesser extent, Asia. The economic, social, and political factors that led to the value creating imperative in the United States are making themselves felt in the rest of the world. Business managers have been late in coming to shareholder value, and while there are local champions of the concept in every one of the advanced market economies, value-based thinking in Europe and Asia still lags the U.S. EVA and similar value-based metrics are catching on fast, but understanding among managers is typically superficial. What's more, the integration of value-based metrics with planning systems, budgets, and incentive compensation schemes is sketchy at best. It can be too in the U.S., but through this author's experiences, the ideas behind EVA, if not the actual metric itself, are more broadly and deeply understood among American managers than among their counterparts in Europe and especially in Asia.

Asia is an interesting case study for students and practitioners of value-based management. Until very recently few Asian managers had even heard of EVA, and those who had cared little for it. The reason is clear. Economic growth rates of 7%, 8%, or even higher made Asian managers indifferent to value-based metrics. In such an environment, you didn't have to be particularly smart or skillful as a manager, you only had to be there (with the right connections, of course). When the economy grows by 8% year after year, just about anyone can make a profit. The Pacific Rim's remarkable economic performance even brought about talk of an Asian management paradigm, one that Western managers would have to learn from if they were to compete in the global markets of the 21st century. But with the 1997-1998 collapse, the Asian bubble burst, and now talk of this magical paradigm has disappeared. We now know that much of the economic devastation in Thailand, Korea, Indonesia, Malaysia, and Japan was wrought by zealous over-lending and the near total disregard for the need to earn satisfactory returns on capital (a cornerstone of the EVA movement). Asian managers who only recently disdained "Western" management thought in favor of some ill-defined "Asian" model, presumably more in tune with the times, have become less smug and, at least in some cases, more open to Western practice, including value-based management. Of course, EVA is not really a Western concept; it's just sound economics. And economic reality has imposed itself on Asia in a big way, a fact that helps to explain the growing interest in the concept even on that once-forbidding continent.

In brief, EVA has grown in popularity outside the U.S. for much the same reason as it did in the U.S. Managers were coming under intense pressure to deliver superior value to investors and needed ways to measure and motivate value creation, at corporate level and in operating divisions. The old concept of residual income was dusted off and given a glossier sheen. One of EVA's great virtues is that it has helped to make the key concepts of value and corporate finance accessible to general managers, and in this way has been an indispensable tool in advancing the wealth creating potential of business.

Chapter 9

EVA and the OECD Principles of Corporate Governance

Robert Straw, Ph.D.
Associate Professor
University of St. Gallen, Switzerland

Simon Peck, Ph.D.
Senior Lecturer
City University Business School, London

Hans-Ueli Keller, Lic. Oec.
Research Associate
University of St. Gallen, Switzerland

INTRODUCTION

Corporate governance has become of increasing interest to academics and practitioners alike in the last decade, as a reaction to, amongst other things, some spectacular corporate failures. This heightened public interest recently led the OECD to release a set of principles on corporate governance. There are still, however, various unresolved issues in this field. In this chapter we analyze whether and what Economic Value Added (EVA) can contribute to good corporate governance taking the OECD principles as a point of reference. The chapter is structured as follows. In the next section we provide an overview of the basic theoretical perspectives on corporate governance. Then we provide a short discussion of the reasons for and the content of the OECD principles of corporate governance. Next, we analyze whether EVA can provide a solution or mechanism in the promotion of the OECD principles. In particular, we review the topics of total value added, executive compensation, and strategic disclosure of information.

THEORETICAL PERSPECTIVES ON CORPORATE GOVERNANCE

The OECD's definition of corporate governance is:

> Corporate governance involves a set of relationships between a company's management, its board, its shareholders and other stakeholders. Corporate governance also provides the structure through which the objectives of the company are set, and the means of attaining those objectives and monitoring performance are determined. Good corporate governance should provide proper incentives for the board and management to pursue objectives that are in the interests of the company and shareholders and should facilitate effective monitoring, thereby encouraging firms to use resources more efficiently.[1]

According to this definition, four actors are involved in corporate governance: the executive management of a company, its board who supervises executive management and corporate performance, the shareholders who own the company, and other stakeholder groups who are affected by or are influential to the company's strategy. Although corporate governance primarily analyzes the relationships between these four actors, it is partly determined by its legal and institutional context. Above all, the concern about corporate monitoring arises from the separation of ownership and managerial control in modern publicly owned corporations. This separation and its problems have been discussed from various theoretical perspectives. These are outlined next.

Agency Theory

Agency theory is the most prominent perspective through which corporate governance is researched. From this perspective, the separation of ownership and control creates the so-called *agency problem*: the shareholders or owners of the company are interested in a maximum return on their investment. But this is not necessarily the main interest of managers who control the corporation. Hence the relationship between the owner (the principal), and the management (the agent) is characterized by this potential conflict of interest.

The motivation of managers — in the absence of proper incentives — rests with factors such as their status, power, and potential for personal growth and income. The status and the power of managers are generally related to the size of the firm. Hence, managers may be more growth-oriented than profit-maximizing behavior would require. Moreover, some top managers sometimes try to increase their income by "above-normal on-the-job" consumption. This problem is best

---

[1] OECD, "OECD Principles of Corporate Governance, SG/CG(99)5" available at http://www.oecd.org/daf/corporate/principles.htm, p. 2.

explained by some extreme examples: J. Stewart, former CEO of Lone Star billed his company $1.1 million for purely personal expenses.[2] Armand Hammer, founder and CEO of Occidental Petroleum, convinced his board to spend $10 million of corporate funds to build a museum for his own art collection and a much smaller sum on a book detailing two years of his own life.[3] Furthermore, managers striving for job security might behave in a risk-averse manner. They may prefer a diversification strategy, in order to spread corporate risks. But this diversification is not in the interests of shareholders who can diversify their portfolio risk much more efficiently in the capital market. Based on the same motivation for security, managers prefer debt financing less than would be optimal from a profit-maximizing perspective. They will propose to retain profits rather than pay them out or invest them in possible loss-making ventures. This potential for self-interested behavior and lack of effort on the part of the agents is called moral hazard.[4]

The first-best solution for these agency problems is an optimal contract between principal and agent ensuring that the agent behaves in the interest of the shareholders. Based on transaction cost theory, such an *ex ante* contract is not possible because — even if all information to set up such a contract was available — the cost of collecting, analyzing, and recording them would be extremely high. On top of that, it would be rather costly to monitor managerial behavior and to enforce activities that are in line with the initial contract. These costs of monitoring, controlling, and interest-aligning are called agency costs. They rise if information is asymmetrically distributed between the agent and the principal, favoring the former. This is certainly the case in corporate governance, where management has a huge information advantage relative to shareholders.

The second-best solution then is to provide sufficient incentives to managers that align their interests with those of the shareholders. Exhibit 1 shows the internal and external mechanisms or incentives mentioned in the corporate governance discussion. Internal mechanisms promote goal congruence between the interests of shareholders and management.[5] From an agency perspective, the primary role of the board of directors is to monitor executive management in the interests of shareholders. In reality, it is the board of directors, rather than the principals, who hire, fire, and undertake the monitoring of top management.

High-powered incentive contracts require that managerial compensation set by the board should be tied to corporate performance. High performance-related compensation transfers risk to the agent, as corporate performance is only to a certain degree a function of managers' behavior. Under the assumption that the agent is risk-averse, this is a further incentive for management to pursue low-risk strategies.[6]

---

[2] Robert A.G. Monks and Nell Minow, *Corporate Governance* (Cambridge, MA: Blackwell, 1995), p. 186.

[3] Monks, *Corporate Governance*, p. 412.

[4] Kathleen M. Eisenhardt, "Agency Theory: An Assessment and Review," *Academy of Management Review*, No. 1 (1989), pp. 57-74.

[5] James P. Walsh and James K. Seward, "On the Efficiency of Internal and External Corporate Control Mechanisms," *Academy of Management Review*, No. 3 (1990), p. 423.

[6] Eisenhardt, "Agency Theory: An Assessment and Review," p. 61.

Exhibit 1: Framework for Good Governance*

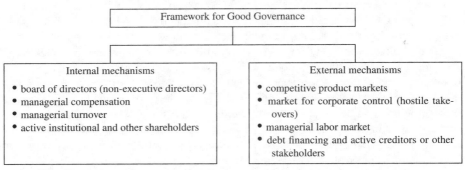

* Based on Oliver Hart, "Corporate Governance: Some Theory and Implications," *The Economic Journal* (May 1995), pp. 678–689; Martin J. Conyon and Simon Peck, "Recent Developments in UK Corporate Governance," in T. Buxton, P. Chapman, and P. Temple (eds.), *Britain's Economic Performance, Second Edition* (London: Routledge, 1997), pp. 253-277, James P. Walsh and James K. Seward, "On the Efficiency of Internal and External Corporate Control Mechanisms," *Academy of Management Review*, No. 3 (1990), pp. 421-458.

Last but not least, the agency problem would be less important if shareholders were active and chose the "voice" option rather than "walk." The importance of institutional shareholders is growing around the world. Furthermore, there is evidence that these institutional investors are becoming more actively involved in the monitoring of corporations. A signal for this can be seen in the investors' demand for codes of best practices in corporate governance and in their lobbying for disclosure requirements that companies have to fulfill, if their shares are publicly traded at a certain stock exchange. However, greater involvement of institutional investors in corporate governance will not be realized without costs. As Jonathan Macey notes: "These costs include: (1) new investments in human capital; (2) significant free-rider problems; (3) loss of liquidity; and (4) potential legal liability for insider trading, or for breach of fiduciary duty to other shareholders where the insiders have assumed a role as a director or an active participant in management."[7]

External mechanisms of control are market-based and contribute to the alignment of the interests of managers and other stakeholders more generally. These mechanisms mainly pose a competitive pressure on top executives. When effective, these mechanisms render monitoring of managers unnecessary.[8] If corporate governance has an influence on corporate performance,[9] then companies with a good governance system would enjoy a competitive advantage in product

---

[7] Jonathan R. Macey, "Measuring the Effectiveness of Different Corporate Governance Systems: Toward a More Scientific Approach," *Journal of Applied Corporate Finance* (Winter 1998), p. 24.

[8] Eric R. Gedajlovic and Daniel M. Shapiro, "Management and Ownership Effects: Evidence from Five Countries," *Strategic Management Journal* (1998), pp. 533-553.

[9] This is assumed by most authors interested in corporate governance. But the relationship between corporate performance and corporate governance is hard to establish empirically.

markets. Certainly in Anglo-Saxon research, hostile takeovers or even the threat thereof are assumed to put considerable restraints on managerial discretion. Whenever a manager is dismissed for low corporate performance or whenever his firm faces bankruptcy, his reputation suffers and his chance of getting a new management job shrinks.[10] This is how the managerial labor market controls managerial behavior. Debt financing forces top executives to stick to the agreed-upon repayment schedule, which constrains managers' ability to dilute corporate cash flows for their personal objectives. For this reason, management-buy-outs and leveraged-buy-outs which normally raise the debt to equity ratio, often result in better corporate performance. The increased ownership incentive of managers is at least of similar importance.

A central assumption of agency perspective is that external markets have the potential to serve as efficient control mechanisms. This assumption is challenged by some academics, particularly as far as financial markets are concerned. The basic argument is that financial markets are biased towards the short term. As outcome uncertainty is high with long-term investments, financial markets might constantly undervalue such corporate behavior, although no one denies that such long-term investments are essential for the firm's survival. Hence, as Keasey, Thompson, and Wright point out: "supporters of this view see the challenge of corporate governance reform as one of providing an environment in which shareholders and managers are encouraged to share long-term performance horizons."[11] It is interesting, however, that there is little supportive evidence for the claimed short-term preference of capital markets.

Managerial Hegemony

The first empirical evidence supporting managerialism was provided in 1932 by Berle and Means who described a process which took place in the U.S. at the beginning of the century.[12] According to their results, enterprises of that time experienced a high growth rate. This growth demanded a great amount of capital, which was raised by attracting small shareholders. Whereas the corporation of the prior century was typically owned by the manager himself or by a small group of shareholders actively participating in corporate control, this process led to dispersed ownership, rendering effective control by shareholders problematic.

A shareholder with a small stake in the company faces a considerable control dilemma: for her, effective control of corporate management is costly. Actions which improve the quality of managerial monitoring are costly to the individual and moreover possess the characteristics of a public good. This implies that

---

[10] R. Charan, "Why CEOs Fail," *Fortune* (June 1999).

[11] Kevin Keasey, Steve Thompson, and Mike Wright, "Introduction: The Corporate Governance Problem — Competing Diagnoses and Solutions," in K. Keasey, S. Thompson, and M. Wright (eds.) *Corporate Governance: Economic, Management and Financial Issues* (Oxford: University Press, 1997), p. 5.

[12] Jürgen Beyer, *Managerherrschaft in Deutschland?* (Opladen/Wiesbaden: Westdeutscher Verlag, 1998), p. 28ff.

every other shareholder profits from this control effort as well. As they cannot be excluded from profit-sharing, other shareholders are certainly unwilling to pay for the control effort. This phenomenon is often described as the *free-rider-problem.*

Hence, it may prove more rational for a minority shareholder not to participate actively in the control of the corporation, but to choose the so-called "walk" option. This means, she will sell her shares as soon as she loses confidence in corporate management.

This perspective led to a research tradition that analyzes the discretion of corporate management as well as the power relations among executive managers, outside board directors, and shareholders. For example Myles Mace has called directors "ornaments on the corporate Christmas tree."[13] The position of the board of directors is weakened by several factors: First, boards suffer from an informational disadvantage. Second, their lack of time is a severe constraint to directional power. Third, strong norms — such as the impoliteness of publicly criticizing executives — hinder open discussion during board meetings.[14] Fourth, the power of the board is influenced by its independence. Therefore, it is important that executives do not participate in the nomination process of directors. Fifth, the board has to be socially integrated as a group to confront executive management. That is why the board of directors should meet regularly and sometimes even without executives. Last but not least, the power of the board is highly dependent on the personality and personal style of the CEO as well as of each director.

Stewardship Theory

Whereas agency theory builds on the economic model of the *homo oeconomicus*, stewardship theory introduces an alternative view of human motivation and decision-making. Having its roots in psychology and sociology, stewardship theory assumes that a manager faces and is conscious of a trade-off between his personal needs and the organizational aims. In agency perspective, the decision of a manager is clearly caring for his personal needs first. On the contrary, stewardship theory claims that — at least in many situations — managers realize that by serving the organizational and social needs first, their personal needs will eventually be met.[15] Hence managers act as the steward, indeed shepherd, of shareholders and other stakeholders.

Agency theory suggests that when conflicts of interest occur, the monitoring and controlling function of corporate boards, particularly of outside directors is very important. But, from a stewardship perspective when managers act deliberately in the interest of shareholders and other stakeholders, an increased controlling effort might be counter-productive. The work of Chris Argyris has

---

[13] Miles Mace, "Directors: Myth and Reality" (Boston: Division of Research, Harvard Business School, 1971), as quoted in Jay Lorsch and Elisabeth MacIver, *Pawns or Potentates* (Boston: Harvard Business School Press, 1989), p. 4.

[14] Lorsch and MacIver, *Pawns or Potentates*, pp. 91ff.

[15] See, for example, James H. Davis, David F. Shoorman, and Lex Donaldson, "Toward a Stewardship Theory of Management," *Academy of Management Review,* No. 1 (1997), pp. 20-47.

shown that control in such circumstances has negative effects on the motivation of the one who is controlled.[16] Other researchers have shown that creative behavior, which is certainly expected from management, is more likely when supervision is non-controlling and supportive.[17]

In relation to corporate governance, it follows from stewardship theory that the board of directors has a strong advisory and consulting function, not just a monitoring mandate. On the other hand, agency perspective is critical about too much *ex ante* board advice on strategic decision-making. It is argued, that if boards, particularly non-executive directors, were strongly involved in strategy formulation, they would lack the ability of independent judgement. This would lead to a situation where outside directors monitor their own decisions.

In considering the agency and stewardship perspectives as complementary, one could argue that it is a central task of the corporate board to balance the degree of control and the amount of advice according to their assessment of managers' main motivation. This of course is an essential task in every leadership situation.

Some recent research provides evidence that the board is more deeply involved in strategic decision making than the traditional managerial hegemony or agency perspective implies. Several factors are said to pose some external pressure on companies for enhanced board involvement in strategic decision making: legal and court systems around the world increase the board's litigation; institutional investors become more active and demanding;[18] the competitive environment of many businesses is increasingly complex; and there is a public controversy about CEO compensation, which is perceived to be too high, and about corporate failures.[19]

Some studies have suggested that there exists a relationship between board composition and board involvement in strategic decision making. For example it was found that board involvement is negatively related to board size and levels of corporate diversification and positively related to corporate financial performance and organizational age.[20] It has also been suggested, that board involvement varies in different stages of strategic decision making.[21] Recently a model has been proposed whereby the entire board takes strategic decisions (i.e., capital investments have to be approved by the board at the end of the investment decision process), but only a subset of the board shapes the preparation of capital investment proposals at

---

[16] Argyris Chris, "Richtig motivieren können wenige Chefs," *Harvard Businessmanager* (no.1, 1995), pp. 9-18.

[17] Gregg Oldham and Anne Cummings, "Employee Creativity: Personal and Contextual Factors at Work," *Academy of Management Journal*, No. 3 (1996), pp. 607-633.

[18] William Q. Judge Jr. and Carl P. Zeithaml, "Institutional and Strategic Choice Perspectives on Board Involvement in the Strategic Decision Process," *Academy of Management Journal*, No. 4 (1992), pp. 767f.

[19] Jay W. Lorsch, "Empowering the Board," *Harvard Business Review* (January-February 1995), pp. 107-117.

[20] Lorsch, "Empowering the Board," pp. 766-794.

[21] See, for example, Sydney Finkelstein and Donald Hambrick, *Strategic Leadership: Top Executives and Their Effects on Organisations* (Minneapolis/St. Paul: West Publishing, 1996), pp. 209-263.

an early stage by consulting executives or by clearly articulating their demands. Moreover, there is a minority of boards actively shaping the content, context, and conduct of strategy. For example, directors can encourage more open discussion about strategy in board meetings and ask for a deliberately formulated strategy.[22]

Stakeholder Theory

Whereas agency theory, which is based on neoclassic economic theory, argues that the only objective of a company is to maximize profit and shareholder value, *stakeholder theory* sees shareholders as just one group of several upon which the company is dependent. The so-called primary stakeholders are characterized by the fact that a company can not survive without their ongoing participation. Shareholders are primary stakeholders, but employees, customers, investors, and suppliers typically belong to the same group. Hence, as Max Clarkson writes:

> the corporation itself can be defined as a system of primary stake-holder groups, a complex set of relationships between them and among interest groups with different rights, objectives, expectations, and responsibilities. The corporation's survival and continuous success depend upon the ability of its managers to create sufficient wealth, value, or satisfaction for those who belong to each stakeholder group.[23]

Although it is often argued that in the long run, the interests of shareholders and other stakeholders converge — which is certainly the case — as Jeff Frooman notes "stakeholder theory is about managing potential conflict stemming from divergent interests."[24] At least in the short run, scarce resources have to be allocated among diverse stakeholder groups. The benefits of a company's investment in a certain relationship to a stakeholder group are often difficult to measure and its costs are immediate and obvious. Yet, there is a broad agreement that a company can capitalize upon contracts with its stakeholders on the basis of mutual trust and cooperation, because such long-term relationships lower transaction costs. This stakeholder perspective is further supported by recent developments in the field of international strategic management: These authors argue that "the most important corporate resources are not the financial funds in the hand of top management but the knowledge and expertise of the people on the front lines."[25] Hence, the relationship to the company's employees is at least as impor-

---

[22] Terry McNulty and Andrew Pettigrew, "Strategists on the Board," *Organisation Studies*, No. 1 (1999), pp. 47-74. The model is based on empirical data from the U.K.

[23] Max B.E. Clarkson, "A Stakeholder Framework for Analysing and Evaluating Corporate Social Performance," *Academy of Management Review*, No. 1 (1995), p. 106f.

[24] Jeff Frooman, "Stakeholder Influence Strategies," *Academy of Management Review*, No. 2 (1999), p. 193.

[25] Sumantra Ghoshal, Christopher A. Bartlett, and Peter Moran, "A New Manifesto for Management," *Sloan Management Review* (Spring 1999), p. 11.

tant as the one to its shareholders. Such relationships might enhance not only corporate financial performance but also corporate social performance.[26]

Resource dependency theory is closely connected to the stakeholder perspective. It is based on the assumption that the corporation is dependent on various stakeholders and that the board and the executive management tries to manage this dependency. Consequently, "the board is considered as an instrument for dealing with the organization's environment."[27] By cultivating close relationships to the owners of resources critical to the firm's success, a company can reduce environmental uncertainty. This underlines the importance of directors' external social ties.

Summary of Corporate Governance

This section has outlined that there are quite a few disagreements on basic assumptions concerning the corporate governance problem. Thus, it is not easy to provide a conclusive answer to the question of what good corporate governance actually is. Yet there are certain characteristics of good corporate governance that are shared among researchers of different theoretical backgrounds.

First, a good system of corporate governance results in enhanced corporate performance, because the company itself gets the full value from its pool of outside directors, and good corporate governance results in minimal agency costs by providing the right incentives to executives to act in the interest of shareholders. But, measuring these two performance attributes of governance systems is not easy. There is a clear need for further improvement in the assessment and measuring of corporate performance. Research has shown that the relationship between certain corporate governance mechanisms and corporate performance is highly sensitive to the specific performance indicator that is used.[28] Performance measurements used in corporate governance should clearly have the ability to show the value that is created at the top level of a company. But, as noted by Prahalad, "the process of value creation, then, requires that firms simultaneously manage three dimensions: performance in the existing business, adaptation to structural changes in the industries in which they operate, and growth in new directions based on their resource and competence endowments."[29] If performance along all these three dimensions has to be assessed, we need to adopt new performance scorecards.

---

[26] Alan J. Richardson, Michael Welker, and Ian R. Hutchinson, "Managing Capital Reactions to Corporate Social Responsibility," *International Journal of Management Reviews* (March 1999), pp. 17-43. These authors conclude that "the literature suggests that there is a consistent positive relationship between CSR and firm performance measured in a variety of ways" (p. 37).

[27] Jeffrey Pfeffer, "Size and Composition of Corporate Boards of Directors: The Organisation and its Environment," *Administrative Science Quarterly*, No. 2 (1972), p. 218.

[28] D. R. Dalton, C. M. Daily, A. E. Ellstrand, and J. L. Johnson, "Meta-Analytical Reviews of Board Composition, Leadership Structure, and Financial Performance," *Strategic Management Journal* (1998), pp. 269-290.

[29] C.K. Prahalad, "Corporate Governance or Corporate Value Added: Rethinking the Primacy of Shareholder Value," in Donald H. Chew (ed.), *Studies in International Corporate Finance and Governance Systems* (New York and Oxford: Oxford University Press, 1997), p. 50.

There are several indicators measuring the ability of a corporate governance system to control agency costs: the level and growth of managerial compensation as well as its sensitivity to corporate performance indicates the degree of interest alignment of management and shareholders; the sensitivity of executive turnover to corporate performance is an indicator for board vigilance; the premium paid for voting stock relative to non-voting stock shows investors' expectation of high private benefits to control that are not shared with non-voting shareholders, and thus points at weak protection of minority shareholders; and the relative proclivity of firms under rival governance schemes to go public measures the well-functioning of capital markets.[30]

Second, there is a wide agreement that good corporate governance should be transparent and that companies should disclose as much information as possible in a comprehensible way. Such corporate behavior enables shareholders and other stakeholders to actively monitor corporate decisions and management. Such active shareholders and stakeholders might be the most efficient way to enhance the quality of corporate governance. As far as shareholders are concerned, concentrated voting power enhances the likelihood of active shareholding, but it has often a negative impact on the liquidity of the stock — at least under the one-share-one-vote rule. Hence, authorities are asked to search for solutions that concentrate voting power, provide liquidity, and protect minorities at the same time.[31]

Third, the board of directors has three sets of interrelated roles: a service function which enhances a company's identity, reputation and standing in the community, a strategy function which helps to ensure that the company pursues specific goals by following carefully chosen strategies and to improve the company's competitive performance, and a control function which attempts to align interests of senior executives and those of shareholders and other stakeholders in order to minimize agency costs.[32] The relative importance of each of these three roles might change over time. However, it implies that the board simultaneously has to be informed well enough to provide advice to executives as well as critical judgement on management performance and to be detached as well as distant enough to assure that its judgement is independent.[33]

Fourth, the effectiveness of a board in performing these functions is highly dependent on the board's relationship to the executives and to the CEO in particular. The board can only act in a mutually supportive and performance-focused manner if the CEO is open for director participation and for board discus-

---

[30] Macey, "Measuring the Effectiveness of Different Corporate Governance Systems: Toward a More Scientific Approach," p. 24.

[31] Marco Becht, "European Corporate Governance: Trading Off Liquidity Against Control," *European Economic Review* (1999), pp. 1071-1083.

[32] J.A. Pearce II and S.A. Zahra, "Board Composition from a Strategic Contingency Perspective," *Journal of Management Studies* (July 1992), pp. 411-438.

[33] Ada Demb and Friedrich F. Neubauer, "The Corporate Board: Confronting the Paradoxes," *Long Range Planning*, No. 3 (1992), pp. 9-20.

sion and if directors are inquiring rather than passive.[34] Team-building processes and personal relationships based on mutual trust should support such behavior on both sides. Many studies have additionally shown how important independent board leadership is.[35] This basically means that the positions of the CEO and the chairman should be filled with two separate individuals, or if they are one in the same, a non-executive should be elected as vice chairman and asked to chair critical board committees.

Last but not least, there should be various effective control mechanisms for managerial behavior. There is no single control mechanism or model of corporate governance that is always superior. Rather certain combinations of different mechanisms are more effective in certain situations than in others. However, executive remuneration is a powerful tool to align executive interests with those of shareholders. A recent study has suggested that proper incentive alignment in executive compensation plans helps boards to capitalize on their mutual personal ties and social integration.[36]

THE OECD PRINCIPLES OF CORPORATE GOVERNANCE

Various Private Initiatives for Principles of Corporate Governance

In Europe throughout the 1990s, there have been various initiatives to formulate some basic rules in corporate governance. The Cadbury report which was released in 1992 contains a code of best practice for British companies. The Cadbury committee was set up by a joint initiative of private sector interests.[37] The Cadbury report's objective was to enhance openness, integrity, and accountability in the British corporate governance system.[38] Therefore, the Cadbury code of best practice mainly called for increasing independence of the board and for a nomination, a remuneration, and an audit committee being comprised of a majority of non-executive directors. A later Cadbury study found that the majority of British companies comply with the Cadbury code. Two further committees were set up in the U.K. The Greenbury committee report of 1995 contains recommendations for executive remuneration, mainly requiring full disclosure of executive compensation. In 1998, the Hampel report was published. It called for improved quality in

---

[34] John D. Aram and Scott S. Cowen, "Reforming the Corporate Board from Within: Strategies for CEOs and Directors," *Journal of General Management* (Summer 1995), pp. 23-38.

[35] Lorsch and MacIver, *Pawns or Potentates* and Robert F. Felton, Alec Hudnut, and Valda Witt, "Building a Stronger Board," *McKinsey Quarterly*, No. 2 (1995), pp. 162-175.

[36] James D. Westphal, "Collaboration in the Boardroom: Behavioural and Performance Consequences of CEO-Board Social Ties," *Academy of Management Journal*, No. 1 (1999), pp. 7-24.

[37] Three organizations cooperated in initiating the Cadbury Committee: the Financial Reporting Council, the London Stock Exchange, and the Accountancy Profession.

[38] John C. Shaw, "The Cadbury Report: Two Years Later," in K. J. Hopt and E. Wymeersch (eds.), *Comparative Corporate Governance: Essays and Materials* (Berlin and New York: Walter de Gruyter, 1997), p. 24.

applying the recommendations of the Cadbury report and basically led to the recommendations being consolidated into a Combined Code which is appended to
the Listing Rules of the London Stock Exchange.

In other European countries, similar initiatives to the Cadbury committee
were launched. The Viénot report (1995) made some recommendations to
improve the French corporate governance system and in the Netherlands the Peter
Committee released a code of best practice (1996). All these reports are based on
the assumption that executives' discretion has to be limited by an independent
board of directors and that the interests of executives have to be aligned primarily
with those of shareholders. Hence, it could be argued that all these reports were
strongly influenced by agency theory and prevailing U.S. style governance
arrangements.

A second group of private initiatives establishing principles of corporate
governance are the institutional investors, of which the most active is CALPERS
from the U.S. Their view of good corporate governance is that governance structures should be fully accountable. Hence, the CALPERS' core principles stress
the importance of an independent board and of independent board leadership,
require several board committees consisting entirely of independent directors, ask
boards to set up formal performance evaluation processes for executives and
directors, and, last but not least, demand full disclosure of governance structures.
On top of that, CALPERS outlines the basic shareholder rights.[39]

Although the CALPERS guidelines were originally designed for U.S.
companies, the pension fund is increasingly promoting global standards of good
corporate governance and even demanding some changes in European corporate
governance systems. This global interest in corporate governance results from the
increasing international diversification of CALPERS' and other U.S. funds'
investment strategy. One major concern of CALPERS is the difference in
accounting standards that is applied in various countries. Consequently, CALP-
ERS calls for a global application of U.S. GAAP. Moreover, CALPERS publishes
a yearly focus list of companies that perform below average in the long run. Their
analysis is partly based on Economic Value Added (EVA) as a performance indicator.[40] According to Ernst Maug, the large, liquid stock markets which we are
currently experiencing, far from being a hindrance to corporate control, tend to
support effective corporate governance. Large shareholders such as CALPERS
will generally extract a rent from the possibility to monitor the firm.[41] As the
impact of institutional investors on corporate governance is growing, it can be
expected that EVA will certainly play an increasing role in this area.

---

[39] The CALPERS principles are available under www.calpers-governance.org (23.06.99).
[40] Compare the following website of CALPERS containing a description of EVA http://www.calpers-gov-
ernance.org/alert/focus/eva.asp (23.06.99).
[41] Ernst Maug, "Large Shareholders as Monitors: Is There a Trade-Off between Liquidity and Control,"
Journal of Finance, No. 1 (1998), p. 89.

Reasons for the OECD Initiative

The OECD became increasingly aware that good corporate governance structures have a positive impact on corporations' overall economic performance. Consequently, the Business Sector Advisory Group on Corporate Governance was established in 1996. Based on the report of this group,[42] which mainly reflects the private sector perspective on governance systems in member countries, the OECD launched an initiative to establish principles to assist governments to improve their legal, institutional, and regulatory frameworks. But the OECD principles also aim to provide guidance for stock exchanges, investors, and corporations.[43]

The principles clearly acknowledge that different countries have different systems of corporate governance and that none of these systems is superior to another. The principles should serve as a common basis which could be considered as the over-arching objectives for each country.[44] Although it is not stated in the principles, they represent something of a compromise given the influence of several, quite diverse, national systems of corporate governance.

The timing of setting up OECD principles of corporate governance was clearly influenced by the financial crisis in Asia and South America. This financial crisis revealed the lack of transparency and insufficiency of the corporate governance systems in the primary countries affected. Furthermore, it revealed how closely related transparent corporate governance and economic stability can be.

The OECD Principles: Content

Basic Assumption of the Principles

The OECD Principles of Corporate Governance are best characterized as being a *least common denominator* summary of diverse national corporate governance systems. Taking these principles as a reference point, national governments as well as companies still enjoy large discretion in designing their corporate governance framework.

In the preamble, it is underlined that the principles are evolutionary in nature.[45] According to the Business Sector Advisory Group, there are three conditions for adaptability in corporate governance. First, regulations should be permissive, which basically means that companies should be allowed or even encouraged to learn from their international experiences and from international governance practices. Second, governance arrangements should provide multiple options as far as ownership structure, internal board structure, corporate owner-

---

[42] Ira M. Millenstein, et al., *Corporate Governance: Improving Competitiveness and Access to Capital in Global Markets; A Report to the OECD by the Business Sector Advisory Group on Corporate Governance*, (Paris: OECD, 1998).

[43] http://www.oecd.org/daf/governance/O&As.htm (28.05.99).

[44] OECD, "OECD Principles of Corporate Governance, SG/CG(99)5" available at http://www.oecd.org/daf/corporate/principles.htm, p. 2.

[45] OECD, "OECD Principles of Corporate Governance, SG/CG(99)5" available at http://www.oecd.org/daf/corporate/principles.htm, p. 3.

ship transaction, and contracts where resource providers are concerned. Third, there has to be a positive public attitude towards diversity and innovation in corporate governance.[46] Such flexibility in corporate governance is certainly beneficial in fast changing, highly competitive markets, as long as corporate governance remains transparent.

The principles cover five areas of corporate governance. For each section, the principles state a basic objective after which several rules are provided indicating how this objective should be realized. The following overview of the five sections has the same structure — first, the basic objective is quoted from the OCED report and then the rules are summarized briefly.

The Rights of Shareholders

> The corporate governance framework should protect shareholders' rights. (p. 5)

This objective is further specified by outlining the basic shareholder rights including access to information, voting and participating at general shareholder meetings, election of board members, a share in the corporate profits and ownership of shares. In order that the shareholder has the opportunity to actively and effectively participate in the general shareholder meeting, he should be well and timely informed, be allowed to ask questions as well as to influence the meeting's agenda, and to vote in person or *in absentia*.

The market for corporate control is considered to protect shareholders' rights as long as it functions efficiently and transparently. Hence, the principles strongly claim that anti-take-over devices should only be used in the shareholders' interest. Furthermore, shareholder rights can be protected by transparent disclosure of ownership transactions or of a disproportionate degree of certain shareholders' control rights.

The Equitable Treatment of Shareholders

> The corporate governance framework should ensure the equitable treatment of all shareholders, including minority and foreign shareholders. All shareholders should have the opportunity to obtain effective redress for violation of their rights. (p. 6)

This section underlines the importance of a legal system providing mechanisms for minority shareholders to bring lawsuits and to obtain redress for grievances at reasonable cost and without excessive delay.

The principles do not argue in favor of a one-share-one-vote system, managers and boards are best able to optimize the capital structure of the firm which then has to be approved by the shareholders. In many countries, financial

---

[46] Millenstein, *Corporate Governance: Improving Competitiveness and Access to Capital in Global Markets*, pp. 33ff.

institutions and other nominees cast votes of those shares which they hold in custody for investors. In such cases, the custodians should be asked to vote in a manner agreed upon with the owner in advance.

Minority shareholders can also be protected by strongly prohibiting insider trading and by requiring directors and executives to disclose any material interest in transactions or matters affecting the corporation.

The Role of The Stakeholder in Corporate Governance

The corporate governance framework should recognize the rights of stakeholders as established by law and encourage active co-operation between corporations and stakeholders in creating wealth, jobs, and the sustainability of financially sound enterprises. (p. 7)

According to this objective, a company's relationship to its stakeholders is determined by two factors: stakeholders' rights guaranteed by law and the profit-enhancing character of these relationships. This more or less minimal consideration for stakeholders' interests is enhanced in the annotations to the principles where the OECD takes the position that corporations should and actually do recognize that long-term stakeholder relationships and co-operation is wealth-creating, and that many companies make additional commitments to their stakeholders. Furthermore, many examples of stakeholder participation in corporate governance are listed on page 18 of the report: employee stock ownership plans, employee representation on boards, creditor involvement in governance in the context of insolvency proceedings, and other governance processes that consider stakeholder viewpoints. All these stakeholder relationships and stakeholder participation mechanisms should be transparent.

Disclosure and Transparency

The corporate governance framework should ensure that timely and accurate disclosure is made on all material matters regarding the corporation, including the financial situation, performance, ownership, and governance of the company. (p. 8)

The principles list a minimal set of areas for which information should be disclosed: financial and operating corporate results, company objectives, major share ownership and voting rights, members of the supervisory and executive board, as well as their remuneration, foreseeable risk factors, employee and other stakeholder relationships, and governance structures and policies. Such information, as well as additional material should be disseminated in a timely and cost-efficient manner. Moreover, an independent auditor should ensure high quality standards in all disclosed materials.

Consequently, a strong disclosure regime — be it mandatory or voluntary — is a tool for protecting investors and for improving the public understanding of the company's activities. It enables active monitoring and participation of investors and stakeholders. The OECD further supports "the development of high quality internationally recognized standards, which can serve to improve the comparability of information between countries." (p.21)

The Responsibilities of the Board

> The corporate governance framework should ensure the strategic guidance of the company, the effective monitoring of management by the board, and the board's accountability to the company and the shareholders. (p. 9)

The following are listed on page 9 of the report as key functions of the board:

1. Reviewing and guiding corporate strategy, major plans and action, risk policy, annual budgets, and business plans; setting performance objectives; monitoring implementation and corporate performance; and overseeing major capital expenditures, acquisitions and divestitures.
2. Selecting, compensating, monitoring, and, when necessary, replacing key executives and overseeing succession planning.
3. Reviewing key executive and board remuneration, and ensuring a formal and transparent board nomination process.
4. Monitoring and managing potential conflicts of interest of management, board members, and shareholders, including misuse of corporate assets and abuse in related party transactions.
5. Ensuring the integrity of the corporation's accounting and financial reporting systems, including the independent audit, and that appropriate systems of control are in place, in particular, systems for monitoring risk, financial control, and compliance with the law.
6. Monitoring the effectiveness of the governance practices under which it operates and making changes as needed.
7. Overseeing the process of disclosure and communication.

The board should perform these functions fully informed, in good faith, in due diligence and in the best interest of the company and its shareholders. But the board should also take into account the equal treatment of all shareholders and the interest of stakeholders. In order that the board is able to exercise objective and independent judgement, the board should consist of a sufficient number of non-executive directors, who are willing to and can devote sufficient time to their responsibilities. Objective judgement is particularly important in responsibilities such as financial reporting, nomination, and executive and board remuneration.

The OECD Principles: Potential Value

It has been shown that several private initiatives for principles of best practice in corporate governance have been launched throughout this decade. Most of them aimed to improve a specific country's corporate governance system. The one glo-bally oriented initiative, the corporate governance principles of CALPERS, only contains the perspective of a single, very large shareholder. The OECD principles of corporate governance, on the contrary, are revolutionary because they have a global scope and therefore could serve as a point of reference for authorities and the private sector. In the light of an increasing interdependence of the world's economies and of the globalization of markets, the development of such princi-ples is not only appreciated but necessary.

Like all OECD resolutions, the principles on corporate governance are not binding. Which means that, at first sight, their value seems to be rather low. Yet, the ministers of all 29 member countries have agreed upon these common characteristics of good corporate governance at the OECD ministerial conference of May 27-28, 1999. In addition, the principles enjoy early support from different organizations. The IMF and the World Bank plan to co-operate with the OECD in the field of corporate governance along two major initiatives: "a newly created Global Corporate Gover-nance Forum, and enhanced structures for policy dialogue and development in regions and individual countries."[47] A further result of this cooperation could be that the IMF uses the OECD principles as best practice guidelines in negotiating debt relief pack-ages.[48] Moreover, other interest groups in the field of corporate governance such as the International Corporate Governance Network support this OECD initiative as a global minimal standard.[49] Hence, the force of the OECD principles of corporate gov-ernance is not based on being binding for national governments, but on their recogni-tion by several institutions and in the overall practice of corporate governance.

Still, a critical test will be how institutional investors like CALPERS react to the principles. The comparison of the CALPERS principles[50] and the OECD principles reveals several commonalties: both principles see themselves as a minimal standard, and companies and national authorities are expected to go beyond it. Both accept the value of various national systems of corporate gover-nance and hence deny that one concept is superior to another. They further agree that good corporate governance is based on principles such as transparency, accountability to shareholders, protection of basic shareholder rights, equitable treatment of shareholders, and effective board oversight.

But, there are also some areas where the two principles disagree. First, CALPERS strongly favors a one-share-one-vote system. Second, CALPERS con-siders executive compensation as the main control mechanism in protecting share-holders' rights. Third, CALPERS wants corporate directors and management to have a long-term strategic vision emphasizing shareholder value. Fourth, CALP-ERS encourages that directors are only accountable to shareholders.

---

[47] http://www.oecd.org/news_and_events/release/nw99-51a.htm (07.06.99).

[48] This was suggested by Joanna Shelton, OECD deputy-secretary general and chair of the task force, quoted in Jane Martinson, "OECD Code to Safeguard Shareholders," *Financial Times* (April 10/11, 1999).

[49] According to a telephone interview with Richard Frederick, OECD, Paris (07.06.99).

[50] http://www.calpers-governance.org/principles/international/global/page01.asp.

The OECD Principles: A Critical Discussion

Taking a closer look at the definition of corporate governance in the principles,[51] one gets the impression that the monitoring role of the board and the alignment of managers' interests to those of shareholders are the most central concerns. Hence, one could argue that the principles are strongly influenced by agency perspective. First reactions to the principles have consequently criticized them for being biased toward the Anglo-Saxon system of corporate governance and its share-holder-value orientation.[52] We do not fully agree with this critique for several reasons. First, the OECD principles acknowledge the important role of stakeholders in the long-term survival of companies. They even support stakeholder participation in corporate governance. Second, the tendency toward long-term shareholder value orientation is due to the fact that capital markets currently seem to be more efficient sources for capital than banks.[53] Therefore, a corporation's relationship to its investors is crucial for securing efficient access to capital. Third, the OECD principles do not prefer the Anglo-Saxon one-share-one-vote concept. Fourth, even as far as accounting standards are concerned, the principles have no preference for the Anglo-Saxon system. And last but not least, the principles are applicable in either one-tier or two-tier board systems.[54]

The Shareholders' Rights

The election of board members is seen as a basic shareholder right. However, if shareholders are not able to actively participate in the nomination process of directors, this right is nothing else than approving the proposal of the current board, and hence rather ceremonial. Unfortunately, the principles make no statement on how the shareholders might be encouraged to actively participate in the nomination process. On top of that, the principles contain no argument on the design of the proxy process.

A further critical aspect of the principles is that the market for corporate control is considered as an efficient control mechanism protecting shareholder rights. Clearly, following the agency perspective, external control mechanisms and particularly the market for corporate control are seen to be the most efficient.[55] Yet, this agency position lacks empirical evidence and there is wide spread doubt on the effectiveness of the markets for corporate control among academics and practitioners. For example, most of the current merger activities

---

[51] This definition has already been cited at the beginning of this section.

[52] Martinson, "OECD Code to Safeguard Shareholders."

[53] Macey, "Measuring the Effectiveness of Different Corporate Governance Systems: Toward a More Scientific Approach," p. 21.

[54] The one-tier board system is dominant in Anglo-Saxon economies, where the board simultaneously consists of executives and outside directors. In a two-tier board system, there are two clearly separated organs at the top of a corporation: a supervisory board and a management board, as it is usual in Germany or the Netherlands.

[55] Compare this to Michael C. Jensen, "The Modern Industrial Revolution, Exit, and the Failure of Internal Control Systems," *Journal of Finance* (July 1993), pp. 831-880.

around the world do not intend to replace weak management teams but are taken for defensive reasons. Furthermore, the effectiveness of the market for corporate control as a governance mechanism is strongly dependent on the institutional context, the ownership structure and the financing preferences. Research in comparative corporate governance has shown that although national corporate governance systems differ in the importance of certain control mechanisms and incentives, their results are quite similar.[56] Such findings imply that different control mechanisms are substitutable.[57] Yet, there is little disagreement that certain control mechanisms work better in a certain institutional context than in another. Finally, in several countries in whose governance system markets for corporate control are central, companies have succeeded in building up effective take-over defense mechanisms. Many of these defense mechanisms can be used either in the interest of shareholders or to protect current management. It is often difficult to judge in advance whether shareholders gain from the take-over defense. Therefore, the principles should instead demand the strengthening of several — internal and external — control mechanisms.

A further critique of the principles is that they do not address two central issues. First, how can active shareholding be supported, without negative impacts on the liquidity of the stock and on the protection of minority shareholders? Second, if the current trend towards more active institutional shareholders continues, it is likely that there will be two classes of shareholders in the future — active institutional shareholders with large, concentrated stock and minority shareholders with small distributed stock? In such a situation, is it beneficial to build special relationships to institutional shareholders? And, if yes, how could the rights of minority shareholders still be protected?

The Role of the Stakeholder

The principles recognize the importance of all stakeholders' interests and argue for the cultivation of special relationships with diverse stakeholders, but only if these mechanisms for stakeholder participation are performance enhancing. The basic assumption of this statement is that in the long run the interests of shareholders and other stakeholders converge. Hence, it is in the interest of the corporation to foster wealth-creating relations with stakeholders. It could be argued that the OECD principles clearly favor a shareholder perspective, though we would note that, unlike most other stakeholders in the firm, it is shareholders who do not have a contract specifying terms and conditions. With fair contracting (and not withstanding the role of long-term or implicit contracting in some economies) this focus is justified. Stakeholder relationships can be seen as profit-enhancing mech-

---

[56] Stephen N. Kaplan, "Corporate Governance and Corporate Performance: A Comparison of Germany, Japan and the US," *Comparative Corporate Governance: Essays and Materials*, pp. 195-210.
[57] Walsh and Seward, "On the Efficiency of Internal and External Corporate Control Mechanisms," and John Kose and Lemma W. Senbet, "Corporate Governance and Board Effectiveness," *Journal of Banking and Finance* (1998), pp. 371-403.

anisms that good boards and management would foster. The positive consequence of this is that the company's management and board enjoy clear accountability to shareholders.[58] The negative consequence of this shareholder bias of the OECD principles is that Europeans might consider them as being too Anglo-Saxon oriented, the result being that the principles might be less accepted in Europe.

Responsibility of the Board

Legally, the Board of Directors constitutes the elected representatives of the shareholders. As Michael Jensen remarks "the board, at the apex of the internal control system, has the final responsibility for the functioning of the firm."[59] In the principles, much is made of the ability of independent, or non-executive directors to undertake informed monitoring of management on behalf of shareholders. These are directors with no, or little, direct financial stake in the company. Their role is crucial, as it seems reasonable to assume that executive (inside) directors will not self-monitor, or monitor effectively the performance of the chief executive officer (CEO). The career of the executive director, after all, is closely tied to the incumbent CEO and so they do not possess sufficient incentives to remove them or to, say, restrict their compensation growth.[60]

There are, however, ample reasons to believe that non-executives have insufficient incentives or power to monitor management. The company equity holdings by non-executives are typically low and so is the willingness to correct managerial mistakes. In addition, the compensation received by outside directors, along with their chances of re-selection as a non-executive director, are influenced by the CEO. So, as Steve Nickell aptly remarks "why should they make a fuss rather than keep quiet and collect their fees?"[61] Second, there seems to be a clear asymmetry of information between executives, as full time employees, and non-executive directors. Typically, non-executive directors spend only a fraction of their time at the company and, indeed, can be executive directors at other companies. This seems to build into the governance system an information bias in favor of the executive directors. In extremis, of course, the shareholders have the power to dismiss the board in a proxy fight organized by one or more dissident shareholders. However, there is a similar free-rider problem here to that which we saw in the case of the monitoring role.

---

[58] Although, even in the U.S. where the shareholder orientation is most prominent, Lorsch and McIver (*Pawns or Potentates*, pp. 37-53) found that directors are somewhat confused about their accountability and that most of the directors they had interviewed, were primarily concerned with the long-term survival of the company and not with current shareholder value.

[59] See Jensen, "The Modern Industrial Revolution, Exit, and the Failure of Internal Control Systems," pp. 831-880.

[60] See G.S. Crystal, *In Search of Excess: The Overcompensation of American Executives* (New York: Norton, 1991); O.E. Hart, "Corporate Governance: Some Theory and Implications," *Economic Journal* (1995), pp. 678-689.

[61] S. Nickell, *The Performance of Companies: The Relationship Between the External Environment, Management Strategies and Corporate Performance* (Oxford: Blackwell Publishers, 1995).

If there are reasons to believe that the board may not constitute, in practice, an effective means of monitoring management, managerial compensation contracts may offer as noted above, a different route for aligning the interests of owners and management. The link between managerial compensation and corporate performance has recently been the subject of much empirical testing.[62] Current evidence points toward a statistically significant though typically small relationship between corporate performance and managerial compensation. The effect of company size is always a more significant determinant of managerial pay. There is a paucity of evidence exploring the relationship in other economies, particularly and predictably in those economies that have fewer disclosure requirements.

So that directors are able to manage the mentioned functions, the principles claim that the board should act on a fully informed basis and should devote sufficient time to their responsibilities. These two requirements seem to reflect wishful thinking rather than actual practice. Throughout the academic literature authors state that the information disadvantage and the lack of time are the two major constraints to the efficiency of the board's work.

Shivdasani and Yermack find evidence consistent with the proposition that firms select directors less likely to monitor aggressively when CEOs are involved in the process. Companies are more likely to appoint gray outside directors who have conflicts of interest and less likely to appoint independent outsiders under these conditions, and also are less likely to make pivotal appointments that give the board a majority of independent outsiders. Stock price reactions to independent director appointments are significantly lower than when the CEO is involved in director selection, and independent appointees are more likely to fit the "busy" definition of Core et. al. A possible interpretation of this evidence is that influence in the director selection process is a mechanism used by powerful CEOs to curb the performance pressures that arise from monitoring by the board. More broadly, their results illuminate how the influence of the CEO serves as an important determinant of the governance structure of firms.[63]

In the CALPERS' principles of good corporate governance, formal performance evaluation processes of executives and directors alike are seen as a central element of improved quality in governance systems. Recent studies have suggested that such formal performance appraisals help the board to clarify its tasks and priorities, to ensure a healthy balance of power and to become better informed about their own contribution.[64] Compared to these efforts and findings, it is a pity that performance evaluation is not mentioned in the principles.

---

[62] For a review of the evidence, see Conyon and Peck, "Recent Developments in UK Corporate Governance," or Finklestein and Hambrick, *Strategic Leadership and their Effects on Organisation*.

[63] A. Shivdasani and D. Yermack, "CEO Involvement in the Selection of New Board Members: An Empirical Analysis," unpublished working paper.

[64] Jay A. Conger, David Finegold, and Edward E. Lawler III, "Appraising Boardroom Performance," *Harvard Business Review* (January-February 1998), pp. 136-148.

Summary of the OECD Principles on Corporate Governance

The OECD principles of corporate governance are the first initiative with truly global reach and support from diverse national governments. They are fundamental for a global adoption of some basic rules in the practice of corporate governance — transparency, accountability, basic shareholder rights, and board functions as well as effectiveness. The discussion of the content has revealed some deficiencies, which basically means some areas where the principles are unclear or that the principles do not consider. This is understandable by recalling the principles as a least common denominator approach. Additionally, hardly any observer of corporate governance calls for more authoritative regulation. From an economic point of view, one could argue that these loopholes leave enough freedom for markets to find efficient solutions. Hence, these gaps should be welcomed. As we will observe below, EVA and similar value-based metrics (such as CFROI) can fill at least one of the deficiencies of the principles as a market-based solution.

EVA AND THE OECD PRINCIPLES

Because the technical issues surrounding EVA® have been adequately explained in other chapters in this book, we will not elaborate here on the calculation of EVA or similar value-based metrics. The strengths and the strategy perspective of EVA have also been elaborated upon in other chapters. Therefore, we will first provide a critique of EVA in light of corporate governance. Then we will take a philosophical turn to analyze global corporate governance as a problem of collective action. Finally, we will specifically address EVA and executive compensation as well as strategic disclosure — two of the critical issues facing global corporations.

Critique of EVA

As stated above, one of the most heavily researched aspects of corporate governance is that of firm performance. According to Pamela Peterson in Chapter 4, "Evaluating a company's performance is much more challenging than looking at stock prices." Dobbs and Koller elaborate stating: "No stock market-based measure truly reflects a company's underlying financial performance."[65] They point out that most believe that total returns to shareholders (TRS) — that is, share price appreciation plus dividends — is the best way to measure firm performance. However if incorrectly used, as it often is, it can lead to misunderstandings about firm performance that in turn distort management incentives, lead to bad decisions, both of which lead to a reduction in value added to the firm. Dobbs and Koller state

> TRS can be likened to the speeding up or slowing down of the treadmill; it measures performance against the expectations of financial markets and changes in these expectations. In effect, it is a

[65] Richard Dobbs and Timothy Koller, "The Expectations Treadmill," *McKinsey Quarterly*, No. 3 (1998), p. 32.

measure of how well a company beats the target set by market expectations — a measure of improvement, in other words. MVA [and we would argue EVA] and market-to-capital, on the other hand, can be likened to the current speed of the treadmill. They measure the financial market's view of future performance relative to the capital invested in the business, and therefore assess the expectations of the absolute level of performance. (p. 36)

The fundamental problem is that traditional market measures tend to lump actual performance and future expectations together, whereas both top management and shareholders — especially those of the institutional type — seek to know if the company is creating *value* in its daily decision making and execution of those decisions.

As Oscar Wilde once said, "economists know the cost of everything, but the value of nothing." EVA and similarly calculated value-based metrics are probably the best metric available at present to provide us with this value measurement. Having said that, these metrics are still all based on *homo oeconomicus*, who we all know is anonymous. The problem is that traditional firms tend to be prostitutes in that they pay for services, labor, goods and so on without needing a relationship with those resource suppliers. Firms based primarily on *homo sociologicus*, however, discriminate and differentiate between their upstream and downstream suppliers based on the strength of their relationships and are therefore more 'accountable to the world *Gesellschaft*.

Despite its novelty and freshness, EVA still subscribes to the age-old strategy-structure-systems management philosophy invented by Alfred Sloan in the 1920s. What is needed is a furthering of the metric to include not only *economic* value, but a new moral contract with society, that is, shareholders and stakeholders alike. Ghoshal, Bartlett, and Moran have gone on record challenging academics and practitioners alike to replace the old strategy-structure-systems mentality with that of purpose, process, and people.[66] That is to say, we need to better account for total value added. In order to do this, the academic challenge is to model a "Schumpeter Index" incorporating the best practices of corporate governance monitoring systems and controls, value-based metrics, and innovation indicators.

Peter Drucker's recent story-telling interview with *Fortune* reveals some of the problems currently confronting top management who are primarily motivated by economic value added principles:

> Marco Polo once asked Genghis Khan what he expects of his officers. And he said, "Of an officer I expect that he takes care of the men before he takes care of himself. Of a general I expect that he takes care of the horse before he takes care of the men." Polo asked

---

[66] S. Ghoshal, C. Bartlett, and P. Moran, "A New Manifesto for Management," *Sloan Management Review* (Spring 1999), p. 15.

why, and he said: "An officer leads by doing; a general leads by example." CEO's should lead by example. But they violate that principle with their exorbitant compensation for eliminating employees. That's a terrible trend.[67]

The problem with EVA and similar metrics is that they encourage the economic aspect of value creation but neglect the total value aspect; that is, such metrics take care of the men, but not the horse. In other words, we could argue that EVA subscribes to the agency theory model of firm performance more than that of the stakeholder model presented above.

To paraphrase a recent and important article by Fama and French, value creation is central to the success of any firm. However, this task is beset with massive uncertainty. The question then is whether there is a measurement that values projects with less error than its competitors. Is the net present value approach (EVA without adjustments), advocated with zeal by textbooks, typically more accurate than a less complicated approach, like payback? And how would one tell? Fama and French's guess is that whatever the formal approach, two of the ubiquitous tools in measuring value are a wing and a prayer, and serendipity is an important force in outcomes.[68] In short, "despite over 40 years of research, we still know surprisingly little about the determinants of capital structure"[69] and therefore about measuring value.

EVA has been used as a methodology to explain stock performance by a large portion of authors writing on the subject; however, several authors have found that traditional accounting metrics appear to do as well or better in explaining stock performance.[70] For example, Bacidore, Boquist, Milbourn, and Thakor have found that other value-based-metrics such as REVA or CFROI — indeed the standard Modigliani and Miller model — work as well or better than EVA.[71]

Of particular importance to the OECD Principles of Corporate Governance in that they affect global corporations, Zimmerman has shown that EVA is not capable of capturing synergies among divisions (and, for that matter, no divisional performance measurement). There is a fundamental contradiction in the very attempt to evaluate the divisions of a multi-divisional firm — as most multinational firms are — as if they were independent companies. For the synergies which multina-

---

[67] "Peter Drucker Takes the Long View," *Fortune* (September 28, 1998).

[68] E. Fama, and K. French, "Industry Costs of Equity," *Journal of Financial Economics* (1997), p. 193.

[69] Robert Parrino and Michael Weisbach, "Measuring Investment Distortions Arising from Stockholder — Bondholder Conflicts," *Journal of Financial Economics* (1999), p. 39.

[70] J. Dodd and J. Johns, "EVA Reconsidered," working paper: http://research.badm.sc.edu/research/bereview/be45_3/evaa.htm; G.C. Biddle, R. Bowen, and J. Wallace, "Does EVA Beat Earnings? Evidence on Associations with Stock Returns and Firm Values," *Journal of Accounting and Economics* (1997), pp. 301-336; S. Chen and J. Dodd, "Economic Value Added (EVA): An Empirical Examination of a New Corporate Performance Measure," *Journal of Managerial Issues* (Fall 1997), pp. 318-333; Randy Myers, "Metric Wars," *CFO* (October 1996); and, Roy Harris, "A Study in Sniping," *CFO* (October 1996).

[71] Myers, "Metric Wars;" Harris, "A Study in Sniping;" and J. Bacidore, J. Boquist, T. Milbourn, and A. Thakor, "The Search for the Best Financial Performance Measure," *Financial Analysts Journal* (May/June 1997), pp. 11-19.

tional firms purport to offer cannot be measured by EVA due to the fact that EVA is not equipped to handle transfer pricing necessary for such synergy to take place.[72]

For example, DaimlerChrysler has many divisions and production facilities literally around the globe. Much of the work of some of the firms under the DaimlerChrysler umbrella are pure internal service companies charging transfer prices for their services, not market prices. The value creation of the buyer of these services from one division is in part dependent on having a lower transfer price; however, exactly the opposite is the case for the seller. Unless an internal service provider charges market prices, there will be distortions when it comes to measuring both the divisional and the corporate-wide value creation. In short, a firm — unless it can provide honest and fair transfer prices — should consider spinning this supplier off in order to create even more value for each division.

Despite these shortcomings, EVA is a strong measurement which is equipped to deal with many facets of measuring performance in the capital markets, for capital investment appraisal, in the evaluation and compensation of managerial performance[73] and even TQM[74] on the operational side of management — all in a single neat number that no other traditional financial measurement can boast to do.

Collective Action Problems: Global Corporate Governance and the OECD Principles

With the radical technological advances making it easier and less expensive for the man on the street to become a global investor, the speed at which international financial markets are growing as well as the ever increasing amount of information that is being disseminated and absorbed (or not) by the markets, it becomes increasingly clear that there is a need for a traffic cop — or at least a safety patrol — to manage the problems confronted by international corporate governance. Stuart Kaufmann provides us with an analogy from the area of technological evolution:

> When the car came in, it drove out the horse. With the horse went the smithy, the stable, the saddlery, the harness shop, buggies, and the Pony Express. But once cars are around, it makes sense to expand the oil industry, build gas stations, and pave the roads. Once the roads are paved, people drive everywhere, so motels are useful. When cars get faster, traffic lights, traffic cops, and parking fines make their way into the economy and our behavior patterns.[75]

---

[72] J. Zimmerman, "EVA and Divisional Performance Measurement: Capturing Synergies and Other Issues," *Journal of Applied Corporate Finance,* No. 2 (Summer 1997), p. 109. See also Ralph Kimball, "Economic Profit and Performance Measurement in Banking," *New England Economic Review* (July/August 1998), pp. 35-53, and Chapter 11 in this book.

[73] For global insights on EVA and value-based management, see Chapter 8 in this book by David Young.

[74] See, for example, J. Bacidore, J. Boquist, T. Milbourn, and A. Thakor, "EVA and Total Quality Management," *Journal of Applied Corporate Finance,* No. 2 (Summer 1997), pp. 81-89.

[75] Stuart A. Kauffman, "Escaping the Red Queen Effect," *McKinsey Quarterly,* No. 1 (1995), p. 126.

From Kaufmann's example, it becomes evident that we need a methodological framework within which we can analyze the various solutions to the global collective action problem of corporate governance in order to answer the question whether the private and global institutional initiatives described above represent adequate solutions to market or state failure in this regard.

Solutions to collective actions vary across the four classic distinctions of political and social thought. The *market system* is best characterized by markets and the price system originally manifested by Adam Smith. The *community system* is identified with communal association and with the general systems of community attributable to Durkheim, Parsons, and Weber. The *socio-cultural system* is typified by evolutionary discourse and bargaining and corresponds to the systems attributed to John Locke as well as recent evolutionary approaches to collective action problems. Finally, the *political system* is characterized by authority and power, and hence by the hierarchical system set forth by Thomas Hobbes.[76] Due to the inherent interrelation of each of these spheres, based on the fact that each solution presupposes the existence of at least one other, none of these approaches or solutions in and of themselves suffice to solve collective action problems such as the provision of a "greater-than-least-common-denominator" global corporate governance system to which all interested parties would agree.[77]

None of these approaches operates in a vacuum, singly they are neither realistic nor desirable solutions to collective action problems. Some mixture of several possible approaches would seem to provide the best solution(s), acting to serve as a general catalyst for understanding the specific problem of international corporate governance. Exhibit 2 provides a general overview of the interplay between the four Denksysteme.

From the point of view of *homo oeconomicus* — the market solution — financial markets should and are working out the details of market-based principles quite adequately. For example, a recent Confederation of Indian Industry (CII) report on 130 Indian blue-chip companies finds that these companies — comprising almost 50% of the total market capitalization of all listed companies and having combined sales accounting for over 35% of total sales revenues of all of the 4,985 listed companies of the Bangalore Stock Exchange (BSE) — have been value destroyers since 1994. Of the 130 companies, 48 gained in EVA and earned return on net worth (RONW) in excess of 20%; 65 companies lost EVA and earned RONW of less than 20%. Their loss in EVA far outweighed the gains by the winners. Global financial markets are good at recognizing growth and reduction in shareholder value, particularly over the long run. Markets have and will continue to punish value destroyers, even more than before with the evolution of global corporate governance principles.

---

[76] See R. Straw, *International Competition Rules? An Economic Analysis* (Bamberg: Difo Druck, 1997), Chapter 4.

[77] See M. Waters, *Modern Sociological Theory* (London: Sage, 1994).

Exhibit 2: Interrelationships in Collective Action Problems: Corporate Governance

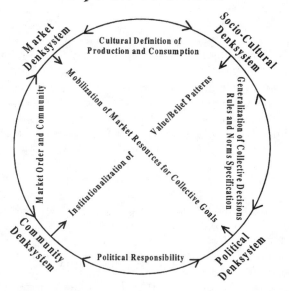

From the point of view of *homo sociologicus* — community-based solutions — the global solution will be based on a common belief system based on the principle of common norms, conventions, solidarity, consensus, and commitments. This typically would be a democratic process in which non-leaders control leaders. With the reduced hegemony of the U.S., it no longer has the power it once had in multinational organizations such as the OECD. One consequence of this is that the new principles were agreed upon by consensus of all member countries.

From the point of view of *homo politicus* — political-based solutions — institutions such as the OECD, and the WTO, etc., exist for the purpose of managing the global society, be it in the economic, political or social spheres. Solutions primarily based on *homo politicus* are characterized by a pre-existing organization of economic and political allies and are denoted by hierarchy, effectiveness, authority, and power in the Hobbesian tradition. Political solutions are best recognized by bureaucracy and differ primarily from market solutions in that they pursue visible hand solutions (often coercive) based on effectiveness as expressed in decision making ability and enforcement. In this regard, it will be interesting to see whether and how the World Bank and IMF utilize the OECD's principles for debt repackaging plans for developing economies in the future.

The similarities and differences of the different legal systems will also be one of the key issues to overcome in finding this "greater-than-least-common-denominator" solution for global corporate governance principles. This issue arises only now in the discussion of corporate governance because the OECD principles are the first global attempt to provide guidelines for corporate governance where there exist very great differences in the fundamental legal systems in the countries which have tabled the OECD principles. Basically, there are two legal structures which provide the background ideology (in addition to culture, history, etc. which we will not discuss here): civil law (found primarily in Europe and Asia) and common law (found primarily in the Anglo-Saxon countries). Civil law places utmost importance on certainty, which is based mainly on a distrust for individual decisions and the reliance on established and detailed rules and solutions. Civil law is based on a set of principles or codes organizing human and social relationships — and corporate governance systems. In this sense, civil law is best understood as being preventative where rules and solutions are pre-organized.

Common law, in contrast, is based on flexibility allowing the freedom to find appropriate solutions to specific individual problems and explains why common law systems are based on an evolving "case law" approach. Common law, then, is primarily curative in its nature: curative solutions are based on the information and outcomes of past cases. Common law seems to reflect stronger trust and confidence in human nature, whereas civil law reveals a greater effort of social organization, in the Lockean and Hobbesian traditions, respectively. In sum, "the idea of a common law process of decision making, as opposed to a centralized regulatory model, is simply unknown on the European continent."[78] Clearly such a fundamental point of friction cannot be solved in the debate over the level, content, and integration of national corporate governance standards or principles into global principles, but is a necessary background to understand many other points of concern in the debate.

In 1996, McKinsey and Institutional Investor, Inc. performed an in-depth survey on the value of board governance. Although their findings were purely descriptive — albeit of investors having a total of $840 billion under management and CEOs from companies with an average of $2.3 billion in average sales — their conclusions were quite insightful in light of the new OECD principles.

> Given that many investors do care about board governance, what action can companies take to improve their own practices? A good first step would be for senior executives, investors, and board members to learn how to talk together about substantive governance issues in a productive way.[79]

---

[78] U. Mattei and R. Pardolesi, "Law and Economics in Civil Law Countries: A Comparative Approach," *International Review of Law and Economics*, No. 3 (1995), pp. 265-297. Also see R. Cooter and J. Gordley, "Economic Analysis in Civil Law Countries: Past, Present and Future," *International Review of Law and Economics*, No. 3 (1995), pp. 261-264.

[79] Robert Felton, Alec Hudnut, and Jennifer van Heeckeren, "Putting a Value on Board Governance," *McKinsey Quarterly*, No. 4 (1996), p. 175.

The OECD principles are a huge step in the right direction, regardless of whether one argues that state or market failure is the reason why we need global solutions to the challenges presented by international corporate governance. Perhaps the next steps could be based on a framework such as suggested here. EVA — although a market-based solution — has strong characteristics of other complementary solutions for some of the issues such as executive compensation and strategic disclosure which will now be reviewed.

EVA and Executive Compensation

One of the problems inherent with global investment markets is that strong, competitive firms often get caught in what Kaufmann refers to as the "Red Queen effect" citing the Red Queen's statement to Alice in *Alice in Wonderland*: "You have to run faster and faster just to stay in the same place."[80] In today's ever stronger growing race for capital and returns, firms which have traditional financial performance measurement systems in place for paying their executives will be forced to re-engineer their current strategies — just to keep running in place. EVA provides a partial — but crucial — measurement in this re-engineering process.

The topic of executive compensation is one of the most prevalently researched subject that breaches both the subjects of value-based metrics and corporate governance. Jensen and Meckling correctly argue that shareholders are expected to tie executives' wealth to firm or stock-price performance in order to reduce agency conflicts with those executives.[81] Compensation schemes which manage the slope of the relation between executives' wealth and stock price by shareholders desiring that executives take actions that increase equity value. Jensen and Meckling pioneered the idea that the convexity or curve of the wealth-performance relation also needs to be managed to induce executives to make optimal investment and financing decisions.[82] However, when this is done according to standard financial theory, no stock market-based measure can really reflect a company's underlying financial performance.[83] Market measures such as stock prices tend to lump present performance with expectations of future performance together. Executives need to be paid according to both of these factors: what they have actually delivered and on the basis of what the markets believe they will deliver in the future.

EVA provides a partial solution to this problem in that it can supplement stock price as a proxy for compensation with a method which compensates managers for producing the underlying performance of EVA. Dobbs and Koller provide an illustrative example ("Tina's Dilemma") in Exhibit 3.

---

[80] Kauffman, "Escaping the Red Queen Effect," p. 125.

[81] M. Jensen and W. Meckling, "Theory of the Firm: Managerial Behavior, Agency Costs, and Ownership Structure," *Journal of Financial Economics*, No. 3 (1976), pp. 305-360.

[82] See Wayne Guay, "The Sensitivity of CEO Wealth to Equity Risk: An Analysis of the Magnitude and Determinants," *Journal of Financial Economics* (1999), pp. 43-71.

[83] R. Dobbs and T. Koller, "The Expectations Treadmill," *McKinsey Quarterly*, No. 3 (1998), pp. 32-43.

Exhibit 3: Tina's Dilemma

Tina Turnaround has been hired as CEO of Widgets'R'Us. The company's margins and growth rate are lower than those of competitors. The market doesn't expect much from it, so its share price is low. Tina hires a top-notch team and gets to work. After two years, Widgets'R'Us is achieving margins comparable to those of its peers, and regaining market share. Its share price has risen twice as fast as those of its peers because the market now expects it to perform as well as they do, and so prices it on the same rating.

Tina and her team continue to work hard. After two more years, Widgets'R'Us has become the industry leader; it boasts the highest margins and a rapidly expanding market share. Its share price has risen at four times the rate of the industry as a whole. The market now expects it to continue earning above-average margins and making market share gains. Tina and her team have done very well out of their share options.

As time goes by, Widgets'R'Us sustains its high margins and market share gains. Two years later, Tina looks back on its share price performance. She is surprised to see that the shares have done no better than those of competitors, even though her company has outperformed its rivals in margins and growth. How can this be?

Tina has been caught out by the expectations treadmill. She and her team have done such a good job that the market now expects Widgets'R'Us to beat its competitors. This expectation has been built into the share price, producing high TRS (total return to shareholders) in earlier periods. The only way Tina can get her share price to rise faster than the market is to exceed this expectation. As long as she delivers results in line with the market's expectations, her company's share price performance will be no better than average. If TRS is the only metric used to measure the performance of a manager like Tina, her natural response will be to look for another company that needs fixing, instead of working harder and harder just to stand still at Widgets'R'Us.

Source: Tina's Dilemma from R. Dobbs and T. Koller, "The Expectations Treadmill," *McKinsey Quarterly*, No. 3 (1998), p. 35.

Much of the recent research in this area supports the idea that residual income — which is measured by EVA — is an essential part of an optimal incentive system. Again, this holds because expected cash flows are not observable, agent and principal have different time preferences, and the agent is protected by limited liability.[84] In fact, Agrawal and Knoesber in investigating seven control mechanisms (insider shareholdings, institutional shareholdings, shareholdings by blockholders, the use of outsiders on the board of directors, debt financing, the external labor market for managers, and the market for corporate control) to control the agency problems between managers and shareholders, found that the use of one mechanism depends on the use of others. Specifically, they found statistically significant relationships between firm performance and insider ownership, outside representation on the board of directors, debt financing, and corporate control activity. Greater insider ownership was positively related to performance, while more outside directors, more debt financing, and greater corporate control

---

[84] Christian Laux, "Performance Measurement in Multi-Period Agencies," *Journal of Institutional and Theoretical Economics*, No. 1 (1999), pp. 176-180. See also, W. Rogerson, "Intertemporal Cost Allocation and Managerial Investment Incentives: A Theory of Explaining the Use of Economic Value Added as a Performance Measure," *Journal of Political Economy*, No. 4 (1997), pp. 770-795.

activity were negatively related to performance.[85] These results are consistent with optimal use of each mechanism and parallel the OECD principles.[86]

Sirower and O'Byrne take the optimal incentives packet based on EVA to its logical and practical conclusion: if managers meet and exceed performance goals as measured by EVA they should be compensated through a plan that pays: (a) a competitive target bonus for achieving the expected EVA plus (b) a fixed share of any excess EVA above target — which may be negative. Their plan is based on the following three factors:[87]

1. *Target bonus:* a competitive bonus opportunity based on labor market compensation practices;
2. *Expected EVA improvement:* the EVA improvement required for the acquirer's shareholders to earn a cost-of-capital return on the market value of their investment;
3. *EVA interval:* the amount of the EVA shortfall that makes the bonus earned zero.

To illustrate this idea, assume that an executive has a target bonus of $200,000, an expected EVA improvement of $63 million, and an EVA interval of $120 — making the executive's share of excess EVA improvement to 0.17%. The bonus in year 1 is $200,000 + [0.0017 × (−139,000,000)] = −$36,300. This amount is debited to a so-called "bonus/debit bank." In year 2, provided the executive makes a positive EVA improvement greater than the resulting $36,300 in year 1, he would receive the difference as actual bonus for her value creation.

Let us again revisit DaimlerChrysler, this time to discuss one of the sore spots of this recent merger: executive compensation. Because of the cultural and legal differences between the countries — as reflected in their respective corporate governance systems,[88] German executives earned far below their American counterparts at the time of the merger. Of course this has led to severe internal power struggles: the German partners cannot seem to fathom why Bob Eaton earns approximately ten times the amount of his counterpart Jürgen Schrempp. Although a very sophisticated model compensation model has been in place in each of the two companies, neither was ready for the culture clash which erupted

---

[85] A. Agrawal and C. Knoeber, "Firm Performance and Mechanisms to Control Agency Problems between Managers and Shareholders," *Journal of Financial and Quantitative Analysis*, No. 3 (September 1996), pp. 377-397.

[86] Except for outside directors which they reason are included for political reasons and the inherent costs thereof.

[87] See Mark L. Sirower and Stephen F. O'Byrne, "The Measurement of Post-Acquisition Performance: Toward a Value-Based Benchmarking Methodology," *Journal of Applied Corporate Finance*, Vol. 11, No. 2 (Summer 1998) pp. 120-121. See also Chapter 5 in this book by Stephen O'Byrne.

[88] See Chew (ed.), *Studies in International Corporate Finance and Governance Systems*; I. Demirag, *Corporate Governance, Accountability, and Pressures to Perform: An International Study* (London: JAI Press, 1998); Dietl, *Capital Markets and Corporate Governance in Japan, Germany, and the United States*; Hopt and Wymeersch, *Comparative Corporate Governance*.

over this point. The Post Merger Integration team is responsible for this issue, but it could only find a second-best solution: the new management of Daimler-Chrysler was in part chosen according to how much he or she made before the merger. That is to say, the top 50 strategic managers of the new corporation could not have income and compensation levels so disparate as to create havoc at the top. So, the merger team chose individuals making relatively the same income. They did not want to give a huge raise to some highly, qualified German managers, nor would their well-earning American counterparts accept a cut in pay. Sadly, it was not the best that were chosen, but the average. The point is this: corporate governance issues — when put into practice on the front lines of real companies, where real people make an income — is very difficult indeed. EVA and similar value-based metrics make the global unification of corporate governance standards easier, but not easy.

Strategic Disclosure

One aspect of the OECD principles which is strongly implicitly as well as explicitly emphasized is transparency. In fact, transparency is addressed in every area listed by the OECD principles. Indeed, section 4 of the OECD principles is dedicated to "Disclosure and Transparency." As David Young points out, EVA is a management communication strategy which provides information to capital markets regarding the financial strength of the firm as well as for capital investment appraisal.[89] To date, only those firms which have bought into the value-creation philosophy go public with their EVA figures. Of course, the private corporate governors such as CALPERS have it in their interest — as well as in their power — to provide this information as a service to their clients as well as the free-riding open markets.

The challenge to companies, investor analysts, as well as internet-based information databanks for investing (because this is the medium through which small, private investors are increasingly choosing to invest), is to provide EVA and MVA as yet another statistic along with the traditional financial data (stock price, price trends, EPS, yield ratios, PE ratios, beta, etc.) used by investors. Furthermore, companies should provide full transparency regarding the calculation methodology of these value-based metrics. Particularly, the specific adjustments — the real heart of EVA and MVA calculations — including how and why they were adjusted should be provided online to the public. Firms such as ValueLine, Datek, and Morningstar and others which are predominantly used by small investors could provide this transparency at virtually no cost in their subpages on "Fundamentals," "Financials," or "Advanced Statistics."

As long as EVA is being used in top managements' communication to capital markets, it is a logical step for the same information to be passed on to the board. Such communication emphasizes management's commitment to value creation and lets an active board of directors know on a regular basis whether value

---

[89] See Chapter 8 for David Young's global views on EVA and value-based management.

has been created or destroyed. This information is obviously a supplement to traditional financial information, but it provides the board the actual breakdown of how much value is due to present actions of management in charge and how much is due to the whims of the market. Practically speaking, the board could use such information in the regular management evaluations, in considering new investment projects as well as capital structure issues.

Provided that the above information structure is established, this information can and should be passed on to capital markets. Such disclosure demonstrates the internal orientation towards value creation in decision making. Simultaneously it serves as an additional external performance "check and balance" system back to management and the board: the market praises value creators and punishes value destroyers.[90]

SUMMARY

The theoretical aspects of corporate governance have been presented with a focus on providing an objective overview of each school of thought. No single theory is adequate, but there exist an optimal mix of the various theories. The OECD's new Principles of Corporate Governance are the first global initiative by a multinational organization. The principles are a huge step toward the transparency and a better understanding of the multiple national systems in place around the globe. The principles are guidelines which provide enough freedom to act upon the principle "think globally, act locally."

EVA and value-based metrics was presented as the best present metric solution to join the disciplines of corporate governance and financial performance measurement. Despite this strength, a new metric including a more balanced emphasis to the other approaches in corporate governance is still needed. Corporate governance is a global collective action problem which can be partially solved by firms employing EVA in the practical areas of executive compensation and strategic disclosure.

---

[90] For empirical evidence on how the capital market values wealth creators and wealth destroyers, see Chapter 2 by Fabozzi and Grant.

Chapter 10

The Implementation of Value-Based Metrics and the Next Steps in Corporate Valuation

Raja Gupta
Principal
World Research Advisory

Craig MacDonald
President
World Research Advisory

INTRODUCTION

Management guru, Peter Drucker, recently wrote:

> Neither preservation of assets nor cost control are top management tasks. They are operational tasks. A serious cost disadvantage may indeed destroy a business. But business success is based on something totally different, the creation of value and wealth. This requires risk-taking decision: on the theory of the business, on business strategy, on abandoning the old and innovating the new, on the balance between the short term and the long term, on the balance between immediate profitability and market share. These decisions are the true top management tasks... But for none of these top management tasks does the traditional accounting system provide any information. Indeed, none of these tasks is even compatible with the assumptions of the traditional accounting model...[Value based metrics]... are based on the new definition of the enterprise as the creator of value and wealth rather than as the possessor of static property, or even, as in costs accounting, as the steward of existing resources.[1]

---

[1] Peter F. Drucker, "The Next Information Revolution," *Forbes ASAP* (August 24, 1998), pp. 47-58.

Professor Drucker is, in essence, calling out for a new way for corporate managers to view and manage the company. It is with this in mind that we consider value-based metrics (VBM) usage within corporations. Metrics such as economic value added (EVA) and cash flow return on investment (CFROI) are offered up as the best way for corporate managers to meet Professor Drucker's observation.

Promoting a value-based discipline leads to an interesting conclusion — VBM deployment is not a project, but a way of life. Implementation is not about shoehorning finance into the company, but instead getting employees to take into account the investments they make to run the company, and capture and manage this knowledge. Too often, companies focus on getting VBMs in, ask where the bump in stock price is, get disappointed, and give up. Those that change the way they operate and those that approach VBMs as building *discipline*, are those that are successful in the long term. More important than the theory is the physical manifestation of these metrics. CFROI and EVA have distinct benefits when it comes to their usage in a corporation. To this extent we provide three detailed case studies on the successful implementation of EVA, CFROI, and an EVA/CFROI hybrid, as well as a series of best practices on how to select, implement, compensate, and manage the knowledge associated with the value-based metrics.

Two issues Professor Drucker did not address, however, are managing the *intangible value* of a company as well as managing *operational risk*. With modern corporations being information rather than capital driven, these issues take on an even greater role. Bill Gates has managed to create hundreds of billions of dollars of shareholder wealth with a few billion dollars of capital. The reason is that he is offering up the intelligence of his employees and those hard to quantify assets of Microsoft such as owning the Windows/DOS standard. Towards the end of this chapter we present a model called Nodal Asset Analysis, a new set of accounting measures that will enhance the traditional accounting model, and bring it in line with today's intangible reality. This new accounting will sit well with VBMs, allowing companies to fill in the holes and drive not only investment discipline but also intangible value discipline. Finally, we discuss enterprise risk, and present a methodology by which to capture and manage this risk using EVA as a template. This methodology allows companies to understand what the chances are to create or destroy value.

VBM CASE STUDIES

We conducted research in depth with a few of our clients concerning their implementation of EVA and CFROI. These case studies, along with more brief conversations, allowed us to compile the list of implementation best practices as discussed later when we cover implementation of best practices.

EVA

We had the opportunity to discuss the implementation of EVA with a senior member of a large U.S.-based transportation company, Alpha Corp. For the purposes of this chapter, Alpha Corporation is a pseudonym for the company with which we spoke, per the request of the company.

To give a brief perspective on Alpha Corp., it is one of the largest transportation companies in the United States. Owning a fleet of over 100,000 vehicles, clients numbering in the tens of thousands, operations conducted worldwide, and revenues in the billions of dollars, Alpha Corp. is a true transportation behemoth.

Why Use Value-Based Metrics?

In 1996, Alpha Corp. underwent a major corporate restructuring in the hopes of turning around a sagging stock price. As part of this restructuring, there was a major emphasis on altering the behavior of the rank and file. Thus, the company was looking for a new set of metrics that would heighten the awareness of all employees to consider the investments required to produce the returns, not just the returns themselves.

During this overall process, the CEO brought in an outside advisor. This advisor concluded Alpha had many metrics, but no one unifying theme. Having considerable experience with EVA and Stern Stewart, he recommended EVA as the right solution for Alpha's needs.

Selection Process

Since the company was looking to drive behavior, it was looking for an easy to understand metric above all. The company settled on EVA because it was dollar denominated and easy to calculate, hence easy for all to use. Being a ratio, CFROI was considered too complex.

Alpha was not concerned about understanding the precise effects of operations on stock price. The company felt that it had a need to simply perform better as a company and the results would show Alpha was looking to instill an internal discipline.

Alpha decided it needed assistance, so it brought in consultants. Two companies made presentations, Alpha's auditors and Stern Stewart. The latter made a powerful presentation demonstrating to Alpha's board and management how the company was losing money over the prior 10 years on an economic basis even though it was producing accounting profits, and hence a sagging stock price. The presentation and the CEO advisor's relationship resulted in Stern Stewart winning the account. Alpha's finance department sees the mathematical analysis behind CFROI and EVA to be the same; the uses, however, were clearly different.

Initial Expectations

Alpha was exclusively looking to drive internal behavior. Therefore stock price expectations were not clearly laid out. The company felt that if it operated better, stock price would increase. Besides, the CEO (in the guise of the CEO advisor) drove the process. The senior finance team did come up with annual EVA improvement targets for the company. The open question at Alpha is how to evaluate success in terms of stock price over time? The company expected to spend in the range of a million dollars for a general VBM implementation.[2]

Implementation

Alpha's goal was to push EVA down to the branch level ($4 to $5 million in sales per branch) by 1999. Exhibit 1 shows the implementation schedule. The implementation team was a cross functional, cross business unit team led by the CFO. It consisted of between 10-20 people, mostly finance, but had representatives of different functions. Stern Stewart stayed for two months, helping with the initial area level implementation. Alpha's own team was along at every step learning while doing. The internal team took over fully when Stern Stewart left, still utilizing the firm on a retainer basis to answer specific questions.

The biggest barrier to the successful implementation was culture. EVA was a major change for the company, and not everyone was on board. Alpha had a culture in which people expected constant change. People acted on the basis that if they did not like something, they would ignore it and it would go away within a year. The implementation team had to do a refresher course within 18 months to reinforce the importance of EVA and its permanence in the corporation.

The implementation ran into IT systems barriers as well with corporate Y2K efforts. The problem was that Alpha did not track balance sheet make-up to the branch level. Ultimately the company had to compromise and back into the numbers rather than collect them.

Exhibit 1: EVA Implementation Schedule for Alpha Corporation

Hierarchy in Company	Size or Hierarchy	When implemented
Divisions	$2 billion each, 10 areas	
Area	$200 million each, 10 business units	1996 (planning went down to business unit previously, when EVA implemented, pulled planning back up to area temporarily)
Business Unit	$20 million each, 5 branches	1997
Branch	$4-$5 million each	1999

[2] In fairness to VBM consultants mentioned in the three case studies, we will not include confidential information about implementation fees. On balance though, the corporate advisory fees were consistent with the initial cost expectations of host firms. In this context, the consulting fees met initial expectations because (1) host firms did not make a complete set of VBM adjustments from highest levels of management on down to lower managerial levels, and (2) because the VBM advisory services were utilized for a short period of time — generally less than a year.

Results

All in all, Alpha is happy with the value-based implementation: "Before nobody considered the balance sheet, now they consider it." The culture has changed; it is now disciplined. Now managers consider all sorts of metrics, not just EVA. They look for insight from all of their financial tools because nobody wants to get into the trap of the project looking good on an EVA basis but not from the standpoint of other metrics. It is likely that if the project looks good on an EVA basis it will look good from the standpoint of the other metrics. There is an understanding that financial metrics are not perfect, not even EVA. This is a very powerful benefit, as many managers in companies manage specifically to the metrics, not considering other issues.

Alpha is a bit disappointed that outsiders do not seem to care that the company has implemented EVA. Earnings per share (EPS) are still Wall Street's primary driver. Consequently, if a company does not hit the EPS forecast it will get hurt, regardless of EVA performance.

Alpha has put into place a team to review the success of the implementation/metric. The team is composed of three business unit CFOs, a senior representative of human resources, the corporate treasurer, the corporate controller, and the corporate CFO.

Compensation Tie-In

Alpha has done an impressive job of tying EVA to compensation. The implementation team has driven EVA all the way down. About 80% of all managers' bonuses are tied to their EVA performance. Salesmen are compensated on EVA performance and if the whole company hits EVA targets, an additional 1% is added to the 401k plan.[3]

Next Steps

Alpha is looking to conduct ongoing refresher courses customized to each unit. Senior management would like to see divisional management customize and run the refresher courses themselves, taking the burden off of corporate. The company is looking to customize the cost of capital rate (weighted average cost of capital) for country/trading region specific and operational risk.

Advice to Others

A representative of Alpha advises the following:

> Stay focused on the initial mission, otherwise it is too easy to run helter skelter and accomplish significantly less than you had hoped. Also, link the metric's implementation to reengineering or corporate restructuring. If the rank and file do not feel they need and value this metric, it will not be successful.

---

[3] The 401k match is now pro-rated, where as before it was all or none.

CFROI

We spoke with J. Robert White, CFO of U.S.-based construction company, Michael Baker Corp., about the company's CFROI implementation. To give a brief perspective on Michael Baker Corp. (MB), it is one of the largest construction services companies in the United States. The company operates in five areas: civil engineering, energy, environmental, general buildings, and transportation industries. The company has sales of approximately half a billion dollars and operates primarily in the Northeast.

Why Use Value-Based Metrics?
In 1996, MB's board was looking for a better way to compensate it's most senior executives, the CEO, and CFO (Robert White). Historically, compensation was based upon ROI and EPS, but these metrics could be manipulated in the short run. The board wanted a long-term metric that mapped to shareholder value creation. Mr. White took the lead in identifying this new metric.

Selection Process
Because MB was primarily looking to change compensation at the highest levels of the company, the board cared less about ease of use/understanding as opposed to accuracy in stock price. Realizing the fundamental finance behind EVA and CFROI was quite similar, MB ignored the specific metrics in favor of the consulting firm. That is, MB would select the firm they felt most comfortable with and implement whatever metric that firm was touting.

With this understanding in place, MB called in four companies to make formal presentations: McKinsey & Co., PriceWaterhouse Coopers, The Boston Consulting Group (BCG), and Ernst & Young. As is typically the case, selection came down to the people. BCG went in with a presentation that showed how well CFROI would have matched MB's operations to its stock price historically, in essence offering a market value simulator — a surrogate for the stock market when evaluating projects. In addition, being a high level strategy firm, BCG offered MB critical analysis as well as the numbers.

Initial Expectations
MB was looking to maximize stock price, hence looking for a metric that would provide new insights as to how to accomplish this. The company was looking to understand the drivers for shareholder value creation, and how those drivers exploded back into the firm's operations.

Implementation
Besides just being a top-level tool, MB chose to push the metric down to the top divisional management. MB had BCG come in and implement the metric across two divisions. BCG implemented the first division with minimal assistance from MB's implementation team. BCG and MB's team worked hand in hand imple-

menting the second division, transferring considerable knowledge. For the third division and onward, MB's team flew solo.

The MB implementation team is made up of a Vice President Robert White specifically brought in for this purpose. The VP's ability to explain the metric and its benefits helped a lot in the successful implementation. In addition, the success the company enjoyed with the first two divisions helped a lot. Besides the VP, Mr. White assigned a director level person to the team full time. The business unit controller of the target unit joins the team when that unit is being implemented. All of the business unit controllers understand how to use the simplified CFROI metric, which has six adjustments, and is the form that is being pushed down the ranks.[4]

The barriers to success were questions about the metrics usefulness and concern about its complexity. The abilities of the VP as described above, the simplified model, and the early successes of the team did much to eliminate those two concerns.

Results

According to Robert White: "The full CFROI model is used as a tool to audit business strategy. It provides management a methodology to break down the company and question the status quo. It forces people to question the fundamental drivers of the CFROI model, ergo the drivers of shareholder value."

CFROI has satisfied MB by providing some new ideas and new insights. It has given MB a basis to move forward in its strategic thinking. In fact, MB was able to take CFROI down to the individual office level, a level it had always wanted to get financial and strategic understanding down to (compensation based upon individual CFROI performance is only at senior levels — there is on overall company CFROI performance compensation tie-in for more employees), to provide more granular business visibility. Currently, MB is looking for a "poster child" best practice office as a basis on which to model its other offices.

One of the greatest behavioral results is that CFROI forces a focus on minimizing cash to cash cycle times.[5] CFROI made employees more cognizant of profitability and return on resources. MB is pleased that CFROI takes into account cash flow, not accounting income.

CFROI has helped management evade many political land mines when it comes to compensation and operations. CFROI allows the company to approach the its "sacred cows" in an impersonal manner, minimizing political vendettas.

CFROI has brought a net positive impact to MB. The metric gives people a set of financial targets, and control over stock (half of the company's stock is owned by an ESOP). Mr. White is a bit disappointed that the model does not take

---

[4] The full version of the metric that MB uses at the top levels has 25 adjustments. They have found 80% of the benefits can be had with a mere six adjustments (the 80/20 rule in practice) and hence have pushed that down.

[5] Cash to Cash Cycle Time = Days Receivable + Days Inventory – Days Payable, a proxy for Working Capital.

into account *operational risk*, and feels that this is one of its primary deficiencies — the reason the model does not fully map to the market.

From an external standpoint, the results have been disappointing. However, Mr. White does not blame the model since there were mitigating factors. The model predicts the stock price should be $2-$3 higher (it is $9 as of this writing), but since the float on the stock is thin and there are only 2 or 3 analysts covering the company, institutional involvement in the stock is limited. However, the company has enjoyed 16 quarters of good earnings growth.

One of the most important benefits for MB has been the new planning process. The old planning process was a bit undisciplined. It took the company till early March of the same year to set objectives. Post implementation, the planning takes place a lot earlier. The operating units put the plans together and top management reviews them (along with the operating units). Corporate revenue objective starts the discussion of the goals. The plans are then run through the CFROI model to see if the targets are optimally structured to increase shareholder value. The process is started earlier, is more quantitative and supported, there is organizational buy-in, and it is concluded in November of the year prior to the year of the goal. Also, there is a lot more focus on the balance sheet, which never existed in the past.

Compensation Tie-In

MB has set CFROI targets. The targets are based on the cost of capital hurdle rate that BCG provides. As of this writing, MB has not put too much weight on CFROI for compensating lower level employees. Only 20% of employee compensation in lower levels is based on the metric (i.e., 20% of lower level employees have incentives based on overall performance of the company on CFROI basis, only senior management has their individual performance measured on a CFROI basis). The reason is that MB did not want to put on too much weight on the value-based metric too fast. MB has wanted people to better understand the metric at first and get a rule of thumb for a good CFROI performance for people to relate to. To do so, MB needs to get some sense of their competitor's CFROIs to provide that benchmark.

Compensation tie goes down to the supervisory levels. Business unit heads that report to CEO have CFROI as major part of compensation. People below that high level (i.e., people lower than corporate executive staff and business unit heads) do not really effect the full range of CFROI, hence are not compensated on it. MB has taken the drivers of CFROI and mapped those into the performance metrics of the lower level people.

Next Steps

MB needs to review in detail the ramifications of the implementation. Mr. White plans on incorporating some sort of operational risk factor into the model, perhaps by using comparables. Its main goal is to maintain the model as a planning/scenario analysis tool, but to push further down to the operational units through further education and training.

Advice for Others

Mr. White advises the following: "Unless the other companies are going to use this [implementation] for political reasons, they can do it on their own. Save a lot of money by just doing good, solid analysis."

EVA/CFROI

We had the opportunity to speak with Michael Keane, the CFO of a large U.S.-based technology company, Unova Corp. This company provides automated data systems and industrial automation systems to customers around the world. It originally was a part of defense contractor Litton Industries. Sales are in the billion-dollar range, with 30% being outside of the United States.

Why Use Value-Based Metrics?

At the end of 1997, some new members joined Unova's board. The new board members, proposed Unova consider value-based metrics to the CEO. Michael Keane, was already researching these metrics, hence the confluence of positive events set Unova forth on a value-based metrics search. The goal was to drive organizational behavior at the divisional level that would create shareholder value.

Selection Process

This mandate set Mr. Keane on a 6-month mission to learn all he could about the various metrics and their applicability to Unova's business. He went through the various steps of reading, attending seminars, as well as conducting detailed internal analyses. In the end, he decided EVA best met the needs of Unova, with two reservations.

Mr. Keane's issues concerned the cost of capital calculation and the process by which to set targets. He was not satisfied with the use of the CAPM to calculate the cost of capital as promoted by the EVA camp. In addition, he did not see the link between EVA and stock price, making it difficult to set EVA targets that would correlate to shareholder value creation.

He had brought in LEK/Alcar and Stern Stewart, but continued to have concerns about these two issues. Neither the shareholder value added (SVA) nor EVA framework was able to provide all the solutions Mr. Keane sought. In his view, they did not seem to provide a solution to the investment disincentive, the cost of capital calculation, and the stock price correlation. Since he had a good relationship with Deloitte & Touche (D&T), he brought that firm in along with D&T's partners, HOLT Value Associates. Working with D&T/HOLT for one day, he felt the answer was to combine EVA and CFROI into a new metric — *Cash Value Added* (CVA).

Initial Expectations

Mr. Keane had a simple expectation: he would get a lot of value, for a very small investment. He did not want to spend a lot of money on implementation, so most of the work would be done in house. He wanted to double stock price within five years.

He felt that the key was to align corporate behavior with the creation of shareholder value. He was satisfied that a broad-based EVA framework would be acceptable, with careful CFROI-derived target setting at the top. Critical to this was the definition of "really justifiable targets." This justification was necessary to get over internal cultural inertia as well as to sell the board. In general his sense was, "People get hung up trying to do the perfect theory, and they miss the point."

Implementation

The implementation team consisted of Mr. Keane (the CFO), the VP of Finance, the Corporate Controller, and the Assistant Corporate Controller. Mr. Keane made two-thirds of all the training presentations; the Assistant Controller was the project manager. After Mr. Keane concluded talking to the divisional executives and left, the Assistant Controller sat down with the divisional finance people and really got into the specifics of how to calculate the metrics. The divisional finance departments did all of the heavy lifting. This was not too difficult, however, as the translation of Unova's internal systems to meet the new metrics was not too involved. The consultants helped at the top levels, setting corporate targets. Ultimately, Unova's goal is to be totally self-sufficient with CVA.

The major barrier to success was acceptance by the divisional. The solution was really one of education. Mr. Keane and his team had to show why this was the right theory, how it would benefit them from a compensation perspective (i.e., show how the new compensation plan could make managers wealthier), and that the plan was fundamentally sound. Of course, there were the expected challenges by the divisional controllers testing the CVA concept.

With the bonus and CVA bank concepts[6] to ensure managers were not penalized for long-term investments, the implementation sailed through in six months (six months of research, six months of implementation). Unova started its consideration at the end of 1997; it went live the first quarter of 1999.

Today, the target setting goes down to the divisional level ($350-$400 million in revenues); that is, divisions set targets based upon a stock performance goal and industry comparables.The company plans to push this target setting down to the sub-divisional level ($50-$60 million in revenues, a few hundred employees).

Results

As the new metrics have only recently been put into place as of this writing, it is premature to assess the results. Mr. Keane and his team are concentrating in 1999

---

[6] The bonus and CVA banks are rather similar in concept. To counteract any investment disincentives, the *CVA bank* allows managers to borrow against future project cash flows to make certain their profit targets are hit today, in essence smoothing out managerial P&L over time. Of course, the use of the CVA bank is actively controlled by the finance department to prevent exploitation. The *bonus bank* is a similar concept, allowing managers to defer bonuses in current years to ensure future bonuses (or borrowing today against future bonuses) and thereby smoothing compensation. This was necessitated by Unova's move to initiate positive as well as negative performance bonuses.

on informing and educating analysts about the discipline that has been created at Unova, and are expecting a payoff of a doubling of the stock's price by 2004.

Within the firm, the impact has already been substantial. Capital projects are being reconsidered and people are actively looking for ways in which to rationalize their balance sheets. Also, the biggest fear — that managers would eschew new investments in favor of short-term profits — has been avoided due to the bonus and CVA bank concepts. Perhaps most importantly and most telling is the new view on the planning process.

In the past, planning was a bit *ad hoc*. Senior managers, in effect, arbitrarily selected targets. Every year they came up with a new plan that was subject to long and arduous negotiations. Now, budgets are somewhat irrelevant. Managers know the targets, and they know the results of meeting those targets. People are told to do whatever it takes to achieve their targets. This avoids the traditional planning pitfalls of managers undershooting goals just to make certain they can make this year's bonus, as well as put themselves in position to attain next year's bonus.

In addition, there is a fundamental re-examination of the company's businesses. If the business cannot make enough money to cover asset replacement costs, is that a business Unova should be in? This insight is similar to that of GE's Jack Welch, with his well-known requirement that GE only be in a business that it can be number one or two. In fact, the old-line divisions did not like the depreciation add back, because it made them look like laggards, when formerly, they looked like stars. These division managers realized the business unit was slowly dying, because their customers were not paying for the replacement costs of the business. As a result, these managers are now considering options such as outsourcing and removing capital from "buffers." In fact, there has been an immediate cash flow benefit as these divisions are pulling cash out of non-performing "buffer" status back to the corporate treasury, where they can be put to proper use.

Another question asked was that if a business unit has a large ROI, but has a size so small as to be meaningless to overall corporate value, should management talent be focused on it? The company has even taken into account businesses it is in which are "loss leaders" that they need to be in order to make the other divisions profitable. In these groups there is target sharing, based upon the subsidies these divisions provide the rest of the company.

In general, Unova has achieved what it wanted to achieve:

1. Get the CVA framework in place by 1999.
2. Provide a framework that is understandable and is used.
3. Allow its IT systems to handle the new framework.[7]
4. Drive corporate behavior.

---

[7] Unova is still tweaking the IT system, but that is because it accelerated the implementation process.

Exhibit 2: Structure of Unova

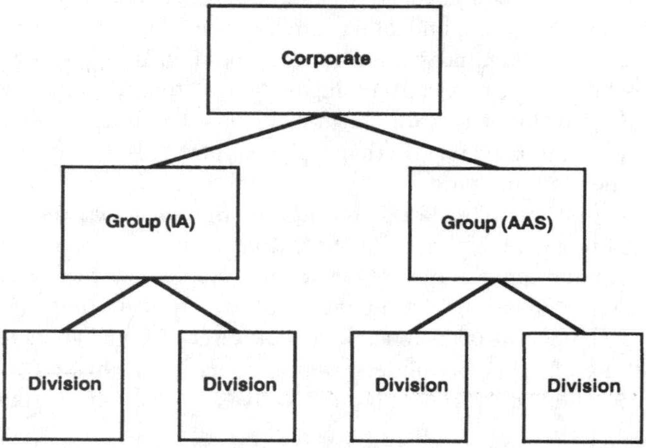

```
                        ┌──────────────┐
                        │  Corporate   │
                        └──────────────┘
              ┌──────────────┐      ┌──────────────┐
              │  Group (IA)  │      │ Group (AAS)  │
              └──────────────┘      └──────────────┘
         ┌─────────┐  ┌─────────┐  ┌─────────┐  ┌─────────┐
         │Division │  │Division │  │Division │  │Division │
         └─────────┘  └─────────┘  └─────────┘  └─────────┘
```

Compensation Tie-In

Unova has a common business structure, and the entire bonuses of the senior people are based upon CVA targets. In general Unova has the structure shown in Exhibit 2.

In corporate the CEO, VPs, and Director levels are affected. At the Group level, the Group Executive and the Group VP Finance are affected. And at the Division level, the Division President or General Manager, the VPs, and the Directors are affected. At the junior levels, CVA affects the discretionary bonus pool and profit sharing. All in all, it was a great example of a company-wide rollout.

Next Steps

Ongoing education is the key to long-term success. Unova is using a method known as "pulsing" — reeducating in needed areas every 3-6 months. This will be necessary for the next two years. In addition, it is forming Intranet best practice discussion groups monitored by a CVA guru. Unova is trying to keep CVA central to the business fabric, touching every aspect of the business.

Unova plans to continue refining the concept through the use of the above-mentioned "pulsing", the Intranet discussion groups, and a feedback loop to bring back information from the divisions.

Advice for Others

Mr. Keane advises the following:

> The management team must be owners of the process, hence must know it better than anybody else. It is like a CFO not knowing accounting; if the management team is not expert at the methodology and its ramifications, it is not really committed.

Exhibit 3: Process to Implement Value-Based Metrics

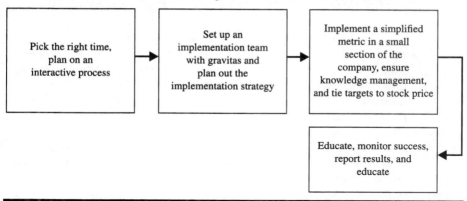

Knowing the methodology inside and out, the management team must take it upon itself to educate others. Do not rely on the consultants. Use consultants as supplements, not as drivers. By the same token, consultants should not be used to fight political battles. If the management team cannot fight the battles, it is not really committed.

IMPLEMENTATION BEST PRACTICES

Implementation into the heart of the corporation is a matter of training junior managers and potentially even lower ranks what the metric is, how to maximize it, how it will affect their lives, and how strategically important the metric's use is to the corporation's future. Of course, implementing the metric at the most senior levels is much simpler since the consultants can explain the theory and provide software tools to aid in the calculation.

Our research has given us a set of best practices that companies must employ when pushing the metric down in order to significantly increase chances for success. We have organized the best practices in VBM implementation in order of appropriateness to the implementation process. See Exhibit 3. Each step is discussed below.

Pick the Right Time To Implement

- Link the metric's implementation to reengineering or corporate restructuring, as the two processes will reinforce each other and make both *stick* better.
- Companies inevitably underestimate the time, the total costs, and the efforts required for the implementation. Firms must realize that imple-

mentation of VBMs is not a project, but an ongoing discipline. Implementation does not stop; it is an ongoing training and re-training process.

Plan the Implementation Process

- Make certain the implementation team has gravitas. For the corporate staff to listen to the implementation team, there must be wide recognition that the implementation team has the ear of the CEO. Without this leverage, the implementation team can never slaughter the corporation's "sacred cows." Hence, it can never be able to really affect change. If the implementation team cannot affect changes in compensation and performance metrics, outside consultants must be brought in to do so. Successful implementations have been led either by outside consultants who earn $250 an hour and are hired by the Board, or are internal teams reporting directly to senior corporate staff with widely publicized CEO/Board support.
- Invest in the education of the decision-makers within the organization early in the process. VBMs can only impact valuation if managers change the way they make decisions. Successful implementations as defined by company stock performance over the longer term have trained managers on how the VBM impacts two variables: (1) cash generation from investments and (2) investments in inventory levels.
- Tie the metrics into compensation for as large a part of the workforce as possible as quickly as possible to maximize the metric implementation's ROI. Successful companies included the VBM as part of decision-maker compensation throughout the organization (the *egalitarian approach*). Non-successful companies made the VBM part of compensation only for senior executives (the *aristocratic approach*).
- Break out the drivers of the metrics. Building a multi-level tree of dependent drivers allows the company to map performance of an individual function to overall corporate shareholder value creation. By compensating the members of the function based on maximizing the driver, corporations can expect that the VBM have a significant impact on the overall value of the corporation. Also, this tree can be used to understand corporate risk as will be demonstrated later in this chapter (see Exhibit 4).
- About 80% of the benefits of accounting adjustments can be had with just six adjustments. There is little need to undergo the entire series of adjustments.
- Push only the simplified versions of the metrics down the line. The fully adjusted complex versions of a VBM is too difficult for personnel not trained in finance to grasp and takes too much time to calculate. Moreover, the additional complexity provides only slightly more accuracy — not enough to justify getting your entire janitorial staff MBAs.

- If external consultants are being used, knowledge transfer to the company is important. Set up an internal implementation team that works hand in hand with the external consultants from the start. This will ensure that knowledge resides within the corporation to continue the implementation once the consultants are gone, as well as improve on what the consultants initially implemented.

The Implementation Process

- Start implementation with a small section of the corporation, not the entire corporation. Successes and feedback from initial implementations will win over skeptics and allow further implementations to proceed smoothly.
- The targets for management to achieve must be justifiable and based upon shareholder wealth creation goals. If the company cannot map the targets back into stock price goals, it will face much internal resistance and not much external support.
- Stay focused on the initial mission, otherwise it is too easy to run helter skelter and accomplish significantly less than the initial expectations.
- Actively report VBM performance and communicate the results internally and externally. This creates a culture of competition based on the new metric and focuses decision-making on improving the VBM.
- Set up a high level team to monitor the ongoing acceptance of the VBM in the corporation.

THE NEXT STEPS

Once a company has embarked upon a path to improve its internal corporate discipline and thereby enhance shareholder value by implementing a VBM, it should continue that momentum and tackle the next big areas: enterprise risk and intangible value. Below we present an overview of two potential solutions.

Enterprise Risk Assessment

Senior managers realize Wall Street values stability in earnings; hence, corporations have a new mantra — "Push assets off the balance sheet while minimizing the volatility in earnings growth." The volatility issue is critical, and often not fully considered. It is with this in mind that we present an enterprise risk framework in this section.

Our research has shown that almost any manager when presented with the need to manage risk, understands its importance, but does not know how to calculate it. We believe that we have come up with an interesting framework that is applicable to all enterprises.

Starting with shareholder value creation as the goal at the top, construct a pyramid of the drivers that influence the goal. The more branches and levels of the tree, the more granular the risk profile the company can construct.

Exhibit 4: Enterprise Risk Drivers Tree

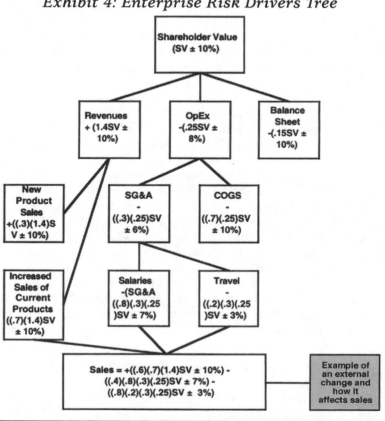

Once this tree is constructed, the tree must be weighted. The question of how much do the sub-drivers influence the driver's maximization must be answered for each and every driver in the tree, starting from the top down. In a four level tree, the bottom most driver will influence the shareholder value creation goal through the drivers above it in the tree. This can be represented by a simple multivariate equation consisting of terms such as the following:

Influence on Shareholder Value = (Weight of level 4 driver on Level 3 driver)
  × (Weight of level 3 driver on Level 2 driver)
  × (Weight of level 2 driver on Level 1 driver) × (Shareholder value)

The above equation will provide the level 4 driver's impact upon shareholder value. This can be seen graphically in Exhibit 4.

The trick is then to map the bottom drivers to the physical operations of the firm. For instance, at a departmental level, identify which of the subdrivers the department has an effect upon, and what is the percentage weight of that driver.

Summing this up across the corporation will provide information as to how each department affects the ultimate goal.

The next step is to develop performance measures whose maximization (or minimization), optimizes the corporate goal. A part of these metrics is a measurement of operational risks. Thus, each department will have an equation consisting of all the drivers it affects, the weights of those effects, along with a variability score as shown below:

$$\sum [(\text{Weight of department on driver})(\text{Value of driver on goal}) \pm (\text{Variability of results})]$$

Summing this up across the corporation will provide the value of each department to the corporation, as well as the risk it creates for the corporation. Note, this same tree can be used for compensation plan development.

While the above steps provide a risk profile, the question still remains, how does management plan how external changes (oil prices go up, bad winter in the Northeastern U.S.) affect the corporation. This requires constructing an inverse external change tree to sit below the above described driver tree. The inverse tree will map external measurements back into the department. When one of those measurements changes, it will flow through to departmental performance, and flow back through to the goal.

Currently, we are working on a simpler method to understand enterprise risk, one most corporations can implement with little additional work or investment. In essence, a risk-adjusted cost of capital charged to each division will incent the divisions to be considerate of the risks they take to achieve their cash flows. However, this is not the rate the corporation pays for capital since the natural hedging that is inherent to a corporation with multiple divisions will lower the overall corporate cash flow volatility, and hence borrowing costs. We propose corporations calculate a risk-adjusted cost of capital for each division both with and without the effects of the natural hedging. The difference between these two rates is the value of the "enterprise risk management program" of the company. The two rates can be calculated as described below:

- *Corporate:* Regress each cash flow against total corporate cash flows to estimate the relationship between each cash flow and that of total corporate cash flow. Use the calculated "beta" (i.e., slope of the regression) to evaluate the risk of the project. This will result in a lower *wacc* for each cash flow as the corporation gets the benefits of natural hedging in the overall company.
- *Divisional:* Calculate the volatility of each cash flow, and assign a cost to that variability. This will result in true risk for each cash flow as natural hedging is not taken into consideration.

The differences between the *waccs* calculated in the first case and the second is the value of the corporation's Enterprise Risk Management.

We are not advocating treasury operate as a profit center (that is a corporate policy decision), rather we advocate using this method to understand and allocate capital based upon the real risks a corporation faces.

This understanding of a corporation's risks is critical to prevent the company from taking on projects that may very well destroy the company, regardless of how glorious the project's potential may be. Besides just understanding the corporate risks, corporations must be cognizant of a whole other area of value, intangible value.

INTANGIBLE VALUATION

With the business environment changing such that intellectual capital is at least, if not more, valuable than physical capital, the traditional view of valuing a company based on its physical, rather than intellectual, assets needs to be reevaluated. In this section we present some ideas on how this can be done.

Nodal Asset Analysis

In our ongoing research into value-based metrics, we have come to the incontrovertible conclusion that the various value-based metrics do not take into account the intangible value of a corporation. To address this need, we have constructed *Nodal Asset Analysis* (NAA) — a tool to help management better understand the corporation and to locate where intangible value is being created or destroyed.

NAA is a very simple tool based upon some human psychology — companies and managers have gone through a certain set of experiences, and their future actions will be based upon the sum total of their learning from those experiences. If one can model the experience of the firm as a whole over time, then it is possible to predict how the firm will respond to external stimuli in the future and how it has organized itself to meet its environment today.

How is this done? How can a company model itself? Using two scientific disciplines — circuit theory and neural network theory (from electrical engineering and biomedical science) — a company can be viewed as a network of assets, be they human or physical capital, whose interactions create value and cash flow. This static system can then be fed into a neural network to dynamically rebalance itself based upon new information.

The way we look at the corporation is very simple: think of it as a virtual network of nodes, whose interaction creates the operations of the corporation. Exhibit 5 is a graphical representation of this concept. In general, the length of a node represents the degree of potential value. Each of these nodes is interlinked, almost like a massive circuit with each node being a capacitor. To this circuit is applied a current, and due to the potential of the capacitors and the resistance along the paths, there is a certain power created, which is the gross cash inflows of the firm. The current is equivalent to the gross cash outflows of the firm. Think of it this way: gross cash inflows are the ultimate and (relatively) easily known and quantifiable results the corporation produces, hence total gross cash inflows are the total power produced by the running of the corporation. The gross cash outflows are the capital needed to allow the corporation to run (i.e., the current flowing through the circuit). The nodes (or capacitors) that make up the corporation are the assets of the firm (a term we will redefine in a moment) and between the nodes are paths, each of which has a resistance. The path represents the process by which one asset interacts with another, the resistance of that path being the less than perfect efficiency of that process by which two assets interact.[8]

Thus there is a series of capacitors, a series of resistances between those capacitors, current flowing through the system, and the total power the network produces. The capacitors are the assets, the resistances are the processes by which information is exchanged between assets, the current flowing through the system is the cash outflow of the firm, and finally the power created by the circuit maps to total cash inflows of the firm. Utilizing circuit theory, all these interactions are calculable, and the corporation is just a complex circuit.

The key to this new model is redefining the term asset. In a traditional accounting sense, an asset is a distinct class of pieces of a corporation that are viewed as holding value over a longer period of time than immediate term. Historically, the idea of intellectual capital has not been a common one, employee salaries were expensed rather than capitalized. Why? Because accounting is still stuck in the industrial age, where employees mostly run factories, with productivity being relatively stable over the life of the employee, hence that employee's efforts are an expensible variable cost, rather than an asset.

Exhibit 5: Corporation as a Circuit

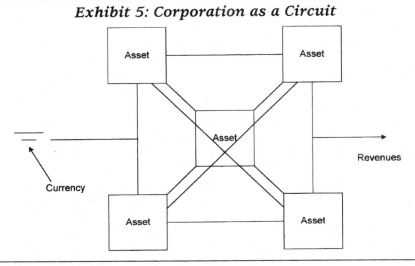

---

[8] By process of interaction we simply mean the process by which knowledge from one asset is transferred to another. Resistance, or process inefficiency, refers to the idea that complete information is not passed, not necessarily a paucity of face-to-face contact.

Today, in the information age this is very different. Experience equates to greater knowledge, and knowledge is power. It is our view that based on a certain criteria, an employee's value depreciates at a rate slower than 100% per pay period. This depreciation will be a function of many items, including age, likelihood to move, type of job they are in, etc. In essence, salary is a proxy for potential of the person, with the assumption that over a large sample set, employees are paid roughly what they are worth by virtue of the position they are able to capture. As time goes on, an employee gains value above what the employee is being paid immediately due to learning — be it corporate policies, classes, experience, and so on. Therefore we view salaries as assets. In addition, things like databases, cash accounts, and patents are assets that should be on the new balance sheet. When all these assets are summed, one obtains the asset side of the balance sheet.

One additional asset needs to be constructed, the Corporate Person (CP). The CP is an ethereal being composed of brand value and history of customer relationships. For many companies, this is perhaps their most valuable asset, and in a world of rapidly commoditizing products and virtual corporations, this will become more and more valuable. We suggest a company consult a marketing consultant with an expertise at valuing corporate brand equity. The ongoing investment is the company's investment in customer service, advertising, and marketing. The decay is the benchmark rate at which customers forget about interactions with the corporation.

Now each of these asset interactions (i.e., processes) has a unique riskiness associated with them. So the cost of capital for running the organization is the weighted sum of all the cost of capital's associated with the assets of the firm. To this we add a market-marking factor which is the perceived riskiness of the company due to imperfect information in the marketplace, hence the total cost of capital for the firm is what it actually pays in the market.

One more major definition is the idea of resistance. It is our view that not only is there current floating through a static defined system, the system itself is changing. When we introduced this theory, we used the term virtual network of nodes. This is conceptually a better way to think than the static circuit theory. Our view is that an asset can only interact directly with one other asset at any given point. Think of the nodes as pulse generators that spin in a three dimensional space. The node is consistently firing a pulse at another asset, the ones it uses more produce the vast majority of the power that node produces for the firm. To simplify our model, and make it mathematically calculable, we have taken this and applied it to electrical engineering theory of circuits. We view all nodes as being always connected, but with a variable resistance over time. Everyone is connected, because there is that one chance that the factory worker will be in the elevator with the CEO and during conversation something may come up that can be of great value to the firm.

Simply put, this is the *nodal asset analysis* of a corporation. In this value-based framework we have constructed a new set of assets. Liabilities, however, stay the same as they measure the cash that the firm owes in the future. With this, the cash flow statement takes on increased significance, as the cash inflow must equal the cash outflow and cash profit (assuming discrepancies will be made up for in the cash reserves or lines of credit). Hence, cash flow is one of the limiting factors; simply put, if a company does not have the cash it cannot perform. With an understanding of the new cash flow statement and balance sheet, let us move to the income statement. The gross cash inflow is the period sales the company makes. In addition to the cost of capital line, there is an in period expense line, made up of costs that are directly used up during the production of that which is sold (such as the steel used in making an automobile). What is left over is a more accurate form of EVA analysis, known as *residual cash flow* (RCF).[9]

Hence, we have developed a methodology for calculating a *fundamental RCF value*, i.e., one that includes both intangible and tangible assets. Using the HOLT Value Associate's CFROI methodology, we can construct a RCF *fade*, allowing the elimination of the perpetuity problem.[10] However, since intangible assets have been accounted for in the NAA, Goodwill need not be accounted for in the calculation. Combining the *fade* with the present values of the RCFs, we have a fundamental value for the firm that incorporates intangible assets and the valuation methodologies of the leading edge value-based metrics.

Why is it Important?

There are several reasons why this is important. We discuss these reasons below.

Eliminate the Cost Center

By mapping each employee, computer, patent, and so on to the final stock price of the company, the idea of the cost center — which was simply a stopgap till each employee's real contribution could be mapped — is eliminated. This will take on greater value as the mapping is pushed further down into the corporation, really allowing the mapping of each individual and other asset to the stock price. As of this writing, we only theorize of mapping an asset class based upon its position in the corporation and to some extent its inherent value (i.e., the computer control system in a factory, while in roughly the same position as a line worker, still has a different potential value).

Optimize Asset Mix and Eliminate Process Inefficiencies

Another reason that the model is important is that it allows a manager to optimize the mix of assets and the processes between them to maximize the value of the firm. Using the insights generated, managers can examine where potential is not being harnessed, and using a form of scenario analysis, can start to understand where some of their energies should be placed in terms of repositioning assets in the company.

---

[9] This is a more accurate metric as reported in B. Douglas Clinton and Shimin Chen, "Do New Performance Measures Measure Up?" *Management Accounting* (October 1998), pp. 38-43.

[10] Discussion of the reversion of company earnings to that of industry means over time due to competition, as well as the methodology HOLT employs to calculate the CFROI *fade* can be found in Rawley Thomas and Laure Edwards, "How HOLT Methods Work," *Corporate Cashflow Magazine* (September 1993). CFROI fade models are also discussed in Chapter 7 by Daniel Obrycki and Rafael Resendes.

This flagging and scenario testing ability is perhaps the greatest value to managers of this model, as it lets them identify where value is being destroyed, giving them the ability to fix it. Basically, the solution will be some form of knowledge management, whether it is getting information at the right time to an employee about how to use a system, or getting the manager access to the right market data as he needs it. Without a model to drive "intangible" valuation down to the asset level, knowledge cannot be measured, hence cannot be managed, as that which cannot be measured cannot be managed. A model such as this allows the understanding of where knowledge adds value, hence allowing an incentive program to be built around sharing and managing knowledge to overcome what the firm of Booze Allen calls the three impediments to knowledge management: sharing (getting someone to share information they have developed), utilizing (using information from others, getting beyond the "not invented here" syndrome), and optimizing (using information to further a specific business goal, not just for information's sake).

Base Corporate Valuation Decisions on Data Not Hunches

The model allows investors to really understand the value of the company, as it eliminates lack of asset visibility. Due to the current *intangibility* of assets, investors are simply taking their best guess as to the true value of the company. By mapping all of the true assets and processes of the firm, investors (and by extension the owners) of a company can understand the true value of what they are buying (own). To do so, requires marking assets to market, a process that can be done through benchmarking.

The model redefines the cash flow statement as the measurement of the inputs to a company. The income statement (or at least the revenues) is used as the measure of the ultimate production (efficiency in use of assets) of the firm, while the balance sheet is employed as the measure of the ultimate (most probably unrealized) potential of the firm. This is perhaps the most unique part of this model. Fundamentally it keeps all the current absolute measurements, such as cash flow, revenues, liabilities, even true cost of capital.[11] In addition, it does keep the three underlying statements together.

Manage Stock Price

In addition, the model results in some interesting insights. One is the importance of stock market brand equity. A lot of the costs and value of the stock of a company are due to its perceived riskiness in the market, relative to alternative stocks. It is critical that companies focus on managing this perception via the use of the Investor Relation (IR) function, so as to keep a steadier and rising stock value while lowering the cost of capital.

---

[11] With this model in effect, the actual cost of capital will more closely match the weighted cost of capitals due to the riskiness of each asset, as the premium (potentially negative) companies pay due to the lack of understanding of true risk on the part of the lender will shrink. Regardless, the true number should always be used.

Capitalize Expenses Including Salaries

What is also interesting is the notion of capitalization of much of what was previously considered R&D and SG&A expense. By capitalizing these as assets, and depreciating them by a unique scale, companies more truly capture the value of the people and knowledge that is being retained in the corporation. This is what makes a running company typically worth more than an idea drawn out on paper, and is often the reason companies are able to survive and flourish. Simply, we are taking assets to the next level. As the Industrial Age added plant and equipment to the asset category, the Information Age demands the addition of knowledge as a store of value, as people are not interchangeable as easily anymore. However, what is unique about intellectual capital is that it is constantly replenished and increased in value as a person stays with a company and learns and becomes more productive.

The NAA in Practice

Now how is NAA used in practice? What makes it effective? Simply, its the ability of NAA to take corporate assets and mark them to market value. For example, a company may have a lot of skilled production workers that it values highly; it may value research scientists less because its focus is on production efficiencies. The company will expect to produce a certain cash flow with its current mix of production workers and research scientists. To maximize that cash flow, it should make the processes that link the production side of its business more effective, hence increasing cash flow. However, if the economy changes and production is less important than innovation, the company needs to change its focus to succeed. By marking asset value to market, it will realize that the value of the skilled production workers has come down relative to the research scientists, so no matter how perfect the production processes are, the cash flow results will never be satisfactory. The company will realize it needs to concentrate on using the research scientists, as only their skills will produce the long-term cash flow the company requires.

A perfect example of this is Apple Computer. In the good old days, Apple was a high flier that practically ruled the personal computer (PC) market. Ultimately, Apple's strategy failed and the company was left near the brink of bankruptcy. Taking a standard path to success, Apple tried to produce low cost PCs, a strategy that just took it down further. With the second coming of Steve Jobs, the company refocused on its design expertise and is now doing well. Why? Apple management recognized that it had overstated the value of the asset/process mix on their production side. When management saw that it could never achieve the cash flows needed from the production side, management revalued the design assets and made the processes connecting the design and production more efficient.

CONCLUSION

We walked through the process to select and implement value-based metrics, as well as explore the next steps of intangible valuation, and enterprise risk. We concluded the best practice for VBMs is for companies to implement a hybrid EVA/ CFROI methodology. This hybrid will give companies the best of both worlds, ease of implementation and understanding as well as targets mapped to valuation. This will allow companies to meet the most important benefit of VBMs, instilling internal corporate discipline. By following the best practices for VBM implementation laid out in this chapter, companies can ensure a successful and thorough implementation, with upfront understanding of costs, time, and manpower requirements. Through the implementation of NAA and enterprise risk assessment, companies can better account for and manage their most important assets and ensure their stock price does not get decimated due to operational failure.

Chapter 11

Allocating Risk Capital in Banking

Ralph C. Kimball, Ph.D.
Associate Professor of Finance
Babson College
and
Economist
Federal Reserve Bank of Boston

INTRODUCTION

While a number of different value-based metrics exist, all are based on some calculation of economic profit. Economic profit differs from earnings by including the opportunity cost of equity capital, which earnings does not. In banking, as in non-financial firms, the amount of equity capital required by a line of business, product, or customer varies with the risk involved, with riskier activities requiring higher proportions of equity to protect the deposit insurance fund and uninsured depositors from loss. Thus while it is possible to describe metrics such as EVA™, CFROI, or TBR as value-based, it is equally appropriate to describe them as risk-equivalent. That is, by incorporating the opportunity cost of equity capital, which varies directly with the risk involved, metrics such as EVA measure each activity on a risk-equivalent basis.

To be effective in reducing agency costs and facilitating the devolution of decision-making, any performance measurement and incentive system must apply not just to senior management and the bank as a whole, but also at the divisional, product, and customer levels. Only by application at the business unit level can a performance measurement system be expected to affect the behavior of managers at these levels. If some variation of economic profit is to be calculated at the business unit level, then the bank's equity capital, as well as its earnings must be disaggregated and divided among the business units. This allocation of equity capital is critical, since without it the opportunity cost of equity cannot be calculated.

The application of any measurement and incentive system based on economic profit to sub-units of a bank is based on a key assumption: that it is possible to isolate the earnings contribution of each business unit of the bank and the proportion of the bank's equity that it uses. In effect, calculation of economic profit at the business unit level views the bank as being the aggregation of individual units, and the earnings and equity capital of the bank as being the sum of the

Parts of this chapter were taken from "Economic Profit and Performance Measurement in Banking," *New England Economic Review* (July/August 1998), pp. 35-53. The opinions expressed are the author's and not necessarily those of the Federal Reserve Bank of Boston or the Federal Reserve System.

individual units and equity capital used by the sub-units. But this "the whole is the sum of the parts" assumption may not be valid if the economic risks faced by different sub-units are imperfectly correlated. This chapter discusses various approaches to allocating equity capital to lines of business and argues that banks need to recognize the ambiguities inherent in the calculation of economic profit and be prepared to create and apply multiple specialized performance metrics.

STAND-ALONE ALLOCATION METHODS

The simplest approach to allocating equity bases the allocations on the capital structure of independent "pure play" peers. To do so, a bank would construct for each line of business a group of publicly-traded peers and allocate capital according to the average capital ratio of the peer group.[1] For example, the mortgage banking business would be assigned equity as though it were an average, independent, publicly traded mortgage banker. While this approach has the advantage of being based on external, and therefore "objective" market data, actual implementation quickly reveals several drawbacks. The number of independent publicly traded peers may be small or in some cases nonexistent, and these peers may differ in important respects from the business being analyzed. And even if a sufficient number of publicly traded peers exist, their capital ratios may vary significantly, so that management must choose among a wide range of possible capital allocations rather than a closely clustered point estimate.

The peer group approach is illustrated for a fictional Last National Bank in Exhibit 1. The Last National Bank is constructed from data for three separate publicly traded mono-line lenders: a mortgage banker, a credit card bank, and a sub-prime consumer lender.[2] In Exhibit 1, the capital allocated under the peer group approach is assumed to be the same as the units' actual equity capital in their true identity as publicly traded independent firms. As shown there, while the bank as a whole has an equity-to-asset ratio of about 15%, the equity-to-asset ratios of the individual businesses vary from about 10% for the credit card business to 33% for the sub-prime lending business.

Exhibit 1: Peer Group Approach to Allocating Equity Capital for Last National Bank

Line of Business	(1) Assets ($millions)	(2) Equity ($millions)	(3) Equity/Assets (Percent)	(4) Return on Assets (Percent)	(5) σ_{ROA}	(6) Z-Ratio
Credit Cards	20,261	2,018	9.96	4.94	1.08	13.80
Mortgage Banking	11,314	1,949	17.23	4.96	2.78	7.98
Sub-prime Lending	5,072	1,666	32.77	14.67	7.96	5.96
Total	36,647	5,633	15.37	5.99	1.29	16.56

Source: *Compustat* and author's calculations

[1] Allocations to products and customers would usually reflect the line of business to which they belong.
[2] This approach is necessary because no bank publishes line-of-business results on a quarterly basis over a sufficient time period to permit calculation of expected returns and their covariance.

While the peer group method of allocation clearly differentiates among the lines of business in terms of the amount of capital allocated, it does not necessarily result in equal probabilities of insolvency across different lines of business.[3] For example, if consumer finance companies have on average a higher probability of insolvency than do mortgage banks, then allocation of equity capital based on the average of their respective capital structure will result in a higher probability of insolvency for the bank's consumer lending business than for its mortgage origination business. One index of the probability of insolvency is the Z ratio,[4] defined as:

$$Z = (ROA^* + K)/\sigma_{ROA} \tag{1}$$

where

ROA^* = the pretax expected return on assets, usually defined as the historical mean ROA

K = the ratio of equity capital to assets

σ_{ROA} = the standard deviation of pretax ROA^*

Thus the Z-ratio is a function of the normal profit margin of the bank, the variation in that profit margin, and the equity capital available to absorb that variation.

In effect, the Z-ratio measures the number of standard deviations by which ROA would have to decline before the book equity capital would be exhausted. The relationship between the Z-ratio and probability of insolvency is an inverse one, with higher Z ratios indicating a lower probability of insolvency.[5] The last four columns of Exhibit 1 calculate the Z-ratio for each line of business and the bank as a whole. As shown there, the Z-ratios differ significantly across the lines of business, with the credit card business having a substantial lower probability of exhausting its assigned equity than do the mortgage banking and sub-prime lending businesses. Thus although the peer group approach results in a directionally correct allocation of equity capital as a function of risk, it does not result in complete risk equivalence across lines of business. To calculate risk-

---

[3] Insolvency for a line of business should be interpreted as the probability that the operating loss of the line of business will exceed the equity capital allocated to it.

[4] This measure was developed in Timothy H. Hannan and Gerald A. Hanweck, "Bank Insolvency Risk and the Market for Large Certificates of Deposit," *Journal of Money, Credit and Banking* (May 1988), pp.203-11. Although Hannan and Hanweck called their risk index "g", in subsequent work it has generally been called "Z".

[5] If the assumption is made that the potential ROAs of the business are normally distributed, then the one-period probability of insolvency can be calculated as a function of the Z-ratio:

$p = 1/(2Z^2)$

However, empirical studies indicate that ROAs are not normally distributed, but instead are "fat-tailed", so that the actual probability of insolvency may be greater than that calculated using the assumption of normality. Moreover, the one-period probability may understate the true probability of insolvency because it measures the risk of a single-period loss being so large it wipes out equity. In reality, insolvency often occurs after a sequence of smaller losses occurring over several periods, indicating that serial correlation between negative shocks may exist.

equivalent measures of economic profit, it is then necessary to apply a variety of hurdle rates, each reflecting the differences in risk, to the capital allocations to calculate the opportunity cost of the allocated equity.

An alternative approach allocates equity capital based on each business's cash flow so as to create an equal probability of insolvency. Equation (1) above can be rewritten to express the capital-to-asset ratio required to achieve a given target Z-ratio, as follows:

$$K^* = Z^* \sigma_{ROA} - ROA^* \tag{2}$$

where K^* is the required capital-to-asset ratio to achieve a target Z-ratio equal to Z^*.

In this approach each line of business will be allocated capital until its Z-ratio equals Z^*. Application of this approach to Last National is illustrated in Exhibit 2, which assumes that each line of business is allocated capital to achieve a Z-ratio of 13.8, the initial Z-ratio of the credit card business. This approach results in substantially higher equity-to-asset ratios for the mortgage banking and sub-prime lending businesses. Indeed, the equity capital-to-assets ratios of the sub-prime lending business increases from about 33% under the peer-group method to about 95% under the equal probability of insolvency approach. Similarly, if the required equity of the bank as a whole is the sum of the required equity for each of the lines of business, then the bank will require almost 89% more equity under the equal probability of insolvency approach than under the peer group approach.

Because it results in all the lines of business having an equal probability of insolvency, this approach permits the application of a single, bank-wide cost of equity when calculating economic profit. In contrast, the peer group approach requires the calculation of unique cost of equity rates for each line of business to reflect the varying probability of insolvency.[6]

Exhibit 2: Capital Allocations for Last National Bank with Equal Probability of Insolvency

Line of Business	(1) ROA (Percent)	(2) σ_{ROA}	(3) Z^*-Ratio	(4) Equity/Assets (Percent)	(5) Equity ($millions)
Credit Cards	4.94	1.08	13.80	9.96	2,018
Mortgage Banking	4.96	2.78	13.80	33.40	3,779
Sub-prime Lending	14.67	7.96	13.80	95.18	4,827
Total Bank	5.99	1.29	27.12	28.99	10,624

Required equity capital for bank to achieve $Z^* = 13.80$:
$K = (13.80)(1.29) - 5.99 = 11.81\%$
Equity capital = $(11.81\%)(36,647) = \$4,329$ million.

Source: Columns 1,2, and 3: Exhibit 1 and author's calculations. Column 4: (Column 3 × Column 2) − Column 1.

---

[6] If done correctly, the dollar opportunity cost of equity for each line of business should not vary between the two approaches. The lower equity capital allocation to riskier lines of business that takes place in the peer group approach should be offset by a higher risk-adjusted cost of equity.

ALLOWING FOR DIVERSIFICATION

A comparison of the Z-ratios for the bank as a whole with the Z-ratios for the individual lines of business, as shown in Exhibits 1 or 2, reveals a drawback to both of these stand-alone methods of allocating capital. The Z-ratio for the bank as a whole is considerably greater than the Z-ratio for any of the three lines of business, indicating that the probability of insolvency for the bank is less than that of any of the lines of business. This occurs because the correlation of the ROAs of the individual businesses is less than perfect. To the extent such correlation is less than perfect, it will tend to dampen the fluctuations in returns for the bank as a whole, so that the risk of the bank will be less than the weighted sum of the risks of the individual businesses. In effect, the business units act as partial natural hedges for each other, reducing the need for equity capital. Thus a bank with a diversified portfolio requires less equity capital to achieve any given probability of insolvency than do the business units on an aggregated stand-alone basis. This is shown at the bottom of Exhibit 2, where the amount of equity capital needed for the bank as a whole to achieve a Z-ratio of 13.8 is calculated to be only $4.3 billion, less than half of the $10.6 billion calculated as the sum of the stand-alone allocations to the individual businesses.

Thus in those situations where the ROAs of the individual businesses are imperfectly correlated, a discrepancy will result between the sum of the individual equity allocations to the different lines of business and the equity capital required when the effects of diversification are incorporated. This discrepancy creates obstacles to the evaluation of businesses and their managers. Ultimately, the larger the capital allocation, the more difficult it is for a line of business to earn an economic profit. If capital allocations to individual businesses exceed the actual capital of the bank, then managers may believe this "ghost capital" unfairly biases downward the reported return on equity and economic profit of each business. The excess allocated equity can also create strategic issues, since the reported economic profit of the business units will not sum to the economic profit of the bank. Theoretically, it would be possible for each line of business to fail to earn its required opportunity cost of stand-alone equity, while the bank as a whole reported positive economic profits based on its actual equity capital. In extreme cases, a bank might choose to exit a business based on an insufficient return on equity earned on allocated capital, while the return on actual capital, taking into account the effects of diversification, might be quite satisfactory.

PROPORTIONAL SCALING

Stand-alone allocation methods can be adjusted for the effects of diversification in two ways. The simplest is to scale back the allocation to the individual businesses so that the sum of the allocations equals the actual (diversified) capital of the bank. Thus if the sum of the individual allocations is 200% of the actual capital of the bank, each allocation is reduced by one-half to make the sum of the individual allocations equal to actual capital. This approach is illustrated for Last National in Exhibit 3, assuming that each line of business has the same probability of insolvency (from Exhibit 2) and that the bank as a whole has a target Z-ratio of 13.8. In effect, this approach spreads the reduction in equity capital due to diversification across the lines of business in proportion to their initial stand-alone allocations.

While simple to implement, this approach to incorporating the effects of diversification has serious conceptual drawbacks. By allocating the reductions in equity capital in proportion to the initial stand-alone capital allocations, inefficient users of capital receive a disproportionate increment to their economic profits. An example of this is shown in Exhibit 4, which compares three lines of business before and after the scaled reductions in stand-alone allocations.[7] All three lines of business have the same adjusted earnings, but they differ in the amount of capital used and thus in their reported economic profits. If stand-alone capital allocations are scaled back by 50% to reflect the benefits of diversification, then the incremental effect on the reported economic profits of Business A, the most inefficient user of capital, will be double that of Business C, the most efficient user of equity capital. As a result, the simple scaling approach obscures the ability of senior management to distinguish among the business units in their efficiency in using equity capital.

Moreover, when the benefits from diversification are allocated in proportion to their initial stand-alone capital allocations, they are being allocated in proportion to the stand-alone total risk of each line of business, weighted by the dollar assets of each business. But the contribution of a particular line of business to the total risk of the bank will depend not only on the stand-alone risk of that line of business, but also on the correlation in returns among the different lines of business of the bank. A line of business with a low or negative correlation of returns with the other parts of the bank will diversify away more risk than will a line of business with a high positive correlation. A simple proportional reduction in stand-alone capital tends to over-allocate capital to lines of business with low or negative correlation, and to under-allocate equity capital to business units with high positive correlation.

Exhibit 3: Capital Allocation for Last National Bank with Equal Probability of Insolvency and Scaled Diversification Effects

Line of Business	(1) Stand-Alone Equity ($millions)	(2) Scaled Diversification Effects	(3) Equity Allocation with Diversification Effect ($millions)
Credit Card	2,018	0.4074	822
Mortgage Banking	3,779	0.4074	1,540
Sub-prime Lending	4,827	0.4074	1,967
Total Bank	10,624	0.4074	4,329

Source: Column 1: Exhibit 2. Column 2: $4,329 (from Exhibit 2) ÷ $10,624 (from Exhibit 2. Column 3: Column1× Column 2.

---

[7] The lines of business shown in Exhibit 4 are fictional and are not those shown for Last National in Exhibits 1,2,3,6,7 and 9.

Exhibit 4: Effect of Scaled Reductions in Capital Allocations on Reported Economic Profit

Business Unit	Adjusted Earnings	Opportunity Cost of Allocated Capital before Diversification Effects	Reported Economic Profit before Diversification Effects	Opportunity Cost of Allocated Capital after 50% Diversification Effects	Reported Economic Profit after Diversification Effects	Incremental Economic Profit due to Scaled Reductions in Capital Allocations
A	100	100	0	50	50	50
B	100	70	30	35	65	35
C	100	50	50	25	75	25

Source: Author's calculations.

INTERNAL BETAS

A second possible alternative to incorporating the effects of diversification in allocating capital is based upon the concept of "internal betas." In this approach, the relative risk contribution of each line of business is calculated as an internal beta, defined as the ratio of the covariance between the business unit's and bank's returns to the variance of the bank's returns[8]:

$$\beta_{Bus} = cov(R_{Bus}, R_{Bank})/\sigma^2_{Bank} = (\sigma_{Bus}/\sigma_{Bank})\rho_{Bus,Bank} \tag{3}$$

where σ_{Bus} and σ_{Bank} are the standard deviations of the ROAs of the business unit and the bank as a whole, respectively, and $\rho_{Bus,Bank}$ is the coefficient of correlation of returns between the business and the bank.

The risk of a bank (σ^2_{Bank}) with n different business units is given by the formula:

$$\sigma^2_{Bank} = \Sigma\Sigma w_i w_j cov_{i,j} \tag{4}$$

where w_i is the proportion of assets used by the i-th business unit, and $cov_{i,j}$ is the covariance of returns between the i-th and j-th business units. This relationship is depicted in Exhibit 5 as the sum of the terms of a weighted matrix of the business unit variances and covariances,[9] with each row representing a different business unit. Then the risk contribution of Business 1 can be expressed as the sum of the terms in row 1, weighted by the assets of the business:

$$\text{Risk contribution of Business 1} = w_1\Sigma w_j cov_{1,j} = w_1 cov_{1,Bank} \tag{5}$$

---

[8] See Kenneth A. Froot and Jeremy C. Stein, "A New Approach to Capital Budgeting for Financial Institutions," *Journal of Applied Corporate Finance* (Summer 1998), pp. 59-69.

[9] Notice that the covariance of a variable with itself equals the variance of the variable.

Exhibit 5: Risk Contribution By Business Unit:
The Internal Beta Approach

Business Unit	1	2	3		N	
1	$w_1^2\sigma_1^2$	$w_1w_2\text{cov}_{1,2}$	$w_1w_3\text{cov}_{1,3}$	—	$w_1w_n\text{cov}_{1,n}$	Risk Contribution $= w_1\Sigma w_j\text{cov}_{1,j}$ $= w_1\text{cov}_{1,\text{Bank}}$
2	$w_2w_1\text{cov}_{1,2}$	$w_2^2\sigma_2^2$	$w_2w_3\text{cov}_{2,3}$	—	$w_2w_n\text{cov}_{2,n}$	Risk Contribution $= w_2\Sigma w_j\text{cov}_{2,j}$ $= w_2\text{cov}_{2,\text{Bank}}$
3	$w_3w_1\text{cov}_{1,3}$	$w_3w_2\text{cov}_{2,3}$	$w_3^2\sigma_3^2$	—	$w_3w_n\text{cov}_{3,n}$	Risk Contribution $= w_3\Sigma w_j\text{cov}_{3,j}$ $= w_3\text{cov}_{3,\text{Bank}}$
	—	—	—	—	—	
N	$w_nw_1\text{cov}_{1,n}$	$w_nw_2\text{cov}_{2,n}$	$w_nw_3\text{cov}_{3,n}$	—	$w_n^2\sigma_n^2$	Risk Contribution $= w_n\Sigma w_j\text{cov}_{n,j}$ $= w_n\text{cov}_{n,\text{Bank}}$
						Total Contribution $= \Sigma\Sigma w_iw_j\text{cov}_{I,j}$ $= \sigma_{\text{Bank}}^2$

To measure the proportion of total risk contributed by Business 1, we divide equation (5) by the overall risk of the bank:

$$\text{Proportional risk contribution of Business 1} = w_1\text{cov}_{1,\text{Bank}}/\sigma_{\text{Bank}}^2 = w_1\beta_1 \quad (6)$$

But this is the internal beta of Business 1. Because the proportion of risk accounted for by all the business units of the bank must equal the risk of the bank, then:

$$\Sigma w_i\beta_i = 1 \quad (7)$$

Thus in the internal beta approach, the equity capital-to-asset ratio for each business unit is equal to the product of the unit's internal beta and the bank's overall equity-to-capital ratio:

$$K_{\text{Bus}} = \beta_{\text{Bus}}K_{\text{Bank}}$$

where K_{Bus} is the capital-to-asset ratio of the business, β_{Bus} is the internal beta of the business, and K_{Bank} is the capital-to-asset ratio of the bank, including diversification effects. This approach is illustrated for Last National in Exhibit 6. As can be seen there, the capital allocations under the internal beta approach differ substantially from the equal scaling approach shown in Exhibit 3. In particular, the business units with relatively low correlation in returns (mortgage banking and sub-prime lending) are allocated substantially less equity capital under this approach than the business unit (credit card) with a relatively high correlation in returns.

Exhibit 6: Allocation of Equity Capital for Last National Bank Using Internal Betas

Business Unit	(1) Standard Deviation of Returns (σ_{ROA})	(2) Correlation Coefficient ($\rho_{Bus,Bank}$)	(3) Internal Beta (β_{Bus})	(4) Equity Capital Ratio of Business (Percent)	(5) Allocated Equity Capital ($millions)
Credit Card	1.08	0.762	0.638	7.54	1,526
Mortgage Banking	2.78	0.423	0.911	10.77	1,217
Sup-prime Lending	7.96	0.429	2.65	31.27	1,586
Bank Total	1.29				4,329

Source: Column 1: Exhibit 1
Column 2: Compustat, author's calculations.
Column 3: (Column 1 ÷ 1.29) × Column 2.
Column 4: Column 3 × (4,329/36,647) (from Exhibits 3 and 1)
Column 5: Column 4 × Column 1, Exhibit 1.

As shown in equation (3), under the internal beta approach the risk contribution of each business will depend on two factors, its stand-alone risk relative to the bank as a whole ($\sigma_{Bus}/\sigma_{Bank}$) and the degree of correlation between the returns of the business and the bank ($\rho_{Bus,Bank}$). The effect of the correlation in returns is unambiguous — the greater the correlation, the greater the risk contribution of the business — but the effect of the stand-alone risk of the business will depend on the sign of the correlation coefficient. If the correlation between the unit's and the bank's returns is positive, then the risk contribution of the business will increase in proportion to its stand-alone risk, but if the correlation in returns is negative, then the risk contribution of the business will decrease as the stand-alone risk of the business increases. Intuitively, if returns are negatively correlated, then variations in returns from the business tend to offset variations in returns on the bank as a whole, and the greater the variation in returns on the business (σ_{Bus}), the greater the reduction in the overall risk of the bank.

While the internal beta approach divides up the risk of the bank and does so in a way that incorporates the correlation in returns between the business unit and the bank, using the internal beta to allocate capital involves two very restrictive assumptions. First, because the risk of the bank is the weighted sum of the risk contribution of the business units, it already incorporates the risk contributions of business 1. That is, the risk contribution of each business is calculated on an *ex post* basis, assuming that the business is already and will remain a part of the bank. If a new business unit is added (deleted) then the variance/covariance matrix depicted in Exhibit 5 will have to add (delete) both a row and a column and the weights of the original entries will change so that each row of the matrix, as well as the overall risk of the bank will change.

Second, the calculated risk contributions for each business unit are only valid for the asset weightings used. Any disproportionate change in the relative importance of a business unit will change the weights on all of the entries in the weighted variance/covariance matrix and thus result in a change not only in the internal beta of that business unit, but also in the internal betas of all the other business units. Thus, capital allocations calculated using the internal beta approach are valid only for a specific mix of business units and cannot be used for other configurations of business units or asset weightings. Moreover, the capital allocation and reported economic profit of each business unit will be affected by the activity of the other business units in the bank.

MARGINAL CAPITAL

Because the internal beta approach measures the risk contribution of a business unit under the assumptions that the business already exists within the bank and that the relative size of the business (and of the other businesses in the bank) does not change, it is most appropriate in a relatively static situation and results in biased allocations in more dynamic situations, such as acquisitions or divestitures, or where the business units are growing at different rates. Thus in situations where the mix of businesses is changing, as a result of either strategic decisions or differential growth rates, capital should be allocated based on the business's marginal risk contribution.

Marginal capital can be defined as the incremental capital (for the bank as a whole) resulting from a change in the scale of operation of a business unit, assuming the probability of insolvency remains constant. For an acquisition or divestiture, marginal capital is measured as the difference between the required equity capital for the bank as a whole, including the business being bought or sold, and the required equity capital for the bank without the line of business. For an existing business that is expanding its scale of operations, it can be measured as the incremental capital for the bank as a whole associated with the incremental increase in volumes.

Marginal capital for each of the lines of business of Last National is shown in Exhibit 7 under the assumption that each line of business is being divested. That is, marginal capital is calculated as the difference in the bank's required capital, with and without the line of business in question. As can be seen in Exhibit 7, marginal capital depends both on the extent of the correlation in returns between the business units in question and on the effect of the change on the diversification of the bank.

Adding a business that has a low positive correlation with existing businesses will require less incremental capital for the bank than will acquiring one with a high positive correlation, and acquiring a business with a negative correlation with existing businesses can actually reduce the required capital, resulting in negative marginal capital. This is shown in Exhibit 7 for the mortgage banking business. Because the correlation in returns between the mortgage banking business and the sub-prime lending business is negative (-0.53), adding the mortgage banking business to an existing combination of the credit card and sub-prime lending businesses actually dampens the variation in the aggregate and therefore reduces the required capital.

Exhibit 7: Calculation of Marginal Equity Capital for Last National Bank

Business Unit	(1) Required Equity Capital for Bank with All Three Business Units ($millions)	(2) Required Capital Ratio for Bank without Business Unit (Percent)	(3) Bank Assets without Business Unit ($millions)	(4) Required Equity Capital for Bank without Business Unit ($millions)	(5) Marginal Equity Capital ($millions)	(6) Marginal Capital Ratio (Percent)
Credit Card	4,329	21.74	16,386	3,562	767	3.78
Mortgage Banking	4,329	19.78	25,333	5,012	(683)	(6.04)
Sub-prime Lending	4,329	12.55	31,575	3,961	368	7.25
Total Allocated Capital					452	
Unallocated Capital					3,877	
Total Bank Capital					4,329	

Source: Column 1: Exhibit 2
      Column 2: Author's calculations, using method from Exhibit 2.
      Column 3: *Compustat*
      Column 4: Column 2 × Column 3
      Column 5: Column 1 − Column 4
      Column 6: Column 5 ÷ Column 1, Exhibit 1

Exhibit 8: Diversification and Marginal Risk

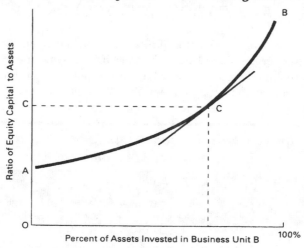

The marginal capital ratio is not constant but will vary as the size of business in question varies relative to the size of the other businesses of the bank. This is shown in Exhibit 8 for a bank consisting of two business units. Business 1 is relatively low-risk and low-return, while Business 2 is relatively high-risk, high-return. Exhibit 8 shows the equity capital-to-asset ratio required to achieve a constant Z-ratio for different asset weightings of Businesses 1 and 2. At point A, 100% of the bank's assets are comprised of Business 1 and the bank's required capital-to-asset ratio is simply the stand-alone required capital ratio for Business 1. At point B, 100% of the bank's assets are invested in Business 2, and the bank's required capital-to-asset ratio is simply the stand-alone required capital ratio for Business 2. The curve AB represents the equity capital-to-asset ratios for all the weightings of Business 1 and 2 to achieve the same probability of insolvency and is thus an iso-insolvency curve. It is convex because the returns of the businesses are assumed to be imperfectly positively correlated.

As shown in Exhibit 8, each point on the iso-insolvency curve shows a different capital-to-asset ratio corresponding to a different mix of business units. If the bank increases the size of Business 2 relative to Business 1 it will move to the right along the curve and its required capital-to-asset ratio will increase. The rate at which the required bank-wide capital-to-asset ratio increases is equivalent to the marginal capital ratio and can be shown as the slope of a tangent to the iso-insolvency curve. At point C, the required capital-to-asset ratio is OC, but the marginal capital ratio is equal to the slope of the tangent at C, which is greater than OC. Thus the marginal capital ratio will not equal the capital ratio of the bank as a whole, nor will it be a weighted average of the stand-alone risks of each of the business units. Instead, the marginal capital associated with a given increment in the size of a business increases as the business unit becomes a larger proportion of the bank.

CAPITAL ALLOCATIONS AND ECONOMIC PROFIT

Exhibit 9 summarizes the results of Exhibits 1, 2, 3, 6, and 7 and shows the equity capital allocated to each of Last National's three businesses using each of the capital allocation methodologies discussed above. Depending on the methodology selected, the allocated equity capital, and thus the reported economic profit of a business unit can vary dramatically.

Exhibit 9: Equity Capital Allocations for Last National Bank, by Allocation Methodology

Business Unit	(1) Stand Alone: Peer Group ($millions)	(2) Stand Alone: Equal Probability of Insolvency ($millions)	(3) Scaled Diversification ($millions)	(4) Internal Betas ($millions)	(5) Marginal Capital ($millions)
Credit Card	2,018	2,018	822	1,526	767
Mortgage Banking	1,989	3,779	1,540	1,217	(683)
Sub-prime Lending	1,666	4,827	1,967	1,586	368
Unallocated Capital					3,877
Bank Total	5,633	10,624	4,329	4,329	4,329

Source: Column 1: Exhibit 1; Column 2: Exhibit 2; Column 3: Exhibit 3; Column 4: Exhibit 6; Column 5: Exhibit 7

Clearly the capital allocation methodology will affect significantly not only the reported economic profit of each business, but also how well the resulting measure captures the true economic contribution of the business and the incremental risk for the bank. For example, if a stand-alone methodology is selected, then the calculated economic profit will be lower than if diversification effects are taken into account, and the sum of the economic profits reported by the individual business units will be less than the economic profit of the bank as a whole. If diversification effects are included by scaling down stand-alone allocations, then the unit economic profits will sum to the bank's economic profit, but the economic profit of inefficient users of capital will be improved more than those of efficient users, and capital allocations will still fail to reflect the actual risk contributions of the businesses. In particular, the economic profit of inefficient users of capital whose returns are highly correlated with the rest of the bank will be biased upwards compared to the economic profit of efficient users of capital with low positive or negative correlation.

If the bank chooses to allocate capital based on internal betas, then the business unit economic profit will sum to that of the bank, and the capital allocation of each unit will reflect not only its stand-alone risk but also the interaction of the business with the other parts of the bank. But the capital ratios calculated using internal betas do not reflect the incremental risk associated with acquisitions, divestitures, or changes in the scale of operations, and thus will result in biased estimates of the associated incremental economic profit. Moreover, if the returns of the unit and the bank are negatively correlated, then the internal beta and capital allocation of the business would be negative.

While some observers have argued that negative capital allocations are nonsensical, in fact they merely reflect the reduction in required bank capital that occurs when a unit with negatively correlated returns is combined with the rest of the bank. The effect of a negative equity capital allocation is to create a negative opportunity cost of capital and increase the economic profit of the unit so that it is greater than its adjusted earnings. This augmented economic profit reflects not only the earnings of the business but the savings in capital costs arising from the unit's function as a natural hedge. However, a negative equity allocation to a particular business may represent a considerable challenge in terms of convincing the managers of the other business units that they have been treated fairly. Moreover, it is questionable whether one would wish to compensate the manager of a business with a negative equity allocation on the basis of the unit's economic profits, since the latter represents not only the economic profit of the business but also its value as a natural hedge, which has nothing to do with the manager's efforts.

Finally, if marginal capital is used as a basis for allocations, then the economic profit of important strategic decisions will more accurately reflect their contributions to the bank, but the sum of the unit marginal capital allocations will be less than the capital of the bank, and the sum of the business unit economic profits will be more than the economic profit of the bank.[10] For example, as shown

---

[10] See Robert C. Merton and Andre F. Perold, "Theory of Risk Capital in Financial Firms," *Journal of Applied Corporate Finance* (Fall 1995), pp. 16-32.

in Exhibit 7, the allocations of marginal capital sum to only about 10% of the total capital of Last National Bank, leaving about 90% of the bank's equity capital unallocated. Thus it would be conceptually possible for each of the businesses to be generating positive economic profit, but for the bank as a whole to be generating a zero or negative economic profit. Moreover, negative capital allocations are more likely to occur, resulting in the communications and compensation issues discussed above. Unfortunately, none of the capital allocation methodologies described above will result in an estimate of economic profit that in all circumstances will reflect the risk-equivalent economic contribution of the business unit.

CONCLUSION: USING ECONOMIC PROFIT TO MEASURE BANK PERFORMANCE

Clearly, the incorporation of an opportunity cost of equity capital into a bank's performance measurement system potentially can offer great benefits in terms of improved risk management, greater efficiency in the use of capital, and quicker and more informed decision-making on the part of managers. But if business units are related, either operationally or in their use of equity capital, then the isolation of the earnings and risk capital used by each business becomes problematic. In such situations, estimates of economic profit may be biased and lead to poor decision-making.

Are there rules of thumb that might help managers address these potential biases? If the assumption is made that the extent of relatedness among businesses can be approximated by the degree of correlation in their returns, then we can distinguish between two polar situations: businesses with a high degree of relatedness and correlation in their earnings, and those with little or no relatedness or correlation. In the case of the former, the earnings of the businesses are likely to be related due to shared operations, products, distribution, or customers, and the economic contribution of units that generate positive externalities for other units is likely to be underestimated, leading to under-investment in these units. On the other hand, the business units are unlikely to act as natural hedges for each other so that each business will need approximately the amount of equity capital required on a stand-alone basis. In this case managers need to focus on identifying cross-unit effects on revenue and expenses, but can apply a relatively simple capital allocation scheme.

In the case of units with low or negative correlation in returns, earnings will not be affected but the units will act as partial natural hedges, reducing the equity capital required for each unit. If the hedging effects of diversification are not taken into account, excessive equity capital will be allocated to these business units, biasing downwards reported economic profit and once again leading to under-investment. In this case managers should focus on the capital allocation methodology to ensure that the allocated capital is proportional to the actual risk contribution of the business.

While the concept of economic profit has powerful conceptual appeal, the ambiguities that surround its calculation indicate that no single measure of economic profit is able to capture all the subtle complexities, and that managers may need to employ multiple specialized measures. For example, marginal capital might be the most appropriate methodology for use in evaluating a potential acquisition, while capital based on internal betas may be better in measuring the economic profit of an existing line of business. While the concept of economic profit may ultimately result in better measurement of bank performance, it is likely to create a more complex measurement process.

Chapter 12

Internal Use of Value-Based Metrics

Bernard L. Lorge, CPA
Senior Financial Manager
Polaroid Corporation

INTRODUCTION

So you have decided that sophisticated investors outside your company are using value based metrics to evaluate financial performance. If that's the case, shouldn't the same concept be applied internally? Would managers or other employees make decisions with better financial outcomes if they were measured on a combination of profit generation and capital employed rather than just "sales," "operating profit" or "costs"? Many companies have concluded that, in general, this would be the case, and have tried to build incentive plans that incorporate value-based metrics to some degree. However, there are a number of organizational characteristics and issues that must be considered before implementation in order to maximize the possibility of obtaining the desired results. This chapter describes some of the areas that have to be carefully addressed in order to design an effective plan.

WHY IS A VALUE-BASED METRIC AN ATTRACTIVE OPTION?

For companies attempting to instill in managers and employees a mindset that focuses on long-term wealth creation, a value-based metric provides a logical foundation. Most employees can easily understand the concept that stockholders are entrusting their funds to corporate management with the expectation that management will employ those funds to generate a desired return. They will also understand that relying on management and employees to accomplish this task is a somewhat less certain proposition than other available options, and that this risk requires a higher return. Establishing and institutionalizing this framework can be very useful in getting employees to pay attention to capital employed to achieve earnings.

Having established this link "in theory" may not necessarily result in behavior consistent with the concept. However, compensation plans that include a "capital to be employed" component can provide that incentive. For example, return on investment (ROI) analyses that are used to justify capital expenditures will be more realistic if the analyst has to subsequently live with a real "capital charge" for the investment. Also, decisions and actions that have not typically required an ROI decision, such as extending payment terms for customers to generate extra sales or scheduling extra production to absorb overhead, will receive the appropriate analysis in light of the cash tied up. Cash outlays that are not normally considered as "capital expenditures," such as research and development or training, although much more subjective, can be given similar consideration. Also, sunk costs should, appropriately, become irrelevant for current decision making.

Designing and executing a plan that joins "value-based" theory with supporting behavior of employees requires careful consideration of several aspects of the related financial metric. Four of the more significant include:

1. the metric itself (what is included in calculating added value),
2. reporting/accountability (what organizations or business units will be measured),
3. compensation (how to tie incentive plans to the financial metric), and
4. value based training (how to present the theory and teach skills needed to apply it).

This manager's "front line" perspective on value-based metric issues is provided below.

METRICS

All value-based metrics attempt to measure the profit generated by an enterprise against the cost of the capital used to generate that profit.[1] One of the more popular measurements is Stern Stewart's Economic Value Added (EVA).[2] In its simplest form, EVA is computed by subtracting a "capital charge," determined by multiplying "capital employed" (net working capital and fixed assets) by an appropriate cost of capital, and subtracting this "capital charge" from operating earnings. To the extent that earnings exceed the cost of capital, value is being created. It's a formula that all members of a business enterprise can easily understand. However, as the creators of this metric observe, "generally accepted

---

[1] This after all is the central message of this book on value-based metrics.
[2] For detailed explanations of the EVA metric developed by Stern Stewart & Co., see G. Bennett Stewart III, *The Quest for Value* (New York: Harper Collins, 1991) and Al Ehrbar, *EVA: The Real Key to Creating Wealth* (New York: John Wiley and Sons, 1998).

accounting principals" may require accounting treatment of certain transactions that do not necessarily reflect their true "economic" impact. In that management designing a metric for internal use can modify this formula to reflect circumstances relevant to their enterprise, a number of "adjustments" to the simple formula may be appropriate.

The most common adjustment is to treat certain expenditures required to be reported as expenses in GAAP financial statements as if they were capital expenditures.[3] These could include investments in research and development, advertising or publicity, restructuring charges, or any other expenditure deemed to have a substantial future benefit to the enterprise. The method is to treat these expenditures for EVA calculations as any other depreciable asset — that is, capitalize the expense and record the "depreciation" over the period benefited (see Exhibit 1). Making such adjustments may give an economically better indication as to whether value is being generated, but it requires keeping a separate "EVA" set of books and explaining differences to those being measured on EVA.

Quite often, EVA practitioners will find that the types of expenditures discussed in the previous paragraph are fairly consistent from time period to time period. Under these circumstances, all the additional record keeping will not have much of an effect on the reported result. A "keep it simple" approach, with adjustments for only significant individual events, could work best.

Another issue that arises around an EVA calculation used to measure financial performance internally is how to deal with items over which operations people have little or no control. The two obvious areas that can impact this measurement of "value creation" are the tax rate and the cost of capital. The question at hand is whether targets for returns on capital employed in operations should be adjusted for changes in the non-operating components of the metric. Again, implementers of an internal EVA financial metric may find it desirable to take a "keep it simple" approach. If a change in the tax rate or interest rate environment is not substantial and/or permanent, annual (or even more frequent) changes to the rates used to calculate "after tax" cost of capital probably cause more confusion than it's worth.

Another issue that seems trivial on the surface but can impact an EVA calculation is the frequency with which the amount of "capital employed" is calculated (see Exhibit 2). If the period between measurements is long, managers may tie up capital for interim periods without the capital charge being assessed. On the other hand, if the balance sheet is measured frequently (for example, monthly) the "off quarter" months seldom have the degree of reliability or review given to the quarter end statements. Also, the more frequent the measurement, the more EVA bookkeeping that is required. A decision on the appropriate interval would depend on how easily EVA capital data can be gathered and how likely it is that there could be significant (and real) short term fluctuations.

---

[3] For an interesting discussion on closing the "GAAP" between accounting earnings and economic profit, see Chapter 3 of this book by Al Ehrbar.

Exhibit 1: Alternative Treatments of Research and Development Expenses
Case 1 - R&D Expenses Relatively Constant
(Assume EVA Measurement Starts in Year 6)

	Cash Outlay	GAAP Accounting		Capitalize for EVA Use 5 year "life"		EVA "Charge" (Expense Plus 12% Capital Charge)	Difference
		Expense	Investment	Expense	Investment		
Year 1	200						
Year 2	210						
Year 3	220						
Year 4	230						
Year 5	250						
Year 6	230	230	0	225	584	295	65
Year 7	240	240	0	231	593	302	62
Year 8	250	250	0	237	606	310	60
Year 9	270	270	0	244	632	320	50
Year 10	280	280	0	251	661	330	50

Case 2 - R&D Expenses Vary Significantly

	Cash Outlay	GAAP Accounting		Capitalize for EVA Use 5 year "life"		EVA "Charge" (Expense Plus 12% Capital Charge)	Difference
		Expense	Investment	Expense	Investment		
Year 1	200						
Year 2	400						
Year 3	250						
Year 4	200						
Year 5	100						
Year 6	150	150	0	225	420	275	125
Year 7	450	450	0	225	645	302	(148)
Year 8	250	250	0	230	665	310	60
Year 9	80	80	0	218	527	281	201
Year 10	300	300	0	226	601	298	(2)

Although in Case 1 there is a difference between EVA on a "GAAP" and "Economic Adjustment" basis, there is not much fluctuation in the difference. In that EVA looks at the trend rather than the absolute measurement, the cost and confusion of making this adjustment may not be justified, compared to Case 2. The same consideration would apply to other expenditures commonly considered to be investments rather than expenses, such as advertising and training.

Exhibit 2: Frequency of Net Asset Calculation for EVA Purposes

	Net Assets
Beginning of year	$50,000
January	$45,000
February	$40,000
March	$52,000
April	$47,000
May	$43,000
June	$53,000
July	$47,000
August	$45,000
September	$54,000
October	$47,000
November	$46,000
December	$55,000
Net assets - 13 point average	$48,000
Net assets - 5 point average	$52,800
Net assets - 2 point average	$52,500

In this example, "net assets" used to calculate the capital charge can differ depending on the frequency with which assets are measured. In a typical company, the quarterly financial statements are generally subject to more scrutiny and are, therefore, more reliable.

REPORTING

Whatever the design of the EVA metric, the reporting of results brings with it another set of issues. For companies wishing to establish a value-based metric like EVA as the financial metric for all parts of an enterprise, another difficult decision awaits. How do you measure the various functional organizations or business units within the enterprise in a way that is relevant to their actions and decisions? On one end of the spectrum, it could be decided to measure just a total company EVA. This method, of course, diminishes the relevance of the concept to smaller organizations and decreases the degree of accountability.

The EVA calculation (operating profit less a charge for capital) essentially requires a full income statement and balance sheet. Therefore, it can be relatively easily applied to organizations with sales and related costs (for example, foreign marketing subsidiaries or domestic subsidiaries or business units with specific product lines). However, the more inter-company transactions there are, the more difficult the accurate measurement of any one unit becomes as its EVA becomes dependent upon conditions of other units.[4]

---

[4] The difficulty of measuring true economic profit from strategic operating units is not limited to manufacturing organizations. For example, value-based measurement limitations caused by EVA "co-movement" effects is examined in a banking context by Ralph Kimball in Chapter 11 of this book.

Exhibit 3: Application of EVA Concepts to a Manufacturing Division/Unit

	Annual Plan	Actual Results
Units produced	10,000	10,000
Material cost per unit	$5.00	$4.75
Overhead spending	$20,000	$19,000
Average inventory	$15,000	$17,000
Average fixed assets (net of depreciation)	$25,000	$25,000
EVA		
Volume Variance	$—	$—
Material Variance	$—	$2,500
Spending Variance	$—	$1,000
Total Variances	$—	$3,500
Capital charge at 12%	$4,800	$5,040
EVA contribution	$(4,800)	$(1,540)
EVA contribution above plan		$3,260

For purposes of measuring a manufacturing unit on a basis consistent with value-based metrics, performance can be measured as illustrated above. Of course, this requires the use of a metric with a result expressed in dollar values (such as EVA) rather than percent returns.

There are several drawbacks to applying this method to a manufacturing unit:

1. The EVA goal always has to be against a "plan," not an improvement over the prior year(s) which carries the issue of a "negotiated target."
2. The EVA plan will always be negative (and in the case of a growing company, will trend more negative as more capital is employed. This can be difficult to explain.
3. The illustration above assumes that units produced were on plan. Sales/Marketing driven volume changes add one more level of complexity (see Exhibit 4).

A partial solution to these issues – tie related incentive plans to a combination of divisional/entire enterprise EVA performance.

Measuring the EVA impact for functional organizations that do not have full profit and loss statements has also been attempted, but significant compromises in the metric have to be made. For example, a manufacturing unit can calculate its "contribution" to the enterprise EVA by using "variances" as a surrogate for "operating profit" and subtract a charge for capital employed in the operation (primarily fixed assets and inventory) (see Exhibit 3). However, without a full profit and loss statement, "value added performance" has to be measured against a plan or budget, not against previous actual results as EVA is intended to do.

Additionally, for manufacturing units, the performance of the sales/marketing organization has a large impact on volume variances and inventories at the plant level, which either results in EVA contribution being beyond the control of the manufacturing organization or requires rather subjective adjustments to the reported EVA results (see Exhibit 4). Neither condition does much to help the credibility of EVA as a financial metric applied to a functional organization. In light of the above, the desirability of driving EVA responsibility to as low a level as possible must be weighed against the compromised integrity of the measurement in deciding whether to apply it to organizations without a full set of financial statements.

Exhibit 4: Application of EVA Concepts to a Manufacturing Division/Unit — Volume Adjustment

	Annual Plan	Actual Results	Adjustment	Adjusted Variances
Units produced	10,000	8,000		
Material cost per unit	$5.00	$5.00		
Overhead spending	$20,000	$18,000		
Average inventory	$15,000	$17,000		
Average fixed assets (net of depreciation)	$25,000	$25,000		
Fixed spending percentage	50%	50%		
EVA				
Volume Variance	$—	$(4,000)	$4,000	$—
Material Variance	$—	$—		$—
Spending Variance	$—	$2,000	$(2,000)	$—
Total Variances	$—	$(2,000)	$2,000	$—
Capital charge at 12%	$4,800	$5,040		$5,040
EVA contribution	$(4,800)	$(7,040)		$(5,040)
EVA contribution above plan		$(2,240)		$(240)

Spending absorption effects of Sales/Marketing driven volume changes can be adjusted by charging Sales/Marketing and crediting Manufacturing for the unabsorbed fixed overhead. However, determining the fixed/variable percentage is not an exact science and adds one more level of subjectivity. Also, inventory effects can be difficult to measure.

COMPENSATION

Assuming that you want to link compensation to a value-based metric, there are a number of concepts to keep in mind and issues that will arise. The most significant is that creating value is a long-term concept, and for a compensation plan to be supportive of an EVA environment, it also must have a long time horizon. Perhaps the purest of EVA compatible compensation components is a maximization of common stock or common stock equivalents in the hands of employees. After all, if over the long haul, positive EVA is going to translate into higher stock prices, and employees have a significant stake at risk, they should pay particular attention to this metric. The drawback is that the cash payoff may be perceived to be too far in the future to be a strong incentive.

On the opposite side, because any one year's EVA is so strongly tied to the "operating profit" component of the metric, incentive plans tied to EVA on an annual basis tend to generate end-of-year thinking and decisions that may help the current year profit picture, but may be poor decisions for maximizing EVA over the long term (see Exhibit 5). In between these two extremes is a variation that the creators of EVA find attractive — calculating an annual incentive payment based on EVA, but leaving a portion of it at risk for a period of years (usually a 3-year time horizon provides a reasonable mix of long-term perspective and immediate incentive).[5]

---

[5] Detailed explanations of the role of EVA in incentive compensation planning can be found in Chapter 5 of this book by Stephen O'Byrne. EVA incentive compensation issues are also explained by Al Ehrbar in *EVA: The Real Key to Creating Wealth*.

Exhibit 5: "Manipulating" an Annual Plan

An annual EVA-based incentive compensation plan with no "bank" provision is not very different from a plan based on "operating profit" and can produce poor EVA decisions like the following:

Impact on current year of producing 1,000 units in excess of demand in the last quarter

Incremental materials in inventory ($5.00 per unit)	$5,000
Favorable volume variance ($2.00 per unit)	$2,000
Unfavorable spending (50% variable spending)	$(1,000)

EVA impact in current year:

Operating profit	$1,000
Capital charge (12% for one quarter on additional materials and spending)	$(180)
Additional reported EVA for the year	$820

However, in the following year, the variances will reverse, but the capital charge will not. Also, there would be an additional capital charge for the period in the following year for which the production remained in inventory. Net result: a larger bonus in the current year for an action that reduces value.

Implementing an EVA-based incentive plan also presents an interesting start-up dilemma. Unlike using a budgeted "profit target" for incentive purposes, EVA has an inherently built in target, the cost of capital employed. Initiating an EVA-based plan requires a reasonable valuation of capital employed (including adjustments to reflect as capital those items of economic value such as research and development or advertising). If an enterprise has assets that are undervalued on the books and underutilized, or has substantial assets that are not earning their cost of capital and can be divested, generating a significant increase in EVA is a little too easy. Although it goes somewhat against the grain of an EVA metric, this problem can be dealt with by setting specific EVA targets in the early years of adoption. It should be remembered that a need to set EVA targets in the long run would indicate that you are using the wrong cost of capital or that you do not believe the valuation of the capital employed.

The last significant decision is how far down in the organization to apply an EVA-based incentive compensation system. Should it be limited to top levels of management or driven down to lower levels? This issue may be most appropriately addressed by looking at the corporate culture rather than EVA theory. It is hard to imagine that applying an EVA-based "bonus" plan to employees that have no opportunity to influence capital employed would be effective in increasing the total company EVA performance. However, in company's that traditionally have provided incentive plans for all employees, EVA can be easily applied in a manner that sets company financial goals that are common to everyone. The percentage of compensation that is at risk can be varied according to employees' level in the organization, but the target financial performance is the same.

Exhibit 6: EVA Training Examples

A couple of simple exercises like these can help illustrate EVA principles in a training session

A marketing manager proposes a plan to increase sales by extending payment terms. He estimates the annual increase in operating profit to be $20,000 and the increase in average receivables to be $100,000. Assuming the "cost of capital" to be 15%, is this a good proposal? What if the increase in operating profit were $12,000 instead of $20,000?

A year ago a project was started that was estimated to cost $200,000 and would result in operating savings of $40,000. There have been difficulties encountered, and as of today, $100,000 has been spent and it looks like another $200,000 needs to be spent. Do you continue with the project? What if the revised estimates of annual savings are $20,000? Again, assume a cost of capital of 15%.

TRAINING

The training design for implementing a value-based plan like EVA will most likely mirror decisions made in the previous sessions and should be considered at the same time. Included below are some issues and questions that arise as a company prepares its population for measuring itself.

In terms of "metrics," the training will at the very least, require educating a substantial percentage of employees on the "accounting" concept of the "balance sheet." This can be a difficult enough chore, but then explaining a variety of adjustments to the "generally accepted" norm can be even more confusing. However, to the extent that "accounting expenses" are reclassified as "investments" for value-based measurement, the implementers had best be prepared to explain them.

Once the nature of the metric is understood, the next challenge (and perhaps the primary focus of training) should be on the levers that are available to increase value generated. The impact on the metric (and the link to shareholder expectations) of levels of receivables, inventories, and other assets, and the related impact on operating profit is key to employees making better financial decisions. Another important notion that is likely to be new to many employees is that "value creating thinking" is always forward looking and cash already gone is irrelevant. This portion of the training is best accomplished with some good examples and a number of hands on training exercises (see Exhibit 6).

Who should present the training? Although this is a financial metric and having the training presented by someone who is knowledgeable and comfortable in this environment is desirable, it is important to avoid the appearance of a new metric as another program "designed by those accountants." To the extent possible, operating managers and supervisors should visibly support (and hopefully, actively participate in) the training. This will emphasize that a value-based metric is not the accountant's view of financial success, but the investor's view.

Should employees in all functions receive the same training? Although the "basics" should probably be similar for everyone and should also establish the principles upon which the company is operating as a whole, there are vast differences between the relevance of the metric in different functional roles. For example, employees involved in "core research" typically have to wait years to see returns on their "investments." The role they play in determining the enterprises' value added, especially when it is measured in rather short time increments, clearly will have to be differentiated from those who have the potential for a much more immediate impact, such as manufacturing or marketing.

What are the most common questions that arise in training? The topic that generates the most questions is the notion of a "cost of capital," particularly as it relates to common equity. The cost used can appear arbitrary, and requires an explanation of "risk" at the same time. Another area that brings about a lot of skepticism is the correlation of value metric to stock prices in the market. Many employees are aware of relatively large short-term market fluctuations that cannot possibly be linked to any financial metric, and will question its usefulness. The third most questioned concept is the notion of an "investment" versus an "expense," of which expenditures for research or employee training are particularly hot buttons. Any implementers would be well advised to have well thought out responses to all of these concerns.

SUMMARY

From an external analytical point of view, value-based metrics such as EVA can be easily modified to fit the user's perception of a company being evaluated and what financial information is relevant under the circumstances. However, for any financial metric to be useful as a focus for internal activities, the target must be well defined, consistent, and understandable. To effect these characteristics, four aspects of implementation must be addressed simultaneously and coordinated:

- The metric itself — specifically, how it is going to be calculated for a company, given the multitude of variations that could exist.
- Reporting — at what level and functional structure will the metric be applied.
- Compensation — how to assure that employees' pay is driven by decisions that are consistent with the metric.
- Training — making sure everyone of influence understands the metric and the impact of their decisions on it.

With these four items considered simultaneously and coordinated with each other, implementation of a value-based metric for internal financial measurement purposes stands a good chance of success.

Index

A

Abate, James A., 1, 2, 5, 23
Accountability, 216
Accounting. See Cash-basis accounting.
 adjustments, 55–63
 book value, 53, 146
 data, 71
 distortions, 73
 earnings, 90
 information, 158
 methods, 70, 72
 principles, 67, 85
 profit, 74
 profit/economic profit, measurement differences, 49
Accounting Principles Board, 51
Accretion policies, 111
Accrued interest, 57
Acquisition, 116, 125, 210, 262
 accounting, 58–59
 company rejection, 119
 cost, metering. See Capital.
 goodwill, 99
 issues, 55
 liabilities, exclusion. See Capital.
Acquisition-created shareholder value, conflict. See Economic profit.
Active investment performance/risk, measurement, 136–137
Active risk, 136
Active strategy, 135
After-tax cash flow, 8, 25
After-tax distribution, 101
After-tax operating income, 142
After-tax present value, 124
After-tax profitability, 37
After-tax return on capital, 21
Agency perspective, 211
Agency theory, 196–199
Agrawal, A., 224, 225
AIMR. See Association for Investment Management and Research.
Allocation. See Banking; Capital.
 methods. See Stand-alone allocation methods.
Amortization, 77, 78, 161
 charge, 58
 policies, 111
Annualized revenue growth, 30
Aram, John D., 205
Aristocratic approach, 242
Asset-based view. See Capital.
Assets. See Intangible assets; Physical assets.
 approach, 20
 cost, 104
 mix, optimization, 249–250
 visibility, 250
 writeoffs, 52

B

Association for Investment Management and Research (AIMR), 20
 Research Foundation, 92
AT&T, 128–129

Bacidore, Jeffrey M., 2, 93, 218, 219
Backloaded forecast, 121
Bad debt recognition, 55
Bad-debt reserve, 17
Balance sheets, 52, 53, 58, 102, 104, 146, 166, 236
 adjustments, 62–63
 data, 74
 make-up, 232
Banking, risk capital allocation, 253
Banks
 diversification, 262
 performance measurement, economic profit usage, 266–267
 returns, variance, 259
BARRA, 25, 83, 140
Bartlett, C., 217
Base salaries, 192
Beaver, William H., 111
Becht, Marco, 204
Benchmark, 133. See also Passive benchmark; Risk-adjusted benchmark.
 portfolio, 136, 137
 return, 136, 137
Beta, 22, 25, 226. See also Internal betas.
 bias, 139
Beyer, Jurgen, 199
Biddle, Gary C., 2, 42, 94, 185, 218
Bilmes, L., 183
Bio-tech companies, 57
Board of directors, 200
 functions, 216
 remuneration, 210
 responsibilities, 210, 214–215
Bond, M.H., 189
Bonus bank terms, 109
Bonus/debit bank, 225
Book value, 86, 118. See also Accounting.
Bookkeeping reserves, 55
Book-to-price ratio, 25
Boquist, John A., 2, 93, 218, 219
Bowen, Robert M., 2, 42, 94, 185, 218
Bretton Woods, 180
Burmeister Ibbotson Roll, Ross, 25
Business cycle, 64
Business risk, 41, 63, 64
 premium, 34
Business Sector Advisory Group. See Corporate Governance.
Business units, 253, 257, 259, 260, 265
 level, 62, 119

C

 product lines, 273
 risk-equivalent economic contribution, 266

Cadbury code, 205
Calculation issue, 164
CALPERS, 206, 211
 principles, 215
CAP. See Competitive advantage period.
Capacitors, 247
Capital, 79–81. See also Debt capital; Equity; Invested capital; Marginal capital.
 access, 212
 acquisition
  cost, metering, 120–121
  liabilities, exclusion, 122–124
 additions. See Working capital additions.
 allocation, 114, 262, 264–266
  decisions, 53
 amount, 255
 asset-based view, 20
 book value, 87, 89
 calculation, 79
 charge, 57, 103, 120, 270
 corporate value-cost, 34
 cost, 56, 84, 106, 113, 157, 276
  calculation, 237
  notion, 278
 discipline, 56
 estimation, cost, 21–22
 expenditures, 93
 flow, 179
 investments, 201. See also Net capital investments.
 providers, 182
 ratio, 263. See also Peer group.
 recovery, 115
 risk-adjusted cost, 245
 sensitivity, 163
Capital Asset Pricing Model (CAPM). See Single-factor CAPM.
 alternatives, 23–25
 anomalies, 22–25
 beta, 82
Capital market, 182
 short-term preference, 199
 value, 70, 89, 91
Capital Market Line (CML), 10, 11
Capital structure, Modigliani-Miller position, 13
Capital-adjusted MVA-EVA results, 48
Capital-intensive firms, 47
Capital-to-asset ratio, 256, 260, 264
Cash, 139. See also Excess cash.
 accounting, 119

279

consequences, 147
generation, 242
operating margin, 115
operating taxes, 74, 148
Cash flow, 118, 166, 250
maximization, 251
measures, 73
volatility, calculation, 245
Cash Flow Return On Investment
(CFROI), 2, 3, 8, 11, 25–27, 46,
68, 234–237
advice, 237
compensation tie-in, 236
implementation, 234–235
initial expectations, 234
link. See Economic Value Added/
Cash Flow Return On Investment.
metric, 235
performance, 236
real world considerations, 26–27
relationship. See Economic margin.
results, 235–236
selection process, 234
steps, 236
valuations, 170–173
Cash Value Added (CVA), 237, 238,
240
Cash-basis accounting, 72
Cash-flow basis, 55
Cash-on-cash yield, 146
CFROI. See Cash Flow Return On
Investment.
Charan, R., 199
Charge-offs. See Net charge-offs.
Chen, Shimin, 93, 218, 249
Chew, Donald H., 203, 225
Chris, Argyris, 201
CII. See Confederation of Indian
Industry.
Civil law, 222
Clark, Myrtle W., 112
Clarkson, Max B.E., 202
Clean surplus, 102
Clinton, B. Douglas, 249
CML. See Capital Market Line.
Cohen, Abby Joseph, 1, 5, 21, 36
Collective action problems, 219–
223
Combined Code, 206
Common law, 222
Community system, 220
Company-specific premium, 23
Company-specific risk score, 23
Compensation, 275–278
tie-in. See Cash Flow Return On
Investment; Economic Value
Added; Economic Value Added/
Cash Flow Return On Invest-
ment.
Compensation opportunities, 110
Compensation plan development,
245
Compensation practices, 190

Competitive advantage period
(CAP), 154, 155
Competitive analysis. See Economic
Value Added.
Competitive bonus opportunity, 225
Compustat, 83
Confederation of Indian Industry
(CII), 220
Conger, Jay A., 215
Construction-in-progress account-
ing, 57
Content. See Organization for Eco-
nomic Cooperation and Develop-
ment.
Control mechanisms, 213
Convexity, 34
Conyon, 215
Cooter, R., 222
Copeland, Thomas, 30, 69, 77, 80–
82, 86, 152
Core competencies, 192
Corporate executives, comparison.
See Money managers.
Corporate finance, 187
Corporate governance. See Interna-
tional corporate governance.
control mechanism, 205
global unification, 226
OECD principles, 195, 205–216.
See also Global corporate gov-
ernance.
summary, 216
practice, 211
principles, private initiatives,
205–206
stakeholder, role, 209
summary, 203–205
system. See European corporate
governance systems.
ability indicators, 204
theoretical perspectives, 196–205
Corporate Governance, Business
Sector Advisory Group, 207
Corporate performance, 55
Corporate Person (CP), 248
Corporate profits, 208
Corporate services, 63
Corporate shareholder value cre-
ation, 242
Corporate strategy, 210
Corporate targets, 238
Corporate taxes, impact. See
Weighted Average Cost of Capi-
tal.
Corporate valuation, 38
decisions, 250
steps, 229
Correlation coefficient, 261
Cost center, elimination, 249
Cost of capital, 63–65, 81–84
change, 33–35, 39–41
Cost of capital estimation, 49
Cost-of-capital return, 225
COV. See Current operations value.
Cowen, Scott S., 205

CP. See Corporate Person.
Creative thinking, 277
Credit card bank, 254
Credit card business, 256
Credit Suisse Asset Management
(CSAM), 23–25
Credit Suisse First Boston, 4
Crystal, G.S., 214
CSAM. See Credit Suisse Asset
Management.
Cummings, Anne, 201
Current non-interest bearing liabili-
ties, 122
Current operations value (COV),
105, 106
Customer Value Added (CVA), 128
CVA. See Cash Value Added; Cus-
tomer Value Added.

D

Daily, C.M., 203
Dalton, D.R., 203
Damodaran, Aswath, 2
Datek, 226
Davis, James H., 200
Dayton Hudson Corporation, EVA
illustration, 141–142
D/C. See Debt to capital ratio.
DCF. See Discounted Cash Flow.
Debt capital, 83
Debt financing, 197
Debt to capital ratio (D/C), 14
Decay. See Economic margin.
Decaying IRR, 174
Decision-maker, education, 242
Decomposition. See Wealth cre-
ators.
Deferred tax reserve, 119
Deferred taxes, 61, 145
Demb, Ada, 204
Demirag, I., 225
Demographics change, 89
Depreciable asset, 271
Depreciation, 28, 29, 60, 77, 78,
271. See also GAAP deprecia-
tion; Negative depreciation; Neg-
ative economic depreciation;
Sinking fund depreciation;
Straight line depreciation.
charge, 30, 31, 60, 61
expense, 151
standards. See GAAP.
Dietl, 225
Dilutive adjustments, 101
addition. See Net Operating Profit
After Taxes.
Dilutive NOPAT adjustments, 120
Disclosure, 209–210
Discount Rate (DR), 103, 171
Discounted Cash Flow (DCF), 100,
111, 117, 118, 134, 168
forecasts, 175
models, 27
valuation, 101–103, 120

Diversification. See Banks; Risk.
  allowance, 257
  benefits, 258
  effects, 257
Divestitures, 129, 262
Dividend Discount Model, 168
Dividend yield, 25
Dobbs, Richard, 216, 223, 224
Dodd, James L., 93, 218
Dollar-based EVA measure, 4
Donaldson, Lex, 200
DR. See Discount Rate.
Driver tree, 245
Drucker, Peter F., 217, 218, 229, 230
Duration estimates, 40
Durkheim, 220

E

Earnings, 51
  growth, 158
  momentum, 25
  press release, 127
  ratio. See Wealth creators.
Earnings Before Interest Taxes
  (EBIT), 127
  Amortization and Technology, 126
Earnings per share (EPS), 226, 233
EBIT. See Earnings Before Interest
  Taxes.
Economic book value, 53
Economic conditions, 67
Economic depreciation, 31. See also
  Negative economic depreciation.
  usage, 115
Economic Margin (EM), 157, 160–
  163
  Cash Flow Return On Investment,
    relationship, 165–168
  decay, 173–176
  EVA, relationship, 163–165
  valuation, 173–176
Economic obsolescence, 28
Economic performance, 158
Economic Profit (EP), 13, 35–36,
  42, 71–72, 89, 103–105, 165,
  172, 257, 264–266. See also
  Expected EP improvement.
  accounting, 118
  acquisition-created shareholder
    value, conflict, 117–118
  adjustments, 120
  bonus plan, 108
  calculation, 73, 124
  conflict. See Shareholder value.
  estimation, 36–38
  pitfalls, 84–86
  forecasts, 174
  improvement, 109
  investment plans, 99
  measures, 101
    relatedness, 11–12
  model, 35–41
  present value, 38–39
  sensitivity, 85

usage. See Bank performance
  measurement.
Economic theory, 90
Economic value, 35, 69
Economic Value Added (EVA), 3,
  36, 51, 68, 90, 179, 184–186,
  195, 231–233
  abandonment. See Performance.
  advice, 233
  application. See Stock.
  bonus plan design. See Stern
    Stewart.
  bookkeeping, 271
  companies, responses. See Share-
    holder value.
  compensation tie-in, 233
  critique, 216–219
  definition, 54, 134–135
  EVA-based bonus plan, 276
  EVA-based competitive analysis,
    151–152
  EVA-based valuation measures,
    152–155
  EVA-based volatility score, 23
  EVA-to-Capital ratios, 45, 46
  executive compensation, 223–226
  illustration. See Dayton Hudson
    Corporation.
  implementation, 232
  improvement targets, recalibra-
    tion. See Incentive plans.
  initial expectations, 231–232
  integration. See Portfolio man-
    agement process.
  interval, 225
  management compensation, 186–
    190
  market value-added reconcilia-
    tion, 89–90
  measure. See Dollar-based EVA
    measure.
  measures, adopters/non-adopt-
    ers, 92
  OECD principles, 216–227
  power, 53–55
  ratio tree, 151
  relationship. See Economic mar-
    gin; Net Present Value.
  results, 233
  selection process, 231
  treatment. See Research & devel-
    opment.
  valuation techniques, 153–155
  valuations, 168–170
Economic Value Added/Cash Flow
  Return On Investment (EVA/
  CFROI), 237–241
  advice, 240–241
  compensation, tie-in, 240
  implementation, 238
  initial expectations, 237–238
  link, 157
  results, 238–240
  selection process, 237
  steps, 240

Economies, interdependence, 211
Edwards, Laure, 249
EE. See Equity Equivalents.
Egalitarian approach, 242
Ehrbar, Al, 5, 19, 51, 69, 270, 271,
  275
Einhorn, Steven G., 1, 5, 21, 36
Eisenhardt, Kathleen M., 197
Eisner formula, 107, 108
Ellstrand, A.E., 203
EM. See Economic Margin.
Employee ownership programs, 190
Employee-focused companies, 183
Enterprise risk assessment, 243–246
Enterprise valuation
  approaches, 27, 49
  process, 33
Enterprise value, 101
Enterprise value-to-earnings ratio,
  decomposition, 44. See also
  Wealth creators.
Environmental liabilities, 120
EP. See Economic Profit.
EPS. See Earnings per share.
Equity
  book value, 79
  capital, 83, 256
  market value, 101
  value, 42
Equity, opportunity cost, 253
Equity allocation, 265
Equity Equivalents (EE), 142, 143
Equity markets, 182
Equity-to-asset ratios, 254, 256
ESOP, 235
  accrual, 148
  trust, 148
Europe, shareholder value, 181–184
European corporate governance sys-
  tems, 206
European Economic Community, 180
European Union, 180
EVA. See Economic Value Added.
Ex post basis, 261
Excess cash, 148
Executive compensation. See Eco-
  nomic Value Added.
Expected EP improvement, 105–107
Expenditures, recognition, 103
Expense policies, 111
Expense recognition, 59
Expenses, capitalization, 251
External control mechanisms, 212
External financing, comparison. See
  Internal financing.

F

Fabozzi, Frank J., 27, 85, 133, 137,
  139, 152, 160, 227
Factor models, 25
Fade, 170–173
Fade to levels, 170–173
Fair market value, 53
Fama, Eugene F., 8, 13, 22, 27, 29,
  35, 41, 86, 105, 218

FASB. See Financial Accounting Standards Board.
FCF. See Free cash flow.
Felton, Robert, 222
FGV. See Future growth value.
FIFO value. See Inventory.
Finance theory, 49
Financial Accounting Standards Board (FASB), 51
Financial data, 226
Financial distress, 135
Financial markets, 199
Financial performance measurement systems, 223
Financial statements, 76
  information, 67
Financial theory, 90
  value-based metrics usage, 7
Financing costs, 73
Finegold, David, 215
Finkelstein, Sydney, 201, 215
Fisher, Irving, 3
Fixed assets, 163, 270, 274
Fixed income market, 34
Fixed interest payments, 64
Foreign currency translation, 55
Foreign marketing subsidiaries, 273
Frederick, Richard, 211
Free cash flow (FCF), 93, 99, 101–103, 122
  approaches, 36
  definition, 100
  model, 28–35, 37, 168. See also Two-stage free cash flow model.
  present value, 32–33
Free cash flow (FCF) estimation
  horizon years, 29–31
  residual period, 31–32
Free-rider problems, 198, 200, 214
French, Kenneth R., 22, 86, 218
Frooman, Jeff, 202
Froot, Kenneth A., 259
Full-cost accounting, 119
Future cash flows, 111
Future growth value (FGV), 105–107

G

GAAP, 52, 53, 58, 61, 112, 206
  accounting, 59, 100, 141
  earnings, 142
  accrual items, 55
  closing, 51
  financial statements, 271
  treatment, 60
GAAP depreciation
  expense, 163
  standards, 100
GATT. See General Agreement on Tariffs and Trade.
Gedajlovic, Eric R., 198
General Agreement on Tariffs and Trade (GATT), 180
General Motors bonus formula, 107

Gesellschaft, 217
Ghoshal, Sumantra, 202, 217
Gibbons, Robert, 56
Global corporate governance, OECD principles, 219–223
Goldman Sachs, 20, 36
  approach, 20
  overview, 21
  client conference, 4
Goods, cost, 122
Goodwill, 55, 80, 146. See also Unrecorded goodwill.
  amortization, 52, 72, 79, 81
  economic treatment, 59
Goodwill-related items, 20
GOPAT. See Gross Operating Profit After Tax.
Gordley, J., 222
Governance structures, 209
Government bond rate, 63
GPV. See Gross Present Value.
Grant, James L., 2, 27, 35, 45, 49, 69, 82, 105, 133, 137, 138, 140, 152, 160, 227
Greater-than-least-common-denominator, 220
Greenbury committee report, 205
Gross annual investment, 29
Gross capital investment, 31
Gross cash outflows, 246
Gross Operating Profit After Tax (GOPAT), 28, 29, 31
Gross Present Value (GPV), 8–10
Growth, 157. See also Earnings.
  conflict, 165
  disincentive, 161
  rates, 153, 154. See also World War II.
  spending, definition, 125
Growth opportunities, 41, 43
  present value, 153
Growth-oriented behavior, 196
Guay, Wayne, 223

H

Hambrick, Donald, 201, 215
Hannan, Timothy H., 255
Hanweck, Gerald A., 255
Harris, Roy, 218
Hart, O.E., 214
Hidden interest liabilities, 122
Hobbesian tradition, 221, 222
Hofstede, G., 189
Hopt, K.J., 205, 225
Horizon
  period, 31, 32, 37
  value function, 35
  years. See Free cash flow estimation.
Hudnut, Alec, 222
Human capital, 246
  investments, 198
Hurdle, 90
  rate, 26, 27
Hutchinson, Ian R., 203

I

IMF, 221
Implementation. See Cash Flow Return On Investment; Economic Value Added; Economic Value Added/Cash Flow Return On Investment.
  best practices, 241–243
  process, 243
    planning, 242–243
    timing, choice, 241–242
Implementation schedule, 232
Incentive payment, 275
Incentive plans
  EVA improvement targets, recalibration, 121
  targets, 112
Incentives, 213
Income statements, 166
Income tax expense, 19, 77
Incremental economic profit, 265
Individualism, 190
Industry bias, 139
Inflation, 55, 164
Information disadvantage, 215
Innovation indicators, 217
In-process R&D, 58
Insider trader, legal liability, 198
Insolvency, probability, 256
Institutional investors, 157, 198
Institutional shareholders, 213
Intangible assets, 28, 55, 146–147
Intangible valuation, 246–251
Intangible value, 246
Intangibles, 116
  investment, value-based management discouragement, 99
Inter-company transactions, 273
Interest
  cost, 144, 145
  rates, 64
  risk-free rate, 34, 82
  tax deductibility, 82
Interest bearing short-term liabilities, 21
Interest-bearing debt, 186
Internal betas, 259–262, 267
Internal financing, external financing comparison, 12–15
Internal Rate of Return (IRR), 5, 25, 26, 114, 166. See also Decaying IRR; Pre-tax IRR.
Internal rate of return (IRR)
  type metrics, 167
Internal Revenue Service (IRS), 61
International corporate governance, 219
Intranet, 240
Intrapreneurship, 183
Intrinsic corporate value, 39
Intrinsic value, 32, 151, 152
Inventory, 274
  FIFO value, 146
  levels, investments, 242
  valuation, 55

Invested capital, 142–144, 152, 186
  impact, 20–21
Invested capital, excess return, 12
Investment, 148
  decision process, 201
  evaluation, 72
  managers, 133
  opportunities, 135. See also Valu-
    ation.
  ratios, 71
  style, 138
  value, 176
Investment Opportunities Approach
  to Valuation (IOAV), 41, 43
Investor Relation (IR), 250
Investor value, creation, 135–140
Investor value added, 133
IOAV. See Investment Opportunities
  Approach to Valuation.
IR. See Investor Relation.
IRR. See Internal Rate of Return.

J

Jackson, Al, 5, 36
Jackson, T., 189
Jacobs, Bruce I., 139
Jensen, Michael C., 15, 187, 212,
  214, 223
Johns, J., 218
Johnson, J.L., 203
Judge, Jr., William Q., 201

K

Kaplan, Stephen N., 213
Kauffman, Stuart A., 219, 223
Keasey, Kevin, 199
Keller, Hans-Ueli, 4, 15
Kimball, Ralph, 219
Klopukh, Steven, 81
Knoeber, C., 224, 225
Kogelman, Stanley, 8, 68
Koller, Timothy, 30, 69, 77, 80–81,
  86, 152, 216, 223, 224
Kose, John, 213

L

Labor market controls, 199
Laux, Christian, 224
Lawler III, Edward E., 215
LBO. See Leveraged buyout.
Lease obligations, 145
Leibowitz, Martin L., 8
Lenders, liquidating perspective, 119
Lev, Baruch, 51, 52, 56, 58
Leverage, 167
Leveraged buyout (LBO), 187, 188
Levy, Kenneth N., 139
Liberalized trade, 181
Liebowitz, Martin L., 68
LIFO reserve, 17, 20, 79, 145–146
Line of sight, 184
Liquidation values, 53
Liquidity
  loss, 198

Locke, John, 220
Lockean tradition, 222
London Stock Exchange, 206
Long duration asset, 35
Long-term bonds, 82
Long-term constant growth, 33
Long-term debt, 186
Long-term investments, 199, 238
Lorsch, Jay W., 200, 201, 205, 214
Low-risk strategies, 197

M

Mace, Miles, 200
Macey, Jonathan R., 198, 204, 212
MacIver, Elisabeth, 200, 205, 214
Macro-factor models, 25
Madden, Bartley J., 2, 171
Management. See Value-based man-
  agement.
  compensation. See Economic
    Value Added.
  performance, 204
  reports, 191
Management buyout (MBO), 188
Managerial hegemony, 199–200
Managerial theme, 48
Managerialism, 199
Managers, decision making, 266
Marginal capital, 262–264
Market
  conditions, 67
  index, 139
  risk premium, 83, 86
  system, 220
  timing, 138
  value, 42, 101. See also Equity.
Market Value Added (MVA), 5, 9,
  12, 46, 68, 69, 86–89, 184–186
  change, 89
  changes, 54
  MVA/EVA rankings, 53
  MVA-to-Capital ratios, 45, 46
  reconciliation. See Economic
    value-added.
Market-adjusted returns, 94
Market-based principles, 220
Market-building expenditures, 119
Market/capital ratio, 102
Marketing expenditures, 55
Markets, globalization, 211
Marshall, Alfred, 3, 50, 72
Martinson, Jane, 211, 212
Masculinity, 190
Mattei, U., 222
Mauboussin, Michael J., 5, 36
Maug, Ernst, 206
MBO. See Management buyout.
McNulty, Terry, 202
Meckling, W., 223
Merton, Robert C., 265
Metering, 120. See also Capital.
Metrics, 270–273. See also Value-
  based metrics.
  non-operating components, 271
  term, 277

Milbourn, Todd T., 2, 93, 218, 219
Millenstein, Ira M., 207, 208
Miller, Merton H., 2, 3, 8, 12–14,
  21, 27, 29, 35, 41, 50, 64, 105
Minow, Neil, 197
Modigliani, Franco, 3, 12, 14, 50, 64
Momentum, 175. See also Earnings.
Money management community,
  165
Money managers, corporate execu-
  tives comparison, 159–160
Monks, Robert A.G., 197
Monsanto, 124–128
Moral hazard, 197
Moran, P., 217
Morningstar, 226
Mortgage banker, 254
Mortgage banking, 260
Mortgage payment, 60, 161
Multinational firms, 218
Multiple-year economic profit, 91
Multivariate equation, 244
Multi-year zero bonus, 110
Murphy, Kevin, 56
Murrin, Jack, 30, 69, 77, 80–82, 86,
  152
MVA. See Market Value Added.
Myers, Randy, 218

N

NAA. See Nodal asset analysis.
Napolitano, Gabrielle, 1, 5, 21, 36
Near-term quarterly earnings, 126
Near-to-current market prices, 17
Negative depreciation, 104
Negative economic depreciation,
  100, 113, 116, 119
Negative economic profit, 108
Net asset base, 163
Net capital investments, 29, 30
Net charge-offs, 148
Net Operating Profit After Taxes
  (NOPAT), 8–10, 13, 16, 20, 28,
  36, 73–78. See also Unlevered net
  operating profit after tax.
  adjustments. See Dilutive NOPAT
    adjustments.
  calculation, 142–144, 148–151
  dilutive adjustment, addition, 121
  estimation, 17–21
  perpetuity, 37
Net Present Value (NPV), 7, 13–16,
  26, 35–36, 39, 43, 48, 73, 176
  EVA relationship, 186
  model. See Two-period NPV
    model.
  economic profit, 10–12
  NPV-EVA combinations, 49
Net working capital, 270
Neubauer, Friedrich F., 204
Nickell, S., 214
Nodal asset analysis (NAA), 246–
  249
  usage, 251

Nodes, 247
Non-cancelable obligations, 144
Non-cash bookkeeping, 119
Non-cash events, 147
Non-depreciable asset, 104
Non-depreciating assets, 161
Non-EVA companies, 61
Non-executive directors, 214
   number, 210
Non-financial managers, 166
Non-interest bearing accounts, 62,
   112
Non-interest bearing current liabili-
   ties, 20
Non-interest bearing liabilities, 120,
   186
Non-operating activities, 148
Non-operating income, 77
Non-performing buffer status, 239
Non-recurring activities, 148
Non-recurring income sources, 19
Non-recurring income/loss, 147
NOPAT. See Net Operating Profit
   After Taxes.
NPV. See Net Present Value.

O

Obrycki, Daniel, 249
O'Byrne, Stephen F., 2, 8, 20, 27,
   60, 73, 102, 105, 108, 110, 163,
   225, 275
OECD. See Organization for Eco-
   nomic Cooperation and Develop-
   ment.
Off-balance-sheet financing, 55
Old Plant Trap, 163
Oldham, Gregg, 201
One-factor expected return-risk pre-
   dictions, 22
One-share-one-vote
   concept, 212
   rule, 204, 208
One-tier board system, 212
Operating capital, 80
Operating income, 73
   adjustment, 84
Operating leases, 144–151
   financing component, 73
   implied interest expense, 76
Operating performance, 102
Operating profit, 77, 275
Operational risks, 245
Opportunity cost, 135
Organization for Economic Cooperation and Development (OECD)
   initiative, reasons, 207
   principles. See Corporate governance; Economic Value Added;
   Global corporate governance.
   assumptions, 207–208
   content, 207–210
   discussion, 212–215
   potential value, 210–211

P

Pardolesi, R., 222
Parrino, Robert, 218
Parsons, 220
Passive benchmark, 138
Passive strategy, 135
Payment streams, 145
Payout rules, 109
P/E multiple, 158
PE ratios, 226
Pearce II, J.A., 204
Peck, Simon, 4, 15, 215
Peer group, capital ratio, 254
Pensions, 55
People Value Added (PVA), 128
Performance, 139. See also Corpo-
   rate performance; Economic per-
   formance; Management.
   comparison, 91
   compensation tie-in, 235
   fees, 140
   indicator, 185
   measure, 95
      EVA abandonment, 124–128
   measurement. See Active invest-
      ment performance/risk; Bank
      performance measurement.
   techniques, 71
   metric, 53, 158, 160
   planning, 128
   scorecards, 203
   traditional measures, 70–71
   Universe, 47
   value-based measures, 67
Perold, Andre F., 265
Perpetuity problems, 173, 174
Peterson, David R., 2, 20, 26, 69,
   92, 142
Peterson, Pamela P., 2, 5, 20, 26, 42,
   69, 92, 142
Pettigrew, Andrew, 202
Pfeffer, Jeffrey, 203
Physical assets, 18
Physical capital, 246
Planning/scenario analysis tool, 236
Political system, 220
Political-based solutions, 221
Pooling-of-interests, 146
Portfolio, 139
   management process, EVA inte-
      gration, 133
   managers, 135, 173
Post horizon, 32
   years, 29, 38, 39
Post-retirement expenses, 55
Post-tax capital returns, 21
Potential value. See Organization
   for Economic Cooperation and
   Development.
Power distance, 189, 190
PPC. See Production Possibilities
   Curve.
Prahalad, C.K., 203
Pre-acquisition year, 121

Preferred stock, book value, 89
Present value, 117. See also After-
   tax present value; Economic
   Profit; Free cash flow; Growth
   opportunities.
   basis, 113
Pre-tax cash operating profit, 19
Pre-tax IRR, 114
Pre-tax net operating margin, 30
Pre-tax operating profits, 61
Price management, 135
Price to Book, 140
Price trends, 226
Price-to-book value ratios, 49
Price-to-earnings ratio, 44, 49, 140
Private-label credit card, 147
   operation, 151
Process inefficiencies, elimination,
   249–250
Production Possibilities Curve
   (PPC), 9, 10
Profitability, 157
   level, 169
   measures, 58
Profit-maximizing behavior, 196
Profit-sharing, 200
Pro-forma base year, 120
   usage, 121
Pro-forma calculation, 121
Project risks/rewards, 184
Proportional risk, 260
Proportional scaling, 257–259
Pulsing, 240
PVA. See People Value Added.

R

Rappaport, Alfred, 2, 30
RCF fade, 249
RCF value, 249
Real-time capital markets, 22
Re-engineering process, 223
Relational capitalism, 181
Relative risk, 259
Remuneration, 209. See also Board
   of directors.
Reporting, 273–275
Research & development (R&D),
   55–56, 99, 116, 251. See In-pro-
   cess R&D.
   EVA treatment, 59
   expenditures, 18
   full expensing, 52
   outlays, 146
   straight-line depreciation, 112
Resendes, Rafael, 249
Reserves, 147–148
Residual period. See Free cash flow
   estimation.
Residual Return On Capital
   (RROC), 12
Residual value, 29, 33, 35
Residual years, 32
Resource dependence theory, 203
Restructuring charges, 52, 55, 60–61

Retention risk, 110
Return On Assets (ROA), 58, 67, 257
Return On Capital (ROC), 12, 42, 81, 170
Return On Equity (ROE), 58, 136, 140
Return on invested capital (ROIC), 81, 114, 134, 140, 150, 151
    forecasting, 154
Return On Investment (ROI), 71, 270
Return on net worth (RONW), 220
Return ratios, 70
Return-risk anticipations, 22
REVA, 218
Revenue base, 30
Revenue growth, 141. See also Annualized revenue growth.
Reverse accruals, 147
Richardson, Alan J., 203
Risk, 71, 191. See also Active risk; Retention risk; Stand-alone risks; Stand-alone total risk.
    adjustment, 137
    assessment. See Enterprise risk assessment.
    capital, allocation. See Banking.
    contribution, 261
    diversification, 258
    function, 255
    incorporation, 96
    level, 84
    management, 133, 243
        discipline, 137–140
    performance. See Active investment performance/risk.
    premium, 82. See also Business risk; Market.
    strategies. See Low-risk strategies.
Risk-adjusted benchmark, 135
Risk-adjusted excess return, 133
Risk-adjusted return, 135
Risk-adjusted stock performance, 94–95
Risk-equivalent economic contribution. See Business units.
Risk-free portfolio, 82
Risk-free rate. See Interest.
ROA. See Return On Assets.
ROC. See Return On Capital.
ROE. See Return On Equity.
Rogerson, W., 224
Rogovsky, N., 189
ROI. See Return On Investment.
ROIC. See Return on invested capital.
RONW. See Return on net worth.
RROC. See Residual Return On Capital.

S

Salaries, capitalization, 251
Scaling. See Proportional scaling.
Schroeder, Richard G., 112
Schuler, R.S., 189

Schumpeter, Index, 217
SEC, 52, 53
Securities fraud, 52
Security analysis, 114
Selection process. See Cash Flow Return On Investment; Economic Value Added; Economic Value Added/Cash Flow Return On Investment.
Senbet, Lemma W., 213
Senior managers, 192
Seward, James K., 197, 213
SG&A expense, 151, 251
Shapiro, Daniel M., 198
Shapiro, Robert B., 57
Shareholder, 49, 63, 118, 134, 199
    accountability, 211
    cost, 110
    equitable treatment, 208–209
    funds, 61
    going-concern perspective, 119
    rights, 208, 212–213, 216
Shareholder value, 116, 165, 181, 184–186. See also Europe.
    accounting, 100
        objectives, 111–113
    conflict. See Economic Profit.
    creation, 234. See also Corporate shareholder value creation.
    economic profit conflict
        EVA companies, responses, 119–124
        straight line depreciation usage, 113–117
    managers, opinion, 191–192
    revolution, global context, 179–181
Shareholder Value Added (SVA), 5, 17, 68
Sharpe, William F., 137
Sharpe ratio, 137
Shaw, John C., 205
Shelton, Joanna, 211
Shivdasani, A., 215
Shoorman, David F., 200
Short duration assets, 35
Short-term debt, 186
Short-term liabilities. See Interest bearing short-term liabilities.
Short-term profits, 239
Single factor model, 22
Single-factor CAPM, 25
Single-period accounting data, 90
Single-period measure, 89
Sinking fund depreciation, 60, 114–116
Sirower, Mark L., 225
Size bias, 139–140
Size-adjusted returns, 94
Sloan, Jr., Alfred, 107
Smith, Adam, 220
Socio-cultural system, 220
S&P. See Standard & Poor's.
Spin-offs, 129
Stakeholder, 200

participation, 209
rights, 209
role, 213–214. See also Corporate governance.
theory, 202–203
wealth-creating relations, 213
Stand-alone allocation methods, 254–256
Stand-alone methodology, 265
Stand-alone risks, 264
Stand-alone total risk, 258
Standard & Poor's (S&P) 500, 139, 140, 158
    Fund, 135
Statutory corporate tax rate, 21
Stein, Jeremy C., 259
Stern Stewart, 19, 20, 36, 54, 62, 68, 89, 133, 179, 270
    approach, 17–21, 79
    EVA bonus plan design, 107–110
Stewardship theory, 200–202
Stewart III, G. Bennett, 2, 17, 36, 69, 73, 82, 119, 122, 134, 142, 270
Stock
    exchanges, depth/liquidity, 180
    liquidity, 204
    options, 188
    price, 67, 226, 231
        goals, 243
    management, 250
    selection, EVA application, 140–155
Stock market
    brand equity, 250
    volatility, 185
Straight line depreciation, 113, 115
    usage. See Shareholder value/ economic profit conflict.
Strategic decision-making, 201
Strategic disclosure, 226–227
Strategic investments, 56–58
Straw, Robert, 4, 15, 220
Sub-drivers, 244
Sub-prime consumer lender, 254
Sub-prime lending, 260
Sub-prime lending business, 254
Sub-units, 254
Succession planning, 210
Sunk cost, 39, 104
Surplus return on capital, 12
Suspension account, 57
SVA. See Shareholder Value Added.
Synergies, capturing, 218

T

T, calculation. See Time period.
Takeover defense, 213
Target bonus, 225
Tax liability, 61
Taxes, 55, 61–62. See also Cash operating taxes.
    expense. See Income tax expense.
    gross-up, 77

TBR, 253
Teitelbaum, Richard, 90
Terminal value, 117
Thakor, Anjan V., 93, 218, 219
Thomas, Rawley, 249
Thompson, Steve, 199
Time period (T), calculation, 168–170
Total returns to shareholders (TRS), 216
Total shareholder return (TSR), 129
Total Stockholder Return (TSR), 2, 5
TQM, 219
Training, 116, 277–278
Transparency, 209–210, 216
TRS. See Total returns to shareholders.
TSR. See Total shareholder return; Total Stockholder Return.
Tully, Shawn, 85, 86, 91
Two-period Fisherian Wealth Model, 7, 9
Two-period NPV model, 8–10, 16
Two-stage economic profit, 36
Two-stage free cash flow model, 29–33
Two-tier board system, 212

U

Uncertainty avoidance, 189–190
Underperforming assets, 187
Unlevered net operating profit after tax, 21, 36
Unova, 238
Unrecorded goodwill, 146
U.S. government debt, 82

V

Valuation. See Economic margin; Intangible valuation.
    decisions. See Corporate valuation decisions.
    investment opportunities, 41–42
    issues, 168
    measures. See Economic Value Added.
    methodologies, importance. See Value-based metrics.
    models, 168
    steps. See Corporate valuation.
    techniques. See Economic Value Added.
Valuations. See Cash Flow Return On Investment; Economic Value Added.
Value
    accounting, objectives. See Shareholder value accounting.
    creation, 186, 187. See also Investor value.
    drivers, 141
    stocks, 49
Value Line, 83, 226

Value-added. See Market value-added.
    evidence, 92–95
    measures, 71–96
        value, addition, 90–92, 95–96
    metrics, 92, 96
Value-adding company, 86
Value-based adjustments, 17
Value-based format, 16
Value-based management principles, 159
Value-based management (VBM), 99, 157, 179
    discouragement. See Intangibles investment.
Value-based measures. See Performance.
Value-based metrics (VBM), 4, 22, 67, 126, 159, 166
    attractiveness, 269–270
    case studies, 230
    framework, 168
    implementation, 229, 241
    internal use, 269
    leading edge, 249
    measurement issues, 16–17
    motivation/practice, 1
    need, 158–159
    players, 3–5
    reflection, 6
    steps, 243–246
    usage, 50. See also Financial theory.
        reason, 231, 234
    valuation methodologies, importance, 249–251
Value-based operating measures, 99
Value-based training, 270
Value/capital ratio, real meaning, 15–16
Value-destroying businesses, 192
Value-destroying company, 86
Value-enhancing projects, 68
Value-to-capital ratio, 15
Value-to-earnings multiples, 45
Value-to-earnings ratio, 45
van Heeckeren, Jennifer, 222
Variances, 274
VBM. See Value-based management; Value-based metrics.
Volatility. See Stock market.
    calculation. See Cash flow.
Voting rights, 209
Voting stock, 204

W

WACC. See Weighted Average Cost of Capital.
Walbert, Laura, 91
Wallace, James, 2, 42, 92, 94, 185, 218
Walsh, James P., 197, 213
Waters, M., 220
Wealth
    creation, empirical evidence, 42–49

    destroyers, 6, 46–49
    destruction, 47
Wealth creators, 42–46
    enterprise value/earnings ratio, decomposition, 43–45
    ranking, 45–46, 48–49
Weber, 220
Weighted Average Cost of Capital (WACC), 8–10, 34, 101, 134, 153, 186
    corporate taxes impact, 14–15
Weighted variance/covariance matrix, 262
Weisbach, Michael, 218
Welker, Michael, 203
Westphal, James D., 205
Wetzker, K., 183
Withdrawals, 111
Wolf, Charles R., 5, 36
Wolin, Jason L., 81
Working capital additions, 28
World Bank, 221
World War II, growth rates, 180
Wright, Mike, 199
WTO, 221
Wymeersch, E., 205, 225

X

Xhonneux, P., 183

Y

Yernack, D., 215
Yield ratios, 226
Y2K efforts, 232
Young, David, 15, 219, 226

Z

Zahra, S.A., 204
Zeithaml, Carl P., 201
Zero-beta portfolio, 82
Zimmerman, J., 219
Z-ratio, 255–257